Military Families and War in the 21st Century

This book focuses on the key issues that affect military families when soldiers are deployed overseas, focusing on the support given to military personnel and families before, during, and after missions.

Today's postmodern armies are expected to provide social-psychological support both to their personnel in military operations abroad and to their families at home. Since the end of the Cold War, and even more so after 9/11, separations between military personnel and their families have become more frequent as a result of multitudes of missions carried out by multinational task forces all over the world. The book focuses on three central questions affecting military families. First, how do the changing missions and tasks of the military affect soldiers and families? Second, what is the effect of deployments on those left behind? Third, what is the structure of national family support systems and how have they evolved?

The book employs a multidisciplinary approach, with contributions from psychology, sociology, history, and anthropology, among others. In addition, it covers all of the services – army, navy/marines, air force – spanning a wide range of countries, including the UK, the USA, Belgium, Turkey, Australia, and Japan. At the same time, it takes a multitude of perspectives, including the theoretical, empirical, reflective, life events (narrative) approach, the national, and the global, and uses approaches from different disciplines and perspectives, combining them to produce a volume that enhances our knowledge and understanding of military families.

This book will be of much interest to students of military studies, sociology, war and conflict studies, and international relations/political science in general.

René Moelker is an Associate Professor at the Netherlands Defense Academy.

Manon Andres is an Assistant Professor at the Netherlands Defense Academy.

Gary Bowen is Kenan Distinguished Professor in the School of Social Work at the University of North Carolina at Chapel Hill (UNC-CH), USA.

Philippe Manigart is Professor of Sociology at the Royal Military Academy, Belgium.

Cass Military Studies

The Tet Effect, Intelligence and the Public Perception of War
Jake Blood

The US Military Profession into the 21st Century
War, peace and politics
Sam C. Sarkesian and Robert E. Connor, Jr. (eds)

Civil–Military Relations in Europe
Learning from crisis and institutional change
Hans Born, Marina Caparini, Karl Haltiner and Jürgen Kuhlmann (eds)

Strategic Culture and Ways of War
Lawrence Sondhaus

Military Unionism in the Post Cold War Era
A future reality?
Richard Bartle and Lindy Heinecken (eds)

Warriors and Politicians
U.S. civil–military relations under stress
Charles A. Stevenson

Military Honour and the Conduct of War
From Ancient Greece to Iraq
Paul Robinson

Military Industry and Regional Defense Policy
India, Iraq and Israel
Timothy D. Hoyt

Managing Defence in a Democracy
Laura R. Cleary and Teri McConville (eds)

Gender and the Military
Women in the armed forces of Western democracies
Helena Carreiras

Social Sciences and the Military
An interdisciplinary overview
Giuseppe Caforio (ed.)

Cultural Diversity in the Armed Forces
An international comparison
Joseph Soeters and Jan van der Meulen (eds)

Railways and the Russo-Japanese War
Transporting war
Felix Patrikeeff and Harold Shukman

War and Media Operations
The US military and the press from Vietnam to Iraq
Thomas Rid

Military Families and War in the 21st Century

Comparative perspectives

Edited by
René Moelker, Manon Andres,
Gary Bowen, and Philippe Manigart

Routledge
Taylor & Francis Group

LONDON AND NEW YORK

To military families worldwide

First published 2015
by Routledge
2 Park Square, Milton Park, Abingdon, Oxon OX14 4RN

and by Routledge
711 Third Avenue, New York, NY 10017

Routledge is an imprint of the Taylor & Francis Group, an informa business

British Library Cataloguing-in-Publication Data
A catalogue record for this book is available from the British Library

Library of Congress Cataloging-in-Publication Data
Military families and war in the 21st century : comparative perspectives / edited by René Moelker, Manon Andres, Gary Bowen and Philippe Manigart.
pages cm
Includes bibliographical references and index.
1. Families of military personnel–Services for–Case studies.
2. Deployment (Strategy)–Psychological aspects. 3. Families of military personnel–Mental health. 4. Families of military personnel–Psychology. I. Moelker, R. (René), 1960–, editor.
UB400.M55 2015
355.1'29–dc23
2014045466

ISBN: 978-0-415-82140-7 (hbk)
ISBN: 978-0-203-40753-0 (ebk)

Typeset in Baskerville
by Swales and Willis Ltd, Exeter, Devon, UK

Contents

Figures

Tables

Contributors

Manon Andres, Ph.D., is an assistant professor and researcher with the Netherlands Defense Academy. She holds a doctorate from Tilburg University. Among other things, her research focuses on understanding military families, and is directed at work–family conflict, well-being, social support, quality of relationships, children's reactions to separation, and the experiences of parents of service members in the course of military deployments.

Jocelyn Bartone holds a master's degree in sociology from the University of Maryland, United States. She undertook extensive research on U.S. military families stationed both in the United States and in Germany.

Catherine Birtles is a research associate with the King's Centre for Military Health Research (KCMHR), at King's College London.

Gary Bowen, Ph.D., is Kenan Distinguished Professor with the School of Social Work at The University of North Carolina at Chapel Hill (UNC-CH). He serves as chief scientist with the Jordan Institute for Military Members, Veterans, and their Families. He also co-directs the School Success Profile (SSP) project with Dr. Natasha Bowen and Dr. Jack Richman. Dr. Bowen received his Master of Social Work (MSW) degree in 1976 from UNC-CH and his doctorate in family studies in 1981 from The University of North Carolina at Greensboro. Professor Bowen is a former president of the National Council on Family Relations.

Helena Carreiras, Ph.D, is a professor of Sociology, Public Policy and Research Methodology at ISCTE-Lisbon University Institute, and a senior researcher at the Centre for Research and Studies in Sociology (CIES-IUL). She holds a PhD in Social and Political Sciences from the European University Institute (2004). She was deputy-director of the Portuguese National Defense Institute (2010–2012) and presently directs the Public Policy doctoral program at ISCTE-IUL.

Julie Coulthard, Ph.D., completed her doctorate in sociology at McGill University, Montreal, and has been a defense scientist with Defense

Research and Development Canada (DRDC) since 2007. Her main areas of research include the impacts of military life on families, and the study of ill and injured service members, with a particular focus on their reintegration back into their pre-accident/illness military duties or their transition from military to civilian life.

Christopher Dandeker, Ph.D., is professor of military sociology with the Department of War Studies, at King's College London, and co-director of the King's Centre for Military Health Research (KCMHR).

Karin De Angelis is an assistant professor with the Behavioral Sciences and Leadership Department, at the United States Air Force Academy. She holds a doctorate in sociology from the University of Maryland. Dr. De Angelis' main research interests include diversity in the military, military families (and the role of diversity), and the intersection of gender with work and family.

Rachel Dekel, Ph.D., is an associate professor with the School of Social Work at Bar-Ilan University, Israel. During the last decade, she has been involved in various research projects that have examined different facets of human coping with traumatic events such as, war, terror, and family violence. Professor Dekel's research focuses on individuals who have experienced secondary exposure to traumatic events. She has conducted studies among spouses of veterans, children of fathers with post-traumatic stress disorder (PTSD), and therapists who work in areas under terrorism. She is currently the deputy director of the School of Social Work at Bar Ilan University and the head of the program for undergraduate students.

Sanela Dursun, Ph.D., is a research psychologist and director of personnel and family support in the Director General of Military Personnel Research and Analysis at DRDC in Ottawa, Canada. Her major projects have included research on the optimal length and frequency of operational deployment, studies of the quality of life of military members, a study of family violence, and studies of ethical decision making. Her current research interests include assessing the impact of military lifestyle demands and deployments on the mental health and well-being of members and their families. She holds a master's degree in social psychology and a doctorate in health psychology.

Meytal Eran-Jona, Ph.D., is the head of the research project on civil–military relations at the Behavioral Sciences Centre (BSC) of the Israeli Defense Forces (IDF). She holds a doctorate from Tel Aviv University. Her research interests include civil–military relations, gender relations in the military, women in the military, military families, military personnel issues, future battlefield challenges, and military operations in civilian environments.

Colonel Yavuz Ercil, Ph.D., graduated from the Turkish Military Academy in 1991, earned his Master of Business Administration (MBA) degree from Istanbul University, and achieved his doctorate on management in 2001. He was appointed to many national and international posts during his period of military service. Dr. Ercil is an associate professor in management and organization, and teaches strategy, communication, cross-cultural management, complexity, and organizations at various military or civilian education institutions, including the Partnership for Peace (PfP) Training Centre, Ankara, the NATO Centre of Excellence Defense against Terrorism, Ankara, and the Turkish Department of Defense.

Claire Eversden was a research associate with the KCMHR, at King's College London.

Sabina Frederic, Ph.D., is professor at the University of Quilmes, Argentina, and an associate researcher with the Argentine National Council of Scientific and Technical Research. She holds a doctorate in social anthropology from the University of Utrecht, Netherlands. Among her main publications are *The Traps of the Past: The Armed Forces and its integration into the Argentine Democratic State* (Fondo de Cultura Económica) and *The Uses of Public Force: Social sciences debates on armed forces and policemen* (UNGS-National Library). She was formerly coordinator of the Gender Policy Council (2007–09) and Undersecretary of Education with the Argentine Ministry of Defense (2009–11).

Atsuko Fukuura, Ph.D. candidate, is an associate professor of anthropology at Shiga University, Japan. She holds a master's degree in education, and a doctoral candidacy from Kyoto University, Japan. Her research interests include the transnationalism of the armed forces, gender ideology, religion and patriarchy, traumatic experiences (war, PTSD, suffering, pain) and organization of memory, and military families. Her 2007 article 'Narratives by the spouses: The imagination and memory about the violence', published in the *Journal of International Security*, is a pioneering study on Japan Self-Defense Forces (JSDF) families, focusing on the wives who share their husbands' suffering experiences.

Jelena Juvan, Ph.D., is an assistant professor at the Defense Studies Department and a graduate research assistant with the Defense Research Centre at the Faculty of Social Sciences, University of Ljubljana. She holds a degree in political science (2001) and a doctorate in defense science (2008), both from the Faculty of Social Sciences, University of Ljubljana. She is an assistant lecturer for the courses 'Sociology and Political Science of the Armed Forces', 'Polemology', and 'Foreign and Security Policies of the European Union'. Her research fields include military families, peace operations, and the human factor in the armed forces.

Hitoshi Kawano, Ph.D., worked as professor of sociology in 2011–2013 with Japan's National Defense Academy. He holds a doctorate in sociology from

Northwestern University, United States, and a master's degree in education from Osaka University, Japan. He also works as a special coordinator with Human Resources Development Division, at the Bureau of Personnel and Education, Ministry of Defense, Japan, in charge of overseeing the organizational reforms of the National Defense Academy. His research interests include the comparative-historical sociology of combat/peacekeeping operations, civil–military relations in contemporary Japan, the mental health of soldiers/veterans, veterans associations, and military leadership education.

Valerian Lecoq, M.Sc., is a research associate with the Department of Behavioral Sciences at the Royal Military Academy, Belgium.

Captain Salvatore Lo Bue, M.Sc., is a research associate with the Department of Behavioral Sciences at the Royal Military Academy, Belgium.

Shelley MacDermid Wadsworth, Ph.D., is professor of human development and family studies with the Department of Human Development and Family Studies, at Purdue University, West Lafayette, IN. She has been director of the Centre for Families from 1996, and director of the Military Family Research Institute from 2000. She is interested in the relationships between work conditions and family life. Over the past twenty years, she has studied differences between small and large workplaces, how adults grow and develop as a result of their work experiences, and how different kinds of organizational policies make it easier or more difficult for workers to be successful at work and at home.

Jay Mancini, Ph.D., is Haltiwanger Distinguished Professor of Human Development and Family Science at the University of Georgia, United States. He also directs the Family and Community Resilience Laboratory. His research and theorizing focuses on families and communities, military members and their families, family systems and adolescent adversity, and the intersections of vulnerability and resilience. Professor Mancini is a Fellow of the National Council on Family Relations.

Philippe Manigart, Ph.D., is professor of sociology and head of the Department of Behavioral Sciences at the Royal Military Academy, Belgium. He is also an assistant professor (part-time) with the Faculty of Economics at the University of Mons. He has a master's degree in sociology from the University of Chicago and a doctorate from the Free University of Brussels. His main research interests and expertise lie in the fields of organizational sociology (with an emphasis on military organizations), survey analysis, and market research. For the Belgian Defense, he has conducted several surveys on job satisfaction among the personnel and on the image of the institution among the public, as well as market researches on the recruitment of personnel. Since 2005, he has been a member of the Council of the Inter-University Seminar on Armed Forces and Society. In 1985–86, he was Jean Monnet Fellow at the European University Institute in Florence and received a NATO Fellowship.

James (Jim) Martin, Ph.D., BCD, is professor of social work and social research at Bryn Mawr College, United States. His scholarship, teaching, and public service focus on social and behavioral health issues, while his research and civic engagements address military and veteran populations. A retired army colonel, Jim's twenty-six-year career in the U.S. Army Medical Department included clinical research, as well as senior management (command) and policy assignments. Jim was the senior social work officer in the Persian Gulf theatre of military operations during the first Gulf War and edited *The Gulf War and Mental Health: A comprehensive guide* (Praeger).

Laura Masson, Ph.D., is professor at the National University of San Martín, Argentina, and a member of the Gender Policy Council of the Argentine Ministry of Defense. She holds a doctorate (2007) and master's degree (1999) in social anthropology from the Federal University of Rio de Janeiro (FURJ), Brazil. She is the author of *Politic in Female: Gender and power in the province of Buenos Aires* (Antroprofagia) and *Feminists Everywhere: An ethnography of spaces and feminist narratives in Argentina* (Prometeo). She was advisor to the Undersecretary for Education, Ministry of Defense, Argentina.

David McCone, Ph.D., is professor with the Behavioral Sciences and Leadership Department at the United States Air Force Academy. He holds a doctorate in clinical psychology from the University of Oregon. Professor McCone has studied marriage and divorce issues, women's integration, and deployment experiences for both Active Duty and Army National Guard soldiers deployed to Iraq and Afghanistan.

René Moelker, Ph.D., is an associate professor of sociology at the Netherlands Defense Academy. He holds a doctorate from the Erasmus University, Rotterdam. His work in military sociology concentrates on the sociology of military families, military technology, military profession, the military sociology of Norbert Elias, military education, conflict in Chechnya, and the media. His latest project focuses on veterans and veteran care.

Laura Sanchez is a research associate with the Military Family Research Institute at Purdue University, Lafayette, IN.

Mady Wechsler Segal, Ph.D., is Professor Emerita of Sociology at the University of Maryland, United States. She earned her doctorate at the University of Chicago. Her research has focused on military personnel issues, with particular attention to military women, military families, and race/ethnicity in the military. Her publications include, among many others, *The Military and the Family as Greedy Institutions* (Armed Forces and Society). She is an author of a report for military leaders on the policy implications of research findings on military families (*What We Know about Army Families*, 2007 update,) and co-author of *How to Support Families during Overseas Deployments: A sourcebook for service providers* (Army

Research Institute). She and David R. Segal co-authored a book entitled *Peacekeepers and their Wives* (Greenwood Press).

Philip Siebler, Ph.D., is a mental health social worker, clinical family therapist, and an Adjunct Research Associate with Child Abuse Prevention Research Australia, Monash Injury Research Institute, Monash University. Philip joined the Australian Department of Defense as a social worker in 1997 and is currently coordinator of the Regional Mental Health Team in Joint Health Command, a position that spans Victoria and Tasmania. He earned his doctorate in social work at Monash University, with a thesis entitled: " 'Military People Won't Ask for Help': Experiences of deployment of Australian Defense Force personnel, their families, and implications for social work."

Unsal Sigri, Ph.D., is an associate professor of management, has the rank of colonel, and has been working as a faculty member at the Turkish Military Academy, Ankara, Turkey, since 1998. He got his doctorate from Marmara University, Istanbul, and completed postdoctoral studies in Bittner School of Business, St. John Fisher College, Rochester, NY. Dr. Sigri teaches management, leadership, group dynamics, cross-cultural management, conflict resolution, negotiation, and mediation in the Turkish Military Academy. In addition, he leads courses, lectures, and seminars in various university, military and civilian academic environments, including other universities in Ankara, the Partnership for Peace (PfP) Training Centre, Ankara, the NATO Centre of Excellence Defense against Terrorism, Ankara, and the Turkish Department of Defense, and some other military and civilian institutions.

David Smith, Ph.D., CDR, U.S. Navy, is Permanent Military Professor and chair of the Leadership, Ethics and Law Department at the U.S. Naval Academy, Annapolis, MD. He received his doctorate in sociology from the University of Maryland in 2010. His dissertation, "Developing Pathways to Serving Together: Dual military couples' life course and decision-making," examined the experiences of dual-career military families and their work–life prioritization strategies. His research interests include military families, gender and culture in the military, identity and efficacy development in leaders, experiential leader development, and qualitative methods.

Kerry Sudom is a defense scientist at DRDC, with the Canadian Department of National Defense (DND). She is currently the leader of the psychosocial health dynamics team, part of the Director General Military Personnel Research and Analysis (DGMPRA). She holds a master's degree and a doctorate in psychology from Carleton University in Ottawa. Since 2005, Kerry has conducted research in areas including military family wellbeing, health and fitness trends among military personnel, transition from military to civilian life, and psychological resilience.

Danielle Swick, Ph.D., is an assistant professor at the University of North Carolina at Greensboro. She received her MSW degree from the University of Michigan and her doctorate from the University of North Carolina at Chapel Hill. Her main research interests include evidence-based practice, school-based interventions, child and adolescent mental health, and community-engaged research.

Maren Tomforde, Ph.D., of the German Armed Forces Staff and Command College, Germany, received her doctorate in anthropology from the University of Hamburg in 2005. For her thesis, she carried out a two-year field research project in Thailand (1999–2000, 2001–02) on the topic of "cultural spatiality." From 2003 to 2007, she was a research associate with the German Armed Forces Institute of Social Research (SOWI) in Strausberg, Germany, where she conducted anthropological research on German peacekeeping missions. Since March 2007, she has been a lecturer in anthropology at the German Armed Forces Staff and Command College in Hamburg. She also lectures with the Institute of European Anthropology at Humboldt University, Berlin.

Kadir Varoglu, Ph.D. is a faculty staff member with the Management and Organization Department at Baskent University, Ankara. He worked for thirty years within the Turkish Army and retired at the rank of colonel. He is vice president of Baskent University.

Janja Vuga, Ph.D., is the Assistant Professor at the University of Ljubljana, a research fellow at the Defense Research Centre and a project manager at the Ministry of Defense of Republic of Slovenia; she gives lectures in peace operations, military sociology and informatics and has been researching cross-cultural relations, work/life balance, children in military families and gender issues in the military. A great share of her research was carried out among service-members in the field (e.g. TChad/CAR, UNIFIL, KFOR). For her work she received a European Cooperation in Science and Technology (COST) scholarship. Currently she is a member of the NATO HFM 258 research group (researching children in military families).

Simon Wessely, Ph.D., is professor of psychological medicine, vice dean, and head of academic psychiatry, with the Department of Psychological Medicine, and director of the King's Centre for Military Health Research Institute of Psychiatry, at King's College London.

Part I

Military organizations and families in transition

1 Introduction

René Moelker, Manon Andres,
Gary Bowen, and Philippe Manigart

Introduction

Since the end of the Cold War, and even more so after 9/11, multinational task forces all over the world have carried out a multitude of missions for more or less extended periods. This implies frequent separations between military personnel and their families. Not only the operational tempo, but also the nature of military missions has changed. The character and organization of new missions imply that military forces face increasingly demanding challenges and must be highly trained. Intensive (predeployment) training necessitates military personnel being away from their families (even more) frequently, even when actual deployment has yet to begin. Furthermore, many Western armed forces face downsizing and restructuring, which further increase the deployment load.

New missions

Being a soldier is a stimulating and exciting job. Better put: it is an ever-demanding profession that changes according to the exigencies of the task to be performed and the organizational structure chosen to fit the task. Considering the exigencies, conscription seems obsolete in many countries (Szvircsev Tresch and Haltiner, 2008), with the exception of nations that face threats from antagonistic neighbors or which aspire to realize domestic and/or international political objectives further reaching than self-defense. Greece and Turkey are two of the largest remaining conscript armies. These countries happen to be allies, but they are friends within a complex symbiotic constellation. Some would teasingly name these countries "frenemies." And there are more examples in the world of "classic" conflict situations: some frozen static ones (such as Cyprus, or the two Koreas); others rapidly emerging in places that often rank high on the Failed States Index. Conscription has evolved out of the objective of territorial sovereignty. It peaked in importance during the Cold War. Although no longer the dominant organizational concept, it remains present.

All-volunteer forces have become the major organizational concept, in part because these forces can be used for purposes other than self-defense. All-volunteer forces are flexible and easier to deploy in intra-state conflicts, which means that it is easier to obtain political support for their deployment, whereas the conscript concept seemed more suited to defending a nation's sovereignty. Mary Kaldor (2012) coined the term "new wars" to describe these conflicts, often between paramilitary, irregular troops, insurgents, and war lord factions. The missions changed in various ways, all of them affecting the home front. One of the consequences is that the casualties that nations suffered in these conflicts did not occur in defense of national boundaries; therefore the framing of these losses had to change. The traditional political rhetoric proved inadequate in explaining the loss of a soldier to spouses, children, parents, and loved ones. Defending vital national interests in places far from national borders is a challenge to a mission's legitimacy (Martinsen, 2013). The construct of "national interest" is thereby becoming ever more abstract.

New missions do impact on the military and their families. According to Shaw (2005), in *The New Western Way of War*, risks are transferred to weaker groups in society, meaning that the costs lie with the indigenous populations, the soldiers, and their families rather than with Western powers or politicians. Not only are new wars network-based (and thus "netwars") – meaning that even when militaries are entangled in distant conflicts, families worldwide are affected – but also missions are globalized, entering our living rooms by means of television and new media, and fought by new methods using cyber capabilities and drone techniques. The home front participates in spectator warfare and, even more astonishingly, the "cubicle warrior" destroys enemies that are thousands of miles away, yet returns home to his or her family each evening and engages his or her children in a leisurely Playstation war game. After the war, soldiers return as veterans and find out that the war continues in their heads. Families that rejoiced during marital reunion experience the long-term effects of war and may even end in divorce.[1]

Many authors state that new missions are not strictly military. Peacekeeping, peace-enforcing, and stability operations share a strong constabulary character (Janowitz, 1960). This Janowitzian constabulary force is still about military tasking, but Oakley, Dziedzic, and Goldber (1998) refer to new missions as "policing the new world order." Nonetheless, geopolitical power relations and hardcore power play will not resile from the political arena easily. Peacekeeping and other missions often are prominent in the specter of violence. Considering recent political developments and the rise of new powers, Christopher Coker (2014) rightly asked, when titling his latest book, *Can War Be Eliminated?*

Missions thus are diverse in character and complex, and put serious strain on military families. Missions are difficult to compare, for one cannot say that missions from the past were "easier" to cope with. But present-day missions do pose problems to the home front that have to be dealt with. The last 15 years of warfare have weighed heavily on families.

The military family

When military personnel are deployed abroad, they leave their families behind. While the institutional armed forces were composed mainly of (drafted) young, unmarried people, most Western military organizations have now been transformed from conscription-based organizations into occupational professional organizations that include a greater proportion of soldiers who are older, married, and have children. Compared to their civilian counterparts, a higher proportion of service members are married and have young children at home; they are also more likely to marry at a younger age (Segal et al., 2011). Moreover, a diversity of family structures coexists alongside the ideal typical nuclear family in the military today. The traditional nuclear family – defined as a married couple with children, running a household together – is no longer the default survival unit in present-day societies. Single-parent households, childless couples, gay couples (with or without children), dual-military couples, and other family structures are common nowadays. Networked informal relationships, fluid patterns of bonding, the role of grandparents during deployments, and so forth pose new challenges to family organizing. Furthermore, the proportion of women in the workforce has increased, implying also a rise in the number of women in the military, and thus of deployed wives and mothers. These families face various challenges and stressors in meeting the dual demands of military and family life.

Work and family interface

A classic theme in the sociology of work and family is the competition between the two spheres that stems from an inherent "greediness" of institutions (Coser, 1974; Segal, 1986). In order to perform well at work or at parenting, devotion is required, and work and family can sometimes compete for the limited time and resources of the individual. The balance between work and family life is particularly difficult to maintain when missions increase in tempo. Stress from either domain can spill over into the other domain or cross over to family members. The nature of this spillover was a major theme of the book edited by Bowen and Orthner (1989), entitled *The Organization Family: Work and family linkages in the U.S. military*.

The covenant between military and society

New missions also affect the relationship between civil society and the armed forces. Sometimes, society does not understand soldiers or their families, who may feel neglected or isolated as a result. Soldiers' jobs are dangerous, and although they receive monetary compensation, the risks that soldiers run and the hardships that their families endure are difficult to compensate in only financial ways. The covenant between soldier and society has changed, and soldiers and families feel that the currency missing in this covenant is recognition. Especially when things turn out poorly, families and soldiers (national guards, reservists, active duty, and veterans) need the support of their communities and wider society.

Family support

Compared to the Cold War period and, to a lesser extent, the era of the mass armed forces, a greater need therefore exists for today's postmodern armies to provide social-psychological support to their personnel in military operations abroad and to their families at home. From a purely military management standpoint, the organization of social-psychological support has become a necessity because, in the short term, the absence of such support impacts negatively on the operational readiness of soldiers and, in the longer term, can have negative effects on recruitment and retention (Bowen and Martin, 2011). As a consequence, in all postmodern military organizations, but to varying degrees, services and/or structures have been progressively developed – or adapted – to provide social-psychological support to military personnel and families before, during, and after missions.

Change in this respect derives from two directions: the supply side of formal support, and the demand side. But people also have higher expectations. Twenty years ago, not being able to communicate with the home front was accepted in the Navy, but nowadays this would be considered backward and a reason for quitting service. The military is not simply a job, because it demands sacrifice from soldiers and families. Therefore the military organization is under a moral obligation to provide support that fits the needs of this special profession. Families also realize that what they sacrifice is above the regular contractual obligations of the labor market, and they seek additional social, emotional and material support.

The focus of this book

International comparisons are the principal aim of this book. It focuses on the most important issues that touch upon families when soldiers are deployed. Writing such a book on military families requires adopting approaches from different disciplines and perspectives, and combining them to produce a volume that enhances our knowledge and understanding of military families. The aim is to push the theory in the field a little bit further, to illustrate the topic empirically, and to add depth to our understanding by cross-national comparative analysis. Contributing to the broad scope of the project, this volume includes all services (army, navy/marines, air force), as well as families from active duty personnel, reserves, and national guard.

The military lifestyle also involves long and unpredictable workdays, and recurrent transfers to new work and living environments, and frequent relocations. In this book, we focus also on work–family conflict and health issues stemming from separation. Three coherent sets of research questions are addressed in the volume, as follows.

How do the changing missions and tasks of the military affect soldiers and their families?

This question relates to the way in which armed forces seek to adapt their structure to the new missions and how military families cope with competing demands from military and private life. Is family–military rivalry, as embodied in the concept of "greedy institutions," still relevant as an analytical concept? What theoretical progress have sociologists made in ameliorating that rivalry? Tensions between the military organization and the family, in terms of work–family conflict, may grow, especially during missions when couples have more difficulty combining work and family obligations. Mass communication (Internet, media, and virtual social networks, including blogs, Facebook, or Twitter) renders operations more transparent to the home front, influencing questions of legitimacy, such as the role of family support in legitimizing military operations.

What is the effect of deployments on those left behind?

Psychologically, deployment weighs heavily on families and deployed soldiers. They face separation, and therefore the stressors and related hardships on the soldier and the military family are relevant research topics. How do soldiers and families deal with these issues? What is the effect on children? Does deployment influence the quality of the marital relationship? Do differences in length of deployment (within and across nations) differently affect the well-being of families? How do community efforts buffer the plight of families? How do families manage marital reconciliation? What is the effect of communication (email, cellphones, virtual support groups) on family outcomes?

What is the structure of national family support systems and what has been their evolution?

Nations have different arrangements in place for taking care of military families. It is not only the structure of these arrangements that differs, but also nations differ regarding family cultures. The role of volunteers and private initiatives in a society is one among the variables. One also needs to know how support fits within the general structure of family life in a certain country, or what the differences are in terms of the organization of support before, during, and after deployment. Leadership is often also different from nation to nation: sometimes, commanders take more initiative; at other times, the community is the pivotal actor. In some cases, military families cope well enough by themselves and show remarkable resilience without any outside support.

Presenting a framework

The framework is interdisciplinary, and stems from both psychology and sociology (with a touch of anthropology). More specifically, the roots in psychology are stress theory, which is inspired by and related to the question of "how to augment or uphold resilience" (Bowen, Martin, and Mancini, 2013). The sociological roots originate from the question of cohesion: how does one hold together a society that is changing rapidly from a holistic entity to a society of individuals? A third traditional strand of study ties the psychological and sociological perspectives together by examining the way in which support relations come into being (Moelker and van der Kloet, 2003). Support relations not only deal with sociological building blocks, but also are the structures around which psychological mechanisms such as coping, stress buffering, and family cohesion revolve.

Family stress and resilience theory

The word "stress" is rather self-explanatory. The concept implies that when pressure is exerted on something or someone, the object or subject will bend or break, and also that when the pressure is lessened, the object or subject will, to a greater or lesser degree, return to its previous state of being. The extent to which the new state of being corresponds to the old one depends on the resilience factor, and the new state can be worse, better, or the same. "Bending," "breaking," "elasticity," and so forth are terms much used in physical analogy. Even terms specific to stress theory have become commonplace, meaning that "stress buffering," "coping," and "adaptation" have become so widely used that stereotypes thrive and may even hamper those who are stressed. For example, veterans are so often associated with posttraumatic stress disorder (PTSD) that future employers might be wary of excessive use of alcohol, violent behaviors, and severe marital problems. Stress – more specifically, family stress – has become commonly known as a concept, but precise definitions are not often given. We will elaborate on family stress mainly, but even within this focus on families, one needs to be aware of the historical and societal context of the concept.

Several authors document the genesis of the concept of "stress." In his study of psychiatric breakdown, Simon Wessely (2006) summarizes all previous studies, while adding his own research. "Shell shock," as a concept, helped people during and after World War I to do away with the value judgment that stress victims were "nothing but cowards" who were "lacking in moral fiber." Treatment had often been so harsh that soldiers had preferred to return to the war front. Acute combat stress reactions were first remedied by allowing the men some rest; by trial and error, more sophisticated treatment methods were then developed.

As a war of high mobility, World War II led to the concept of "fatigue." Cohesion not only helped soldiers to retain combat motivation ("men fight for their buddies"), but also helped to prevent stress symptoms later in life. By serendipity, it was found that the long journey home by ship contributed to coping, because soldiers were able to share their experiences and talk about them. Symptoms that we now recognize as PTSD were, at the end of World War II, diagnosed as "concentration camp syndrome" and treated by progressive psychiatrists with hallucinogenic drugs such as LSD.

After Vietnam, PTSD became part of the psychiatrists' vocabulary; in 1980, it was included in the Diagnostic and Statistical Manual of Mental Disorders (DSM). The fifth revision of the DSM was released in May 2013 (DSM-V). Labeling, diagnosis, and treatment have thus varied over time and across cultures. Different societies deal differently with the phenomenon. Sociologist Withuis (2004), to a degree, fears that PTSD has become a "trendy" disease, with the media, politics, insurance companies, armies, and all other societal institutions not only acknowledging it, but almost propagating identifying as a stress victim.

The ABC-X model of stress among families (Hill, 1949) and its more recent elaboration, the double ABC-X model (McCubbin and Patterson, 1982), are the fruits of military psychological research. Civilian family therapy and ideas on the operation of stress in civilian families are also based on this research. Surveys among the female population in general reveal that a period of separation ranks third on the list of the most stressful events (Holmes and Rahe, 1967). Only the death of a partner and divorce score higher. This means that every military family experiences a fairly high level of stress during the period for which the service member is deployed abroad. That separation is inherently stressful becomes clear in light of the effects of doubling the deployment in length (as was the case in Iraq and Afghanistan for many American soldiers, for example). Spouses of soldiers that were deployed for a year reported that the length of deployment was the premier stressor, while spouses of soldiers participating in shorter deployments were more concerned about the safety of their partners (Bartone and Bartone, 1997).

The ABC-X model for family stress, developed shortly after World War II by Hill (1949), is attractive because of its simplicity. In the model, "A" stands for the stressful event and "B" stands for the resources that people have for solving their problems (financial resources, the help of friends and family, help from the organization, etc.). Because an event may be much more problematical for one person than it is for another, the model also includes subjective perception. The subjective definition of the stressor is indicated by the letter "C." "X" stands for the crisis – that is, the disorganization and chaos results from the combination of A, B, and C.

The double ABC-X model of McCubbin and Patterson (1982: 46) expands Hill's original model by addressing both the pre- and postcrisis components of the stress process. It takes into account the piling up of problems as a dynamic process: over the course of time, one problem piles up on top of the other. The doubling of stressors is often evidenced in old adages such as "it never rains, but it pours"; pile-up is often attributed to "Murphy's law." A similar doubling may also occur with regard to the availability of resources. Besides the existing resources, new resources can be tapped to remediate the problems ("double Bs"). Doubling also occurs regarding the perception of the problem ("double Cs"). The first problem is perceived to be more stressful because of the second problem.

People can learn to cope with stress. Coping behavior can be defined as "the management of a stressful event or situation by the family as a unit, with no detrimental effects on any individual in that family. Coping is the family's ability to manage, not eradicate or eliminate, the stressful event" (Gelles, 1995: 429). The ability or inability to apply coping mechanisms results ultimately in adaptation to the crisis situation. Alongside all of the numerous negative coping strategies that do not solve the problem (drinking, sleeping tablets, denial, or flight) are positive coping strategies, such as keeping family ties intact, developing self-confidence and self-esteem, developing social support, developing a positive attitude, learning about a problem, and reducing tension by involvements and activities (McCubbin, 1979).

Military sociology: From "greedy institutions" to the work–family conflict

Military personnel have become increasingly trapped between two "greedy institutions": the armed forces and the family. The traditional military family fits in with armed forces that have many institutional features. According to Moskos (1977), this means that the spouse and the military family are part of the military community. Private life is not separate from military life. The service member, partner, and children are all involved in military activities. This is the situation that one still typically finds when military units and their families are posted at foreign military bases (Durand et al., 2001; Hawkins, 2001). The isolation, or inability to connect with a foreign culture, drives military families into a community that is closed in character. In such communities, the privacy of family life is constantly under pressure. Social checks are paramount. Gossip is the instrument for exercising social control (Soeters, 1994).

The more the military profession becomes a job like any other, the fewer the partners who will be integrated into the military community. The soldier's job has become more occupational (Moskos, 1977). Service personnel's partners are much more likely to have jobs and circles of friends of their own. They are no longer morally obliged to participate in the military community.

The evolution of the traditional institution into the modern occupation is important for the claims that are made on service personnel by the military organization and the family. Mady Segal (1986) stated that the military family and the military community are both "greedy institutions." Lewis Coser (1974) defines the "greedy institution" as "a pattern of absolute devotion."

The armed forces and the family both claim the devotion of the individual. In the past (in the institutional model), the armed forces were the most dominant and most greedy institution of the two: duty was meant to override love. Officially, service personnel had to be available 24 hours a day. The shift in the armed forces from the institutional model toward the occupational model is the reason why the armed forces and the family both make strong claims on the devotion of the individual, who is appealed to, on one hand, in his or her role as a member of the armed forces and, on the other hand, in his or her role as partner, parent, or member of the family. The individual is caught between two greedy institutions and has a dual loyalty problem: if one is given priority, the other is given short measure. If the person in question opts for the armed forces, the military family is confronted with a specific problem: the problem of family stress. The armed forces of different countries vary in terms of degree of greediness, and there are, of course, also variations in greediness over time. In times and places where tradition prevails, greediness is higher.

In a historical analysis of class-based role expectations, Harrell (2001) developed the hypothesis that military wives – and especially officers' wives – are engaged in volunteer action to secure the status position of their husbands. This hypothesis holds particularly true among commissioned officers' wives at West Point Military Academy, who try to uphold upper-class status by fulfilling role expectations such as mentoring younger wives, attending ceremonial gatherings, entertaining guests, and participating in family support. Other researchers have noted this aspect of greediness, but from a different perspective. For instance, Weinstein and White (1997) offer a feminist explanation for the same phenomenon, whereas Jessup (1996) points toward the fact that the British Armed Forces benefit the most from expectations towards military wives: military wives who participate in family support and other forms of assistance are providing the armed forces with free services.

Greediness among the institutions could easily lead to conflicts between the family and the military organization. Using items from previous surveys undertaken by Bourg and Segal (1999), Moelker and van der Kloet (2003) found that this family–military conflict was a reality for some families in the Netherlands. Sixteen percent of spouses were not able to attend family activities because of the obligations connected with the soldier's job. An important finding was that supportive policy among the armed forces and support offered by the unit commander lessens family–military conflict.

Conflict between work and family life has been defined as a form of inter-role conflict in which the role pressures from the work and family domains are mutually incompatible in some respects (Greenhaus and Beutell, 1985: 77). It is considered a multidimensional construct (Rode et al., 2007), distinguishing work roles interfering with family roles (work–family conflict) from family roles interfering with work roles (family–work conflict). Many researchers have demonstrated positive relationships between job and family stressors and conflict between work and family demands (Greenhaus and Beutell, 1985; Ilies et al., 2007; Vinokur, Pierce, and Buck, 1999). Generally, it is assumed that work–family conflict is produced by features of the work environment – that is, job stressors, such as long working hours – whereas family stressors, such as having children, may underlie family–work conflict. Yet there is some evidence suggesting that both job stress and family stress produces work–family conflict (for example Westman and Etzion, 2005).

Support relations

Seeking social support is one of the ways in which people cope with stressful situations. But societal structures differ from nation to nation (and also within nations), and therefore a typology can be helpful for international comparative studies. The theory on which this typology is based is derived from sociology and anthropology.

Sometimes, people have extensive social networks and do not need support from the organization. Sometimes, the organization can stimulate and facilitate informal family support groups. The effectiveness of social support has been much discussed by many scholars (Bell, Segal, and Rice 1995; Bowen and Martin, 2011; Cohen and Wills, 1985; Rosen and Moghadam, 1990). Desivilya and Gal (1996) were among the first to explore solutions for overcoming the conflict between families and the military organization. They focused mainly on family structures.

We can distinguish four support relationships on the basis of the "dependency" axis and the "individualized–communitarian" continuum. Dependence and independence form the extremes on the dependency axis. This axis refers to the relationship with the providers of support. The second axis refers to two traditions in social exchange theory: one is individualist; the other, communitarian.[2] The first is rooted in the work of George Homans, which represents an almost economic individualist conceptual framework under which each gift or service has to be reciprocated by the recipient in the form of a service in return, a gift, or money. The communitarian tradition builds on the concepts of Durkheim, Mauss, and Lévi-Strauss (Ekeh, 1974). This tradition states, for example, that even in economics there are communitarian issues – such as trust – that are essential to exchange transactions. Exchange cannot solely be analyzed by using the calculative logic of contributions versus retributions.

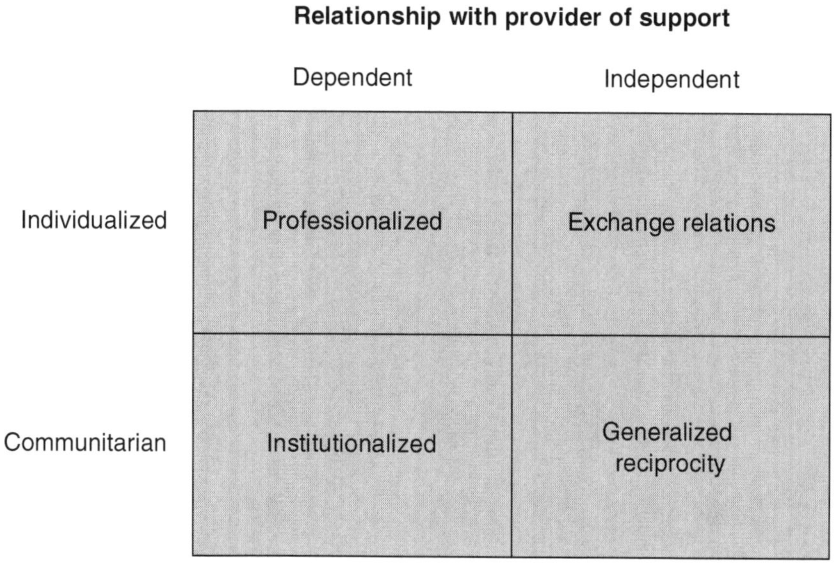

Relationship with provider of support

	Dependent	Independent
Individualized	Professionalized	Exchange relations
Communitarian	Institutionalized	Generalized reciprocity

Figure 1.1 Structure variables determining social support network types

The two structure variables, "dependency" and "individualism–communitarian," together form a taxonomy that defines four types of social support network: professionalized social support relations; institutionalized social support networks; exchange relations; and social support networks based on generalized reciprocity (see Figure 1.1).

In *professionalized social support relations* (see Table 1.1), the individual spouse becomes dependent on support offered by professionals such as psychologists, social workers, or members of the medical profession. Services by professional helpers are reciprocated by means of private payment or insurances, or are paid for by the military organization. This dependency arises because spouses are isolated and are not connected with other army wives, family, or friends. When confronted with problems with which they are unable to cope, they resort to professional workers. Hence the size of the support network is small and few others are available to whom the spouse can turn for help. The marital quality and the authority relation between family members may vary from family to family. Commitment is limited to the family only. One of the problems that might weigh heavier on such types of family is the conflict with the military organization. Whilst the family is inner-directed and highly "greedy," the spouse may not accept the justified demands of the military organization regarding the duties of the service member. Deployments especially will lead to a sharp conflict between family and the military organization. Support from professionals is effective, but costly. When high demands or

Table 1.1 Ideal typical approach of social support networks

Variables/social support network	Professionalized	Institutionalized	Exchange relations	Generalized reciprocity
Dependent–independent	Dependent of professional care	Dependent of military community	Independent: bargaining for own position	Independent: strength of weak ties
Individualized–communitarian	Individualized: individual versus bureaucracy	Communitarian: service to community	Individualized: quid pro quo	Communitarian: citizenship behavior
Network structure	Individualized/isolated	Military community serves as extended family	Dyadic structure	Friendship circles
Network size	Small – isolated	Large	Small	Medium to large
Status spouse	Does not apply: family is separated from military community	Depending on rank of serviceman	Depending on the possibilities to reciprocate	Depending on own occupation/personality
Authority relation within the family	Varies for all families	Patriarchal/traditional	Depending on what the other can offer	Egalitarian
Commitment	To family only	To military community	To one's self	To friends and loved ones
Greediness: conflict family–military organization	Family is most greedy: sharp conflict when organization demands deployment	Military organization is most greedy: sharp conflict when spouses do not accept traditionalism	Low conflict if balanced: "give and take" kind of balance	Low conflict if balanced: balanced if there is mutual acceptance – "a two-sided affair"
Effectivity and efficiency of the support network	Professional help is effective if spouse cannot cope; not efficient because of costs and capacity problems	Effective and efficient if "institution" character is accepted	Not effective and efficient: when families are in trouble, they are not attractive exchange partners	Effective and efficient: support is offered on basis of friendship, without expectation of immediate reciprocation

emergency situations arise, professional support will probably encounter capacity problems.

Institutionalized social support networks are common where the traditional "institution" model (Moskos, 1977) has persisted. Communitarianism is strong and the individual is dependent on the military community for social support. Often, the military community is – to a certain degree – isolated from civilian society (that is, it is a closed, inner-directed community). This community is characterized by strong social control, a high commitment to community among its members, and hierarchic relationships. The military community serves as a surrogate extended family. The family itself is also traditional and is characterized by patriarchal authority relations. Civilian spouses of service members usually do not have jobs, but devote their time to housekeeping and raising children. The status of the spouse is derived from the rank of the service member. The network can be very large, which contributes to effectiveness and efficiency of the support rendered, but this support is effective and efficient only when the spouse accepts the traditional "institution" character. When the "institution" character is not accepted, a sharp conflict may exist between the family and the military organization. In contrast to the first type of social support network, the military organization in this type is highly greedy.

In *direct exchange relationships*, individual spouses bargain for their own position in a way that is ruled by the "quid pro quo" principle. Calculations are based on whether or not investments in relationships are profitable, considering the costs. The support network is structured in dyads. There can be several dyads – that is, relationships of support between provider and recipient – but the number of dyads will be limited as a consequence of the investments and costs needed to maintain them. Status and authority relations with others depend on what those others can offer and on the "market value" of the spouse. Commitment is primarily to one's self. The attitude towards the military organization is not conflictuous, provided that there is a balance between "give and take." The dyads are not very effective and efficient support systems. When someone experiences a problematic situation over a considerable period of time, his or her "market value" will diminish and he or she will lose attractiveness as an exchange partner. In fact, the dyadic structure will dissolve and revert to the professionalized support relationship, meaning that the needy will now have to knock on the doors of professional support workers.

Social support networks based on generalized reciprocity (Sahlins, 1972) combine a communitarian character with a great independence among participating individuals. In fact, the strength of the support network is derived from what Granovetter (1973) called the "strength of weak ties": a rather large community of friendship circles with members who support each other, but the ties between whom are not so strong that they would cause the support network to become greedy or to threaten the independence of the individuals in the network. There are many weak ties between people to make the network strong. The exchange principle is not based on direct reciprocation. Sometimes, help may never be reciprocated – which "is not to say that handing over things in such form, even to 'loved ones' generates no counter-obligation. But the counter is not stipulated by time, quantity, or quality: the expectation of reciprocity is indefinite" (Sahlins, 1972: 194). This results in a behavior that can be described as "citizenship behavior." People make contributions to society that are not altruistic, but stem from the well-understood self-interest that, one day, they might receive support from someone with whom they perhaps are not personally acquainted. The principle of generalized reciprocity enables networks to be of medium or large size. Relationships within the network, but also within the family, are egalitarian. Spouses derive their status from their own occupation or their personality. When the military organization and the family both believe the relation to be a two-sided affair, the chance that the family–military relation will be conflictuous is low. Support is offered on basis of friendship without the expectation of immediate reciprocation, which causes the support network to be stable. Prolonged support is enabled because support is offered without the expectation of immediate reciprocation. The friendship circles giving support, in fact, very much resemble the volunteer groups, or "home front groups," in the armed forces. In short, social support networks based on generalized reciprocity are effective and efficient.

The structure of this book

The organization of this book corresponds to the three main research questions and therefore is divided into three parts, as follows.

- Part I Military organizations and families in transition
- Part II: Military families under stress
- Part III National social-psychological family support

Part I (Chapters 2–5) focuses on how military families manage the demands of military and private life, in light of societal and military changes and developments that have occurred during the past several decades. The framework of Segal (1986), viewing the military and the family as greedy institutions, provided a significant basis for studying work and family relations in military contexts. In the first chapter of this part of the book (Chapter 2), De Angelis and Segal discuss the current applicability of Segal's original application of the "greedy institutions" concept to the military and the family. In view of the transitions that both social institutions have undergone, the authors address the contemporary military work–family interface. Chapter 3 deals with the interrelationship between the military and the family in Israel, where "home" is sometimes just a few miles away from the "battlefield." In this chapter, Eran-Jona explores the role of the military culture in constructing gendered role divisions in officers' families. In Chapter 4,

Smith examines dual-military couples' strategies and decision-making to achieve a work–family fit, given that coordinating two military careers with a family is likely to involve additional challenges. The first part of the book concludes with the contribution of Frederic and Masson (Chapter 5), who focus on changes in military–family relationships in Argentina.

Part II (Chapters 6–11) focuses on how soldiers and their family members are affected by, and deal with, family separations caused by military deployments. This part of the book starts with a description of the emotional cycle of deployment. In this chapter (Chapter 6), Tomforde discusses the stressors and coping strategies used during the various stages of deployment, illustrated by data collected among families of German service members. In Chapter 7, Dandeker, Eversden, Birtles, and Wessely describe the experiences of British Army wives before, during, and after service members' deployments to Iraq. Among other things, they address work–life tensions, adaptation to the separation, experiences of rest and recreation (R&R), well-being, the impact on children, support, and satisfaction with military life. Subsequently, in Chapter 8, Dursun and Sudom assess the impact of military lifestyle demands on spouses of Canadian Armed Forces members, and the effects of appraisals and coping styles on their well-being. In Chapter 9, Andres, De Angelis, and McCone address how military deployments affect relationship quality and stability among couples, from an international perspective. The authors stress the diversity of intimate relationships, describe their unique challenges, and focus on the different approaches to different types of couple. Dekel, MacDermid Wadsworth, and Sanchez (Chapter 10) then focus on family dynamics should soldiers return home with stress symptoms. More specifically, they describe the effects of deployment-related posttraumatic stress on couple relationships. Their review includes international research, conducted among families of active duty military personnel, as well as families of national guard and reserve forces. The final chapter of this part of the book (Chapter 11) deals with the effects of deployments on children. In this chapter, Andres and Coulthard make international comparisons between military families with children in Canada and the Netherlands.

Part III (Chapters 12–19) assesses the evolution and organization of national structures of family support systems. This part of the book starts with a chapter from the United States (Chapter 12) in which Bartone explores significant changes in the level of support given to American military families during the last two decades. In Chapter 13, Bowen, Martin, Mancini, and Swick present a framework of community capacity. The authors argue that community members have a shared responsibility in supporting military families and promoting their well-being. In this chapter, they examine the role of community capacity in the psychological well-being of married U.S. Air Force members. Subsequently, in Chapter 14, Juvan and Vuga examine the support provided to members of the Slovenian Armed Forces and their family members. Chapter 15 focuses on social-psychological support services provided by the Belgian Defense. In this chapter, Manigart, Lecoq, and Lo Bue examine the extent to which support services are known and used by military families before, during, and after long-term operations abroad, and families' satisfaction with these services. In Chapter 16, Carreiras addresses the Portuguese case, in which families are "invisible" components of the military social landscape and where there are no specific programs or policies aimed at supporting families of deployed service members. Varoglu, Ercil, and Sigri focus, in Chapter 17, on military families in Turkey, and the support systems that help them to cope with family separation and the injury and death of a family member. Because of the increased involvement of Turkish military personnel in peacekeeping and counterterrorism operations, service members and their families face increasing demands and challenges, and family support has become a necessity. However, research and attention to military families in Turkey is scarce. Similarly, little is known about support supplied to military families in Australia and Japan. In Chapter 18, Siebler describes the organization of the support provided to Australian military families, as well as families' deployment experiences, and perceptions of formal and informal family support in the context of deployments to East Timor. Kawano and Fukuura (Chapter 19) then address the organization and effectiveness of family support in Japan, where service members and families have faced increased operational tempo as a result of a wide range of missions overseas, along with domestic disaster relief operations related to the earthquake, tsunami, and nuclear power plant disaster in 2011.

We conclude this book with an epilogue (Chapter 20), which presents a synthesis of the main findings and insights presented.

We hope that the chapters in this book stimulate a rich dialogue among military family scholars worldwide, as well as lead to greater collaboration among scholars from different disciplines, perspectives, and locations in expanding the science of what we know about military families.

Notes

1 Ample references substantiate the point of "change" in missions, conflict, and warfare. Just a cursory selection, necessarily incomplete, serves as an illustration. This paragraph was based on Arquilla and Ronfeld (2001), Kaag and Kreps (2014), McInnes (2002), Shaw (2005), and Singer (2009).

2 For a discussion on these traditions, see Ekeh (1974).

References

Arquilla, J., and Ronfeld, D. (2001) *Networks and Netwars: The future of terror, crime, and militancy*. Santa Monica, CA: Rand.

Bartone, J.V., and Bartone, P.T. (1997) "American Army Families in Europe: Coping with deployment separation." Paper delivered at the International Workshop on The Importance of Research on the Home Front and the Need for Family Support. Brussels: Royal Military Academy.

Bell, B., Segal, M.W., and Rice, R.E. (1995) "Family issues in the assignment of Reservists to peacekeeping duty." Paper presented at the Inter-University Seminar on Armed Forces and Society, October, Chicago, IL.

Bourg, C., and Segal, M.W. (1999) "The impact of family supportive policies and practices on organizational commitment to the Army." *Armed Forces & Society*, 25(4): 633–52.

Bowen, G.L., and Martin, J.A. (2011) "The resiliency model of role performance for service members, veterans, and their families: A focus on social connections and individual assets." *Journal of Human Behavior in the Social Environment*, 21: 162–78.

Bowen, G.L., and Orthner, D.K. (eds.) (1989) *The Organization Family: Work and family linkages in the U.S. Military*. New York: Praeger.

Bowen, G.L., Martin, J.A., and Mancini, J.A. (2013) "The resilience of military families: Theoretical perspectives." In M.A. Fine and F.D. Fincham (eds.) *Family Theories: A content-based approach*. New York: Routledge, pp. 417–36.

Cohen, S., and Wills, T.A. (1985) "Stress, social support, and the buffering hypothesis." *Psychological Bulletin*, 98: 310–57.

Coker, C. (2014) *Can War Be Eliminated?* Cambridge: Polity Press.

Coser, L.A. (1974) *Greedy Institutions: Patterns of undivided commitment*. New York: The Free Press.

Desivilya, H.S., and Gal, R. (1996) "Coping with stress in families of servicemen: Searching for 'win–win' solutions to a conflict between the family and the military organization." *Family Process*, 35: 211–25.

Durand, D.B., Burrell, L., Knudson, K., Stretch, R.K., and Castro, C. (2001) "Living OCONUS in a high OPTEMPO environment: How are families adjusting?" Paper presented at the Inter-University Seminar on Armed Forces and Society, October, Chicago, IL.

Ekeh, P. (1974) *Social Exchange Theory: The two traditions*. London: Heinemann.

Gelles, R.J. (1995) *Contemporary Families: A sociological view*. London: Sage.

Granovetter, M. (1973) "The strength of weak ties." *American Journal of Sociology*, 78: 1360–80.

Greenhaus, J.H., and Beutell, N.J. (1985) "Sources of conflict between work and family roles." *Academy of Management Review*, 10(1): 76–88.

Harrell, M.C. (2001) "Gender- and class-based role expectations for Army spouses." Paper presented at the Inter-University Seminar on Armed Forces and Society, October, Chicago, IL.

Hawkins, J.P. (2001) *Army of Hope, Army of Alienation: Culture and contradiction in the American Army communities of Cold War Germany*. Westport, CT: Praeger/ Greenwood.

Hill, R. (1949) *Families under Stress*. New York: Harper & Row.

Holmes, T.H., and Rahe, R.H. (1967) "The social readjustment scale." *Journal of Psychosomatic Research*, 11: 213–18.

Ilies, R., Schwind, K.M., Wagner, D.T., Johnson, M.D., DeRue, D.S., and Ilgen, D.R. (2007) "When can employees have a family life? The effects of daily workload and affect on work–family conflict and social behaviors at home." *Journal of Applied Psychology*, 92(5): 1368–79.

Janowitz, M. (1960) *The Professional Soldier: A social and political portrait.* New York: The Free Press of Glencoe.

Jessup, C. (1996) *Breaking Ranks: Social change in military communities.* London/ Washington, D.C.: Brassey's.

Kaag, J., and Kreps, S. (2014) *Drone Warfare.* Cambridge: Polity Press.

Kaldor, M. (2012) *New and Old Wars: Organised violence in a global era.* Cambridge: Polity Press.

Martinsen, K.D. (2013) *Soldier Repatriation: Popular and political responses.* Burlington, VT: Ashgate.

McCubbin, H.I. (1979) "Integrating coping behavior in family stress theory," *Journal of Marriage and the Family,* 41(May): 237–44.

McCubbin, H.I., and Patterson, J. (1982) "Family adaptation to crisis." In H.I. McCubbin, A.E. Cauble, and J. Patterson (eds.) *Family Stress, Coping and Social Support.* Springfield, IL: C.C. Thomas, pp. 26–47.

McInnes, C. (2002) *Spectator Sport War: The West and contemporary conflict.* Boulder, CO: Lynne Rienner.

Moelker, R., and van der Kloet, I.E. (2003) "Military families and armed forces: A two-sided affair." In G. Caforio (ed.) *Handbook of the Sociology of the Military.* New York: Kluwer Academic/Plenum Publishing, pp. 201–24.

Moskos, C.C. (1977) "From institutions to occupation." *Armed Forces & Society,* 4(1): 41–50.

Oakley, R.B., Dziedzic, M.J., and Goldber, E.M. (1998) *Policing the New World Order: Peace operations and public security.* Washington, D.C.: National Defense University Press.

Rode, J.C., Rehg, M.T., Near, J.P., and Underhill, J.R. (2007) "The effect of work/family conflict on intention to quit: The mediating roles of job and life satisfaction." *Applied Research in Quality of Life,* 2: 65–82.

Rosen, L.N., and Moghadam, L.Z. (1990) "Matching the support to the stressor: Implications for the buffering hypothesis." *Military Psychology,* 2(4): 193–204.

Sahlins, M.D. (1972) *Stone Age Economics.* London: Routledge.

Segal, D.R., Blum, R.W., Gorman, G.H., and Maholmes, V. (2011) *The Effects of Military Deployment on Family Health.* Washington, D.C.: National Press Club.

Segal, M.W. (1986) "The military and the family as greedy institutions." *Armed Forces & Society,* 13(1): 9–38.

Shaw, M. (2005) *The New Western Way of War: Risk-transfer war and its crisis in Iraq.* Cambridge: Polity Press.

Singer, P. (2009) *Wired for War: The robotics revolution and conflict in the 21th century.* New York: Penguin.

Soeters, J. (1994) "Roddel in organisaties [Gossip in organizations]." *Sociologische Gids,* 5: 329–45.

Szvircsev Tresch, T., and Haltiner, K.W. (2008) "New trends in civil–military relations: The decline of conscription in Europe." In A. Weibull and B. Abrahamsson (eds.) *Heritage and the Present.* Stockholm: National Defense College, pp. 169–88.

Vinokur, A.D., Pierce, P.F., and Buck, C.L. (1999) "Work–family conflicts of women in the Air Force: Their influence on mental health and functioning." *Journal of Organizational Behavior,* 20(6): 865–78.

Weinstein, L., and White, C.C. (1997) *Wives and Warriors: Women and the military in the United States and Canada.* Westport, CT: Bergin and Garvey.

Wessely, S. (2006) "Twentieth-century theories on combat motivation and breakdown." *Journal of Contemporary History*, 41: 268–86.

Westman, M., and Etzion, D.L. (2005) "The crossover of work–family conflict from one spouse to the other." *Journal of Applied Social Psychology*, 35(9): 1936–57.

Withuis, J. (2004) *Does PTSD Really Exist? On trauma, trauma culture, and trauma abuse.* Utrecht: Stichting ICODO.

2 Transitions in the military and the family as greedy institutions

Original concept and current applicability

Karin De Angelis and Mady Wechsler Segal

Introduction

Military families live at the intersection of two major social institutions, both of which involve a complex set of roles and rules, and both of which make great demands on the individual's time, loyalty, and energy as "greedy institutions" (Coser, 1974; Segal, 1986). The military is the primary organization for providing a common defense against external threats. Service members, who are the military's most important tool, complete this charge within the confines of a professional code and leadership decisions that determine how, when, and where they serve. Families, which encompass great diversity in their form and roles, serve the important social functions of protecting property rights, providing protection to their members and legal legitimacy for childbearing and childrearing. They also disproportionately carry the social burden of member care, regardless of age or location (Bianchi and Casper, 2000). When functioning well, family members also provide psychological gratification and social support to each other.

Separately, the military and the family impose substantial demands on their members; together, the intersection of these two social institutions creates the potential for spillover, both positive and negative, and conflict.[1] It is this capacity for spillover and conflict that was first captured by Segal (1986) when applying the concept of "greedy institutions" to both the military and the family. Since then, the original application has been used to provide conceptual understanding and a policy-relevant framework to a complex intersection; however, its usefulness and applicability also have evolved as these social institutions have undergone considerable change.

In this chapter, we examine Segal's original application of the "greedy institutions" concept to the military and the family, with attention to the wartime and family trends that were occurring during its conceptualization. We then transition to the major social and demographic trends currently shaping the military and families, and we revisit the work–family interface. We argue that the greediness of the military lifestyle for modern families in the United States and its allied nations has at least remained constant, if not grown, since Segal originally applied this concept. In her oft-cited article, Segal (1986: 9) argues that, "due to various social trends in American society and in military family patterns, there is greater conflict now than in the past between these two greedy institutions." At this point in history, we extend this original application and argue that the suggested tensions of the 1980s American military and American military family have been even more exacerbated. We make this argument because of demographic and cultural shifts in families, as well as accompanying organizational changes in the American military that have occurred since the time of the article's publication – changes that we highlight in subsequent sections of this paper.

Greedy institutions and military families: Original conceptualization

Families have always been connected to the American military, yet the military institution has had varying definitions of and approaches to the families of its personnel. At times, the military has viewed the family (generally spouses and children) as an obstacle competing for the service member's time and interest, and has ignored familial contributions as well as the overall well-being of service members (Albano, 1994). From the Revolutionary War until World War I, the military neglected family concerns, especially since the overwhelming majority of military members were young, unmarried men. As a consequence, there was less recognized conflict between the military and the family during this time, although for those with families there is evidence of spousal involvement in, and sacrifice for, the war mission. Between World War I and World War II, the military's approach changed to ambivalence, with service members formally encouraged not to marry. However, the military did provide informal services and allowances to those who did so; this support was mainly limited to the officer corps.

A major transition in the relationship between the military and the family occurred after World War II, as the United States greeted the looming Cold War with a commitment to building and maintaining a large standing army rather than the mobilization model of past conflicts (Segal, 1989). The mass armed forces of the early-to-mid twentieth century were based on a model of national mobilization during wartime and demobilization during times of peace, since it was considered an inefficient use of financial and staffing resources to keep large militaries in place permanently, especially in democratic societies (Segal, 1989). When needed, the expansion of these forces was achieved mainly through selective conscription, which was justified by male citizenship responsibilities. The reliance on conscription soured after the United States' negative experience with the Vietnam War. There were, for example, perceptions that certain groups of men, especially African American men, disproportionately bore the burden of service (Badillo and Curry, 1976). As a consequence, the government transitioned to a volunteer model of a smaller, professional force built around labor market principles and the prioritization of free will.

This transition from selective conscription to an all-volunteer force, coupled with a newfound focus on career-oriented service members, changed the interdependence between the military and families. This transition occurred of necessity, as the bachelor military was slowly being replaced by highly skilled and more educated service members, who, by virtue of their time in service, were older and thus more likely to be married with children (Segal and Segal, 2004). Women also began to fill the ranks in greater numbers, particularly as the legal mandates limiting their participation were lifted and women were no longer automatically discharged upon becoming pregnant (Manning, 2008).

The Cold War, although demanding and stressful, was a unique conflict for the American military because of its focus on arms accumulation and deterrence. Deployments were a part of the military lifestyle, especially for Navy and Marine Corps personnel who participated in routine seafaring missions, but these deployments were relatively short and ample time was provided in between missions for rest. Additionally, much of the wartime focus was on short-lived regional conflicts and on ready exercises in the continental United States (Segal, 1989). Large numbers of Army and Air Force personnel were stationed overseas. Those of sufficient rank were able to have their spouses and children accompany them, with one-year tours in Korea a notable exception. The majority of service members were not enduring the pace of deployments experienced today.

Because of the arms race, weapons systems were becoming increasingly complex, creating the need for a more educated force capable of operating and maintaining them. As a consequence, attracting and then retaining high-quality accessions became an issue of national security, leading to the increased use of formal benefits, such as family support, in line with labor market principles of recruitment and retention. For example, partly in response to grassroots movements among military families (Stanley, Segal, and Laughton, 1990), the 1980s brought new support services such as child development centers, spousal employment programs, advice for new parents, and programs to prevent and treat domestic violence (euphemistically called "family advocacy"), relocation information and sponsorship (including information on schools), and counseling centers focused on balancing the demands of the military lifestyle. The military relied upon these formal support systems as a way of furthering individual service member and family well-being, as well as offering familial support (Segal and Harris, 1993). A cultural change had also taken hold across the officer and senior enlisted ranks, with the expectation that career service members would settle down, marry, and bring into the organizational fold a committed spouse ready to serve both the family and the military (Harrell, 2001).

The average American military service member is now much more likely than in years past to be married with children and to have an employed spouse, and the military organization has had to respond to these demographic shifts with formal policy changes that recognize the sacrifices experienced by military families. Building on these trends, and because both research and experience demonstrate a connection between family satisfaction and service member commitment and retention, the military now formally recognizes with policies and programs the contributions and needs of military families (Booth et al., 2007; Segal and Harris, 1993). These policies and programs are aimed at helping service members and their families to adapt to the military's greedy demands, not at reducing those demands.

It was toward the end of the Cold War when Segal proposed the application of Coser's theory of "greedy institutions" to the military and the family. At this time, the American military was in the midst of a unique wartime environment, in which it was fighting with an all-volunteer force of demonstrably higher quality than the fighting forces of past conflicts. Further, as a large standing force, the military continued as a major institution in the American social structure (Segal, 1989). As noted by Coser (1974), most modern social institutions, which are in competition with each other for survival, make only limited demands on their members because it is unrealistic to expect more. In the case of the economy and paid labor, employers are restricted in terms of the time demands that they can make on workers, and employees have some legal protections that create space for family care (Coser, 1974; Segal, 1986). Work–family conflict does exist at a significant level, especially in connection to broad cultural and demographic shifts in the American population, and the trends regarding this conflict apply to both civilian and military families.[2] However, in contrast to other occupations, the military, which also functions as a major employer, is unique in terms of the "greedy" demands that it is able to make legally on its employees and how these demands interact with other major social institutions, such as the family. For example, service members do not have the same protections as other federal employees regarding work time: they can be expected to be on duty continuously and to work "overtime," or shift time, without extra compensation. Leave can be cancelled instantaneously in the event of a local or national emergency, and service members can be in deployed situations that prevent them from attending major family events, such as weddings, funerals, births, and graduations (Segal, 1986). Even while at their home stations, duties can interfere with spending time with families for routine and special occasions.

In addition to the difference between formal work protections among military and civilian employees, the military is also unique in terms of the combination of demands that it makes on the service member and, by extension, his or her family. The pattern of demands that characterizes the military lifestyle includes risk of injury or death, geographic mobility, separations resulting from deployments, training, and temporary duties, residence in foreign countries, and normative constraints that dictate proper behavioral norms, including a masculine environment that can affect family socialization and organization norms (Segal, 1986). It is this combination of demands that largely explains the differences in work–family conflict, stressors, policy, and support programs between military and civilian work organizations. Although people in other occupations experience some of these characteristics, the military is unique in that service members and their families are likely to experience all of these over the course of a career.

During the time of Segal's original conceptualization, the spillover from this combination of demands had become more pronounced, because it was occurring internationally against the backdrop of changing gender norms regarding the proper familial and occupational roles of men and women. Since the 1970s, women's participation in the labor force has been increasing steadily and occupations previously closed to women, whether because of formal restrictions or cultural norms, have been opening up in greater numbers (Bianchi and Spain, 1996; Bureau of Labor Statistics, 2011; Segal and Knudson, 1985). These changes also apply to the military, with incremental changes shaping the roles and representation of female service members.[3]

Thus the original application of "greedy institutions" to the military and the family came at a time of rapid, important social change regarding gender. This major cultural shift also influenced the expectations of service members as members of both the paid labor force and families, even if only indirectly, because they and their families witnessed greater flexibility in familial and work roles. These tensions have continued since the time of Segal's original application of the concept and, we argue, are even more pronounced among today's American military families, who have had to navigate two wars lasting over a decade.

Changing military missions and organization

The intersection of the military and the family as greedy institutions is not a stagnant relationship, but rather is shaped by broader social change, including the changing missions and tasks of the military, and it is most pronounced at certain occupational stages, such as wartime deployment. In the United States in particular, the military has experienced great change from the mass armed forces of the major world wars, through the Cold War period, to the postmodern military force of the subsequent era. During the 1980s and 1990s, the military was involved in conflicts and missions such as in the Sinai Peninsula, Somalia, Bosnia, Kosovo, and the Persian Gulf, as well as multiple humanitarian missions. Some of these wars resulted from destabilization following the dissolution of the Soviet Union, despite predictions of a "warless society" at the end of the Cold War (Moskos, 1992). Today, the United States has a professional all-volunteer force that has been involved in two wars in Iraq and Afghanistan. The catalyst for these concurrent, ongoing wars was the terrorist attacks of September 11, 2001. In line with its purpose of providing defense against external threats, these attacks forced the military to transition from the more regional conflicts of the 1980s and 1990s to the expeditionary conflicts of today's global "war on terror."

As a consequence, today's military forces face a new type of war – unlike the conventional world wars or regional conflicts of the past – that challenges them to master military operations other than war, such as counterinsurgency and nation-building. The area of expertise of the American service member and the doctrinal focus of the American military has grown even larger, from war-making, through peacekeeping, to managing civilian institutions in a foreign country. Military personnel are experiencing a deployment pace not seen since World War II, with many service members – especially those in the Army and the Marine Corps – serving multiple deployments with little rest time in between (Booth et al., 2007). Finally, they are doing so using a new, untested manpower model known as the "total force," which encompasses active duty personnel, reservists, and civilians. All of these changes affect how the military, as a social institution, intersects with the family.

The terrorist attacks of 2001 brought an irregular type of war counter to the training, doctrine, and expectations of the conventional warfare studied and perfected by the American and other Western militaries. Relying on the preferred model of engaging an enemy nation-state equipped with a traditional army, navy, and air force, the United States and its allies entered into the wars in Iraq and Afghanistan using the weaponry, strategy, and tactics that had guided their engagement in past conventional wars. What the American military and its allies found was an enemy that did not use the traditional organizational structures of Western militaries – there were no uniformed service members or major operating bases that could be targeted – and which intentionally broke the restrictions of international laws of war, such as those protecting civilians or humanitarian/religious centers, as a way of gaining strategic advantage. With the exception of the Vietnam War for the United States, and other colonial-era wars such as Algeria and Afghanistan, the Western militaries had little experience with guerrilla warfare and even less demonstrated success.

This initial lack of preparation for irregular warfare also brought new stressors and new injuries, both physical and mental. Unsure of who the enemy was or where it was embedded, troops deployed to Iraq and Afghanistan had to negotiate the possibility that their enemy was hidden among the innocent civilian population and that engaging in conventional warfare tactics would further feed into the insurgent cause. They also had to negotiate an enemy who capitalized on arms, such as improvised explosive devices (IEDs), which were random and deadly, and created a constant stress. Conventional weaponry, such as tanks and fighter jets, provided little relief against evolving homemade weapons that could be hidden in the ground and detonated remotely. Thus one characteristic of today's military mission and of the experiences of deployed service members is the unceasing unpredictability of irregular warfare, which defies conventions agreed upon internationally and creates a grating mental and physical stress.

Although mental stress or posttraumatic stress disorder (PTSD) are not new phenomena during warfare – terms such as "shell shock" and "battle fatigue" are labels used in the past – they have become the signature injury of these wars. Research suggests that at least 18.5 percent of service members returning from Iraq and Afghanistan have PTSD and/or depression, making detection and treatment primary issues for service members and their families (Tanielian and Jaycox, 2008).

In addition to the changes in military mission, this new type of warfare has brought new types of physical injury that, in conjunction with PTSD, have become the hallmarks of these wars and pronounced stressors for military families. As a result of improved science and technology, the gear and transportation options issued to service members provide increased protections against IEDs. Service members who, in previous conflicts, would have died from combat exposure are now surviving – but they are doing so with the increased possibility of traumatic brain injury, which can be caused by multiple concussions and the pressure changes created by IED explosions. It is estimated that approximately 19.5 percent of service members experience a traumatic brain injury during deployment (Tanielian and Jaycox, 2008). Loss of limb also has increased, with more than 1,000 service members becoming amputees (Davenport, 2010; Tan, 2012). The increase in these injuries not only strains the traditional treatment centers of the U.S. Department of Defense and the Department of Veterans Affairs, but also makes increased demands on military families, who, in many cases, are at the center of diagnosis, treatment, and ongoing support (RAND Corporation, 2008). Whether in regard to physical or mental injuries, the risk of injury and/or death is one of the characteristics that (perhaps even without the others) certainly makes the military a greedy institution.

The change in the military's mission has increased not only the risk of injury or death for service members, but also familial separation resulting from deployments and training requirements. During peacetime, these separations mainly involve professional military education, occupational training, unaccompanied tours, routine field training, and rotational sea duty (Segal, 1986). During wartime, these required separations continue, but they occur alongside more unpredictable and longer wartime deployments. Since 2002, more than 1.7 million U.S. service members have been deployed in support of operations in Iraq and Afghanistan, with approximately 150,000–200,000 troops deployed in hostile locations each month (Hosek and Martorell, 2009).

Service members are not in combat areas for an unspecified time, as was the case in wars such as World War II, but are rotated in and out of the wartime environment – that is, they are deployed on a rotational basis. However, because of the unprecedented length of these wars, many service members – especially those in the Army and the Marine Corps – experience multiple deployments with little recuperation and/or training time in between. The deployment rate is highest for Army soldiers, who often experience wartime deployments that range in duration from 12 to 15 months, with the possibility of even longer service. For example, in 2006, of those Army soldiers who had deployed, nearly 20 percent had been in the area of operations (AOR) for 18 or more consecutive months. Forty-four percent of Marines have served for 12 or more months, with the Navy and the Air Force having typical deployments of six months (Hosek and Martorell, 2009). These long-term absences have demonstrated negative effects on military families, with a measurable decline in well-being for service members and spouses, and an increase in anxiety for military children (Booth et al., 2007; Meadows, 2012). These separations also occur in tandem with other stressors cited by Segal as unique to the military institution; thus not only are military families negotiating wartime deployments, but also they are doing so alongside other demands, such as relocation.

In addition to the changing wartime mission and the influence that it has on the combination of demands experienced by military families, today's all-volunteer force is also fighting these wars under a new, untested manpower model: the "total force." At 39.4 percent of the total force, active duty personnel are the largest portion of the American military's total end strength, followed by the ready reserves at 29.2 percent and, to a lesser extent, civilian personnel (Office of the Deputy Under Secretary of Defense, 2012). This equates to approximately 1.1 million reserve service members (Meadows, 2012). Owing to this compositional breakdown, the American military cannot go to war with the active component alone. By relying on a total force, the military aims to avoid overuse of active duty forces by resituating the reserves as equal partners meriting on-par training, responsibility, and support, and by necessitating public support for even minor military operations. This policy, also known as the "Abrams Doctrine," was put into action in the 1990s during the first Gulf War, because active duty forces at that time had been reduced by 30 percent.

This model moves the reserve component from a strategic to an operational force; it must now be mobilized if the military is to accomplish its wartime mission (Segal and Segal, 2005). For example, reserve personnel are the core of many essential functions, such as transportation, medical service, and civil affairs, in which they provide 80 percent, 75 percent, and 98 percent, respectively, of military personnel (Wipfli and Owens, 2008). Thus the military (the Army in particular) has many units that cannot deploy without the activation of reserve personnel. Although the reserves have always been a key operational force (with the Vietnam War being an exception), their role has changed substantially during the current wars in Afghanistan and Iraq, as a result of the intense operations' tempo and the accompanying long – and sometimes unpredictable – deployments of these operations. In mid-2008, reserve forces constituted 40–50 percent of U.S. military personnel serving in the AOR for counterterrorism operations (Segal, 2006).

The continuous deployment schedule also highlights the need to implement a realistic mobilization schedule for reservists and their families.

To prepare for the counterinsurgency and stabilization missions of Iraq and Afghanistan, reservists often require more preparation time prior to deployment than their active duty counterparts. This process adds an additional six months to tours that are already 6–15 months in duration – a time requirement that is particularly burdensome for citizen-soldiers. Past research suggests that although separations, and especially deployments, are stressful for all families, they are even more so for families of reserve component members. This stems partly from these families being removed from the formal resources and support networks built in for active duty families and available via the closest military installation. Children may be isolated in their deployment experiences, and spouses may be unaware of what resources are available or where to go to receive them (Castaneda et al., 2008; Meadows, 2012). Like their active duty counterparts, families of reserve personnel negotiate the combination of demands detailed by Segal; however, they must also contend with potential isolation from active duty military communities. On the positive side, they are more likely to be integrated in the civilian community, to live near extended family and long-term friends, and to relocate less frequently than active duty families. Their experiences are one example of how the changing missions of the military and the accompanying manpower strategies used to accomplish them affect the intersection of the military with the family.[4]

Changing families

Changes in the military, especially in regard to the missions that it fulfills and its accompanying organizational structure, have important implications for how the military intersects with other social institutions. However, the military is not the only social institution that has experienced meaningful, measurable change. In the United States and internationally, families also have experienced major shifts, especially in demographic trends and cultural norms. This shift is most pronounced in the changing definition of who constitutes a "family." Diverse family structures continue to challenge, both numerically and culturally, the once-dominant "separate spheres" model of a breadwinner husband and a homemaker wife. In this section, we describe these major social changes in families broadly. We then highlight the similarities and differences between American families and those connected to the military.

In the United States (as well as other Western countries), the structure of the family has been subject to rapid change in the last few decades. Segal (1986) noted some of these changes and their effects on the relationship between the military and family institutions. Some of these trends have continued, further increasing the conflicts in this relationship. Some of the changes were not addressed in Segal's original analysis, but we examine them here.

The most noticeable change over time is that marriage rates continue to decline steadily. In 2010, approximately half of the adult population in the United States was married (51 percent), and there are now more young adults who have never been married than those who are married (Cohn et al., 2011; Taylor, 2010). Age at first marriage continues to rise for both men and women. Accompanying these changes in marriage is the rise in cohabitation, which is now a majority experience for most age cohorts, either as a new step toward marriage or as its replacement. There has been an increase in couples having children outside of marriage, with the share of births to unmarried women increasing from 5 percent in 1960 to 41 percent in 2008 (Taylor, 2010). Although public opinion holds the "traditional" family of a married man and woman with children to be the preferred model, there is an increased acceptance of different family types, such as single parents.

Changes in family structure, and public acceptance of them, are connected to attitudinal changes about the proper roles for men and women in the family, and in the paid labor force. More women now envision their life course as involving family and career; men have also shown a greater desire to participate actively in family life. Although once relegated to the domestic sphere, women continue to enter higher education and the paid labor force in greater numbers. They also are entering occupations once closed to them, including the military. The pay gap between men and women has been closing, and public opinion regarding women's labor participation has become more egalitarian (Cotter, Hermsen, and Vanneman, 2011; England, 2010). Men have increased their role in the domestic sphere, especially active parenting. Although fatherhood is still epitomized by providing for the family financially, men are becoming increasingly involved with domestic life and especially child care (Bianchi, Robinson, and Milkie, 2006; Townsend, 2002). Military families reflect these attitudinal changes, with more women, either as civilian or military spouses, expecting to participate in the paid labor force and more men expecting to share domestic responsibilities.

Although demographically distinct in several key ways, military families are embedded within society and, as such, are affected by these broader changes in work and family life. Women's participation in the military, for example, has increased in line with women's overall increased presence in the paid labor market. This has implications for both male and female service members, who are now more likely than in past decades to be part of a dual-earner couple. Many of these couples, and especially those that include a female service member, are dual-military couples, in which both spouses serve in the military. Currently, 6.5 percent of U.S. active duty personnel are in dual-military relationships and 11.5 percent of active duty marriages are dual-military (Office of the Deputy Under Secretary of Defense, 2012). There also has been an increase in single-parent families in the U.S. military. Currently, 5.3 percent of the active duty force comprises single parents; this is in stark contrast to the 17.4 percent of U.S. households that were single-parent households in 2010. However, despite this difference, the rate of single parenthood among female service members has increased steadily, with the highest figure occurring in 2011. The rate for male service members has been decreasing since its high in 2000.

Despite the similarities that military families share with American society, they also differ from broader societal trends in important ways, especially in regard to marriage and childbearing. Whereas marriage rates have been declining and cohabitation rates have been increasing in Western countries generally, military service members tend to have higher marriage rates than their age-matched civilian peers, with the greatest difference among groups (such as African Americans) who have the lowest rate of marriage as civilians (Lundquist, 2004). Military couples also marry at a younger age than their civilian counterparts (Segal and Segal, 2004). At the time of recruitment and initial entry into the military, however, service members are less likely than their age-comparable civilian peers to be married. This suggests that there may be something distinct about this population that makes it more receptive to marriage, or that there may be motivators toward marriage inherent in the military lifestyle (Segal and Segal, 2004). Research supports both hypotheses, suggesting that these differences may be linked to the availability of benefits to married families that are not available to cohabiting couples and the importance of military accession standards in screening out populations who are less likely to be married (Karney, Loughran, and Pollard, 2012). In addition, required relocations often force service members to make a decision about the future of an ongoing romantic relationship, choosing among ending the tie, maintaining a long-distance relationship, or getting married. The increased likelihood of marriage among military service members means that the military, as an employer, has more people affected by organizational demands; in fact, at a ratio of 1:1.4, there are more family members than service members attached to the military (Booth et al., 2007; Office of the Deputy Under Secretary of Defense, 2012).

The earlier age at first marriage plus the benefits offered to married heterosexual couples are connected to increased fertility for military families and an earlier age of first childbirth than comparable civilian peers (Kelty, Kleykamp, and Segal, 2010). In 2011, 43.9 percent of U.S. military personnel had children. Employment difficulties may also play a role in encouraging military wives to have children. Of those military families with children, approximately 68 percent have children aged 11 or younger (Office of the Deputy Under Secretary of Defense, 2012). Note, however, that these trends reflect the experiences of male service members, rather than female service members: military women have lower marital rates and fertility than their male military peers, suggesting the unique challenges faced by this group in negotiating a masculine work organization that uses a traditional family model in its approach to work–family conflict.

The military work–family interface

With the growing number of military families, as well as the increased diversity in these families, there is the potential for increased conflict between the military and the family. Aided by formal support programs, the family is expected to adapt to the military institution, rather than the military to adapt to the family. However, this assumption becomes more problematic as military families change in terms of expectations, structure, and norms, leading to increased difficulty with or outright rejection by service members and their families of organizational demands and prescribed roles (Segal, 1986). The military increasingly acknowledges a moral responsibility to military families, while also noting that, by recognizing and fulfilling family needs, it may engender greater organizational commitment from them (Bourg and Segal, 1999). Coupled with the changing military mission involved in fighting two decade-long wars, we argue that military families now experience increased spillover and potential in comparison with past decades.

The unique combination of demands outlined by Segal still applies to military families, with its impact in many cases being measurable and demonstrable of their continued greediness. Perhaps the demand most indicative of this increased conflict is the repeated, ongoing war deployments required of service members, especially those in the U.S. Army and Marine Corps. This demand is experienced alongside other required separations, such as training and military education, as well as ongoing frequent relocation. Military families move, on average, every two or three years – a rate that is 2.4 times higher than that among civilian families. They also move further distances than civilian families and are more likely to be separated from extended family – a situation that can be especially problematic for single-parent families who rely on the extended family for support (Cooney et al., 2011).

Dual-military couples face special challenges as they try to maintain two careers and have a reasonable family life. They have to work hard to get assignments in the same geographical location (known as "collocation"), contend with twice the number of separations resulting from deployments and training, and deal with institutional expectations of fast-track careers (Smith, 2010; Smith and Segal, 2012).

For dual-earner couples, the frequent relocation is especially challenging for spouses who need or want to participate in the paid labor force. To keep the family together in a joint domicile, spouses become both tied stayers and tied movers, with their employment locations determined by the military requirements of the service member, rather than the employment location that is most advantageous to the family (Cooney et al., 2011). Civilian wives also experience human capital penalties if they work in the labor market areas surrounding military bases, with higher unemployment and lower wages than in other labor market areas without a military installation (Booth, 2003).

These employment challenges are more pronounced now than they were in past decades because of the increased expectations that families should be dual-earner and that women, who previously were discouraged from labor market participation, will have employment goals and needs.

Despite this changing of social roles, families make different demands on different members, with women experiencing higher demands than men in the domestic sphere and increased social pressure to do the family work. There also is evidence that men experience increased pressures to participate fully in the paid labor force and that women are still more likely to opt out of paid work to take care of their families at home. Those women who stay in the workforce are more likely than men to take advantage of family-friendly policies designed to reduce the work–family conflict; this is especially pronounced during greedy periods such as childbirth (Glass, 2004). Unfortunately, there are no formal protections for military family members who need to reduce this conflict during times of separation and are expected to manage all domestic responsibilities (in addition to, or as a replacement of, paid labor) in the service member's absence.

This potential conflict between the military, as the lead employer, and the family is important because spousal employment – and whether this employment meets the spouse's expectations – is a major determinant of overall family satisfaction with military life and a key predictor of retention decisions (Segal and Segal, 2004). These challenges, which are a consequence of the "greediness' of the military institution, demonstrate the increased pressures that service members face in balancing work and family demands.

Even as more military spouses attempt to participate in the paid labor force, there may be limitations to their full participation because of the behavioral expectations connected with being part of a military family. Despite the increased presence of military women and of dual-earner (including dual-military) couples, family members may feel pressure to accommodate certain social roles in line with a traditional family model, which the military still favors. If the service member is married, this model often assumes a "two-person single career" approach to military life, positioning the husband as the military service member (or breadwinner) and the wife as the supportive homemaker (Papanek, 1973). This framework favors one spouse's career at the expense of the other spouse's professional life, as demonstrated by the military assumption that the service member always has an immediate support system for domestic responsibilities. The military utilizes this model by requiring unfettered availability from service members, who, in turn, frequently rely upon their spouses to provide unlimited – and often unscheduled – domestic labor.

This model disadvantages family types that are increasing in the military: dual-earner, dual-military, and single-parent. Husbands in dual-earner couples may not enjoy the benefit of having someone manage the home front; they are men within a greedy institution who do not have the privilege of living the "two-person single career" model. Likewise, married military women do not experience the same advantages as their male counterparts because there is no role counterpart for their husbands. Single parents do not have a spouse to manage any part of the domestic home front. Service members in these types of family may find themselves in stressful positions because of the often incompatible demands between home and the workplace, and the military's continued reliance on the "separate spheres" model of family life.

Research on officer and senior enlisted wives demonstrates an increase in gender-egalitarian attitudes within families, with civilian spouses less likely to subvert their careers to the demands of the military lifestyle (Durand, 2000). However, this increased unwillingness to accommodate traditional gender roles is accompanied by ongoing recognition of institutional demands on the family as necessary contributions to the service member's career (Durand, 2000). This recognition is especially acute for the wives of senior officers, who understand that their performance within gendered roles is an important consideration for service member success, particularly within command assignments (Harrell, 2001). The military assumes the participation of unpaid spousal labor in public relations and ceremonial duties, mentoring, entertaining, and socializing, and unit and readiness support. For example, military wives – particularly those married to senior officers – are responsible for planning functions such as "hail and farewells," balls, and spouse coffees. Despite the increase in women's labor force participation, these demands assume that spouses (usually wives) do not have career demands and are able to donate significant amounts of time to unpaid labor in support of the military. Although they have eased somewhat in their power, behavioral expectations for military family members remain firm and have not adjusted to broader social changes regarding gender, work, and family roles.

Because family satisfaction has a significant influence on retention, the military operates formal family support mechanisms at each military installation. However, despite the additional attention and support that these programs offer, they rely upon the traditional military husband–civilian wife model, leading to support services that do not account for the unique needs of the growing number of dual-career, dual-military, single-parent, or same-sex families. Harrison and Laliberte (1997) argue that family support centers, which are formally run by the military, not only facilitate the military's gendered organization, but are an example of it. It is common for civilian wives to lead these centers, particularly during deployments. Additionally, active duty wives and husbands and civilian employed spouses are often excluded from the informal spouse networks that provide instrumental and affective support (Marriott, 1997). In the United States, there was a news report in December 2012 of a U.S. officers' wives' club banning the wife of a woman officer, demonstrating the disconnect between the formal support services provided by the military and the increased diversity of military families.

If implemented effectively, organizational support of military families decreases the conflict experienced between work and family by creating an environment in which military personnel can express high commitment to both the military and the family (Bourg and Segal, 1999). However, there also is the possibility that formal and informal supports provided by the military will fail to alleviate many of the demands experienced by families that do not conform to the traditional family model. This problem is exacerbated in today's wartime environment and with the increased diversity of today's military families.

Cross-national issues

The book that contains this chapter is one of the first to cover military families in a cross-national context. Very little research and writing has been dedicated to analyzing the extent to which the experiences and reactions of military family members are similar or different among nations. In this section, we explore some comparisons for which some research exists, to develop hypotheses that might be tested with further cross-national analyses.

There are cross-national similarities in experiences with deployments. Some soldier reactions and family dynamics seem to be common across nations, at least among those with similar cultures. For example, all stages of the deployment process appear to be stressful for families in all of the nations studied, including the Netherlands, the United Kingdom, and the United States. The nature of the stress varies by deployment stage, with predeployment stress resulting from the anticipation of separation and the necessity to prepare for it, as well as anxieties about safety and other worries.[5] During the deployment, a common spousal emotional reaction is loneliness. Reunion is often not the ideal that spouses expect, but rather a time of readjustment in their relationships.

Research on the U.S. Army has shown that the longer a deployment – and the more time for which a soldier is away from home – the greater the stress for soldiers and their families, and the less satisfied spouses are with army life (Booth et al., 2007). Family separations have ranged from 1 to 18 months or more, with satisfaction levels decreasing with each additional increase in separation time. Some research in other nations may not have corroborated this relationship (Andres, 2010), but that may be because the separations were not nearly as long. Therefore it is important, in cross-national comparisons, to analyze the effects of specific deployment lengths, as well as time at home between separations.

The impact of injuries incurred in war zones reverberates throughout service members' families.[6] The specific effects of context need to be studied, such as the ameliorative processes of formal and informal support mechanisms. Indeed, cross-national research can be valuable in measuring the extent to, and the conditions under, which social support functions to alleviate stress caused by various aspects of the military family lifestyle.

Relocation of service members and their families is frequent in the United States, with negative consequences for families (children's schooling, spouse employment and income, maintaining friendships, etc.). Because the United States covers a large geographic area, moves even within the contiguous states can cover thousands of miles, making in-person contact with friends and family difficult (both expensive and time-consuming).

The effects of relocation in other nations are likely to be a function of several variables. We expect that the greater the distance moved, the more difficult the adjustments for families. For nations with smaller geographic area, moves are likely not to be as far, and therefore may be less stressful for service members and their families. The longer the time spent in one location, the better are spouse employment outcomes and satisfaction (Cooney, De Angelis, and Segal, 2011) and family adjustment (Booth et al., 2007). These findings need to be tested cross-nationally.

The wars in Iraq and Afghanistan have taken a toll on military families because of family separations, but there are tragic consequences in terms of the thousands of cases of fatalities and injuries to service members. Serious injuries, such as loss of limbs, traumatic brain injuries, and PTSD have become the primary responsibilities of military family members. Parents, spouses, and children of the wounded feel the effects of these wars quite directly. Cross-national research is needed to analyze how the effects vary by nation, including the effects of culture and institutional supports available to these families.

Beyond considering the differential impact of specific demands in different nations, we must also consider the nature of the military institution and organizations in each nation. Countries with military conscription of youths are likely to have fewer married service members, while those that rely on volunteers and long-term retention are likely to have mostly married personnel. Incorporating reserve personnel, who tend to be older and therefore are more likely to be married, also increases the number of military family members. All of these have implications for the intersection of the military and the family in the national context.

Conclusion and looking toward the future

Unless the demands of the military on service members and their families decrease substantially over the next decades, we can expect increased conflict between the military and family institutions. In some nations, the military demands less of families than is true of the United States, but among the United States and those nations with continued military demands, we are likely to see pressures from service members and their families for changes in the military. These increased pressures stem from the changing missions of the military, which have become more expeditionary and which – at least for the wars in Iraq and Afghanistan – confront an enemy that uses unconventional war tactics. Many countries also rely upon a volunteer military, which is expected to deploy and fight repeatedly, with little chance for rest and retraining in between missions.

Accompanying this change in military missions has been a change in family structures and expectations. Whereas the traditional family of a breadwinner husband and a homemaker wife was once the dominant model, there has been an increase in cohabiting and same-sex couples and single-parent families, all of whom potentially have different stresses and needs. Attitudinal changes have also occurred regarding the proper social roles of men and women. More adults now expect to participate in both domestic life and in the paid labor force, regardless of their gender.

As the military and the family change, the potential for conflict increases, especially as the greedy demands of these institutions continue. As part of the military organization, families are expected to absorb and accommodate the combination of demands unique to the military lifestyle. To facilitate this adaptation and as an acknowledgment of the importance of familial satisfaction, the military provides formal support services to spouses and children. These resources, however, cater to traditional families, with less formal support available to other family types. Consequently, we can anticipate further pressure for the military to do more to accommodate other family types if it wants to retain committed service members.

Regarding dual-military couples, for example, some U.S. services have been adding flexibility to "fast track" careers, such as leaves of absence and parental leave, with the U.S. Coast Guard leading the way. Assuring that couples are assigned near to each other would decrease these couples' stress and allow them to have a semblance of normal family life. Other nations provide society-wide government-supported long paid parental leave, so the situation for parents is quite different.

Reducing the frequency of relocations would likely make the military lifestyle more appealing to many families, including those with school-age children (especially teenagers), as well as civilian spouses who need or wish to be employed (and certainly those who aspire to a professional career or who are in occupations that require state licenses). Clearly, it would reduce the stress on dual-military couples and enable them to be together more. It also would allow single-parent families to remain close to their established support system.

With the repeal of the "don't ask, don't tell" policy, gay men and lesbians are now permitted to serve openly in the American armed forces. In addition, some states have passed laws allowing gay marriages. Regardless of the definitions of these couples, they further increase the diversity of military families, and will likely join other civilian spouses in pressing for recognition and change.

Sometimes recognized and sometimes ignored are military family members other than service members' spouses and children – especially service members' parents. In the United States, support groups for military families have sometimes included soldiers' parents, such as during the first Persian Gulf War. In some nations, soldiers' parents have been a political force. This can be seen in antiwar protests led by American parents of service members killed in action in recent wars (such as Cindy Sheehan protesting the war in Iraq in August 2005 outside President George W. Bush's Texas ranch). In Israel, bereaved parents of captive, missing, and fallen soldiers have organized against the government institution (Lebel and Rochlin, 2009). Parents of service members often become the primary caregivers if their children are wounded in combat. Because of their political clout and the military's reliance on them for service member well-being, parents may become increasingly vocal in their need for support and resources.

Military families, in all of their diverse forms, exist at the intersection of two major social institutions that make great, often competing, demands on their time, energy, and loyalty. Segal's original application of the "greedy institutions" concept captured this potential for spillover and conflict. Even as the military and the family have undergone considerable change, the greedy institutions framework continues to provide conceptual clarity and policy relevance to the challenges of the military family lifestyle. With this model in hand, we are better equipped to consider the increased demands encountered by military families and to provide workable solutions.

Notes

1 See Milkie et al. (2010) for a review of these concepts.
2 See Bianchi and Spain (1996) and Kanter (1977) for more information.
3 See Manning (2008) for a summary of gender integration in the American military.
4 For more on the characteristics and experiences of reserve component Army personnel, see Booth et al. (2007).
5 See Booth et al. (2007) on the United States and Tomforde, Chapter 6 in this book, on Germany.
6 See, e.g., Dekel, MacDermid Wadsworth, and Sanchez, Chapter 10 in this book, on the United States and Israel.

References

Albano, S. (1994) "Military recognition of family concerns: Revolutionary war to 1993." *Armed Forces & Society*, 20: 283–302.

Andres, M. (2010) "Behind family lines: Family members' adaptations to military-induced separations." Ph.D. dissertation, University of Tilburg. Breda, Netherlands.

Badillo, G., and Curry, G.D. (1976) "The social incidence of Vietnam casualties: Social class or race?" *Armed Forces & Society*, 2: 387–406.

Bianchi, S.M., and Casper, L.M. (2000) *American Families*. Population Bulletin #55, Washington, D.C.: Population Reference Bureau.

Bianchi, S.M., and Spain, D. (1996) *Women, Work, and Family in America*. Population Bulletin #51, Washington, D.C.: Population Reference Bureau.

Bianchi, S.M., Robinson, J.P., and Milkie, M.A. (2006) *Changing Rhythms of American Family Life*. New York: Russell Sage Foundation.

Booth, B.H. (2003) "Contextual effects of military presence on women's earnings." *Armed Forces & Society*, 30: 25–52.

Booth, B.H., Falk, W.W., Segal, D.R., and Segal, M.W. (2000) "The impact of military presence in local labor markets on the employment of women." *Gender & Society*, 14: 318–32.

Booth, B.H., Segal, M.W., and Bell, D.B., with Martin, J.A., Ender, M.G., and Nelson, J. (2007) *What We Know about Army Families*, 2007 update. Fairfax, VA: ICF International.

Bourg, C., and Segal, M.W. (1999) "The impact of family supportive policies and practices on organizational commitment to the army." *Armed Forces & Society*, 25: 633–52.

Bureau of Labor Statistics (2011) "Women at work." *Spotlight on Statistics*, March [online], available from http://www.bls.gov/spotlight/2011/women

Castaneda, L.W., Harrell, M.C., Varda, D.M., Hall, K.C., Beckett, M.K., and Stern, S. (2008) *Deployment Experiences of Guard and Reserve Families: Implications for support and retention*. Santa Monica, CA: RAND Corporation.

Cohn, D., Passel, J., Wang, W., and Livingston, G. (2011) "Barely half of U.S. adults are married: A record low." *Pew Research Social and Demographic Trends*, December 14 [online], available from http://www.pewsocialtrends.org/2011/12/14/barely-half-of-u-s-adults-are-married-a-record-low

Cooney, R., De Angelis, K., and Segal, M.W. (2011) "Moving with the military: Race, class, and gender differences in the employment consequences of tied migration." *Race, Gender & Class*, 18: 360–84.

Coser, L. (1974) *Greedy Institutions: Patterns of undivided commitment*. New York: Free Press.

Cotter, D.A., Hermsen, J.M., and Vanneman, R. (2011) "The end of the gender revolution? Attitudes from 1974 to 2006." *American Journal of Sociology*, 117: 259–89.

Davenport, C. (2010) "Ranks of amputees have risen steadily in 8 years of war." *The Washington Post*, March 21 [online], available from http://www.washingtonpost.com/wp-dyn/content/article/2010/03/20/AR2010032001225.html

Durand, D.B. (2000) "The role of the senior army wife: Then and now." In J.A. Martin, L.N. Rosen, and L.R. Sparacino (eds.) *The Military Family*. Westport, CT: Praeger, pp. 73–86.

England, P. (2010) "The gender revolution: Uneven and stalled." *Gender & Society*, 24: 149–66.

Glass, J. (2004) "Blessing or curse? Work–family policies and mother's wage growth over time." *Work & Occupations*, 31: 367–94.

Harrell, M.C. (2001) "Army officer's spouses: Have the white gloves been mothballed?" *Armed Forces & Society*, 28: 55–75.

Harrison, D., and Laliberte, L. (1997) "Gender, the military, and military family support." In L. Weinsten and C.C. White (eds.) *Wives and Warriors: Women and the military in the United States and Canada*. Westport, CT: Bergin & Garvey, pp. 35–54.

Hosek, J., and Martorell, P. (2009) *How Have Deployments during the War on Terrorism Affected Reenlistment?* Santa Monica, CA: RAND Corporation.

Kanter, R.M. (1977) *Work and the Family in the United States: A critical review and agenda for research and policy*. New York: Russell Sage Foundation.

Karney, B.R., Loughran, D.S., and Pollard, M.S. (2012) "Comparing marital status and divorce status in civilian and military populations." *Journal of Family Issues*, 33(12): 1572–94.

Kelty, R., Kleykamp, M., and Segal, D.R. (2010) "The military and the transition to adulthood." *The Future of Children*, 20: 181–207.

Lebel, U., and Rochlin, Y. (2009) "From 'fighting family' to 'belligerent families': Family–military–nation interrelationships and the forming of Israeli public behavior among families of fallen soldiers and families of MIAs and POWs." *Social Movement Studies*, 8: 359–74.

Lundquist, J.H. (2004) "When race makes no difference: Marriage and the military." *Social Forces*, 83: 731–57.

Manning, L. (2008) *Women in the Military: Where they stand.* Washington, D.C.: Women's Research and Education Institute.

Marriott, B. (1997) "The social networks of naval officers' wives: Their composition and function." In L. Weinsten and C.C. White (eds.) *Wives and Warriors: Women and the military in the United States and Canada.* Westport, CT: Bergin and Garvey, pp. 19–34.

Meadows, S.O. (2012) "Military families: What we know and what we don't know." *National Council on Family Relations Report Magazine*, March 2 [online], available from https://www.ncfr.org/ncfr-report/focus/military-families/what-we-know-and-dont-know

Milkie, M.A., Denny, K.E., Kendig, S., and Schieman, S. (2010) "Measurement of the work–family interface." In S. Sweet and J. Casey (eds.) *Sloan Network Work and Family Encyclopedia* [online], no longer available.

Moskos, C.C. (1992) "Armed forces in a warless society." In J. Kuhlmann and C. Dandeker (eds.) *Armed Forces after the Cold War.* Munich: SOWI, pp. 13–23.

Office of the Deputy Under Secretary of Defense, Military Community and Family Policy (2012) *2011 Demographics: Profile of the military community.* Washington, D.C.: Department of Defense Printing.

Papanek, H. (1973) "Men, women, and work: Reflections on the two-person career." *American Journal of Sociology*, 78: 852–72.

RAND Corporation (2008) *Postdeployment Stress: What families should know, what families can do.* Santa Monica, CA: RAND Corporation.

Segal, D.R. (1989) *Recruiting for Uncle Sam: Citizenship and military manpower policy.* Lawrence, KS: University Press of Kansas.

Segal, D.R. (2006) "Military sociology." In C.D. Bryan and D.L. Peck (eds.) *21st Century Sociology: A reference handbook.* Thousand Oaks, CA: Sage, pp. 353–60.

Segal, D.R., and Segal, M.W. (2004) *America's Military Population.* Population Bulletin #59, Washington, D.C.: Population Reference Bureau.

Segal, D.R., and Segal, M.W. (2005) *U.S. Military's Reliance on the Reserves.* Washington, D.C.: Population Reference Bureau.

Segal, M.W. (1986) "The military and the family as greedy institutions." *Armed Forces & Society*, 13: 9–38.

Segal, M.W., and Harris, J.J. (1993) *What We Know about Army Families.* Alexandria, VA: U.S. Army Research Institute for the Behavioral and Social Sciences.

Segal, M.W., and Knudson, K.H.M. (1985) *Scientific Knowledge Applicable to Decisions Regarding Women in the Military.* Report to the Secretary General of NATO, prepared under the auspices of the Committee on Women in the NATO Forces, Washington, D.C.: U.S. Department of Defense.

Smith, D.G. (2010) "Developing pathways to serving together: Dual military couples' life course and decision-making." Ph.D. dissertation, University of Maryland, College Park, MD.

Smith, D.G., and Segal, M.W. (2012) "Changing family norms: Dual military couples navigating institutional structures." Unpublished paper.

Stanley, J., Segal, M.W., and Laughton, C.J. (1990) "Grass roots family action and military policy responses." *Marriage & Family Review*, 15: 207–23.

Tan, M. (2012) "DoD says amputations reached wartime high." *Army Times*, March 14 [online], available from http://archive.armytimes.com/article/20120314/NEWS/203140318/DoD-says-amputations-reached-wartime-high

Tanielian, T., and Jaycox, L.H. (eds.) (2008) *Invisible Wounds of War: Psychological and cognitive injuries, their consequences, and services to assist recovery.* Santa Monica, CA: RAND Corporation.

Taylor, P. (ed.) (2010) "The decline of marriage and rise in new families." *Pew Research Social & Demographic Trends*, November 18 [online], available from http://pewresearch.org/pubs/1802/ decline-marriage-rise-new-families

Townsend, N. (2002) *The Package Deal: Marriage, work, and fatherhood in men's lives.* Philadelphia, PA: Temple University Press.

Wipfli, R., and Owens, D.D. (2008) *Colloquium Brief: State of the U.S. military reserve components.* Carlisle Barracks, PA: U.S. Army War College and 21st Century Defense Initiative of the Brookings Institution.

3 Organizational culture and military families

The case of combat officers in the Israel Defense Forces

Meytal Eran-Jona

Introduction

This study attempts to make a hidden group visible, a group that, until now, has been largely ignored in organizational research: workers' spouses – especially the wives of combat officers in the Israel Defense Forces (IDF).

The chapter is based on a study carried out in the IDF of military personnel and their wives. The aim has been to examine how the military, as a state institution and work organization, participates in gender processes that shape the interrelationship between family and work, and marriage relations within the family. The study examines a number of aspects of the militarization of women's lives in the case of military wives in Israel.

The research objective was to explore whether or not the military culture shapes, produces, and reproduces gendered role division in the officers' families. The findings indicate that the IDF, as a state institution and workplace for combat officers who represent hegemonic masculinity in Israeli society, employs practices and patterns of activity that shape the military culture and the combat officers' role, and produce and reproduce a gendered role division in the officers' families. The construction of the officer's role is a central element in the "justification regime" and stands at the core of the husbands' "exemption" from "household chores," and the expectation that their wives will subordinate all of their time, energy, and personal resources to household chores (so, ipso facto, to the military).

Literature review

The study is based on a sociological analysis of the meeting point between gender and three theoretical fields: family, the labor market, and civil–military relations.

The analysis of the interrelationship – which forms the foundation of the research – between the military and the processes taking place in the family is based on a number of assumptions. One, following Pateman (1989), is that practices in both the public and private spheres are interdependent and mutually linked.

Another assumption is that the military is not only part of the labor market or an instrument of the state, but also, in the case of Israel, a labor organization and social institution that represents national and state ideologies. Therefore the study also discusses the state's part in shaping the mutual relations between labor and family.

In this sense, the military is presumed to be not only a political institution closely linked to the state, as Giddens (1985) claims, but also a labor organization having its own culture, norms, and activity patterns, some of which are identical to those in other public or private labor organizations. Therefore the study of the triangular relationship between military–soldier–family can also teach us about the complex, generally transparent, relations in contemporary labor organizations between organization, worker, and worker's spouse.

My analysis is based on Giddens' view that the military is not "merely another social institution," but one that is intimately connected to the state. Indeed it is difficult to imagine another social institution as closely identified with the state – and its ideology and policies – as the military.

The military, however, is more than a state institution, as Barrett (1996) and others claim; it is a central player in constructing gender in all areas of civilian life. It constructs masculine images and defines the woman in relation to them. Enloe (2000) claims that the military has a special role in the ideological construction of patriarchy because of the central weight that combat plays in the construction of masculine identities and justification of male superiority. According to Enloe (1988), analysis of the relationships between women and the state, and women and the military, reveals the depth at which the state and military are based not only on women's support of the troops, but also on the entire gender division of labor in society. This is the case in Israel, where the conscription model is still compulsory for all men and women, and the military plays a central role in the ideological construction of patriarchy, the institutionalization of the power of the state, and definitions of masculinity (Ben-Ari and Levy-Schreiber, 2001; Sasson-Levy, 2011).

The few studies that deal with the influence of work organizations on their employees' wives are, at best, only fragmentary. Kanter (1977) was one of the first scholars to examine employees' wives and the impact of the work organization on their family and personal lives. Kanter discussed managers' wives and the organizational and social role that they played, and assumed that the labor world had an influence not only on those directly involved in it, but also on those who shared their lives with the organization's employees. Kanter noted the unspoken aspect in the distribution of housework, which grants the working men freedom in their career conditioned on the gender-based division of labor at home and the emotional, social, and technical support provided by their wives.

Be this as it may, a small number of sociological studies have focused on the work that employees' wives perform for the organization. Janet Finch (1983) produced one of the pioneering studies in this area. Finch examined different forms of wives' inclusion in their spouses' work and the processes that made this possible. Additional literature has been published in a relatively new area of research: the militarization of women – that is, the work that soldiers' wives perform for the military and the use that militaries made, and still make, of them (Enloe, 2000; Harrell, 2001; Weinstein and White, 1997).

Most of the research dealing with the relationship between the military and soldiers' families has been carried out in the American, Canadian, and British military services. Segal (1986) was the first scholar to address military–family relations as a relation between contesting organization and interests. Segal refers to the military and the family as "greedy institutions" that compete for the commitment, loyalty, time, and energy of their members. Studies carried out for the military generally investigated the degree of satisfaction with and commitment to military life, and its influence on the female spouse and children (Bell and Schumm, 2005; Blankinship, 1990; Howe, 1983; Jans, 1988; Segal, 1986; Segal and Harris, 1993). Studies taking a critical view show that the relations between the military and the soldiers' wives were never on an equal footing, because the military always had to maintain its control and domineering role over the family (Stanley, Segal, and Laughton, 1990). Moelker and van der Kloet (2003) explained modes of military control over the family by manners of "cooptation" – that is, that whenever armed forces realize for themselves that outside groups are uncontrollable and unstoppable, they will try to bind, commit, and even incorporate them.

Military–gender relations were also examined in Israeli sociological literature, although research in the field is limited and relatively new. The heart of the research and observations was women IDF soldiers in compulsory military service, and research dealt mainly with the women's place in the internal division of labor and their marginality in the military organization (Czerniak, 2006; Izraeli, 1997; Sasson-Levy, 2006; Tubi and Eran-Jona, 2002; Yuval-Davis, 1997). In the early twenty-first century, a number of works were published on the construction of masculinity among male soldiers in compulsory service (Ben-Ari and Levy-Schreiber, 2001; Gross, 2000; Kaplan, 2003; Lomsky-Feder and Rapoport, 2003; Sasson-Levy, 2002, 2006; Sion, 1997).

The first comprehensive studies of the military's status in Israeli society and its influence on gender relations were carried out by Nira Yuval-Davis (1997) and later expanded by Hanna Herzog (1998). Herzog's work examined the influence of long-term military conflict and the term "national security" on the development and preservation of gender division of labor. Ben-Ari and Levy-Schreiber (2001) claimed that the gender–military relationship is critical in Israeli nation-building. A small number of studies have dealt with the link between the military and the families of military personnel, but here too the emphasis was on soldiers in compulsory service and the connection between the military and soliders' families (Doron and Lebel, 2003; Herzog, 1998).

Research on families of career personnel was prepared mostly by and for the IDF, and most was unpublished (Israelshvili, 1987; Paz, 1982; Syna-Desivillia and Gal, 1988). These studies dealt mostly with the micro aspects of relations between the career soldier and his family. Most of the works were psychologically oriented, focusing on the family's views of military service. Few of the studies examined military–family relations from a sociological point of view (Manor et al., 2006), or discussed the implications of these relations in terms of power relations, gender aspects, and civil–military relations in Israel.

The absence of critical research on the families of Israeli career soldiers and the IDF's role as a state institution that influences all aspects of life in Israel forms the background and motivation for this study. This chapter is part of what Sasson-Levy (2011) calls the "third wave of feminist criticism" in scholarship on the military and gender in Israel, as introduced by the studies of Izraeli (1997) and Jerby (1996). It indicates that the military gender regime has broad ramifications for both men and women in Israeli society (Eran-Jona, 2007, 2011).

Methodology

The study used mixed methodology, and combines qualitative and quantitative methods. The research is based on in-depth, half-constructed interviews held with 20 combat officers and 20 wives of combat officers – all married and with children. It is also based on a quantitative survey of combat officers' families, which included two main populations: the wives of combat officers, and the wives of military personnel in general – both officers and noncommissioned officers (NCOs). The survey examined various issues related to the spouses' military careers, such as: the wives' attitudes to their spouses' military service, their attitudes to various issues regarding military–family relations, the ability to integrate family and career, role distribution patterns in the family, as well as background questions regarding the wives' socio-demographic and occupational characteristics, and background questions on the characteristics of their husbands' service. Altogether 965 respondents took part in the survey: 130 wives of combat officers, 598 wives of military personnel, and 237 husbands of career women in the military. In this chapter, emphasis is on the wives of combat officers. In addition, the study also drew on various organizational documents related to programs designed by the military for families, and so forth.

Findings

Combat officers' wives: Basic characteristics

The quantitative findings show that the combat officers' wives are a rather homogenous group of young women (with an average age of 33.1), whose socio-economic status is middle class and higher, most of whom are nonreligious Jews (82 percent), the majority (74 percent) of whom have an academic education, and all of whom have young children (an average of 2.1 children per wife).

Most of the combat officers' wives (78 percent) work outside the home; half (55 percent) work full-time and the rest (23 percent), part-time. Their employment rate is high, equivalent to that of the wives of all military officers and women with similar characteristics in the Israeli labor market. Furthermore, it was found that a third of the wives (30 percent) are employed in demanding roles (as professionals, in the security services, and so forth).

Despite the high level of employment and labor characteristics, it was found that the pattern of the division of roles in the combat officers' families was conspicuously traditional. Unsurprisingly, the findings indicate that it is the women in those families who are almost exclusively responsible for "family work." Almost all (98 percent) of them reported that they had prime responsibility for the children and most of them (70 percent) expressed dissatisfaction with this situation.

Today, such a role division occurs only in a minority of civilian Israeli families, as demonstrated by Oren (2001). Oren found that the pattern of "traditional" role division, in which the wife is mainly responsible for household chores, exists today in only 16 percent of Israeli families in which the woman works full-time. The usual pattern in most Israeli families combines some degree of shared management with a degree of the woman's dominance in performing household tasks (68 percent).

Gender arrangements and the military organizational culture

In light of these findings, it was pertinent to discover how a situation is created in which intelligent young women, in 21st-century Israel, where men are significantly more active than they were in the past in taking responsibility for the children and the family work, agree to live like their mothers did in households with a "traditional" gendered division of labor. In addition, it was worth exploring the connection between the division of roles in the private sphere and the characteristics of the husband's service and the military culture.

Before describing the findings, it is important to stress the special characteristics of the Israeli case, considering the features of the combat officers' service in the IDF. As opposed to their colleagues from the United States, the United Kingdom, and various European countries, who are deployed on missions far from home, whilst their homeland and borders remain safe from threats, the Israeli combatant's missions are within the Israeli borders, defending it from missile and terror attacks. The combat officer leaves his home to go on mission at the beginning of the week and comes back home at the weekend. Since Israel is a relatively small country, "home" may sometimes be just a few miles away from the "battlefield" (and the average commander comes back home once a week, but at least

once every two weeks). This situation creates circumstances in which families are both close and yet far, unreached in many aspects. Theoretically,
officers could take an effective part in their families' lives, but the reality
in most cases is very different. In Israel, military families do not live on
military bases, but in civilian towns, and do not have a military community
to support them (other than in the case of the Air Force, which is not part
of this study).

The main argument in this study is that since the IDF is a social institution and militaristic ideology exists in Israeli society, then it informs gender
arrangements in the families of the combat officers. These arrangements
are produced and reproduced in the couples' relationships through daily
practices linked to the cultural features of the military and to the ways in
which the role of the "ideal commander" has been constructed.

What are these daily practices? To answer this question, we can examine
the daily practices that construct the officer's role in combat units. The
findings reveal that it was constructed as a "total role" – that is, that there is
only one "right way" in which to carry it out successfully. This "ideal type"
is based on the inherent assumption that care of home and children is the
women's exclusive responsibility. Women are at home to provide for the
needs of the men and children. In other words, the "ideal model" of a "top-
notch commander" derives from a single "ideal model" in which the wife
works laboriously in the private sphere and is solely responsible for it, while
the man functions primarily in the public sphere. This implies that the realization of men's civilian commitment to the state depends on the women
bearing the entire burden of the private sphere.

The "culture of sacrifice"

The term "culture of sacrifice" is used to refer to all aspects of the organizational culture in field units that construct the role of the commander.
Gilmore (1990) claims that sacrifice is one of the outstanding features of
"masculinity" and that it frequently appears in cultures throughout the
world. Sacrifice is connected to the role that positions men as defending
family and society, even at the cost of their lives. According to Yagil Levy
(2003: 316), sacrifice always has a civilian objective, since it is defined in
terms of "the home" – the place that warrior leaves and to which he returns.

The culture of sacrifice plays a major role in the justification regime –
that is, the system of explanations and legitimacy that justifies the gender
regime created in the officers' families. The interviews revealed that the
"sacrifice culture" has six characteristics that influence the construction of
the combat officer's role: exhaustive workload and lack of sleep; physical
hardship; combat situations and life endangerments; the inability to plan
one's time; uncertainty regarding the career track; and absence from home.

We will now describe the characteristics of this "culture of sacrifice" and
then discuss its implications for gender relations in the officer's families.

Exhaustive workload and lack of sleep

All of the men interviewed mentioned the complexity of their roles and the enormity of the accompanying workload. Work continues round the clock even when they are at home on leave. For all practical purposes, almost their entire lives are devoted to work. The officers, who have to make do with minimal sleep, defined this as an "organic" part of their job.

The strain of their assignments and the chronic lack of sleep influence the amount of time that they can take off and their ability to function at home. Many officers admit that they arrive home utterly exhausted. For example, "Omri," a battalion commander, acknowledges that when he comes home, he is usually very tired and sometimes easily peeved by his children:

> One time I came home at 5 in the afternoon and stretched out on the living room rug. I didn't wake up till nighttime. The kids were running all over me, the TV was blaring, and I was totally zonked out – I'd slept through it all.
>
> (Omri, infantry battalion commander)

Physical hardship

The second characteristic is physical hardship. In Israel, service in combat units is characterized, inter alia, by sparse conditions and physical hardship. Rundown buildings, limited infrastructure, and harsh working conditions are standard features of this reality. Officers have to meet rigorous physical, mental, and organizational challenges, including combat operations, long marches, dwelling in tents for lengthy periods, lack of showers, few hours of sleep for days on end, and perpetual equipment shortages. Under these conditions, they have to carry out complex missions, often in areas populated by hostile civilians.

The ability to overcome the "grueling conditions," as the officers themselves describe them, points to the toughness, endurance, and ability to handle physical adversities that characterize military service in general. Good soldiering is linked, inter alia, to firmness and the ability to surmount hardship without complaint (Barrett, 1996). These conditions, which make it difficult for career officers' families to lead normal lives, explain why many officers prefer not to invite their families to the base at weekends.

Combat situations and life endangerments

The third characteristic is combat situations and life endangerments. Engaging in warfare is the combat soldier's ultimate objective and what distinguishes the combat officer's role from all others. Furthermore, participation in combat is also the ultimate test of a man's political commitment – since it expresses his willingness to sacrifice his life for the state (Pateman,

1989: 11). In other words, the willingness to die for one's country is the means by which to achieve the status of "ultimate soldier" and "ultimate man," with all of its implication vis-à-vis society, the military, and the officer's family. The individual's readiness to risk his life for the defense of the state is closely linked to national and militaristic perceptions in Israeli society, which put the value of "security" above and before all other values – including one's life and family.

A majority of combat officers' wives (83 percent) stated that the role their husbands fulfill is a life-risking occupation. This is not surprising. From the beginning of 2000 to 2005 (and after), during what is termed the "Second Intifada," 240 security personnel were killed and thousands injured, including a number of high-ranking officers. The officer's occupation and the life-endangering situation that it entailed had an influence on the family, for example in the anxiety experienced by family members – especially the wives. It can be assumed that the danger to life is a central factor in constructing the hegemonic masculinity of combat officers in the military, while a parallel mechanism creates and reproduces distinguished gender identities between spouses in combat officers' families. For example, the wife of a battalion commander described the special nature of her husband's profession thus:

> From the family's point of view the psychological elements are tough to deal with. When your husband is in the territories, or when Omer was in Lebanon, I was scared to death . . . I was frightened of a telephone call, a knock on the door at night, it was something that I internalized, and still have.
>
> (Shanit, battalion commander's wife)

The inability to plan one's time

The fourth characteristic is the inability to plan one's schedule. The interviews show that the organizational culture is such that although the unit generally has fixed and well-defined tasks, many parameters can alter the daily schedule: operations and initiated activity in which the officers are often required to participate; military exercises; bureaucratic and operational contingencies; prescheduled meetings with senior commanders that are cancelled on short notice; and so forth.

This characteristic of organizational culture has a powerful impact on a family's daily life. It generates instability during the officer's leave at home, since, for all practical purposes, he is on constant standby. His presence at home is on "borrowed time," perpetually in doubt, dependent on the ring of the phone that can send him racing back to his unit in the middle of the night. The family is unable to make vacation plans, and the officers cannot participate in children's holiday activities and attend family events. In many interviews, we hear of family vacations being cut short and personal plans cancelled at the last moment. Shanit, a battalion commander's wife and economist by profession, describes the uncertainty in her daily life and the inability to plan a normal schedule as characteristics of the organization's culture. Shanit also notes their implications for her ability to lead an independent career parallel to her spouse's:

> This [the army] is not an 8 to 5 workplace. (I can't even imagine what this would be like!) [The army] demands that its personnel devote their entire lives to the system, a system that sets up meetings on short notice, regardless of what you've already decided or if you have to cancel previously made arrangements. *It's a totalitarian system.* I can understand why the divorce rate is so high [among military personnel] in a system that only knows how to make demands. Last week there was a battalion commanders' meeting. Attendance was compulsory. I had a course that I'd planned three months in advance so that my husband could be home to take care of the kids. Suddenly, out of the blue, I had to find alternative arrangements; he washed his hands of the problem. He had to be at the meeting and that took precedence over everything else in our lives. This is what the organization requires of its members – it demands priority status.
>
> (Shanit, battalion commander's wife)

This uncertainty factor, as expressed in the interviews, is based on a central feature of military organization: the military's appropriation of time so that private/personal time is subordinate to organizational/public time. Under these conditions, the organization governs the officer's time as though it were its own, while private or family time – such as that of the spouse – is not taken into consideration. On the other hand, the organization instinctively assumes that officers will be prepared to perform all assignments regardless of schedule changes, even if this means canceling personal or family plans. In this light, the uncertainty factor can also be defined as a mechanism of organizational control, as Shenhav (1995) notes.

Uncertainty regarding the career track

Another aspect of the military culture is uncertainty regarding the officer's career track. Although a field assignment is limited to two years and new roles are posted during the summer, a new position is often decided at the last minute. In other words, some officers have no way of knowing even a month or two ahead of time what their next position will be. The organization's chronic deficiency in planning also means that the individual frequently has to cancel his career plans on short notice – such as beginning or even continuing academic studies – because of the uncompromising demands of the new assignment. These features of the organizational culture are endemic to the "culture of sacrifice," and create a situation in which the officer finds it difficult to arrange his time and is frequently subject to sudden changes in his professional and personal plans. Even more importantly, they point to the organization's near-absolute control over the officer's private/personal time, which is, in part, family time.

The nagging uncertainty over the serviceman's career track limits the ability to plan the family's place of residence, the wife's occupation, family expansion, and so forth. Each interview recalls a story of last-minute changes in the husband's next assignment or the cancellation or postponement of his leave, which basically means, inter alia, that the family has to revise all of its plans for a new apartment, the wife's employment, the children's school, and so forth – various aspects of managing family life that are "transparent" as far as the military is concerned. Jonathan, an army brigade commander, describes the problems through which his family goes each time it has to look for a new apartment because his next assignment is decided only at the last minute:

> You can't even plan a year ahead of time. In fact, you can't plan anything! If the army needs to transfer you from one place to another, then it does so. My wife is unwilling to leave her job. We didn't want to drive our child crazy by frequently moving to a new house. This [way of life] places heavy restrictions on a wife's career . . . At present the family's needs are a nonissue in the [army's] decision-making system and in its considerations for the officer's next assignment. If they told us a year ahead of time what my next job was going to be, we'd know what to do, and this would mitigate the uncertainty, which makes people despise the system. We always find ourselves having to rent a flat and arrange things at the last minute.
>
> (Jonathan, brigade commander)

The officers' stories reveal that the military is intolerant of an officer's refusal to accept a particular posting; refusal is practically a nonoption. The military culture expects absolute obedience from its commanders even when this affects them or their families adversely.

Absence from home

The last characteristic of the "culture of sacrifice" is prolonged absence from home. More than half of the combat officers' wives reported that the spouse comes home once a week or less (compared to only 6 percent of the wives of all officers in the military).

In the military culture, the longer the officer is away from home, the more he is perceived as a "devoted" officer and racks up organizational credit, which can be translated, among other things, into fast-track promotions. Even if many officers declare that they would prefer to be home more often, some proudly speak of their long periods of absence from home. According to Ron, an infantry brigade commander:

There's an unwritten culture in the military that looks unfavorably on anyone going home early on leave, it's as though he's shirking responsibility. The guy who makes a real effort is the one who works late hours and is absent from home. I overheard a conversation between two generals about who came home later, and whose wife throws him out of the house and has him sleep in the doghouse.

(Ron, brigade commander)

Absence from home not only is a matter of physical absence and relegating the onus of "household chores" to the wife, but also means the absence of attention and emotional resources with which the officer can provide his family. In other words, absence increases the physical work that the women are compelled to perform (taking care of the children and maintaining the home), as well as the emotional energy that they have to invest in supporting their children and officer-husbands – energy that their spouses are too busy to exert because of the nature of their work.

Discussion: The "culture of sacrifice" and its gender implications

The "culture of sacrifice" and construction of the combat officer's role, which involves an exhausting workload, physical hardship, life-risking situations, lack of control over time, uncertainty regarding the career track, and absence from home, create a situation in which the time spent by the officer with his family is, in the vast majority of cases, limited, partial, and uncertain, even though the officers serve close to their homes and come home for weekends. Furthermore, this situation creates expectation for more involvement in family lives, which remains unfulfilled. Although they are not deployed for a mission in a distant country, Israeli officers' wives cannot rely on their spouses to take an active part in family life, household chores, or child care, since practically and emotionally most of them are out of reach.

The appropriation of the combat officer's private/personal time by military/public time creates a situation in which a wife is tacitly recruited into the military by assuming her husband's role at home and providing him with all of the support necessary for his successful work performance.

But is the situation described in combat officers' families basically different from that in other Israeli families? Apparently not. We may assume that some of the features in combat officers' families are not inherently different from those in families with husbands employed in similarly demanding fields, such as hi-tech, business, administration, and others. In many ways, this study offers a general critique of the "greediness" of work organizations, which points to the capitalist order and its implications in both the public and the private spheres.

Nevertheless, military service has special characteristics – lengthy and consistent absence from home, engagement in combat, and life-risking situations – and it can be argued that the key difference between the families of combat officers and other families lies in the "justification regime." This regime imposes a system of assertions and legitimacy that justifies the gender regime in these families.

The data reveal that construction of the officer's role is a central element in the "justification regime" and stands at the core of the husband's "exemption" from "household chores." It seems that many strings bind the daily practice to the militaristic ideology prevalent in Israeli society: the officer is seen to be performing a national mission that entails his willingness to devote all of his time and energy, and even sacrifice his life, for the sake of the collective. In this way, he earns "exemption" from the private sphere, as expressed in his almost total freedom from "family work" and daily chores. But as Moelker and van der Kloet (2003) argue, the military's contract with its personnel cannot be one-sided: the other side of the "justification regime" includes financial compensation and, in the long term, social status for both officers and their families (compensation comes with the promotion to high rank, but only for those who achieve it).

The "justification regime" operates in other places too. In the hi-tech industry, for example, the system of assertions and legitimacy to the gender regime is likely to be based on high material recompense in the present and the opportunity to gain great wealth in the future.

This study has explored how the military organization culture is made up of daily practices that create a dominant, almost exclusive, pattern in families of combat officers whereby most of the wives have sole responsibility for the housework and care of the children, while the men are primarily obligated to the military. Moreover, the division of gender roles is a condition (albeit unstated and informal) for a career of military command. The gendered division of roles is constructed by the "culture of sacrifice," which is represented as a condition for the career success of the officers. In this way, the wives are recruited to provide all of the necessary assistance for their husbands' work, so that they become, in effect, invisible workers in the military.

This research has shown how young, educated, religiously nonobservant women are positioned in a traditional patriarchal order by means of the military culture and practices that subordinate officers' wives to their spouses' military careers. It indicates that the military gender regime has broad ramifications for these young women in Israeli society.

References

Barrett, F.J. (1996) "The organizational construction of hegemonic masculinity: The case of the U.S. Navy." *Gender, Work & Organization*, 3(3): 129–42.

Bell, D.B., and Schumm, W.R. (2005) "Balancing work and family demands in the military: What happens when your employer tells you to go to war?" In D. Halpern and S.E. Murphy (eds.) *From Work–Family Balance to Work–Family Interaction.* Mahwah, NJ: Lawrence Erlbaum, pp. 83–114.

Ben-Ari, E., and Levy-Schreiber, E. (2001) "Body-building, character-building and nation-building: Gender and military service in Israel." *Studies in Contemporary Judaism*, 16: 171–90 [in Hebrew].

Blankinship, D.A. (1990) "Army families and installation leaders." *Military Family Research Review*, February.

Czerniak, O. (2006) "The pink today is very blue: The integration of women soldiers in technical units of the Air Force." Unpublished thesis, Tel Aviv University, Tel Aviv, Israel.

Doron, G., and Lebel, U. (2003) *Politics of Bereavement*. Tel Aviv: Hakibbutz Hameuchad [in Hebrew].

Enloe, C. (1988) *Does Khaki Become You? The militarization of women's lives*. London: Pandora.

Enloe, C. (2000) *Maneuvers: The international politics of militarizing women's lives*. Berkeley, CA: University of California Press.

Eran-Jona, M. (2007) "The 'woman of valor' and the 'new man': Two models of the ideal family and their implications for gender arrangements in families of women and men who serve in the Israeli military." *Sotzyologyah Yisra'elit*, 8(2): 209–39 [in Hebrew].

Eran-Jona, M. (2011) "Married to the military: Military–family relations in the Israel Defense Force." *Armed Forces & Society*, 37(1): 19–41.

Finch, J. (1983) *Married to the Job: Wives incorporation in men's work*. London: G. Allen & Unwin.

Giddens, A. (1985) *The Nation-State and Violence*. Berkeley, CA: University of California Press.

Gilmore, D.D. (1990) *Manhood in the Making: Cultural concepts of masculinity*. New Haven, CT: Yale University Press.

Gross, A. (2000) "Sexuality, masculinity, military, and citizenship: The service of gays and lesbians in the Israeli Army in comparative perspective." *Pelilim*, 9: 95–183 [in Hebrew].

Harrell, M.C. (2001) "Army officers' spouses: Have the white gloves been mothballed?" *Armed Forces & Society*, 28(1): 55–75.

Herzog, H. (1998) "Homefront and battlefront: The status of Jewish and Palestinian women in Israel." *Israel Studies*, 3(1): 61–84.

Howe, H.M. (1983) "Children of the military: New support to families improves their lives." *Children Today*, 12(3): 12–14.

Israelshvili, M. (1987) *Wife's Support of Husband's Military Service*. Tel Aviv: IDF Behavioral Sciences Center.

Izraeli, D.N. (1997) "Gendering military service in the Israeli Defense Forces." *Israel Social Science Research*, 2(1): 129–67.

Jans, N.A. (1988) "The career of military wife." *Human Relations*, 42(4): 337–52.

Jerby, I. (1996) *The Double Price: The status of women in Israeli society and women's service in the IDF*. Tel Aviv: Ramot [in Hebrew].

Kanter, R.M. (1977) *Work and Family in the United States: A critical review and agenda for research and policy*. New York: Russell Sage Foundation.

Kaplan, D. (2003) *Brothers and Others in Arms: The making of love and war in Israeli combat units*. New York: Haworth Press.

Levy, Y. (2003) *The Other Army of Israel: Materialist militarism in Israel*. Tel Aviv: Miskal, Yediot Aharonot [in Hebrew].

Lomsky-Feder, E., and Rapoport, T. (2003) "Juggling models of masculinity: Russian-Jewish immigrants in the Israeli Army." *Sociological Inquiry*, 73: 114–37.

Manor, D., Amram-Katz, S., Mechani, E., and Lerer, Z. (2006) *Torn between Commitments: The veneration of suffering and family life among male and female career officers*. Paper for the IDF Advisor on Women's Issues to the Chief of Staff [online], available from http://www.aka.idf.il/SIP_STORAGE/files/1/62681. pdf [In Hebrew]

Moelker, R., and van der Kloet, I. (2003) "Military families and the armed forces: A two-sided affair?" In G. Caforio (ed.) *Handbook of the Sociology of the Military*. The Hague: Kluwer Press, pp. 196–218.

Oren, A. (2001) "Structuration of gender inequality in the labor market." Unpublished Ph.D. thesis. Tel Aviv University, Tel Aviv, Israel.

Pateman, C. (1989) *The Disorder of Women: Democracy, feminism and political theory*. Cambridge: Polity Press.

Paz, A. (1982) *Families in the Home Front: A survey of military servicemen's families*. Tel Aviv: IDF Behavioral Sciences Center [in Hebrew].

Sasson-Levy, O. (2002) "Constructing identities at the margins: Masculinities and citizenship in the Israeli Army." *Sociological Quarterly*, 43(3): 353–83.

Sasson-Levy, O. (2006) *Identities in Uniform: Masculinities and femininities in the Israeli military*. Jerusalem: The Hebrew University Magness Press [in Hebrew].

Sasson-Levy, O. (2011) "Research on gender and the military in Israel: From a gendered organization to inequality regimes." *Israel Studies Review*, 26(2): 73–98.

Segal, M.W. (1986) "The military and the family as greedy institutions." *Armed Forces & Society*, 13(1): 9–38.

Segal, M.W., and Harris, J.J. (1993) *What We Know about Army Families*. Alexandria, VA: U.S. Army Research Institute for the Behavioral and Social Sciences.

Shenhav, Y. (1995) *The Organization Machine*. Tel Aviv: Schocken [in Hebrew].

Sion, L. (1997) *Images of Manhood among Combat Soldiers*. Shaine working paper #3, Hebrew University, Jerusalem [in Hebrew].

Stanley, J., Segal, M.W., and Laughton, C.J. (1990) "Grass roots family action and military policy responses." *Marriage & Family Review*, 15: 207–23.

Syna Desivilia, H., and Gal, R. (1988) *Coping with Stress in Families of Servicemen*. Zikhron Ya'akov: The Israeli Institute for Military Studies.

Tubi, S. and Eran-Jona, M. (2002) *Women in the Israeli Military: Status, explanations and future directions*. Tel Aviv: IDF Behavioral Sciences Center [in Hebrew].

Weinstein, L.L. and White, C.C. (1997) *Wives and Warriors: Women and the military in the United States and Canada*. Westport, CT: Bergin and Garvey.

Yuval-Davis, N. (1997) *Gender and Nation*. London/Thousand Oaks, CA: Sage Publications.

4 Dual-military families

Confronting a stubborn military institution

David Smith

Introduction

The intersection of the advent of the all-volunteer force, the socio-historical context of more women entering the workforce, and more dual-earner families in society in the 21st century has created a tension between military institutional demands and changing military family needs. Indeed, despite these important societal changes, the military continues to deploy and manage forces the way it has for the past 60 years.

While the military and family as institutions continue to exhibit many of the same greedy characteristics discussed by Segal (1986),[1] the family as an institution has new demands and expectations of the military as an institution. Dual-military couples, in which both husband and wife serve in the military, have become more common in the U.S. military. The demographic shift parallels the greater percentage of women serving in the military services and increasing diversity of other family types (such as dual-earner/career couples, single parents, and same-sex couples). Interviews with 23 dual Navy officer couples show that work and family decisions are influenced by organizational constraints. However, dual-military couples coordinating two careers with a family expect flexibility that is vital to achieving work and family goals. For many of these nontraditional families, work–family conflict is inevitable in a military organization with far-reaching control in most aspects of work and family life. Couples' discourse focuses on maintaining control of their lives and being collocated, while managing two intertwined careers, an increased number of sea duty tours and deployments, perceived low priority of collocation in the job assignment process, and concerns about when and how many children to have.

This research uses a life course perspective to examine how work–family decisions influence life course pathways of U.S. Navy dual-career officer couples. The study focuses on military family life aspects in which adaptation and compromise are employed so that couples can continue their military service. This chapter provides evidence that dual-military couples are aware of structural constraints imposed by rigid military career paths encouraging a fast-track culture in the U.S. military's "up or out" promotion system. These couples also cope with twice as much time away compared to most military families. Rigid military officer career paths and increased family separation leads to a family emphasis on maintaining a collocated household – often the focus of effort for these families contending with a stubborn military institution while finding strategies to fit their family into the military lifestyle.

Stubborn military institutional structures

Entrance and promotion in the U.S. Navy is based on an internal labor market in which most accessions are brought in at the bottom and there is little opportunity for lateral entry (Rosen, 1992). Officers promote within their own unique promotion system and according to specific career requirements. Officer promotions are statutory, prescribing the number of officers, effectively establishing the military's "up or out" promotion system (Rostker et al., 1993).

The Navy's officer corps is organized by designators assigning officers' warfare specialty, career path, and promotion opportunities (Navy Personnel Command, 2010). Designators are grouped into three major categories: unrestricted line, restricted line, and staff corps. Unrestricted line officers are eligible for command at sea of ships and aviation squadrons, and have no promotion limitations. Unrestricted line warfare specialties make up the majority of the Navy officer corps and include surface warfare, submarine warfare, aviation warfare, special warfare, and special operations (Navy Personnel Command, 2010).

Officer career paths are specific to warfare specialties and determine standard tour length, type and level of job, required rank, and relative timing to next promotion opportunity. These career paths are rigid, based on timing of career milestones being achieved prior to statutory promotion boards. Career paths also determine when officers are assigned to sea duty and shore duty. "Sea duty" is defined as assignment to a deployable ship or aviation squadron. During sea duty tours, officers can expect to spend up to 50 percent of their time away from home as part of their training or deployment. "Shore duty" is defined as an assignment to a unit not normally deployable. During these tours, officers can expect to spend most of their time at their home duty station.

Dual-military couples

While proportions of women (48 percent) in dual-military marriages are higher than those of men (7.2 percent), based on overall higher proportions of men there are obviously equal numbers of men and women in dual-military marriages (Office of the Under Secretary of Defense, 2008). Dual-military couples comprise 12.1 percent of all married personnel in the military and 9.9 percent of married Navy personnel (Office of the Under Secretary of Defense,

2008). The implications of increasing numbers of dual-military couples are challenges with deployment schedules, collocation assignments, childcare arrangements, work schedules, and maintaining a high level of satisfaction with military life (Office of the Under Secretary of Defense, 2006).

For this study, dual-military couples are defined as two married military officers. Dual-military couples are restricted in career choices based on warfare specialization. These professionals' career paths often conflict with their spouses' career paths if not in the same career field. Work and family options are reduced because of institutional policies not usually allowing "sabbaticals" or lateral transfers. Military assignment policies force service members and their families to make work–family decisions on a regular basis – every two to three years. The assignment process can be emotional, since it often results in one spouse leaving months earlier to set up home at a new location, including overseas locations, while the other spouse maintains a separate home at the old duty station. This assumes that they are able to negotiate orders to the same location. "Collocation" is the term used to describe both spouses having duty station orders in the same geographical location, normally within 90 miles (Chief of Naval Personnel, 2009).

Although dual-military couples have become increasingly common in the past 30 years, there is little research on this type of military family and how their work and family roles are interrelated in achieving a work–family fit. Examining the work–family decision-making of these couples situated in the institutional structure of the U.S. Navy provides an understanding of how the timing and sequencing of role transitions varies based on strategic adaptation to the structures that shape these decisions. These couples' awareness of structural constraints is implicit in their desire to find creative solutions to reach their personal, professional, and family goals.

Previous research highlights differences in retention, promotion, work and family commitment, satisfaction, spouse collocation, and spouse support for career (Farkas and Durning, 1982; Lakhani and Gade, 1992; Orthner, 1980; Orthner and Bowen, 1982; Teplitzky, Thomas, and Nogami, 1988). Members of dual-military couples are more likely to have higher commitment to their military role if their spouse also has high commitment to the military role (Lakhani and Gade, 1992). In interviews of dual-military couples, Stander et al. (1998) find evidence that roles and family structure are understood in terms of the military organization. The couples organize and manage family time under the influence of military culture. Couples explain the interface between military and family roles in a positive context, suggesting that role meaning is found in family and career strategies. Their commitment to work roles can be explained through career goals. However, the authors find wives more likely to consider leaving their military role than husbands. Wives who are contemplating leaving the military are more likely to be making the decision based on family concerns; husbands leaving the military are more likely to be leaving the military based on promotion opportunities or financial concerns.

The gendered life course: Finding a good "fit"

Traditionally, the work–family interface is conceived in terms of conflict, spillover, and strains (Britt and Dawson, 2005; Eby et al., 2005; Grzywacz and Bass, 2003; Hammer et al., 2005; Ilies et al., 2007; Karasek and Theorell, 1990). Recently, work–family theorists are taking a more systemic view of family in relation to work demands and needs that is termed "work–family fit," or "life course fit" (Grzywacz and Bass, 2003; Moen, 2011; Moen et al., 2008a, 2008b; Voydanoff, 2005). This holistic approach to understanding how families and work "fit" together in terms of resources and demands, and in relation to gender, age, life stage, and upcoming role transitions, provides a means to examine the military (work)–family rivalry as greedy institutions (Moen, 2011). Dual-military couples may have different perspectives on how they enact their roles as officer, spouse, and parent. Because the U.S. Navy does not differentiate between husband and wife for career needs, these couples adapt their combinations of roles in creating their life course fit while adapting to a gendered life course in a male-dominated institution.

Gender is reproduced in social institutions such as families and creates boundaries to define appropriate behavior in the context of role identities, values, beliefs, and expectations (Ferree, 1990; Potucheck, 1992; West and Zimmerman, 1987). Results from the research of Zvonkovic and colleagues (1996) finds that gender roles within marriages follow traditional norms and beliefs, the meaning of which can be understood by means of how partners make work–family decisions.

The hypermasculine military institution reproduces socially defined gender roles and behavior in itself and its families. These gender roles create boundaries between work and family, so that conflicts are resolved in favor of work. Papanek (1973) defines the work–family dichotomy as the institutional blending of formal and informal requirements into the "two-person single career." If work and family are structured by gender roles, dual-military couples and other nontraditional families must adapt their role performances to achieve work–family goals to be successful. Choices related to parenthood, timing of children, and priority of work careers and family help to explain how gendered roles are influential in developing life course fit.

Williams (2000) ideologically constructs "domesticity" as based on the "ideal worker" norm, and as requiring a high level of commitment of time and energy to the employer's market work. Domesticity expects overtime and those who cannot devote themselves fully to their job are viewed as not committed. Dual-military couples are likely to confront this gendered ideology based on the total commitment and extreme demands placed on time by the military, availability for work, and the structured nature of the work career. However, since mothers and fathers both deploy, there is opportunity for both men and women to experience the effects of domesticity and the norm of the ideal worker while the spouse is deployed. In this case, the gender ideology may pose different challenges for mothers and fathers in dual-military couples.

Work–family decisions are shaped by social and cultural constraints when couples attempt to fit their everyday lives into their external reality. Hochschild and Machung (2003) use "gender strategy" to explain how husbands and wives create a decision-making framework within their family. The "second shift" is the strategy that Hochschild and Machung (2003) find operating in most working couples, among whom domestic work at home and child care usually falls to the wife to perform after a shift at work. Dual-military couples may face different challenges based on their motivation to have two successful careers, each constrained by the same organizational demands and structures. A couple's concerted focus of effort and energy may be devoted to finding a fit that leaves little room for gender and power differences observed in other civilian couples' gender strategies.

In response to what popular media began depicting as the "opt-out revolution" by working women, work and family researchers studying working couples find that most women are not leaving work for family reasons; rather, working women are being forced away from paid market work by the workplace (Stone, 2007). After the completion of their initial service obligation, "opting out" is a normal decision point in every military officer's career. All officers are faced with the decision to stay or leave the military regardless of family status. In a life course fit construct, "choice" may be more influenced by whether the family wants and is able to have children, as well as being able to serve and live together. Gendered career paths created by the military institution may be a constraint to finding a good fit for these families.

Research methodology

Using a life course perspective, a sample of 23 U.S. Navy officer dual-military couples, with and without children, are analyzed based on life course concepts of historical and cultural context, linked lives, human agency, and timing of lives or strategic adaptation (Giele and Elder, 1998). The analysis is sensitized to these families attempting to improve their situation in life, exerting personal control, being able to manage uncertainty, and creating structural change by reforming social institutions. Grounded theory is employed to let the data tell the story for these couples. In the tradition of Glaser and Strauss (1967), there is a continuous process of collecting and analyzing data while developing theory emerging from the data. Through data analysis, themes and categories connect the experiences of participants. Using a constant comparative method, data are collected, analyzed, and coded for emergent themes.

A purposive sample was created with help from Navy Personnel Command to achieve maximum variation within the stratified sample. Couples were recruited based on warfare specialty, when they entered military service, and presence of children. Semistructured, in-depth interviews were used to collect life histories. Interviews were conducted separately for each husband and wife to allow for differences in how couples experience the decision-making process without the influence of their partner. To aid in the analysis of the timing and sequencing of individual and couple's work–family decisions across the life course, a life history calendar was used to recall important decisions and life events (Axinn, Pearce, and Ghimire, 1999). To protect participants' anonymity, they have been assigned pseudonyms using a different letter of the alphabet for each couple. All children and Navy personnel discussed in the interviews have also been assigned pseudonyms. Any command, school, or job-specific information that may identify a participant has been altered.

Results

In support of the "greedy military institution" hypothesis, results show that work constraints influence every aspect of dual-military families. Work constraints for participants are the prescribed career path, with timing and sequencing to achieve the highest ranks. The military officer career path, while designed to meet promotion timelines and to accommodate the military's "up or out" promotion policy, also supports the breadwinner–homemaker family type. Participants find that exerting agency by choosing nonstandard career paths is met with institutional resistance. The career path that they follow also maintains a fast-track culture that does not serve officers' needs equally. Family formation and role transitions are unique to each couple's life course, based on timing and sequencing that may not always fit with a fast-track culture and structured career path. Specifically, managing two intertwined officers' careers is restrictive and maintains the relevance of the greedy military institution.

Institutional structures are a frustration and challenge for officers to exert control of their lives. The overarching cultural constraint is the Navy's institutional fast track, which essentially sets a gendered life course for women since there are perceived "acceptable" times at which to have children. Men also find the fast-track culture a challenge in supporting their wives' careers.

Coordinating the careers of a dual-career couple is all-encompassing and time-consuming. Managing two work careers requires long-term planning to meet career and family goals. Negotiating the military job assignment process leads to developing strategies to achieve collocation.

Timing children within institutional timelines for career paths, biological time for fertility, and life stage for marriage influence some officers toward career transitions that allow for having a career and family. However, many couples feel that their career paths have no "right time" at which to have children. Indeed, the dual-military family is privileging the greedy military institution with little accommodation by the military institution.

Fitting into the stubborn military institutional career path

These officers are expected to follow the career path that presents the best opportunity for promotion to the highest ranks. The culture to push people toward the most competitive career path is limiting for dual-military couples, who are balancing two careers while being in collocated job assignments. In Ike and Isabel's family, Ike is following Isabel and giving her career priority, so he is willing to accept the best job available that keeps them collocated while supporting his wife's career. Ike recounts his experience:

> [T]here are people who have other life priorities and not everybody wants to be an Admiral . . . I think if we shift the culture to where . . . you can take a job over here and enjoy your quality of life but it's not going to get you promoted and it's not the end of the world, I think that's a cultural thing that we've got to shift . . .

Kirk relates a similar experience and emphasizes the constraints of the fast-track culture in relation to the life course trajectory that he and his wife have chosen:

> [T]his notion that . . . every single person . . . should aspire to be a [Commanding Officer] . . . it's damaging in the realm we're talking about because . . . it limits your choices on what you can do . . . that mindset is not a policy per se, but it's a culture you have to work against . . .

Institutional structures and career flexibility vary based on each warfare community's career path. However, unrestricted line communities (aviation, surface, submarine) generally have more sea duty tours with stringent timing. Additionally, there are shore duty tours that are considered more competitive and milestones, such as joint duty tours (serving with a command that comprises another service) and joint education tours (which are requirements for being promoted to admiral). Other communities (restricted line, special duty, staff corps) have more flexible career paths and generally fewer sea duty tours.

Kirk is at a point in his career at which the next tour will be critical to his next promotion and selection to command, but he knows that the choices he will be expected to make for his career are not aligned with his family plans and he is struggling with how to deviate from the norm:

> I am supposed to, as a milestone for my next job, do one of a series of jobs . . . So I sense I'm going to be herded that way . . . I just know that's what I'm supposed to do . . . having been educated through my career that I'm expected now to be at milestone X . . . if my Mom was out here or there were joint jobs out there, it would be no issue for me to do the normal path, but that's not what's going to work best for a dual military career. So I feel like I have to make a different decision.

Couples in which at least one officer is not unrestricted line generally have better experiences with staying collocated and meeting both spouses' career milestones. Less structure in a career path translates to having more control of work–family decisions and timing of role transitions. Kate is in the Medical Service Corps and she offers a perspective on the flexibility that her community provides:

> [I]n the [unrestricted] line they just value moving around in the pipeline . . . in medical it's not. They value doing whatever you do well. And then part of it's . . . the politics that play into it . . . But it's definitely way more flexible than I would say the [unrestricted] line is . . .

The institutional structures of Navy officer career paths support the traditional breadwinner–homemaker family in which the stay-at-home spouse is available to provide full-time support to the service member, and the service member can devote complete energy and time to the Navy and a career. However, the most difficult aspect of the structured career path is related to coordinating two intertwined work careers.

From a life course perspective, coordinating the relational careers of a dual-career couple requires complex, long-term planning to achieve career and family goals as they negotiate the job assignment process, necessarily leading to developing strategies to achieve collocation. Because these couples have twice as many factors to coordinate, they plan well in advance to reduce uncertainty, to maintain control of their lives, and to provide flexibility for assignment changes. The assignment process is the mechanism for managing careers and negotiation with the assignment officer as a representative of the organization. In their negotiations, they employ strategies that help them to achieve work and family goals and control of their lives. Harry describes the work–family management problem thus: "[B]ecause now you're dealing with not one, but two systems, two squadrons, two frustrations, two [supervisors], I mean it's dually cumbersome."

Having twice as many factors to manage, couples view career planning and associated decision-making from several perspectives. From a responsibility perspective, just as many women as men are involved in career planning for both careers. Collocated job assignments are an assumed goal for most of the couples. The potential of not being collocated or not being available to support a spouse is stressful for many people. Kate illustrates her frustration with managing two careers:

> That's what [couples who are not dual military] do, they're not managing . . . when I deploy, when . . . I'm going to be eligible to deploy . . . these are the things I manage as a female officer with a husband who also deploys. So no one else is dealing with that.

The daily schedule also has twice as many commitments that Kirk describes thus:

> [W]hen you have duty, she has duty too; it's twice as much duty. It's twice as much I'm deployed now you're deployed. It's twice as much phone call in the middle of the night. You know it's the mandatory fun at the cocktail party when you're forcing a smile after a long day at work and you don't want to be there times two.

As these couples plan for children, the complication of two careers adds a third dimension from a life course timing perspective. Children are an additional responsibility and planning consideration that is related to the career timing and marriage, as Wendy depicts:

> The decisions you make, it's not all about you anymore. It's about another child and you can't just do whatever you want, you have to consider . . . when you get married, you have to consider your husband and now with your children you have to consider what's good for them.

Planned relocations and timing of children in the family life course and work career path have overlapping implications when the children reach school age, reinforcing the concept of a life course fit. Zoe includes school and childcare considerations in work and family planning as they change job assignments every two to three years. She conveys her concern for her children in this process when she says:

> [T]hat motherhood thing . . . you're always thinking about it, hoping what you do doesn't negatively impact them . . . deciding where to live, make sure it's near a good school . . . When I was single, I didn't have to worry about any of that . . .

To reduce uncertainty while managing two intertwined work careers, these couples find it necessary to use a long planning time horizon. Being able to plan well in advance of normal timelines, couples allow for twice as much negotiation and coordination. Finding ways in which to control any aspect of their career and family life course is important to the satisfaction of these couples. Nora explains in terms of balance:

> I think you can completely achieve your work–life balance very easily as long as you kind of think ahead about what needs to be happening or what you need to be doing for the Navy, as well as what you need to be doing for your family.

Using all available resources to exert agency into a structured process, dual-military couples use their informal support networks to find collocated jobs. Ike feels that a longer planning timeline facilitates this process:

It generally takes a lot of lead time. Where the normal process they tell you to start calling a year to six months [ahead], we generally try to start maybe a year and a half, two years out to at least get feelers of . . . where are they going to send her . . . so I can start scrubbing the database or making phone calls to friends. You sometimes have to go outside of the Navy [assignment] system . . .

Kirk expands this strategy of a longer planning timeline when he describes planning a career as a continual process to stay in control of their choices:

The whole being dual military is an ongoing thing. In my mind . . . the day I execute any future orders, I'm going to be looking for the next set of orders, that's just the nature of . . . being dual military. You gotta plan ahead more so than anybody else . . .

The institutional mechanism to obtain new jobs is negotiated through the assignment process. Collocation is the most common concern for couples and they have distinct feelings about how this is handled in the assignment process. A common theme among couples in unrestricted warfare communities is that the assignment officer is not concerned about their work–family situation. Rick rationalizes this perspective:

[Assignment officers have] jobs they need to fill, and they have a certain career path that they want you on. And they're just putting pegs in holes. They're saying . . . this guy, he's a department head so he's gotta go here; this guy's gotta go there . . . So I mean they're not nearly as flexible.

However, most of the couples explain that the single part of their life over which the Navy has the most effect and could similarly improve is the assignment process. Zoe expresses her desire for improvement:

To me the biggest deal about dual military couples is the [assignment process]. Whether your [assignment officer] is sensitive or even cares about trying to keep you collocated. Because if you can't be near each other, that's going to make that whole tour that much harder . . .

Officers in restricted line communities feel that their communities are more interested in keeping them happy from a work–family perspective, and work closely with each officer to assign jobs that develop the officer and provide a professionally rewarding experience. As an example of taking a more holistic approach to considering work–family fit, some warfare communities have started to include children and spouses in their career planning, allowing officers to plan a life course pathway with their assignment officer – although it is not likely to be coordinated with the spouse's assignment officer. Laura demonstrates how her community is able to provide flexibility and overcome conflict caused by her husband's community:

I think they can do that partly because it's shore-based and then also because it's a small community. And the [restricted line] community is a lot more flexible in terms of tour lengths too. And they actually have on their . . . career planner; they have children in there, when they start high school, when they start grade school.

Given the importance of collocation, these dual-military couples create strategies to exercise agency and control in the assignment process. The most common strategy was bargaining with capital. In some cases, the capital was staying in the Navy if their spouse were able to be collocated. Mark discusses how Melissa uses this strategy: "I think Melissa had something to do with it where she told the detailer that she . . . would think about staying in if I got some [collocated] orders. So I think that definitely helped the process."

Another common strategy is to negotiate an assignment for the spouse who can get the desired location and then use the collocation policy to attempt to force the spouse's collocated assignment. Laura recounts how she used this strategy to have Lance reassigned to her location, saying: "[S]ince I was six months ahead of Lance, I did get my orders before he did and so he had to be collocated, but collocated with Annapolis is still considered Washington, D.C."

Similarly, couples use power differential between assignment officers in different communities to negotiate for their spouse. For example, Isabel states that "we would tend to negotiate with my detailer first because we knew that they would eventually get his detailer in line."

Having expert or detailed knowledge of the assignment process allows couples to take advantage of informal business rules employed by assignment officers. Isabel explains how her assignment officer has a smaller number of officers to assign, which creates a situation in which she says:

[T]hey're more forceful [assignment officers], they have been pretty demanding. "We are sending her to a ship; she will live with her husband. Now what are you going to do about it?" . . . a year and a half out, [my assignment officer] saying we want to send you here next. So I tell my husband . . . can you start asking your [assignment officer] about it? His [assignment officer says], "you're not in the window; I don't want to talk with you." [My assignment officer said], "we'll take care of this."

Managing two interdependent work careers combined with family is a complex task that highlights the family adaptation needed for dual-military families to succeed in the stubborn military institution. To ease the stress, couples increase planning and lengthen the time horizon to cope with the regular frustration of negotiating collocated assignments and maintaining competitive careers. Strategies developed to negotiate assignments keep them together as a family, while working toward achieving their personal and professional goals. Instead of internal couples' negotiation for the greedy family institution, much of these families' time and energy is focused on the negotiation with the greedy military institution.

Dual separation and time demands

The cumulative time that these couples spend apart is measured in years. Each dual-military couple describes time away from family as their most important sacrifice. Spending, maximizing, and protecting time together, are variations that describe the importance of time. Deployments and time away are central to these couples' decisions and experiences, and lead to developing coping strategies. Dual-military families depict how they deal with time away as being collocated, but deployed, maximizing time together when they are home, adjusting and readjusting from being gone, and being away from children. To summarize these couples' experiences, Olivia says: "We spend twice as much time away as other [Navy] couples."

Many couples are collocated and able to live in the same house, yet spend a significant time apart because of deployments and operational schedules. When this occurs early in careers and the family life course, it influences later work and family decision-making in determining pathways that fit their changing circumstances. Accommodations take the form of delaying or not having children, transitions to warfare communities that are less sea duty intensive, separation from the Navy, or strategically adapting their work and family careers to find a better work–family fit. Lance describes his experience during their early years of marriage:

> [Surface nuclear] tours are hard tours, especially when every time her ship pulled in, my ship pulled out. Every time my ship pulled in, her ship pulled out. I estimate the first two years we were married, we saw each other six or seven months' total.

Claire rationalizes the experience of being separated by looking back and placing the separations in the context of their entire career and marriage:

> We did multiple back to back deployments, so that would be a year apart, six months together, a year apart . . . But a year in the grand scheme now looking back on it, because we've been married for 15 years, doesn't seem like that big of a deal, but at the time it definitely was a big deal . . . especially the first few deployments not knowing what to expect.

Because dual-military couples spend so much time apart, they maximize their time together by developing strategies to make the most of any time together. Charles says that this started early in their careers and marriage, and became integral to their perspective on life: "Claire had to [relocate] and that really got us discussing how we were going to facilitate the next opportunity to be together which is definitely kind of the mindset as a young married couple in maximizing time together."

When separated, these couples spend more hours at work and find it helpful to keep busy while their spouse is gone. When they are together, Dana explains: "But when Doug was home, it was the exact opposite. It's ticking on 4 o'clock, see you later. I'll do the paperwork tomorrow." Although a spouse might be deployed, when their ship makes a port visit overseas, their spouses often take time off from work to fly out and meet them for a couple days to help to break up the long separations. One couple even devised a way in which to see each other while they were both deployed and on different ships, as Patrick recounts during one deployment: "But when the ships got close enough together, we were doing [underway replenishment] and . . . we would do sign language back and forth."

Dealing with time away gives the concept of time a different meaning for dual-military couples. Time for these couples is not related to the typical division of labor or household and childcare duties of other dual-career couples. These couples talk about time in the context of months and years more often than the daily schedule of hours. The strategies that they use to protect time together are often innovative, and display their human agency and knowledge of the greedy military institutional structure within which they work and live.

Conclusions

In this research, the greedy institutions of the military and family still exist with many of the same characteristics described by Segal (1986). What has clearly changed is the focus of families competing with the military. Diverse military families in the 21st century are resisting military demands to be controlled by military policy and structure. At the forefront of family issues are military women, since they are most likely to confront gendered career paths ingrained in a historically male-dominated institution. This analysis demonstrates the need for military family research and policy to shift focus from trying to integrate women and their families at the periphery of the military institution by means of making exceptions toward a more holistic approach that accommodates a diversity of families in the mainstream military–unrestricted line for the Navy (Kelly and Moen, 2007).

By challenging the military cultural and institutional structures, these couples influence change within the military institution. Examples of institutional policy in which active involvement or feedback from dual-military couples has been influential in change include addition of 21 days of parental leave for adopting parents, 10 days of paternity leave, 12 months of operational deferment for new mothers, partial funding of an in vitro fertilization program, telework policy, compressed work schedules, the addition of Task Force Life–Work, the Career Intermission Program, and integration of children into career path planning by some assignment officers (Chief of Naval Operations, 2007; Navy Personnel Command, 2012).

This study suggests a need for military family researchers and policy-makers to consider a more temporal perspective of work and family that considers the gender, age, life stage, and roles transitions of service members to more effectively support diverse military families, while maintaining readiness to complete required missions. For dual-military families, there tends to be a period of time (usually in the couples' late 20s) that overlaps both the career decision point after initial service obligation and family role sequencing, timing of marriage, and having children. The military lifestyle also creates more opportunities in the early formation and launching years to combine important work–family decisions that have long-term impacts beyond the Navy, such as number of children or childlessness. Frequent relocations are a contributing factor to challenges faced by dual-military couples and the collocation policy, but is also noted in previous research for all military families. As noted at a recent conference (Booth, Segal, and Place, 2010), frequent relocations are an important concern for all military families and one of the top five issues to be addressed by the U.S. Department of Defense. Reducing the number of relocations to only those that are mission-essential could have a positive impact of the work careers and family life of dual-military couples, as well as all military families.

Note

1   See also Chapter 2 in this book.

References

Axinn, W.G., Pearce, L.D., and Ghimire, D. (1999) "Innovations in life history calendar applications." *Social Science Research*, 28: 243–64.

Booth, B., Segal, M.W., and Place, N. (2010) *National Leadership Summit on Military Families: Final report.* Prepared for the Office of the Deputy Under Secretary of Defense, Military Community and Family Policy, Washington, D.C.: U.S. Department of Defense.

Britt, T.W., and Dawson, C.R. (2005) "Predicting work–family conflict from workload, job attitudes, group attributes, and health: A longitudinal study." *Military Psychology*, 17: 203–27.

Chief of Naval Personnel (2007) *Navy Guidelines Concerning Pregnancy and Parenthood.* Doc. No. OPNAVINST 6000.1C, Washington, D.C.: U.S. Department of the Navy.

Chief of Naval Personnel (2009) *Military Couple and Single Parent Assignment Policy.* Doc. No. MILPERSMAN 1300–1000, Washington, D.C.: U.S. Department of the Navy.

Eby, L.T., Casper, W.J., Lockwood, A., Bordeaux, C., and Brinley, A. (2005) "Work and family research in IO/OB: Content analysis and review of the literature (1980–2002)." *Journal of Vocational Behavior*, 66: 124–97.

Farkas, A.J., and Durning, K.P. (1982) *Characteristics and Needs of Navy Families: Policy implications.* San Diego, CA: Navy Personnel Research and Development Center.

Ferree, M.M. (1990) "Beyond separate spheres: Feminism and family research." *Journal of Marriage and the Family*, 52: 866–84.

Giele, J.Z., and Elder, G.H. (1998) "Life course research: Development of a field." In J.Z. Giele and G.H. Elder (eds.) *Methods of Life Course Research: Qualitative and quantitative approaches.* Thousand Oaks, CA: Sage Publications, pp. 5–27.

Glaser, B., and Strauss, A.L. (1967) *The Discovery of Grounded Theory: Strategies for qualitative research.* New Brunswick, NJ: Aldine Transaction.

Grzywacz, J.G., and Bass, B.L. (2004) "Work, family, and mental health: Testing different models of work–family fit." *Journal of Marriage and Family*, 65: 248–61.

Hammer, L.B., Cullen, J.C., Neal, M.B., Sinclair, R.R., and Shafiro, M.V. (2005) "The longitudinal effects of work–family conflict and positive spillover on depressive symptoms among dual-earner couples." *Journal of Occupational Health Psychology*, 10: 138–54.

Hochschild, A.R., and Machung, A. (2003) *The Second Shift.* New York: Avon Books.

Ilies, R., Schwind, K.M., Wagner, D.T., Johnson, M.D., DeRue, D.S., and Ilgen, D.R. (2007) "When can employees have a family life? The effects of daily workload and affect on work–family conflict and social behaviors at home." *Journal of Applied Psychology*, 92: 1368–79.

Karasek, R.T., and Theorell, T.T. (1990) *Healthy Work: Stress, productivity and reconstruction of working life.* New York: Basic Books.

Kelly, E.L., and Moen, P. (2007) "Rethinking the clockwork of work: Why schedule control may pay off at work and at home." *Advances in Developing Human Resources*, 9: 487–506.

Lakhani, H., and Gade, P. (1992) "Career decisions of dual military career couples: A multidisciplinary analysis of the U.S. Army." *Journal of Economic Psychology*, 13: 153–66.

Moen, P. (2011) "From 'work–family' to the 'gendered life course' and 'fit': Five challenges to the field." *Community, Work & Family*, 14: 81–96.

Moen, P., Kelly, E., and Huang, Q. (2008a) "Work, family and life-course fit: Does control over work time matter?" *Journal of Vocational Behavior*, 73: 414–25.

Moen, P., Kelly, E., and Huang, Q. (2008b) "Fit inside the work–family black box: An ecology of the life course, cycles of control reframing." *Journal of Occupational & Organizational Psychology*, 81: 411–33.

Navy Personnel Command (2010) *Navy Officer Manpower and Personnel Classifications, Vol. 1.* Doc. No. NAVPERS 15819I, Millington, TN: Navy Personnel Command.

Navy Personnel Command (2012) "Life/work integration" [online], available from http://www.public.navy.mil/bupers-npc/support/tflw/Pages/default.aspx [accessed January 10, 2013].

Office of the Under Secretary of Defense, Personnel and Readiness (2006) *Population Representation in the Military Services: Fiscal year 2004.* Washington, D.C.: Department of Defense.

Office of the Under Secretary of Defense, Personnel and Readiness (2008) *Population Representation in the Military Services: Fiscal year 2006.* Washington, D.C.: Department of Defense.

Orthner, D.K. (1980) *Families in Blue: Implications of a study of married and single parent families in the U.S. Air Force.* Greensboro, NC: Family Research and Analysis.

Orthner, D.K., and Bowen, G.L. (1982) *Families in Blue: Insights from Air Force families in the Pacific.* Washington, D.C.: SRA Corporation.

Papanek, H. (1973) "Men, women, and work: Reflections on the two-person career." *American Journal of Sociology*, 78: 852–72.

Potuchek, J.L. (1992) "Employed wives' orientations to breadwinning: A gender theory analysis." *Journal of Marriage and the Family*, 54: 548–58.

Rosen, S. (1992) "The military as an internal labor market: Some allocation, productivity, and incentive problems." *Social Science Quarterly*, 73: 227–37.

Rostker, B., Thie, H., Lacy, J., Kawata, J., and Purnell, S. (1993) *The Defense Officer Personnel Management Act of 1980: A retrospective assessment*. Santa Monica, CA: RAND Corporation.

Segal, M.W. (1986) "The military and the family as greedy institutions." *Armed Forces & Society*, 13: 9–38.

Stander, V.A., McClure, P., Gilroy, T., Chomko, J., and Long, J. (1998) *Military Marriages in the 1990s*. Scranton, PA: Military Family Institute, Marywood University.

Stone, P. (2007) *Opting out? Why women really quit careers and head home*. Berkeley, CA: University of California Press.

Teplitzky, M.L., Thomas, S.A., and Nogami, G.Y. (1988) *Dual Army Career Officers: Job attitudes and career intentions of male and female officers*. Alexandria, VA: U.S. Army Research Institute.

Voydanoff, P. (2005) "Toward a conceptualization of perceived work–family fit and balance: A demands and resources approach." *Journal of Marriage and the Family*, 67: 822–36.

West, C., and Zimmerman, D.H. (1987) "Doing gender." *Gender & Society*, 1: 125–51.

Williams, J. (2000) *Unbending Gender*. New York: Oxford University Press.

Zvonkovic, A.M., Greaves, K.M., Schmiege, C.J., and Hall, L.D. (1996) "The marital construction of gender through work and family decisions: A qualitative analysis." *Journal of Marriage and the Family*, 58: 91–100.

5 Profession and the military family in the Argentine Armed Forces

Generational differences and socio-cultural changes

Sabina Frederic and Laura Masson

Introduction

Argentina is a large country, with 38.8 percent of its total population of 40 million living in the Buenos Aires metropolitan area. Transport, education, and healthcare systems are concentrated in that small area, causing regional inequalities. However, its Armed Forces – especially the Army – were built and developed on the "territorial defense" model, making it necessary to spread military units across the country. Although these conditions also existed in the past, increasingly military officers have asked the Argentine Ministry of Defense whether their domiciles might be adapted to fit their needs. Three types of officer can thus be distinguished: those who accept separation from their families, but express suffering and discomfort; those who demand a posting nearer to their families; and those whose families have always relocated with each and every new posting, but who recognize how these frequent changes have stressed their family members.

Using an anthropological perspective to analyze qualitative interview data,[1] this chapter addresses the following questions.

- What changing conditions have given rise to this new challenge to family organization?
- How have new social family arrangements and new cultural values defeated the traditional "military family" concept?
- Do Argentina's Armed Forces have institutional instruments with which to ameliorate undesired effects?
- Does the meaning of the "military profession" and its relationship with the "military family" differ across generations?

Disgrace, military dispersion, and population concentration in Argentina

Since their constitution early in the twentieth century, the Argentine Armed Forces have adhered to the concept of territorial, marine, and air defense, which explains their current dispersion across the territory, particularly with regard to the Army. The localization of Argentine Army units was based on a 9,376 km defense frontier, as well as on the protection of extensive, sparsely populated, and isolated regions. In some cases, the Army also positioned regiments with the purpose of colonizing areas in which public services were absent, laying the groundwork for the arrival and settling of a civilian population.

During the twentieth century, this phenomenon was accompanied by an irreversible demographic trend toward extreme concentration of the population, public transport, public services, and resources in the Buenos Aires metropolitan area. Currently, an area of 2,681 km^2 supports more than 12.8 million inhabitants – that is, almost a third of the country's entire population. Such hyperconcentration brought about great disparity in terms of access to education, health, and work opportunities. Since the 1970s, a lack of investment and the dismantling of the railway system have also led to a public transport network that is increasingly deficient.

Presently, many military units – especially in the region of Patagonia, where population is particularly sparse and isolation more acute – become the nucleus of all civilian life. They are also the fundamental support base in times of snowstorm and other natural hardship, representing a source of local income for those supplying them. Hence attempts to close military units and apply a model of swift territorial deployment by specialized forces are not yet feasible.

For the deployment of effectives, the Argentine Armed Forces rely on two systems: one for officers, and a different one for noncommissioned officers (NCOs). The former remain at their posts for periods of two or three years. Consequently, an officer, on average, moves with his family 10 or 12 times during his career. On the other hand, the NCOs remain in the same post throughout practically their whole careers. In these cases, the institution tends to post NCOs in places from which they originally come, if they are required there.

Every time officers move their belongings, the institution will cover a percentage of supplementary removal expenses. At the moment, however, there is no other institutional benefit to support the mobility of officers and their families.

This was not the case two decades ago. Members of the military enjoyed benefits deriving as much from the prestige of high rank as from the fact that the national education system was also federal. As with employees of the Argentine Mail Service, or the National Bank, or the Argentine Federal Police, it was possible for military wives, many of whom were primary or secondary school teachers, to transfer their jobs across any schools in the country. At the same time, the children of military families would easily find places in schools wherever the family was posted.

The military was, however, increasingly discredited as a consequence of the part that it played in violent repression during state terrorism in the 1970s and the military dictatorship's economic failure during what it named the

"Process of National Reorganization" (1976–83), as well as the maltreatment of conscripts in the Army and its defeat during the Malvinas War (1982). The resulting disgrace was to the detriment of the prerogatives and privileges enjoyed by military members during the twentieth century (Frederic, 2012).

It was also increasingly difficult to satisfy the professional and educational needs of wives and children as a result of the transference of public education authority from the national to the provincial level. With this change and the increasing privatization in educational institutions, the disparity in standards of education in favor of Buenos Aires was strengthened. These factors, plus others deriving from the social changes within the organization of family life, have led to officers reluctant to be transferred, the previous consent of family members to follow wherever the institution might send the officer now weakened.

Military organization and family life

As holds true for armed forces within the Western world during the Cold War, in Argentina the family of the military constituted, until recently, a highly significant social unit.[2] Several factors have contributed to the constitution of the Argentine military family as a sphere of highly symbolic and social value.

From the initial training phase of officers and subofficers, during which they are separated from their family of origin, the sentimental value of this bond unfolds, promoted by military instructors; the emotional impact of the nostalgia of being far away from loved ones is considered in depth. At the same time, in this initial stage, the notion of a "great military family" is engendered, first, with their peers, and then progressively consolidated with spouses and children, with whom the officers and subofficers develop recreational activities throughout the training period.

The intervention of Catholic religious support, Argentina's official religion,[3] through its representatives within the military units has also played a fundamental role regarding the concept of family as a source of spiritual and affective support in the military profession.

At the same time, the organization of social life on military barracks and bases was centered around the family nucleus and the social networks of these families, especially in underpopulated regions with scarce educational, cultural, and entertainment options. Here, wives have played a key role, supplying affective stability to spouses and children, and creating bonds in social and recreational activities together with other wives and families. The networks formed by the attention and care in cases of illness of direct family members and the absence of the husband is a fundamental aspect of the value that soldiers attach to family. Many among those with most seniority in the Armed Forces highlight the support that their wives received during pregnancies and childbirth, as well as during illness, while the husband was posted far from home. The soldiers favor and defend this system, because they derive peace of mind from it. It allows them to continue to perform their military duties without having to worry about the situation at home.

It is also important to point out how the family model has contributed to engendering leadership among the older generation. The fatherly task of understanding, supporting, sustaining, and counseling subordinates has been one of the pillars of military leadership. Throughout generations, it is not possible to conceive a member of the military with "ascendency" over subordinates that does not derive from a daily investment in showing concern: listening to subordinates' problems, comforting them, and giving advice. Knowing details of subordinates' lives and families is considered to be a necessary element of a leader's role. In fact, this study reflects a strong conviction among higher-ranking officers that the maturity engendered by the experience of fatherhood, generally consolidated by the age of 40, is a necessary precondition to assuming unit commands – that is, command of regiments, ships, or squadrons.

The social and symbolic web woven by each of these families lessened the negative impact of transferring officers to new postings bi- or triennially, and of NCOs less frequently (every eight or ten years). That very social net-work built within the family, and within the military units, had to maintain its balance and stability – a balance that depends on receiving a portion of newcomers every year, whilst parting with others. No doubt it operated as a social "cushion," particularly in more isolated military units, such as those at more remote distances or those located in very small towns. It was there ready to mitigate the impact of leaving a place of residence – that inevitable disturbance of intimacy undergone by those having to move. It had to work precisely to sustain the web and the sense of protection that it offered in spite of the constant renewal of its members. The hospitality offered to the newly arrived was a basic institutionalized principle of care and attention that higher-ranking militaries, and particularly their wives, had to offer.

In this scenario, a military would hardly be able to distinguish specifi-cally between personal, family, or professional aspects of his life. The mili-tary organization itself elided those three dimensions of life as one, and made sure that the effectives and their families were able to function. This demanded a very active role on behalf of the wives of the militaries, thus limiting their ability to choose other jobs, professions, or tasks that would interfere with this main duty as "wife of a military."

We should consider also that this life pattern of short periods of residen-tial stability, not very common in other professions, could manifest with very little perceivable conflict whether within the heart of the family or outside the domestic sphere, owing to certain conditions also evident within civil-ian family arrangements in which the wife had to fulfill her traditional role as a mother. The study found that duty toward the mandate of "supporting family unit" subordinated the individual interests and desires of family mem-bers. Family, as the paramount value, is found even at an institutional level. The military authorities responsible for ensuring compliance with the service requirements expected subordinates to abide fully by these requirements, demanding no particular conditions, terms, or considerations. In the same vein, the rules and values that guided the mores and customs of the institution clearly reflected the family model that its members (and their wives) were expected to follow if they wanted to stay in the Armed Forces and/or have a successful career.

During the course of the twentieth century, the dominant obligation to the male parent and his authority subjugated the personal aspirations and affections of spouses or children. Similarly, individuals in the military scene were subordinated to the needs of the institution, with individual desires and interests excluded from consideration. Without doubt, this family model and exercise of authority was certainly not uniform, being distributed unevenly among the different social groups. It certainly dominated the military concept of family, however, while at the same time being the ideal promoted by the more conservative wing of the Catholic Church in Argentina.

In this regard, it is worth pointing out that, in some recently developed debates on family and relatives, specialists have noted a crucial shift in the formation and social valuation of families. As the anthropologist Martine Segalen (1992) states, obligation as the intra-family link that subdued the needs of the person within the unit to the demands imposed by those in command has given way to the consideration of individual needs within the unit as more important than contracted obligations.

Along with these changes in social values within the family, since the return of democracy in 1983, several legal transformations have challenged the model formerly encouraged by the Armed Forces. The first modification was the re-establishing of the Shared *Patria Potestad* Law in 1985 (Ley 23.234).[4] Two years later, the Divorce Law was passed in Argentina (Ley 23.515).[5] However, despite the changes in legislation that attempted to democratize relationships within the family, until quite recently the Armed Forces continued to use the term "irregular family" to designate all those couples living together without being legally married, those divorced couples who had children outside legal marriage, or single mothers. In 2007, the Argentine Ministry of Defense modified the regulations for staff administration to allow these cases to be brought under consideration; in 2008, it revoked directives of the Air Force and the Army demanding information on the matter. That same year, the regulations that made approval of a superior necessary if a military were to get married were also revoked, together with distinctions between biological children and adoptive ones, as well as children born inside the marriage or out, with the distinct purpose of eliminating stigmatizing rules that contradicted the right to equal treatment (Ministry of Defense, 2010). As it can be seen, hierarchical and authoritative values that formally guaranteed the subordination of women to their husbands' personal and professional projects have gradually been replaced by values of equality and the acknowledgment of individual rights.

Recently, legal changes have been even more challenging to the traditional family model and the Ministry of Defense has already required that
the Armed Forces adapt internal regulations to meet legal requirements.
Such is the case of the modification of the Civil Law Code, which states
that marriage will hold the same requisites and effects independent of
whether those concerned be of the same or different sex, and the 2012
Law of Gender Identity (Ley 26.743) under which anybody may register a
sex rectification, and request the consequent change in name and image
when these do not coincide with "self-perceived gender identity." As a
result, there has been an institutionalization of a perspective that favors
gender equality, respect for sexual diversity, and the acknowledgment of
individual rights that contradicts the family ideal historically favored by the
Armed Forces. This process is related to a professional tendency dominat-
ing the Western world, defined as a "postmodern" military trend (Moskos,
Williams, and Segal, 2000).

Military perceptions and generational change:
Everyday tensions in family, professional, and personal life

In this process of gradual change within the social conception of families,
the blurring of professional and family life that leads to a conception of
the military profession as all-encompassing is challenged. The following
analysis was offered by an officer, who portrays the loss of what he calls the
"concept of one big family" and introduces "social demand" as one of the
possible explanations:

> [E]vidently something has been lost. As members of society we have
> had to give in to changes that have modified this "one big family"
> notion. Perhaps the pace of life today makes us focus more on our own
> personal problems? Maybe we're more selfish or society's demands on
> study, work and family are wearing out the sense of unity we felt before?

On reviewing the causes, the officer describes the problem as the dissolution of what he calls the "idea of one big family" under which, in the past,
the military sphere of demands and missions subdued all other demands.
But this totalizing force, comprehensive of military life and producing
bonds analogous to those that lace a family together, loses relevance. As the
officer points out, the "great union" among members of the military has
been distorted by other demands that they must satisfy, those of the family
among them.

Another officer portrays this experience as one of tension between his
professional life and his family life. In his opinion, family arrangements and
unspoken agreements are causing this tension. Above all, he highlights the
place held by women and how they are valued within this arrangement, as
well as expressing the need for a father's attention – something quite rare
among older generations of civilians and militaries:

For me, my family is the most important thing I have in the world, but so is my profession. So you realize that your children need you but you can't not attend the force . . . I've been in the force for almost 20 years . . . [F]ortunately I've had few postings . . . [W]e decided with my wife what we would have to do and decided I should travel alone, 'cos my kids were at school, and she had a job here . . . We decided I was going to travel and I'd come over to Bahía Blanca . . . It was necessary for me to be close to my family at least that way, because they were the ones who kept me going to be able to keep working. The trouble is, in those comings and goings, my oldest daughter got sick . . . then the other one. Now I've requested permission to leave the office at 7 p.m., but still I feel bad because I know my mates have to stay on until the boss leaves, at 10 p.m. or later. I think the postings issue in the Navy affected many families.

The postings have indeed become a problem in the last years. The functioning of the social network has been jeopardized. The strength of regulations and traditions regarding the military organization, indicating that families had to travel with officers to their posts and leave affective bonds and professional commitments behind, has started to weaken. It has now become evident that the father's professional career is his own interest and no longer a reason to drag other family members along in pursuit of that interest. Before, such an idea would have been unconceivable: both the family, as well as the officer, would have been trained emotionally and socially to rely, theoretically, on the necessary backup.

For the generations of militaries under the age of 40, the family and professional experience have a different meaning from that which they have for the older generation. During our field study of military units, in an informal situation during a meal with younger officers, they asserted their "right to also be interviewed," since they claimed to have an opinion that differed from those of commanding officers. The "issue about wives" was one point mentioned. When faced with difficulties in family life, the younger officers described how their commanding officers advised them in light of the decisions that they once made themselves: "In my time, we used to do so and so . . ." But according to the younger generations, they have to deal with different issues today: "It's alright that they learned that way, but we face a different reality. They earned their authority that way, but it's different now." Older officers mention, for example, that they used to arrive at the base and had to stay there for the whole weekend, and that they thought that was fine; officers under the age of 40 could not understand why they were made to attend ceremonies or social events, or had to stay at the institution without real necessity. Younger officers all agreed that it is absurd to stay at the military base if there is no specific duty to perform, mentioning some such tasks as those activities related to promoting the socialization between families and officers. It is worth noting, in that respect, that collective life in military units has diminished. According to data revealed, only 11.6 percent of the interviewed staff declared themselves to be living in collective institutions (barracks), while 15.2 percent declared that they lived in a military neighborhood and the majority (67.9 percent) declared themselves to be living in a civilian one (Frederic et al., 2008).

Regarding their relationships with wives, younger officers exchanged a few jokes on how they exercise their power over them: "[W]e always have the final say: 'Yes, dear.' " And they mentioned ironically that their wives often threaten to abandon them, using expressions such as "I might just leave." They pointed toward the experiences of two unit officer colleagues who were, in fact, abandoned by their wives. Seeing that the welfare of the couple and the children was no longer mainly subordinated to that of the husband, many military men felt that they could no longer assert their full authority over the members of their families. The members' different wishes, social ties, and interests had to be taken into consideration, thus increasing the possibility of household breakups and divorce.

Together with generational changes in the constitution of hierarchical relationships inside the family, younger officers also account for changes in the definition of leadership and command itself. According to their experiences, they think that it is harder to make people obey orders simply on the basis of rank or seniority – "applying the stripes," as they put it. In this sense, they feel that many of the superior officers have not yet severed ties with the old way of exercising command and refuse to accept that "because I say so" is no longer sufficient justification. Supplying grounds and explanations for orders appears, among the younger generations, to be a prerequisite to the exercise of command.

Currently, the pressure exerted by the institution to abide by moral values that sustain the ideals of the military family sound, to the ears of younger officers who have experienced a different family model, to be ever less adequate in the context of military life today. A vice-commodore aged 48 and divorced (after his wife left him), now living with the children of his first marriage and with a new spouse and son from this second marriage, comments:

> Ten years ago, having a divorce would affect your career prospect; it's no longer thus. We have to admit that, with the kind of lives we lead, the number of divorces is increasing. An old commodore once asked me, "How did you manage to get a divorce?" Well . . . I just did! He replied: "But it's such a hard thing to do!"

In this case, the sacrifice made to keep the family together is no longer valued in the same way: "We have to admit that, with the kind of lives we lead, the number of divorces is increasing." Besides, personal well-being requires values similar or superior to those that the institution held for decades and which were functional according to the social context at the time. The trends toward greater equality between men and women and the consequent democratization of family relations are a threat to sustaining the balance between the historic demands of the service and a harmonious family life.

According to Philippe Manigart (2006), at a socio-cultural level, individualism and hedonism have become central values: there is a broader respect for cultural diversity, people's work expectations have changed, and there seems to be more attention given to working conditions than before. In the cases observed, this is particularly noticeable among young officers in the Air Force. It is common to hear that they are the "more civilian-inclined of the forces," or that they do not apply differences between officers and subofficers with the rigor that can be seen in the Army and the Navy. The officers consulted mentioned considering professional performance a priority, and they found the value of "sacrifice" frequently mentioned by seniors not to be as important as "defending" what is their own (the national territory), performing their duties with the highest degree of professionalism, and then being able to "enjoy life in the same way that any of their civilian friends do."[6]

Thus the results of the study point toward it being the younger or more modern officers and NCOs who are least prone to sacrifice themselves and their families, and least willing to bear the personal costs of this tension between family and professional life:

> [M]y house is in Puerto Belgrano, on the base itself, and I have a very hard time with the postings issue, 'cos when I was posted in Buenos Aires I decided that my wife should stay there, because she has her mother and her brothers and the baby is still too small. She wanted to come but I convinced her to stay . . . I even thought of leaving the force because there was a time when I really missed them, especially as my son was so tiny . . . I've often asked myself what I'm doing here, what am I leading this life for, if what I want is to be with my wife and my son and they're so far away. On the other hand, I do know that the Navy is what I want, that postings are good to prepare you in case the moment should arise when you have to go and defend your country.

Two aspects can be highlighted as a result of this experience of tension between family and professional life. First, the wives of NCOs or commanding officers now more frequently hold down their own jobs, which they want to develop and which men can also appreciate – both for the personal fulfillment that they offer to the wives and because they significantly increase family income. But there is another aspect: the growing importance of the wishes of the children. Although moving them from city to city is easy when they are small, it becomes harder when they reach adolescence. Their wellbeing and their relationships with friends are now being taken into account by parents. Hence, over the last 15 years, the idea of subordination of the military family to the professional career has gradually become more and more untenable.

Final considerations

The social and cultural transformations, as well as the democratization of society, have had a strong impact on the family organization of soldiers and thus on the military profession, without the institution being able to reorganize itself as a consequence. It is important to point out that the domestic arrangements that allow a man to deal with the demands of unit postings are adopted with more difficulty in younger couples – that is, those under the age of 40 – because of the increasing importance of women's work within these couples, but also because these parents are strongly committed to raising their children. These values and the difficulties that they bring with them (which multiply when both parents are in the military institution) constitute a major concern for most officers of the Argentine Armed Forces.

As our study shows, a generational line divides those who assimilate all personal and family sacrifices in order to construct their military identity and those who are able to distinguish personal and family matters from work matters. The comparison with other professions and with acquaintances or friends who have not continued in the military profession is a key factor in this process. Without doubt, this line separating the senior officers (those with more than 15 years' service) from the younger ones (those with less than 15 years' service) accounts for how socio-cultural forces affect the professionalization of the military. The resulting set of transformations in the labor market, the greater participation of women within it, and the variation of male–female, father–son, and old–young dynamics, among others, is particularly important. These transformations intervene in the personal lives of those in the Forces, and modify the professional concepts and practices of some. This allows us to disagree with the most conservative views of the military profession, such as those expressed by Samuel Huntington (1957), which affirm the refractory nature of functional imperatives to societal imperatives. On the contrary: the current situation of the Argentine military profession, as well as that in other countries, indicates that social and cultural values have been absorbed by the military institution – albeit that they have been incorporated rather later than in other social spheres and institutions, as Bernard Boëne (1990) or Christopher Dandeker (2003) argue.

Notes

1   Qualitative data given in this chapter is derived from an ethnographic study on family, gender issues, and the military profession in Argentina, developed during 2007 (Frederic, 2007).
2   For an analysis of the value of family organization within military life in Western armed forces before the Cold War, see Moskos, Williams, and Segal (2000).
3   Freedom of creed is practiced in Argentina and public education is secular. However, the Catholic Church takes part in official ceremonies – particularly

military ones. The origins of the Catholic Church's penetration into the lines of the Argentine Army dates back to the 1930s, with the expansion of the denominated Catholic Nationalism (Zanatta, 1996).

4 The Law had been established in Argentina in 1949, but was derogated in 1956 by the military government, thus re-establishing the inequality between men and women in terms of responsibilities regarding decisions about their children.

5 Before 1987, there was a legal form of divorce in Argentina, but the bond of marriage was not dissolved. Those divorced within this legal framework were unable to remarry, and children born of these new couples were considered "extramarital."

6 The notion of a job for life has weakened in the context of the Armed Forces as it has in society as a whole during the last decade and a half; hence the Armed Forces' decision in 1996 to incorporate its institution into the national education framework, submitting the Armed Forces' official degree to the requirements of the Ministry of Education, enabling graduates to obtain a degree that was valid in the civilian labor market. The intention was to grant a university degree that allowed officers leaving the Forces to enter into the civilian working world.

References

Boëne, B. (1990) "How unique should the military be?" *European Journal of Sociology*, 31: 3–39.

Dandeker, C. (2003) " 'Femmes Combattantes': Problèmes et perspectives de l'intégration des femmes dans le armée britannique." *Revue Française de Sociologie*, 44(4): 735–58.

Frederic, S. (2007) "Report on family, gender and the military profession in Argentina: Socio-cultural devices of the democratization of the Armed Forces." Unpublished report for the Argentine Defense Ministry, Quilmes National University, Buenos Aires, Argentina.

Frederic, S. (2012) "Fotografías de la configuración profesional de los militares en el contexto de su declinación como elite estatal." In M. Plotkin and E. Zimmerman (eds.) *Las Prácticas del Estado: Política, sociedad y elites estatales en la Argentina del siglo XX.* Buenos Aires: Edhasa, pp. 210–34.

Frederic, S., Masson, L., Soprano, G., and Di Tomaso, R. (2008) "Socio-professional situation of the militaries in Argentina." Unpublished report for the Argentine Defense Ministry, Quilmes National University, Buenos Aires, Argentina.

Huntington, S. (1957) *The Soldier and the State: The theory and practice of civil–military relations.* Cambridge: Cambridge University Press.

Manigart, P. (2006) "Restructuring of the Armed Forces." In G. Caforio (ed.) *Handbook of the Sociology of the Military.* New York: Springer, pp. 323–43.

Ministry of Defense (2010) *Equidad de Género y Defensa: Una política en marcha (IV).* Buenos Aires: Argentine Defense Ministry.

Moskos, C., Williams, J.A., and Segal, D.R. (eds.) (2000) *The Postmodern Military: Armed forces after the Cold War.* New York: Oxford University Press.

Segalen, M. (1992) *Antropología Histórica de la Familia.* Madrid: Taurus.

Zanatta, L. (1996) *Del Estado Liberal a la Nación Católica. Iglesia y ejército en los orígenes del peronismo 1930–1945.* Bernal: Editorial de la Universidad Nacional de Quilmes.

Part II

Military families under stress

6 The emotional cycle of deployment[1]

Maren Tomforde

Introduction

Any prolonged separation from partners (spouses) and families places mental stress on those involved. This is also true for military families who, owing to peacekeeping and peacemaking missions abroad such as those in the Balkans and in Afghanistan, face separations to an increased extent. The absence of partners and husbands, of friends and fathers, puts the families[2] left at home to a test that is as tough as that which the soldiers who are separated from their loved ones and their familiar environment at home have to pass. During a separation, knowing that the family at home and/or the soldier[3] in the theater of deployment are well is of great importance for all persons involved. If problems occur or if communication between the two sides is impaired (perhaps because of technical problems), the stress on those involved – which, owing to the separation, is very high anyway – will even increase. Military sociology studies (Biehl et al., 2004; Pittman, Kerpelman, and McFayden, 2004; Rosen et al., 1995) have already shown that the motivation of soldiers during a mission abroad is highly correlated with the well-being of their partners and families at home. No soldier who has problems with his or her family at home or who is permanently worried about their well-being can fully concentrate on the tasks that he or she has to perform during deployment. The family also must know for sure that the soldier is well. In a survey conducted by the former Bundeswehr Institute of Social Sciences (SOWI),[4] German soldiers stationed in Bosnia-Herzegovina often said: "It is my wife back home who runs the real mission." This is an opinion that is also shared by the families, as an open remark by one of the wives shows:

> There is no need for the politicians to fly to the countries of deployment for the umpteenth time in order to thank the soldiers and feel sorry for them. The soldiers do their job after all. Rather, the politicians should go to the family service centers and thank the families who have to cope with twice the workload at home, and feel sorry for the children who cry for their daddies for months!

As previous SOWI studies have revealed (Biehl, Keller, and Tomforde, 2005), deployment-related stress not only undergoes various phases, but also affects different areas: the partner, for example, is missed as a person to whom to relate, as an interlocutor and sexual partner, as well as a family member and educator. The objective of this chapter is to demonstrate which concrete stress the spouses and families of deployed German military members face prior to, during, and after the four–six-month period of separation and which coping strategies are used in the individual phases of separation.

Since the early 1990s, the Bundeswehr has been confronted with new missions in the field of "military operations other than war," which now have to be accomplished in addition to the two "classical" forms of employment of the German Armed Forces (deterrence and defense). These new operations cover missions of most different kinds, which include peacekeeping and peacebuilding tasks, as well as involvement in the war in Afghanistan.

Having existed for 50 years and experienced various transformation processes, the Bundeswehr is evolving into a global operational army. Over the past 15 years, it has been among the armed forces to contribute the largest troop contingents to international peace missions. When employed to maintain security in the new theaters of operation, the German military predominantly acts in cooperation with its allies and supports the governmental bodies of the theater of deployment in maintaining security. In January 2013, approximately 6,200 German service members were deployed to countries or regions such as Afghanistan, Kosovo, the Horn of Africa, Turkey, Lebanon, and (South) Sudan. Previously, military personnel were deployed to the theaters of operations for a period of six months (including three weeks' home leave), which was the normal tour of duty. As a result of the high pressure exerted by soldiers' representatives and based on research findings, the duration of deployment was reduced to four months in May 2005, which cannot in principle be interrupted by a home leave. Despite this rule, quite a number of service members are still deployed to Afghanistan for six months and longer because their professional expertise is also needed before and after a contingent starts/ends. German military personnel (in particular those serving in the Navy) and their families had experienced absences for several weeks – in some cases even several months – as a result of training courses, training area periods, or maneuvers also during the Cold War era. The separation over a period of six and/or four months owing to a deployment, which is accompanied by a preparation and training period lasting several months, however, constitutes a new and unusual situation – not only in terms of quantity. Short-term volunteers and regulars of the now professional, all-volunteer Bundeswehr[5] have to participate in deployments abroad several times as a rule, with a minimum period of two years between two subsequent deployments promised by the military organization, which promise cannot, however, always be kept.

As a consequence of the increased participation in deployments abroad, German soldiers now are even more torn between the two "greedy institutions" (Segal, 1986) – that is, the family and the military. Both areas place high demands on the soldier, which he or she often cannot meet simultaneously. This may lead to loyalty conflicts between the priorities given to the occupation and the family.[6] Owing to a step-by-step shift from an "institutional" to an "occupational" focus (Moskos, 1988; see also Bourg and Segal, 1999) within the Bundeswehr, German military families tend to be less integrated into the everyday military routine than they were two or three decades ago. Owing to frequent changes of duty stations and the more intense integration of women into the labor market, many German service members no longer live in their garrisons with their families, but instead commute between home and workplace. More often than not, service members serve far away from the families so that they can spend only the weekends at home. For this reason, the Bundeswehr is now often called a "commuter army" (Schwarz, 2011: 105; see also Wendl, 2011). As a result, it has become rather the exception than the rule that family members take part in the life in the barracks. As in many other countries, most soldiers leave the barracks immediately after end of duty to live their private lives. The occupational and the private spheres are no longer connected with one another.

Accordingly, it is to be stated that the armed forces, owing to deployments abroad and separations for several months, demand more support and understanding of the military families, while spouses and families are less integrated into supporting Bundeswehr–internal networks than during East–West conflict times.[7] This fact confronts the armed forces with new challenges, because they have to secure the support of the wives and families, which is a central factor contributing to the soldier's motivation and work during deployment. Authors such as Bourg and Segal (1999) assume that the fundamental attitudes of wives and partners towards the armed forces exert major influence both on the professional planning of the husband and on his motivation during deployment abroad.[8] The Bundeswehr has taken up the new challenges evolving not only in the theater of deployment, but also at home, by setting up a comprehensive family service organization in Germany, started in 2001. It maintains 31 full-time and more than 50 additional points of contact throughout Germany for military families. They provide information about mission-related issues and facilitate establishing contacts among those left at home (Lüder, 2004). These so-called "family support centers" are part of a larger "network of help" – a network consisting of formal social institutions provided by the armed forces, as well as of several voluntary support organizations maintained by military spouses.[9] The measures taken to support families within the framework of the family service organization will be only briefly addressed in the following, because this chapter takes a closer look at the tensions to which military families are exposed prior to, during, and after a deployment abroad.

The chapter is structured as follows: first, the database of the surveys upon which this study is primarily based will be introduced; after this, the four phases of separation, with their specific stress and coping strategies, will be addressed. The findings of the analysis of the different stress phases will be summarized in the final section and evaluated in terms of future prospects.

Research project and database

Between July 2003 and December 2012, the former Bundeswehr Institute of Social Sciences (SOWI) conducted the research project "Sozialwissenschaftliche Begleitung der Auslandseinsätze der Bundeswehr [Social Science Monitoring of Deployments Abroad of the Bundeswehr]" on behalf of the Federal Ministry of Defense (FMOD). The project was designed to contribute to the improvement of the preparation for deployments abroad, of the mission accomplishment on the ground, of the support provided to the military families during the period of deployment, and of the reintegration of soldiers in everyday military life.

Within the scope of this project, a long-term qualitative study to monitor the partners of military personnel of Tenth KFOR [Kosovo Force] Contingent was conducted. Thirty women whose boyfriends/husbands were employed in Kosovo from November 2004 to May 2005 in the scope of the KFOR mission had volunteered for this study. The women were questioned four times using semistructured interviews: the first time in October 2004, four weeks before the deployment; the second time in January 2005, about two months after the beginning of the deployment; the third time in April 2005, four months after the beginning of the deployment (following the home leave of the soldiers); and the fourth and last time in August 2005, two months after return. The interviews were carried out mainly at the women's homes and lasted 1.5 hours on average. To better evaluate the situation of the soldiers on deployment, the husbands and/or boyfriends of the women interviewed were interviewed in Kosovo in April 2005, using unstructured questions on their experiences of deployment and of the separation from home (Tomforde, 2006). Additionally, in order to update and review the research findings, in-depth and focus group interviews were held at the German Armed Forces Staff and Command College between April 2012 and February 2013 with officers who had been deployed to Afghanistan (the International Security Assistance Force, or ISAF) in 2010–11. These new, additional interviews revealed – in line with current publications on deployment and military families – that the research results of the 2006 publication were still very valid and needed only to be complemented in a few ways, because experiences of service members and their spouses had not changed drastically since 2006; on the contrary. Yet additions need to be made when it comes to coping with fear, high-risk situations, and use of force during deployment, because these are new aspects of the deployment in Afghanistan, which the KFOR mission did not have.

The four phases of separation

The amount and kind of stress imposed on the soldier and his family vary during a deployment. Conversations with the women have shown that the difficulties that occur prior to and at the beginning of a mission differ from those that occur during the deployment or after the return of the soldiers. This section addresses the stress imposed on, as well as the coping strategies applied by, the families, which were mentioned by the women questioned prior to, during, and after the deployment. In accordance with the four interview phases (prior to, twice during, and after the deployment), the section is broken down into four subsections. This structure makes sense not only for the presentation of the results of the interviews in question, but also reflects the four phases that a deployment, in my view, involves in terms of different emotions and stress factors.[10] In this deployment-related "emotional cycle of deployment" (Pincus et al., 2004), through which all of the families go in a more or less similar way, some authors distinguish between not only four, but sometimes even seven, different stages of stress factors that affect those involved (De Soir, 2000).

Each of the four phases introduced in the following covers a certain period of time and is marked by specific emotional challenges that are to be mastered by those left at home. Early information about, and preparation for, these stages can allow the soldiers and their family members to cope with deployment experiences in a positive way.

Predeployment

The predeployment phase ideally begins with the first notification of the imminent deployment and ends with the departure of the soldier. The first interviews with the partners involved in the KFOR study took place in early October 2004, a month and a half before the soldiers left for Kosovo (in the second half of November 2004). Most of the Bundeswehr service members and their families were informed of the planned deployment abroad at the beginning of 2004, while the exact date of departure had not yet been fixed when the interviews were conducted. It was announced only two weeks before the beginning of the deployment. The news of the imminent mission causes a mental attempt to come to terms with the forthcoming separation and the difficulties resulting from it. Many service members and their families see this period as stressful, because it is accompanied by additional training courses and military exercises away from home (Gravino, Segal, and Segal, 1993). Therefore the service members and their partners call it "deployment prior to deployment," which already involves long periods of absence from home and can prolong the mission-related time of separation by up to six months. These periods of absence from home prior to deployment, which are interrupted only by short stays at home during the weekends, often make it impossible for the service members and their families to jointly and deliberately prepare for the imminent prolonged separation. Accordingly, a mother of two children put it as follows during an interview: "Prior to the deployment, one appointment is on top of another. You have a busy schedule; the preparation is probably more frantic than the deployment itself. Everything is like in a beehive." Another respondent also perceived this period before the departure as very strenuous: "Oh, I wish they [the men] had already left. I will heave a sigh of relief when he has gone at last. I simply find the time before the departure too strenuous. I wish he had already left." A 31-year-old woman added:

> It would be best if he left spontaneously! It is good that it is going to start soon, then I can start counting the days down again. Currently, it is as if he had left long ago, apart from the fact that he comes home for a few days now and then. This is like going on a roller coaster.

The phase before the departure is emotionally very demanding, because neither the men nor their partners know what will be in store for them during the deployment. The service members attempt to come to terms mentally with the dangers and various challenges of their duty during the mission, while the women prepare for several months or longer without their partners and fathers of their children. The uncertainties that the imminent separation, as well as the security situation during deployment, involve often also cause fears of what is to come. Even though new data show that about 45 percent of the Bundeswehr soldiers and their families have at least one previous deployment experience (Seiffert, Langer, and Pietsch, 2012), families agree that the situation is not easier to cope with each new mission; on the contrary. It becomes even harder when new missions are more dangerous than those in the past and fear becomes omnipotent (Rosenfeld, 2010).

However, it is particularly the uncertainty *before* the deployment that places an enormous stress on those involved and sometimes even leads to emotional outbursts or psychosomatic diseases, as was the case with some people included in the 2006 SOWI study. While the time before the departure is marked by mental stress and uncertainty for some women and their husbands, there are also girlfriends/spouses who regard this phase as unproblematic. A 26-year-old woman declared during an interview: "I feel guilty about being so well although I ought to be depressed because my husband is departing in four weeks." The leaflets prepared by the family service organization of the Bundeswehr mainly address problems, so that those women who do not have any deployment-related difficulties wonder whether they deviate from the norm. Therefore they demand that the information leaflets refer not only to problems, but also to the positive aspects of preparation for deployment and separation, thus enabling a more differentiated view of deployments abroad and the surrounding circumstances.

During the period preceding the departure, the service member and his family have to prepare for the deployment organizationally and emotionally. Moreover, possible problems that might occur as a result of the absence of the husband have to be anticipated and the following four–six months planned properly. Besides the bustling, which results from the various tasks to be performed, couples also have to manage the emotional stress of the imminent separation. As shown in numerous spouses' letters to their partners deployed,[11] many couples wish for a calm and warm farewell, but instead quarrel and sometimes even get into serious fights because of their high stress levels before departure (Schwarz, 2011). It is younger couples in particular who have not yet been separated for a prolonged period who may be confronted with fear of loss during this phase. Interestingly, 5 out of the 30 partners questioned in 2004 and 2005 stated before the deployment that their husbands had felt exaggerated jealousy and had often addressed their wives reproachfully over insignificant matters. This jealousy certainly is an expression of the uncertainties and fears of loss felt by the service members, who will not only be sent to an unknown and insecure theater of deployment, but also for have to leave their partners alone for a prolonged period the first time. In all five cases, the jealousy and the urge to exercise control felt by the men died down during the first weeks of deployment after the soldiers had noticed that their wives at home continued to be there for them and also provided major support.[12]

Coping strategies

To better manage the insecure and turbulent period of time prior to the beginning of the deployment, the women interviewed in 2004 and 2005 applied various coping strategies. First, the couples settled all important organizational matters together, for example completing bank mandate forms and other authorization forms, making their wills, preparing telephone number lists that included important points of contact, or conducting (overdue) repairs in the house and garden and/or on the car.

Second, the women planned special activities, such as visiting friends and relatives, performing special tasks, or practicing sports to spend the time of the deployment in a meaningful way and to render it more manageable.

Third, half of the respondents used the so-called "cuddle week" (seven days' special leave before the beginning of deployment) granted to the soldiers for a common holiday at home or somewhere else. Those involved regarded this holiday as very important because it offers "a lot of rest and time for communication," as a 17-year-old respondent put it positively. Obviously, it was good for the couples to have had this common time of rest after the stressful, emotional, and exciting time of preparation, which allowed them to better prepare mentally for the impending departure. Those couples who did not have the opportunity to spend this holiday together for duty commitments or other reasons (perhaps child care) were stressed until the very departure; some of them even had to part against a backdrop of unresolved problems.

At the beginning of deployment

As a general rule, the initial phase of deployment covers the period from the departure of the soldier until about one–two months after the departure. For the girlfriends/spouses, the first days and/or weeks of separation are marked by the pain of parting and the feeling of loneliness, of being abandoned, and the experience of disorganization. Their usual lives have got in a muddle; the women have to come to terms with their own everyday life without their partners (Schwarz, 2011). The time of being separated from their familiar partners seems to be endless and hard to get over. Particularly in this phase, it is helpful for the families when the dates of holiday or return flights are already known, so that the period of separation is transparent.

The soldiers are relieved of many everyday things in their camp (for example preparing food, doing laundry, and cleaning accommodations and sanitary installations). In contrast, the families at home often have to carry double the workload because the husband cannot make his contribution. Moreover, women with children do not only have to play their part as mothers, but to a certain extent they also have to replace the fathers and explain to their children the absence of their father in a comprehensible way. The girlfriends/spouses have to reorganize their everyday lives. Although the women remain in their usual environments, they have to cope with the absence of an important person to whom to relate. "I do find it strange to get up alone now, to have breakfast alone, to lie in bed alone in the evening and not to have the opportunity to communicate any longer. Suddenly, I feel like a single again": this is the way in which a 42-year-old spouse summarized her feelings in the initial period of her husband's deployment. The partner is missed as a contact person: "I miss him as a human being. I missed the affection, I missed the physical contact. Sometimes I do feel as a loner, some evenings are boring and dull, with the weekends sometimes being particularly depressing" (statements made by a 51-year-old). Many women without children suddenly feel like singles again, while mothers mimic the experiences of single parents who have to bring the everyday tasks and the needs of the children into line on their own.

Children

The women who took part in the long-term study in 2004–05 expressed highly different opinions about the role that children play during deployments abroad. Some of the women without children thought that it was good not to have children yet, because this prevented the absence of the husband from bringing about additional stress also on other persons.

Moreover, as childless persons, they have to care only for themselves and not additionally for their offspring, who perhaps would miss their fathers unbearably.[13] However, some of the childless women also expressed their regret at not having children who could render the period of deployment easier for them. The mothers take a similar attitude: they are either glad not be left home alone, or they find it difficult to carry the burden of suddenly being single parents.

The children themselves seem to perceive and manage the absence of their fathers differently: babies and infants up to 2 years old do not understand the separation from their fathers consciously and are not yet able to estimate it correctly. However, even the smallest ones obviously seem to miss their fathers, which becomes clear when babies show pleasure when seeing strange men wearing a uniform, for example in the supermarket. The 2–4-year-old children seem to be hurt the most by the absence, because they miss their fathers consciously, while not being able to fully grasp the duration of the deployment period. Accordingly, a 4-year-old said, when hearing about her father's deployment: "Oh cool, can I sleep in daddy's bed then?" A 2-year-old regularly had tantrums during the separation and phoned her father imaginarily to ask him when he would come home at last. Although older children and juveniles also suffer from the separation from their fathers, they can be diverted and calmed down by extra activities and weekly mail/parcels from their fathers.

Coping strategies

It is not only the knowledge of a planned home leave or the foreseeable end of the separation, but in particular also good communication between the soldiers and their girlfriends/spouses that are important to get over the first phase of emotional disorientation and loneliness (Ender and Segal, 1996). In contrast to this, a difficult or impossible communication can lead to disappointment, misunderstanding, and disgruntlement, which put a heavy stress on the subsequent period of separation (Schwarz, 2011). Correspondingly, Peter Wendl (2011) found in his study of long-distance relationships that functioning communication forms one of the basic prerequisites for the stability of a partnership that is burdened by separation.

Many of the women interviewed stated that they talked to their deployed husbands over the phone at least several times a week, if possible. Thanks to these frequent phone calls (fixed, Internet, or cell), events can promptly be conveyed to the theater of deployment and vice versa. This may render the separation easier for some people; it can, however, also involve new stress. Personal interviews in the theater of deployment have shown that confronting the soldier with everyday issues of his family, which he often cannot influence at all, may burden him with additional concerns and, in the worst case, even cause a feeling of helplessness. The Internet is also used frequently for the communication between the partners. Emails are exchanged; couples also use Instant Messenger services such as Skype. Moreover and most importantly of all, the couples "relearn" how to write letters during the separation; some women even write to their husbands daily (Schwarz, 2011). Other women keep a diary for their partners in which they record the "daily little things and activities" that one cannot recapitulate in their entirety in conversations after the deployment. The women either send excerpts of the diaries to their husbands in the theater of deployment or give them the complete diaries upon return. Although it is not always easy for the partners to write to the soldiers so regularly (partly on a daily basis), this kind of alternative communication is nevertheless important for the women. By writing, they can give free rein to their emotions – a chance that they are not offered too often. Accordingly, one of the respondents stated:

> I write daily because there is nobody I can really refer to. My girlfriends who are not separated from their husbands cannot understand me. But I have to be tough for my 4-year-old daughter and also for my husband, although my own emotions are going on a roller coaster too.

Women partly structure their day around the letters that they write to their deployed husbands. Sometimes, they start a letter early in the morning and continue it during the day, to finish it just before the next emptying of the nearby mailbox. Walks with the dogs or trips to town are planned according to the "pick-up times" of mailboxes, as well as according to their locations. The day has been a good one if the spouse has received either a letter or a telephone call, and has been a hard and sad one if the last letter, text message, mail, or call has been too long ago (Schwarz, 2011). The German Armed Forces officially recognize the high importance of communication between the partners at home and in theater, and provide good and inexpensive cellphone and Internet services. The German Army Postal Service, which has existed since 1716, is quite efficient and fast, and it is officially well recognized that this method of communication between soldiers and their partners is essential for the motivation of the service members deployed. In 2010, the Bundeswehr transported 1.1 million postcards and letters, as well as 270,000 parcels, between the mission areas and Germany (Schwarz, 2011).

The monthly meetings arranged by the family support centers of the Bundeswehr, during which those left home can meet "fellow sufferers," constitute another kind of support for the women, in particular during the initial period of the deployment. Those women who have met military wives also affected by deployment already before the start of the mission mutually exchange telephone number lists in order to inform each other as quickly as possible in an emergency or in case of an accident in which their husbands might be involved. Women who have not met other military wives before the deployment, however, state that the meetings arranged by the family service center should not start at the beginning of deployment, but a few months before. This would provide the women with the opportunity to already meet "fellow sufferers" when the deployment is imminent, and to receive more support and exchange of thoughts. Another forum, which is very important for the spouses, is the online platform "FrauzuFrau.de" ("from woman to woman") founded in 2000 by Katrin Schwarz, a wife of a soldier and mother of three who wanted to facilitate contacts and the exchange between spouses. This forum is widely used and appreciated by the women; in 2010, the platform had approximately 18,000 "unique visits" per month (Schwarz, 2011 171). Women not only exchange instant information after an attack in the mission areas, but also chat about their personal experiences, the hardships of the separation, and the feelings that they cannot easily share with other people who are not going through the same experience in life. Some women whose partners have been deployed more than once even offer their advice to newcomers and thus support them especially in the beginning of a deployment.

During deployment

For the 2004–05 study, the third round of interviews with the military wives took place in the fourth month of the six-month deployment period. Interviews were conducted after the soldiers' home leave (one–three weeks) – that is, when the women had to endure "only" two more months of separation. While the first two rounds of interviews had been characterized by accounts of stress, emotional ups and downs, and the feeling of being alone and missing someone, the third phase of interviews now found the women mostly in a good mood. On the one hand, they were relieved about the fact that the mission so far had been so peaceful and relatively unproblematic, that they had noticed only minor changes in their partners during their leave, and that they had already overcome the longest part of the separation period. During this interview phase, those questioned made the following statements:

> The feeling of missing him and the loneliness are getting less intense. After all, he is coming home soon.
>
> In the past months, there had been days when everything was really crappy. Apart from that, I feel well and happy.
>
> I feel very well today. We have almost made it, haven't we?
>
> During the past months, I had been sad now and then, but I did so many things so that I had only little time to think. Only the weekends were hard, when little was happening. But this will be all over soon.

When reviewing these statements, a certain euphoria about the imminent return of the partners can be noted. Inter alia, this is possibly a result of the fact that the women in this phase were, to some extent, proud to have mastered the period of separation and the challenges accompanied by it so well. The great strain, which was present before and shortly after the departure, seemed to have vanished. The respondents themselves stated as the reason for this that they had got through the longest part of the separation period, and that the real climax of excitement and uncertainty had been reached with the (first) leave. For a six-month deployment, German soldiers are entitled to 21 days' leave, and can visit their families and partners once or twice. Most soldiers either split up their leave between the second and fourth months of deployment, or take it completely at mid-term. Service members deployed to Afghanistan, however, mostly decide against a mid-term holiday, because the long return journey to Germany (with Bundeswehr aircrafts) would take up a substantial part of the holiday time.

When service members choose to spend their leave at home, it appears that most couples do not spend the time in a relaxed and positive atmosphere, but in an atmosphere loaded with problems. Both the women and the soldiers obviously have misplaced hopes for the "time out" during the deployment period. While the women expect their partners to be there for them and to compensate to some extent for the separation by their presence and bodily closeness, the soldiers obviously need distance from the theater of deployment, and rest and recreation. They are not always able to readjust smoothly to their families or to accept the changed male and female roles. Only those couples who go to a different place during the home leave perceive it to be relaxing and refreshing. Concerning this, a master sergeant told us:

> I feel we were among the few who did it the right way during the leave: I came home and relaxed for two days during which my wife still went to work. Then we went on a skiing holiday together with the children. This was exactly the right thing because we were on neutral ground there: I could neither meddle in my wife's affairs at home nor did she have to readjust to my role as "master of the house" for a short time.

Even though some couples spend the home leave loaded with problems and quarrelling, most women do highly appreciate this time out. The leave is a focal point that makes the deployment period more manageable, even though the return of the husband is not imminent yet. Moreover, the temporary return of the husband makes it possible to revive the relationship and the mutual confirmation.[14]

Coping strategies

The third round of the 2004–05 interviews with military wives clearly showed that only few girlfriends/spouses were confronted with severe problems during the deployment. Quite the opposite: it became clear that the respondents settled in their new "everyday life without a husband" relatively successfully, although they were missing their partners and sometimes felt alone. While, at the beginning of the mission, attending the meetings arranged by the family service organization was still important for many women to receive as many pieces of information as possible about the theater of deployment, in the course of deployment cultivating social contacts with "fellow sufferers" became more and more significant. For many women, it was important to maintain relations with other women who were in the same situation and would not tell them that the additional tax-free foreign duty allowance more than sufficiently compensated for the separation from their husbands. "Don't forget about the tidy money" obviously is a well-intended and oft-repeated remark that is of little help for the partners. In this context, a woman told us:

> The exchange between military spouses is important. Some of my friends say: "This would be nothing for me at all, I would not manage that." Friends just don't understand the situation we are in. But we military wives help each other. They are the women who understand you quite well. I think that this contact will be maintained also after the deployment, because the husband may go on a deployment again at any time.

Individual networks composed of family members, friends, and neighbors can make the separation from the soldiers more bearable by means of emotional support and physical closeness, while the professional assistance provided by the armed forces within the framework of the family service organization is rather regarded to be a safety net for severe problems (illness, injury, death).[15] The assistance provided by the Bundeswehr is also an important signal to the families indicating that their central part during a deployment is officially recognized and enjoys support. Here, it is important that not only wives and parents, but also girlfriends and current partners, receive help and win recognition as target groups.

Coping with danger and fear

Especially the Bundeswehr mission in Northern Afghanistan has become quite dangerous with a growing number of different sorts of attacks by insurgents since 2008, some of them injuring and killing German service members.[16] Thus eminent and constant fear of attacks, injury, and death is not only prominent among soldiers deployed, but also among their spouses at the home front. This constant fear is a new challenge with which the women have to cope and was not a prominent topic in the SOWI study of 2006, because the Bundeswehr missions then were much calmer and less dangerous. However, since 2008, the German Armed Forces have been part of the war in Afghanistan and, for the first time since World War

II, they are not only being attacked, but they also shoot and kill. How do the women at home cope with this new situation and with the mission's new nature? While the 2006 study showed that the predeployment period was one the most stressful for the women at home, new interviews with service members and literature research underlines that it is most stressful for the spouses at home when they know that their partners have left camp (for a day or longer) for an operation. The women relax only when they know that their men have returned safely to the more or less "safe haven" of the camp, or that they have returned to quiet Masar-e-Sharif from dangerous Kunduz. Military partners have different ways in which to cope with their fear. Some want to be as well informed about the where-abouts of their husbands/boyfriends as possible and claim that knowledge is the best way to fight fear (Rosenfeld, 2010). Once they hear about an incident in Afghanistan in the news, they get in contact with other women by phone or more often in chatrooms (Wendl, 2011). They try to find out about the details of the attack and are thus, at times, quite well informed about occurrences in theater even though this is, owing to security risks, unintentional by the Bundeswehr. Nonetheless, more often than not, information leaks via text messages (sometimes even via YouTube movies of attacks) even before all telephone and Internet lines are shut down to prevent leakage.

Other women, on the contrary, do not want to know any details of the mission nor of the operations in which their partners might be involved. By not knowing, they protect themselves from "going crazy with worry," as a staff officer stressed in an interview at the Staff and Command College in February 2013. The women simply hope that everything will be all right, and they believe their partners when they promise before deployment that they will return home safely. Some women even start to believe in the "protective spirit" of guardian angel figurines or other lucky charms that they give to their partners before departure. It appeases them to know that their husbands/boyfriends carry these talismans with them. They believe in the protective power of these artifacts in an attempt to feel that they can control a situation over which, in fact, they have no control whatsoever. Other "relearn" to pray and become more religious during deployment times. Some start to go to church again and regularly light a candle for the spouse abroad. One woman states in a forum run by the MOD: "God gives me the strength to bear the time alone here at home."[17] Nonetheless, the women suffer from news about assaults and (improvised explosive device (IED) attacks in theater.

Women try to be as strong as possible for their deployed partners, trying to avoid showing their overwhelming anxieties and also preventing themselves from calling their men every few hours to check that they are safe. When anxieties grow unbearable, women either vent their emotions in numerous, endless letters, or in chatrooms. Some of them even have their own blog,[18] and update it daily to share their feelings and experiences with other people. Wives and girlfriends not only try to be strong for their partners (and children), but also try to support and motivate their deployed partners. They recognize that the men are also likely to suffer from anxieties and psychological stress, especially after an attack. More often than not, women write in their letters to their spouses in theater, "You are my hero" (Schwarz, 2011: 42), acknowledging the hardships that their partners have to endure and offering support "from the home front." Interestingly enough, in the 2006 SOWI study, women did not refer to the soldiers as "heroes" or anything similar. These soldiers also had to endure hardships, but they did not fight and did not have to cope with wartime experiences.

How stressful it can be for the women "on the home front" when fears are high owing to dangerous incidents in theater is expressed by one partner on the MOD forum: "The mission is not only concentrated to war and conflict areas. You can also find the war mission at home, behind closed doors, and nobody knows how unbearable it is."[19]

Women not only acknowledge the work that they think their partners accomplish during deployment, but also offer their help in times of stress. For example, after an assault on a German military convoy in 2010 in Afghanistan, a woman wrote a letter to her husband expressing her sorrow about those killed and her parallel relief about the fact that her husband was unscathed (Schwarz, 2011: 110):

> I hope that you talk with your comrades about what happened. As a leader you are also allowed to show weaknesses, by doing so you show that you are strong, indeed. I will not ask if you knew the comrades personally. If you want to talk about it, then do so. I am always open for this, always, and I always have a telephone alongside my bed. Please talk to me if you want to talk and please remain silent if you feel like remaining silent.

As a major stressed in an interview at the Staff and Command College (January 2013), it is especially after an attack that service members discuss how they should inform their partners at home. They feel that they should tell their women what happened to allay fears. They also know that the news will rapidly spread and that it is very likely that people in Germany will learn it anyway. However, they hesitate to share the news of an attack, partly because they have a heavy conscience towards their spouses and partly because they do not want it to be said, after their return, that an attack has changed them as a person. However, having heard and read enough reports about service members returning with posttraumatic stress disorder (PTSD) after deployment,[20] this is exactly what many women fear is happening. To counter this concern, many soldiers choose to inform their partners about attacks, but they omit the horrifying and troubling details.

After the return

Both for the soldiers and the families, the last month of deployment is generally marked by joyful expectation and preparations for the reunion, if the situation in theater is calm and quiet. Especially at home, the "perfect return" is planned – but the expectations and needs of the women and their returning partners might drastically differ (Schwarz, 2011). The women long for twosome and tender times, while the service members might simply look forward, next to seeing their spouses (and children), to a long, hot bath, some time alone or with friends, or time to tinker at their hobbies. However, there are also concerns that the relationship or the partner might have changed, as already noted. Great challenges are waiting for the soldier and his girlfriend/spouse after the deployment, because relationship problems and adjustment difficulties may occur. Readjusting to one another can take several weeks, or even months. Upon return from deployment, many soldiers want to resume their previous roles within the family as soon as possible, which leads to tensions if the family has restructured as a result of the deployment (Drummet, Coleman, and Cable, 2003). Sometimes, the women find it difficult to lose the greater independence that they acquired during the period of separation (Rohall, Segal, and Segal, 1999). Many children have problems accepting their fathers as an authority again. For the soldier and his girlfriend/spouse, this phase of readjustment therefore constitutes a difficult, although very important, test from which many couples emerge strengthened.

During the last round of interviews after the deployment with women participating in the SOWI study, astonishingly the following opinion was very often expressed: "It is as if he had never been away now." The last interviews took place two months after the return of the soldiers, so that, by that time, service members and their families had got accustomed to one another relatively well again and found their way to a shared everyday life. Only 2 out of the 30 women questioned – both of them in their early 50s – reported serious problems with their husbands. For one, the husband had returned relatively aggressive and, for the first time ever, had beaten his 18-year-old son. The other soldier, one-and-a-half months after his return, no longer showed any physical interest in his wife – a situation with which the woman had never been confronted in the course of their 25-year relationship and for which she had no explanation.

Apart from these two "problem cases," the return of the soldiers obviously turned out to be very positive. The women were not only pleased to have their partners and fathers of their children back, but also relieved that they had returned unscathed. Many of the women interviewed even indicated that the period of separation had had a positive effect on the relationship, because now they appreciated each other more highly.

Conclusion

This chapter tried to illuminate in more detail the challenges and stress with which military families have to cope during deployment. Soldiers' participation in deployments abroad confronts them and their families with manifold tests. The separation involves major emotional, social, and family stress. The women have to (have no other choice but to) support the mission and their partners deployed, and thus become part of the military "culture of sacrifice" that their partners developed a long time ago and to which they willingly succumbed as service members.[21] The families back home have to carry a substantial part of the heavy burden connected to deployment. It appears that the predeployment period and the immediately subsequent phase confront the women with major challenges and involve emotional ups and downs. This is also the case during deployment when attacks occur in theater and German service members are injured, or even killed.

In general, four phases of separation can be distinguished. Before the deployment, first attempts to come to terms with the absence are made, which are hampered by the manifold professional obligations of the respective soldier. The real beginning of the deployment constitutes an enormous change for the family at home, which has to adjust to its new role. The fact that service members are aware that their girlfriends/spouses have to carry the heavy burden of the deployment is also confirmed by the interviews. While the Bundeswehr relieves the deployed soldiers of many everyday chores and organizational tasks, their girlfriends/spouses at home have to carry the real burden of the deployment and to accomplish many tasks that the husband would otherwise perform. The phase of getting accustomed to the separation generally lasts until the end of the deployment; it can, however, be interrupted by the home leave of the soldier. Upon return, many partners have to get accustomed to one another again. Often, fathers and children have to reconcile their differences. In spite of all of these impediments, the majority of the families cope well with the separation, with only a few families really facing more severe problems.

Deployment-related separations cannot be avoided, but comprehensive information about help or support provided, the exact planning of the deployment period, and other measures can minimize the associated stress. The units and the chain of command can also make a substantial contribution to the better management of deployments abroad (Bartone et al., 1993; Pittman et al., 2004). When planning, military leaders should consider the personal and family interests of their soldiers in a responsible and conscious way to ensure the motivation of the service members and the positive support by their families in the longer term: "From research we know that the conflict between the family and the military is a reality but we also know that it can be alleviated by the organizations [*sic*] effort to provide family support and by supportive commanders" (Moelker, 2004: 22).

In the future, it will become even more important than before also to consider the effects of any organizational and military decision on the family, and to take those effects into account. Otherwise, it might become difficult to recruit personnel with family into the Bundeswehr. From this point of view, the 2005 decision to reduce the length of deployment from six to four months was a right step toward the best interests of military personnel and their family members. But even with all of the efforts made by the armed forces, deployments will, by nature, remain a heavy hardship for military personnel and their families.

Notes

1 This chapter is based on the study *Einsatzbedingte Trennung: Erfahrungen und Bewältigungsstrategien* [*Separation Resulting from Mission Deployment: Experiences and coping strategies*] (Tomforde, 2006). Research material has been updated for this book by means of further in-depth and focus group interviews with numerous service members in 2012 and 2013, as well as thorough literature research.

2 During the past decades, the relationships of soldiers have changed in so far as they no longer follow only traditional patterns. For this reason, the term "family" will be used in a global sense, to refer to both married and unmarried heterosexual, as well as homosexual, couples, with children or without any children, who either have common or separate residences.

3 The proportion of females participating in Bundeswehr missions abroad is approximately 6 percent (Seiffert et al., 2012). General statements concerning deployed service members naturally include both men and women. Since male soldiers outnumber female personnel during deployments abroad, the following text will be based on the most common case in which a soldier (male) goes on a mission, while his partner (female) remains at home.

4 As part of the current transformation process of the German Armed Forces, the Bundeswehr Institute of Social Sciences was merged with the Military History Research Institute in Potsdam (Germany) in January 2013. The new institute is called the Center for Military History and Social Sciences of the Bundeswehr.

5 In July 2011, the Bundeswehr became an all-volunteer force when conscription was abandoned.

6 See also Bourg and Segal (1999), and Goffman (1973).

7 See also Chapter 2 by De Angelis and Segal in this book.

8 See also Coolbaugh and Rosenthal (1992), and Orthner and Pittman (1986).

9 See http://www.bundeswehr.de, "Das Netzwerk der Hilfe," [accessed February 4, 2013]. See also Reitz (2011) and Wendl (2011).

10 See also Gravino et al. (1993), and Wood, Scarville, and Gravino (1995).

11 Katrin Schwarz (2011) has published outlines of letters and mails sent by spouses to service members deployed abroad between 2000 and 2010. Women volunteered this correspondence for her publication.

12 Concerning the statistics of people deployed, research in Afghanistan among personnel of the Bundeswehr in 2011 (Seiffert et al., 2012) has shown that 45 percent of the men were aged 18–30, 30 percent were aged 31–40, 18 percent were aged 41–50, and 7 percent were over the age of 50. More than three-quarters of the service members were in a relationship, 15 percent were single, and "only" 3 percent were divorced, currently separating, or widowed. Thus, contrary to myths of high separation rates among military families owing to deployment stress, numbers were relatively low – especially considering the fact that almost half of the service members deployed were under the age of 30, at

which time relationships tend to break up more easily and separation rates are usually higher.

13   See also Rosenfeld (2010).
14   See also Chapter 7 by Dandeker et al. in this book about UK experiences with "rest and recuperation" during deployment.
15   See also Rohall, Segal, and Segal (1999); Wood et al. (1995).
16   At time of writing, since 2001, 52 German service members have been killed in the war in Afghanistan. Even though this number is relatively low in comparison with casualty rates of countries such as the United States, United Kingdom, Canada, or France, the death of every single soldier means great loss and unimaginable grief for his or her family and friends. For casualty statistics, see http://www.icasualties.org [accessed February 6, 2013].
17   See http://www.bundeswehr.de, "Ernstfall für die Familie: Leserreaktionen (2)," [accessed February 10, 2013].
18   See, e.g., http://www.afghanistan-blog.de
19   See http://www.bundeswehr.de, "Ernstfall für die Familie: Leserreaktionen (1)," [accessed February 10, 2013].
20   Since 2001, the number of service members treated for PTSD in the Bundeswehr has been constantly rising, reaching the 1,143 people treated in 2012 (194 new cases and 949 cases in which treatment was being continued). See http://www.50-jahre-bundewehr.de, "Belastungsstörung: Aktuelle Zahlen," [accessed February 9, 2013].
21   See also Chapter 3 by Eran-Jona in this book.

References

Bartone, J., Harris, J., Segal, D., and Segal, M.W. (1993) "Paratroopers' wives." In D. Segal and M.W. Segal (eds.) *Peacekeepers and Their Wives: American participation in the multinational force and observers.* Westport, CT/London: Greenwood Press, pp. 129–39.

Biehl, H., Keller, J., and Tomforde, M. (2005) "Den eigentlichen Einsatz fährt meine Frau zu Hause: Belastungen von Bundeswehr-Soldaten und ihren Familien während des Auslandseinsatzes." In G. Kümmel (ed.) *Diener zweier Herren: Soldaten zwischen Bundeswehr und Familie Kümmel.* Frankfurt am Main: Peter Lang, pp. 79–107.

Biehl, H., Keller, J., Kozielski, P., Reinholz, C., and Tomforde, M. (2004) "Einsatzmotivation im 7. und 8. Einsatzkontingent SFOR: Ergebnisbericht." Unpublished report for Unveröffentlichter SOWI-Bericht, Strausberg.

Bourg, C., and Segal, M.W. (1999) "The impact of family supportive policies and practices on organizational commitment to the Army." *Armed Forces & Society,* 25: 633–52.

Coolbaugh, K.W., and Rosenthal, A. (1992) *Family Separations in the Army.* Technical report, Alexandria, VA: Army Research Institute for the Behavioral and Social Sciences.

De Soir, E.L.J.L. (2000) "Hoe beleeft het thuisfront een uitzending? De emotionele stadia bij langdurige inzet [How does the home front experience a deployment? The emotional stadia during prolonged deployments]." *Kernvraag,* 123: 19–26.

Drummet, A., Coleman, M., and Cable, S. (2003) "Military families under stress: Implications for family life education." *Family Relations,* 52: 279–87.

Ender, M., and Segal, D. (1996) "V(E)-mail to the foxhole: Soldier isolation, (tele) communication, and force-projection operations." *Journal of Political & Military Sociology,* 24: 83–104.

Goffman, E. (1973) *Asyle: Über die soziale Situation psychiatrischer Patienten und anderer Insassen.* Frankfurt am Main: Suhrkamp Verlag.

Gravino, K., Segal, D., and Segal, M.W. (1993) "Lightfighters' wives." In D. Segal and M.W. Segal (eds.) *Peacekeepers and Their Wives: American participation in the multinational force and observers.* Westport, CT/London: Greenwood Press, pp. 140–56.

Lüder, A. (2004) "Das Leit-Familienzentrum in Potsdam: Visionen für die Zukunft." *Streitkräftebasis* [online], available from http://www.streitkraeftebasis.de/C1256C290043532F/docname/rep_fbz_II [accessed September 6, 2004].

Moelker, R. (2004) "Military families: A theoretical framework." Paper presented at the Biannual Conference of the International Sociological Association, Ankara, Turkey, 6–9 July.

Moskos, C.C. (1988) "Institutional and occupational trends in armed forces." In C.C. Moskos and F.R. Wood (eds.) *The Military: More than just a job?* Washington, D.C.: Pergamon-Brassey's, pp. 15–26.

Orthner, D.K. and Pittman, J.F. (1986) "Family contributions to work commitment." *Journal of Marriage and the Family,* 48: 573–81.

Pincus, S., House, R., Christenson, J., and Adler, L. (2004) "The emotional cycle of deployment: A military family perspective." *Hooah4Health* [online], available from http://www.hooah4health.com/deployment/familymatters/emotionalcycle.htm [accessed September 5, 2004].

Pittman, J., Kerpelman, J., and McFayden, J. (2004) "Internal and external adaptation in army families: Lessons from Operations Desert Shield and Desert Storm." *Family Relations,* 53: 249–60.

Reitz, C. (2011) *Auslandseinsatz: Dein, mein, unser Einsatz – Ein Ratgeber für Soldatenfamilien.* Koblenz: Zentrum Innere Führung.

Rohall, D.E., Segal, M.W., and Segal, D. (1999) "Examining the importance of organization supports on family adjustment to army life in a period of increasing separation." *Journal of Political & Military Sociology,* 27: 49–65.

Rosen, L.N., Durand, D., Westhuis, D.J., and Teitelbaum, J.M. (1995) "Marital adjustment of army spouses one year after Operation Desert Storm." *Journal of Applied Psychology,* 25: 677–92.

Rosenfeld, D. (2010) "Schießt der Papa auch auf Menschen?" *Zeit,* July 18 [online], available from http://www.zeit.de/2010/29/Afghanistan-Soldaten [accessed July 18, 2010].

Schwarz, K. (ed.) (2011) *Ich kämpf mich zu dir durch, mein Schatz: Briefe von der Heimatfront (2000–2010).* Sankt Augustin: adatia Verlag.

Segal, M.W. (1986) "The military and the family as greedy institutions." *Armed Forces & Society,* 13: 9–38.

Seiffert, A., Langer, P., and Pietsch, C. (eds.) (2012) *Der Einsatz der Bundeswehr in Afghanistan: Sozial- und politikwissenschaftliche Perspektiven.* Wiesbaden: VS Verlag.

Tomforde, M. (2006) *Einsatzbedingte Trennung: Erfahrungen und Bewältigungsstrategien.* Forschungsbericht #78. Strausberg: Sozialwissenschaftliches Institut der Bundeswehr.

Wendl, P. (2011) *Soldat im Einsatz – Partnerschaft im Einsatz: Praxis- und Arbeitsbuch für Paare und Familien in Auslandseinsatz und Wochenendbeziehung.* Freiburg/Basel/Wien: Herder Verlag.

Wood, S., Scarville, J., and Gravino, K. (1995) "Waiting wives: Separation and reunion among army wives." *Armed Forces & Society,* 21: 217–36.

7   The British military family

The experiences of British Army wives before, during, and after deployment, their satisfaction with military life, and their use of support networks[1]

Christopher Dandeker, Claire Eversden, Catherine Birtles, and Simon Wessely

Introduction

Work–life balance is a persistent issue in the UK Armed Forces, which have been overstretched for 15 years. Guest (2001) highlights five models of the relationship between work and life: (1) "segmentation," in which the two are distinct spheres with no influence between them; (2) "spillover" – either positive or negative – from one sphere to the other; (3) "compensation," in which people may find rewards in one area to make up for being unfulfilled in the other; (4) "instrumental" – that is, using one sphere as a means of making gains in the other, for example using work as a means to an end outside work; and (5) "conflict," which proposes that, with high levels of demand in all spheres of life, some conflicts and possibly some significant overload of an individual occur. This latter model can be linked to the concept of "greedy institutions" (Coser, 1974).

Armed Forces are not the only "greedy institutions," but deployment commitments and the assumption that soldiers will, when required, go into harm's way result in a contract of "unlimited liability" (Dandeker, 2000a; Hockey, 1986). The traditional family is also a greedy institution (Segal, 1988; Shields, 1988), and the traditional military family has been part of an institution in which it supports and gives priority to service life (Jessup, 1996; Moelker and van der Kloet, 2003). Military wives contribute an unpaid and often "invisible" contribution to the armed services (Harrell, 2000). Since the 1970s, the military has become less institutional. Women have played a wider, more integrated role in service employment (Dandeker and Segal, 1996), while military spouses have become less dependent upon their service partners, tending to build lives of their own, but expecting more time and attention from their service partners – particularly in terms of family duties (Deakin, 1994). Military families have also become more diverse: there are dual-service couples, both with and without children; couples in which the female is the service member; and same-sex couples.[2]

While the family has become more demanding, so has the military in the last three decades, with forces performing an increased number of operational commitments (Dandeker, 2000b), but with fewer human resources, so that families have been separated more frequently (Rohall, Segal, and Segal, 1999; Segal and Segal, 2003). Those "left behind" during deployments may have to adapt suddenly to being alone – such as to paying bills or looking after children. They may have limited support mechanisms, may experience financial difficulties (Andres and Moelker, 2011; Eran-Jona, 2011), may be unaware of the duration of the deployment, and may experience additional stress about whether their loved ones will return. Stress levels can vary over time and are related to the perceived risk of the deployment (Milgram and Bar, 1993). U.S. research indicates that the "stress-buffering" effects of social support networks are important factors in the general well-being of military wives during their spouses' deployment (Cohen and Willis, 1985; Rosen and Moghadam, 1990; Rosenberg, 1989).

Research aim and objectives

This chapter investigates the experiences of British Army wives during a six-month deployment period to Iraq in 2004–05 (known as "Op Telic," this fifth deployment of which was called "Telic 5"). It focuses on the following questions.

- Do soldiers and their spouses feel trapped between the competing demands of the military and family?
- How do spouses "draw a line" between work and family life?
- How do spouses adapt to separation during periods of deployment?
- What part is played by informal and formal networks in how spouses deal with the stresses that occur during deployments?
- Are spouses who are satisfied with the quality of military life, their marriages, and their own personal development more likely to be supportive of their partners' military careers?

Social support for families is a buffer against stress, and this can be provided by official channels (normally a "top-down" process), by informal social networks (normally a "bottom-up," grassroots approach), or by a combination of both mechanisms through partnership or a process of cooptation of the informal by the formal mechanisms. For this deployment, the great majority of the spouse sample (89 percent) was drawn from German garrisons in which spouses were closer to, and dependent on, Army support services. Thus the study provides a representative sample of the units that deployed to Iraq rather than a sample of the British Army as a whole.

Methods

Study design

The study combined both qualitative and quantitative research methods, and comprised three distinct phases: face-to-face interviews at the start and the end of deployment (Phases 1 and 3), and a mid-deployment postal questionnaire (Phase 2). The sample of service wives derived from a parallel study investigating the health and well-being of regular British Army personnel deploying to Iraq in 2004. For the parallel study, 193 soldiers took part, of whom 80 (42 percent) were married and cohabiting. All spouses of married participants were invited to take part in this study via an invitation forwarded to them by their respective unit welfare office (UWO) and 51 (64 percent) spouses were recruited.

The sampling strategy was to identify patterns and differences across ranks and length of service, with the aim of differentiating wives who were new to Army life from those more experienced, who had progressed through the rank structure. The sample was stratified by those with less than 4 years' service, between 4 and 12 years' service, and more than 12 years' service. These groups were then proportionally stratified by rank.

Data collection process

In Phase 1, study participants were interviewed shortly after the main departure date of each of the deploying units. The face-to-face interviews (as with Phase 3) mainly took place in the privacy of each UWO, although spouses were offered the choice of being interviewed in their own home. Interviews covered socio-demographics, employment, support networks, general health (including the 12-item General Health Questionnaire, or GHQ-12[3]), marital satisfaction using the Enrich Marital Satisfaction (EMS) Scale,[4] and deployment issues including the perceived well-being of children.

For Phase 2, spouses were sent a brief mid-deployment postal questionnaire, which further investigated support networks, reactions to "rest and recuperation" (or R&R, a two-week leave period granted to soldiers deployed overseas), potential deployment stressors, and perceived adjustment of children, and repeated the GHQ-12.

In Phase 3, a postdeployment interview took place between four and six weeks after the return of the service partner, and once postoperational tour leave (POTL) had ended. Interviews with spouses during POTL were logistically impossible, because many families went on holiday during this period. Interviews covered issues such as patterns of family readjustment, the EMS Scale, sources of support, employment, health, and well-being (repeating the GHQ-12), and feelings about Army life.

All Phase 1 and Phase 3 interviews were audiotaped with participants' permission and later transcribed. In cases in which husbands returned home prior to mid-deployment, spouses were interviewed over the telephone, to investigate the early return of the husband and any readjustment difficulties. These data were analyzed together with the main group. At Phase 3, participants who were not available on the day of the scheduled visit were, where possible, interviewed over the telephone.

Methods of analysis

Quantitative data were double-entered on to SPSS statistical analysis software and, where relevant, paired sample *t*-tests were undertaken to compare mean values. Qualitative data from the transcripts were analyzed using the constant comparative method (Glaser, 1965). In the results, quotations showing a nonidentifying respondent identification (ID) have been used to illustrate the generated themes.

Ethical approval

The study received ethical approval from King's College Hospital Research Ethics Committee and from the British Ministry of Defense (Navy) Personnel Research Ethics Committee.

Results

Response rates were as follows. In Phase 1, of the 80 spouses invited to participate, 51 Army spouses opted into the study (64 percent response rate). The three spouses whose husbands did not deploy, along with the single male spouse, have been excluded from the analysis, giving an adjusted sample of 47 Army wives. In Phase 2, 44 mid-deployment questionnaires were posted to wives and 40 (89 percent) completed questionnaires were returned. Three wives, whose husbands returned prior to the questionnaires being sent out, were followed up with a postdeployment interview. For Phase 3, 42 wives completed a postdeployment interview. The five active refusals were reportedly the result of "busy schedules" ($n = 4$) and ill health ($n = 1$). As far as matched couples were concerned, of the total wives and husbands who were interviewed, 37 couples both completed a pre- and postdeployment interview. The demographic profile is presented in Table 7.1.

The average length of marriage of the sample was 7.7 years, while the average length of time that the husbands had served in the Army was 8.7 years, highlighting the fact that many spouses had "married into" the Army, their husbands having been serving soldiers before marriage. The large majority of wives (89 percent) resided in Germany, with the remaining five wives living in the United Kingdom. Most of the wives lived in service accommodation, with only three choosing to live in their own private accommodation. All of the wives except one lived in close proximity to other military families.

The results were used to generate five main categories of data.

Table 7.1 Wives' demographic profile, Phase 1

Variable	n = 47	%
Age of participants		
19–24	7	14.9
25–29	11	23.4
30–34	10	21.3
35–39	15	31.9
40–44	3	6.4
45–49	1	2.1
Ethnic group		
White	43	91.5
Other	4	8.5
Country of residence		
Germany	42	89.3
United Kingdom	5	10.6
Rank of spouse		
Officer	4	8.5
Other ranks	43	91.5
Role of spouse		
Combat	32	68.1
Combat support	7	14.9
Combat service support	8	17.0
Length of marriage (yrs)		
<5	14	33.3
5–10	12	28.6
11–15	11	26.2
15+	5	11.9
Missing	5	
Time spent in Army whilst in relationship (yrs)		
<4	5	11.9
4–12	20	47.6
13+	17	40.5
Missing	5	
No. of children under age of 18 who reside with participant	8	17.0
0	39	83.0
1 or more		
Type of accommodation		
Service accommodation	44	93.6
Own home	3	6.4
Level of education		
No qualifications	1	2.1
O level/GCSE/equivalent	20	42.6
A level or above	26	55.3
Employment status		
In paid employment (incl. those on maternity leave)	23	48.9
Not in paid employment	24	51.1
Of those in work (*n* = 23)		
Full-time	8	34.8
Part-time	15	65.2

1. Work–life tensions between Army wives and the British Army

Just over half the sample (51 percent) considered their marital relationship to be negatively affected by their husband being in the military, and 47 percent considered their husband's career to be in conflict with family life. Emotional conflict accounted for the majority of comments (63 percent). Examples of this type of conflict included emotional stress caused by long periods of separation, and husbands missing special family occasions because of work commitments. It also included volatile marital and family relationships, and estrangement from children following husbands' return from deployment. Practical conflict (37 percent of comments) included military routines clashing with family ones, making it difficult to coordinate or plan family activities and time together, and husbands not being able to share the responsibilities of married and family life.

> Sometimes it's upsetting if there [are] things going on. He was there when our children were born but I know people who didn't have that same luck, that kind of thing and that's gone on all our married life – "Is he going to make it for whatever or is he not?" – There's no end to what they can ask him to do really.
>
> [W7828]

> Yes his career is in conflict with family life, obviously he's trying to get on and get a higher rank, he's having to take on more responsibilities and be doing these tours. They [soldiers] live a separate life from what we have here. They're almost single and we're left with all the responsibilities.
>
> [W2124]

Of the wives who thought that there was conflict, 91 percent had talked to their husbands about this issue. Only one wife said that her husband was attempting to address the conflict caused by his career. The rest of the couples had taken no action, largely because they felt that very little could be done – it was "just the way the Army is" – combined with accepting conflict in favor of the financial security provided by the Army.

> Husband was going to get out the Army and I persuaded him not to do it because he's only got another six years left and if he got out now he wouldn't get his pension straight away and I think he'd only get about £8,000, but if we wait until his time's up – the full 22 years – he'll get £40,000 plus his pension straight away, so finance does come a great deal into it.
>
> [W3214]

Of the 37 matched couples who both completed a pre- and postdeployment questionnaire, 41 percent of the wives thought that their husbands' careers were of equal importance to home life, whereas 89 percent of husbands felt that home life was more important.

Most wives thought that their children both benefited from and were disadvantaged by military life. When asked in what way, the most common response was "frequently relocating due to husband's postings," which exposed children to different cultures, but also meant that children repeatedly lost their networks of friends and had to start again.

2. Factors that moderate and aggravate work–life tensions

Wives identified numerous factors that aggravated and moderated conflict between themselves and the Army.

Relocations

Relocation resulting from military postings was the most common factor that wives reported as an example of the ups and downs of Army life.[5] The mean number of times that wives had relocated as a result of husbands' postings was 3.74. Relocations were reported as offering variety to life and giving wives greater self-confidence; however, they also caused problems, such as disruptions to children's schooling, loss of social networks, and loss of wives' employment.

Of the 23 wives in paid employment, 20 reported themselves happy with their job, but 19 said that the demands of their husband's career had a negative impact on the kind of work available to them. Of the 24 wives not in paid employment, 22 looked after children full-time; however, just under 90 percent expressed a desire to be in employment or education, but reported a lack of (affordable) childcare and employment opportunities in the local area. Over 70 percent of Germany-based wives admitted that their employment status would have been better if they were living in the United Kingdom.

> There are no career prospects for spouses when you're in the Army because you're moving around all the time . . . It [the Army] limits your opportunities and your qualifications and training and everything.
>
> [W9714]

> We're subject to moving around with our husbands, you're not here in your own right. You haven't come because there's a job you want to do, you come because of your husband.
>
> [W1516]

Deployments and separation

Separation from husbands as a result of operational exercises and deployments was reported as the main cause of work–life tension. Over 70 percent of wives reported themselves satisfied with the period of notice given for

Telic 5, but 53 percent felt that they did not have enough quality time with their husbands before departure, primarily because of an increase in workload or training prior to deployment.

> They knew they were going so their training and everything should have been done, not left to the last minute so we see less of them . . . They were working long hours and they had days here and there and some of the leave they were supposed to have they didn't get. We all thought as wives, they [the Army] knew they were going, deal with it and then give their families time together before they went . . . it was just a total nightmare.
>
> [W7143]

Of the 31 wives whose husbands had served on previous deployments, two-thirds felt that the lack of quality time before Telic 5 was worse than previously encountered.

Nonnegotiable demands of the Army

All of the wives except one reported that they had no say in their husbands' work commitments, but 53 percent accepted this as the nature of the Army. Other responses were frustration with the nonnegotiable demands of Army life, a belief that civilian jobs are also demanding, and – for a few wives – feelings that it is not the place of a wife to say:

> If you marry a soldier you marry their job, it's the way it is. You can't argue with the Army.
>
> [W8842]

> I feel like a second class citizen basically. It's not down to me what I want regards his [husband's] working hours and when he is away, but at the end of the day he can't listen to me because it's his job . . .
>
> [W1114]

Wives commented on uncertainty of family life owing to their lack of control over their husbands' absences, postings, housing, health care, and children's education.

Belonging to the wider military family

A fifth of all moderating comments were related to "perks" to which wives were entitled and which they enjoyed as members of the wider military family. These included tax breaks, quality of living, subsidized schooling, good medical care, generous block holidays, and the improved social status that came with their husbands' promotion.

Housing – it's much cheaper [than civilian housing] and it's close to his workplace and it's in an accessible area because you've got all the shops and education center and the crèche that my daughter goes to, so I think it's a great advantage for us. My husband and I don't know how to drive so most of the time we make use of the military transport because it's free of charge.

[W2117]

Schooling here is very good. They get funded quite well and my son is doing very well at school here . . . so that's a big advantage.

[W7935]

Conversely, some wives expressed frustration at the way in which they were often expected to adhere to military rules and regulations in areas such as housing and family welfare. Some wives also perceived rank as a social stigma, and resented the fact they were categorized and judged by the rank of their husband rather than their on own merits.

Here it's your husband's rank that's rammed down your throat. You're under military rule; you have to have permission for your family to come to your house!

[W412]

Of the total sample of wives, only one did not live in close proximity to other service families. As a result, another fifth of all aggravating comments were related to lack of privacy arising from living within a tight-knit military community.

You get the goldfish bowl syndrome as I like to call it, where everybody seems to know what everybody else is doing all the time . . . and when your husband's home you can never get away from work, you're always bumping into people to do with work.

[W6816]

However, wives also reported the social framework provided by the military community as a benefit of Army life, especially during periods of deployment.

Financial security

Wives appreciated the job stability and financial security provided by the Army – the perceived good wages and pension at the end of service. Many wives believed that their quality of life was better than if their husband were a civilian, in which case he might have limited choices of employment with poorer pay.

> Pension when he gets out – the security, that's a big factor in the Army. You know you're not going to get made redundant like on Civvy Street.[6] You know you'll always have a roof over your head and a regular wage and I know the soldiers moan but it's a decent life . . .
>
> [W2521]

3. Wives' adaptations during deployment

In Phase 1, the absence of the husband was an important concern. The majority of wives (81 percent) felt that the length of deployment was acceptable, although 71 percent felt that the husbands' absence was not easy to deal with. Also 41 wives (87 percent) said that, as a result of their husbands' absence, additional demands would be placed on them at home. Of these 41 – approximately a third – worried about how they would cope, because the majority of their husbands usually took a share of the household chores and child care. Nearly all husbands (95 percent) were confident that their wives could handle key responsibilities in their absence.

In Phase 2, the theme of R&R emerged as a topic. Of the 40 wives who completed a mid-deployment postal questionnaire, 37 husbands had already been home for the two-week period of R&R granted to soldiers whilst deployed. Of these 37, over 90 percent ($n = 34$) of wives reported that their husbands spent all the R&R with them and over 80 percent ($n = 30$) of the wives reported this as being a good experience for both of them.

> Both relieved to be a whole family unit again and they [children] could see their dad was safe and well for themselves, rather than telephone calls.
>
> [W8636]

Negative feelings about R&R resulted from no choice of dates for R&R, and having to readjust and say goodbye for a second time.

> I found that after R&R it was hard to get back to routine. In the two weeks I settled into family life again and found it quite depressing and lonely to face three more months without him again.
>
> [W4310]

Of the wives with children living at home, 80 percent reported that their husbands spent time with the children during R&R and 70 percent of wives thought that the R&R was a positive experience for their children. However, most wives, along with those who thought that R&R was a negative experience, considered it difficult for the children to say goodbye and adjust for a second time.

My daughter is too little to understand where he [daddy] is and why he went away again after R&R, although we remind her that daddy is just away at work and that he loves her very much.

[W9039]

R&R is positive for children as they get to see their dad [but] it upsets them . . . they're just getting used to the idea of dad being home and he has to go away again.

[W4133]

The majority of wives (61 percent) expressed a preference for no R&R in return for a shorter deployment period. In contrast, 100 percent of husbands who returned a mid-deployment questionnaire said R&R *was* an important part of deployment. Most soldiers worked a seven-day week whilst deployed and R&R was perceived as a crucial period during which soldiers could unwind away from operational stressors. Even the small minority who suggested shortening the tour by a couple of months stated that a period of R&R was still required.

We work seven days a week . . . I have noticed that I am less tolerant of people than usual and get frustrated more easily but put that down to not having much time off . . . R&R is very welcome.

[Husband A13]

It's better if the men stay away and not get R&R until deployment is finished as it only upsets the apple cart more for both wives and children, as you are just getting used to being a family again when they have to go away again.

[Wife W1133]

In Phase 3, a key point was wives' perceptions of the positive and negative aspects of the deployment period. Postdeployment, 26 of the wives (62 percent) reported a positive gain whilst their husband was deployed. The majority of comments regarded personal development, for example weight loss, learning new skills, and acquiring greater self-confidence as a result of coping without the husband. Wives also spoke about being able to save money and expand social networks because of having more free time. Of the 23 wives who were in paid employment at the start of the deployment, none of the wives' employment status changed as a direct result of the deployment.

So far as negative experiences were concerned, over three-quarters of wives reported feeling lonely during the deployment. Just over a fifth of wives reported difficulty comforting children and explaining "daddy's absence" and another fifth reported a lack of regular contact with their husband especially during Christmas. (Just over 40 percent of husbands reported problems contacting home whilst deployed as a result of a lack of telephones/Internet terminals and unreliable telecommunication systems.) Just over a third of wives stated that they found it difficult to run a home alone and deal with finances. Both wives and husbands were alert to the benefits of good communications during deployment. They agreed that better telecommunication facilities for soldiers in Iraq was an important factor in reducing deployment-related stress, and reported problems communicating with each other because of insufficient and unreliable systems.

Wives also reflected on the question of how the husband might best be reintegrated into the family. The majority of wives (89 percent) supported a period of decompression for soldiers postdeployment; believing that it helped readjustment to normal military routine, but felt that husbands should have access to their families during this period because family readjustment was also important. Married soldiers perceived decompression differently, believing that they did not need or benefit from it.

In terms of the overall impact of the deployment, one important dimension was marital satisfaction. Of the 37 matched couples, four husbands felt that the deployment had a detrimental effect on their marriage, whereas none of the wives thought that the deployment had an overall detrimental effect. Interestingly, of the four wives whose husbands thought the deployment had been detrimental, three of the wives thought the opposite – that is, that the relationship had been strengthened by the deployment.

With regard to the EMS Scale (Fowers and Olson, 1993), Table 7.2 shows that, of the 37 matched couples, average EMS scores for both wives and soldiers did not show a statistically significant change across the deployment period.[7]

However, soldiers' mean scores for overall marital satisfaction across the deployment were slightly higher than their wives', and, by the end of the deployment, husbands were on average significantly more satisfied with their marriage than their wives (see Table 7.3). There were no statistical differences between the mean positive couple agreement (PCA) scores.

Table 7.2 Mean marital satisfaction scores for wives and soldiers across the deployment period

	n	*Phase 1*	*Phase 3*	*Difference*	
		(start of the deployment) *Mean score*	*(end of the deployment)* *Mean score*	*Mean (95% CI)*	*p-value*
Spouse	37	56.57	55.12	1.45 (−1.97 to 4.88)	0.396
Soldier	35*	58.40	60.66	−2.26 (−6.00 to 1.49)	0.229
PCA**	35	44.29	47.43	−3.14 (−9.85 to 3.56)	0.348

* Of the 37 matched couples, two husbands refused to complete the EMS Scale at Phase 3.
** Positive couple agreement (PCA) scores provide the percentage of EMS Scale areas that both partners agree are a strength for them, e.g. "communicating," "parenting," "sexual relationship."

Table 7.3 Mean differences of marital satisfaction scores between matched couples across the deployment period

	n	Paired differences	
		Mean (95% CI)	p-value
Soldier–spouse, Phase 1	37	1.86 (−1.91 to 5.64)	0.324
Soldier–spouse, Phase 3	35*	6.11 (2.19 to 10.04)	0.003

* Of the 37 matched couples, two husbands refused to complete the EMS Scale at Phase 3.

EMS scores across the deployment were also examined by the education levels of wives (see Table 7.4) and the rank of their husbands.

At Phase 3, couples whose wives had lower levels of education (GCSEs[8]/equivalent or lower) had significantly improved mean PCA scores (with a mean change of −10.77, $p = 0.047$). The main agreed area of improvement was how they related sexually, followed by management of leisure activities. However, when comparing mean scores between couples at Phase 3, wives with lower levels of education were significantly less satisfied with their marriages than their husbands, despite their improved PCA scores (see Table 7.5). This was not apparent in wives with higher levels of education. Differences in rank were not found to be a factor, although the officer sample size ($n = 3$) was too small for meaningful comparisons.

Table 7.4 Mean marital satisfaction scores for wives and soldiers across the deployment period, grouped by level of wives' education

	n*	Phase 1 Mean score	Phase 3 Mean score	Difference Mean (95% CI)	p-value
Wives					
GCSEs/equivalent or lower	14	57.50	53.47	4.03 (−1.89 to 9.94)	0.165
A levels/equivalent or higher	23	56.00	56.12	−0.12 (−4.52 to 4.29)	0.957
Soldier					
GCSEs/equivalent or lower	13	59.69	63.38	−3.69 (−12.70 to 5.32)	0.390
A levels/equivalent or higher	22	57.63	59.05	−1.41 (−4.94 to 2.12)	0.416
PCA					
GCSEs/equivalent or lower	13	41.54	52.31	−10.77 (−21.37 to −0.17)	0.047
A levels/equivalent or higher	22	45.91	44.55	1.36 (−7.32 to 10.04)	0.747

* Of the 37 matched couples, two husbands refused to complete the EMS Scale at Phase 3.

Table 7.5 Mean differences of marital satisfaction scores between matched couples across the deployment period, grouped by level of wives' education

	n	*Paired differences*	
		Mean (95% CI)	p-*value*
Soldier–spouse, Phase 1			
GCSEs/equivalent or lower	14	2.07 (−5.95 to 10.09)	0.586
A levels/equivalent or higher	23	1.74 (−2.50 to 5.98)	0.404
Soldier–spouse, Phase 3			
GCSEs/equivalent or lower	13	10.09 (1.68 to 18.50)	0.023
A levels/equivalent or higher	22	3.77 (−0.32 to 7.85)	0.069

When considering the overall impact of deployment on children, in Phase 1, 23 wives (61 percent) with children living at home reported negative changes in their children's behavior following their husband's departure, including: tantrums and displays of aggression (78 percent, $n = 18$); sleeping problems, such as nightmares, not being able to sleep alone, and bed-wetting (70 percent, $n = 16$); being more emotionally upset (52 percent, $n = 12$); general insecurity (30 percent, $n = 7$); and fixations with death (26 percent, $n = 6$). Most wives stated that, during the period of their husbands' deployment, they tried to shield their younger children from the media's reports of Iraq, which tended to dwell upon the negative aspects of the deployment.

> The biggest one, he's been dry for two years, out of nappies but now he's bedwetting. If my husband phones in the night to say goodnight, then my little boy is OK, otherwise he wets the bed. This started a week after he left.
>
> [W1147]

> It really hit them that [daddy] had gone away. Strange behavior, tantrums, saying they didn't want him to go. It was my eldest really, he was saying [daddy] was going to die in Iraq and he'd just do really strange things; he'd sit and put my husband's uniform on . . . he has been starting drawing picture of tanks and people in tanks with blood all over them and that quite upset me, but my husband said he used to do things like that when he was younger and I actually talked to social workers about that.
>
> [W1127]

Of the 15 (39 percent) who reported no adverse changes in their children's behavior, three mothers stated that their children (under 12 months old) were too young to notice their father's absence, and those mothers with

Table 7.6 Wives' mean GHQ-12 scores across the deployment, by education and rank

	n	Mean GHQ-12 scores		
		Phase 1	*Phase 2*	*Phase 3*
Overall	42	3.26	2.37	1.00
Education				
GCSEs/equivalent or lower	16	2.56	1.75	1.06
A levels/equivalent or higher	26	3.69	2.78	0.96
Rank				
JNCOs or lower	17	3.47	1.75	0.82
SNCOs	22	3.23	2.87	1.27
Officers	3	2.33	2.33	0.00

JNCO = junior noncommissioned officer; SNCO = senior noncommissioned officer

several months' advance warning of the deployment said that it had helped to "prep" the children in advance, so that they were more mentally prepared for the deployment. Five of the Germany-based mothers also applauded the local military school for helping the children to adapt to fathers' absences:

> She [daughter] was helped by the school . . . the school invited the padre in to talk about it [Iraq] and he'd been to Iraq and brought back photos and spoke about what he'd seen there and what their dads and mummies would be doing when they were out there and we've never looked back since . . . It's been ok with her since then.
>
> [W119]

By the end of the deployment, nine wives and five husbands individually thought that the deployment had been detrimental to their children, but only one husband and wife together agreed that this was the case.

Another consideration is the overall impact of deployment on mental health – that is, the GHQ-12 scores. The overall mean scores for wives' GHQ-12 decreased (from 3.26 to 2.37 to 1 over the three phases), so their mental health improved as the deployment progressed (see Table 7.6).

There was a significant drop (that is, an improvement in mental health) in overall mean scores between Phases 1 and 3 (see Table 7.7). However, a significant decline of scores across the deployment was not found in wives with the lowest levels of education (that is, GCSEs/equivalent or below), although this group had the lowest mean score for GHQ-12 at Phase 1.

4. Spouses' networks of support during the deployment period

The majority of wives felt that, by staying within the local military community during the deployment, they were better informed about regimental

Table 7.7 Differences in the wives' mean GHQ-12 scores across the deployment, by education and rank

| | Paired differences | | | | | | | | |
| | Phase 3–Phase 1 | | Phase 2–Phase 1 | | Phase 3–Phase 2 | |
	Mean (95 % CI)	p-value	Mean (95 % CI)	p-value	Mean (95 % CI)	p-value
Overall	-2.26 (-3.11 to -1.41)	0.000	-0.93 (-2.09 to 0.22)	0.109	-1.53 (-2.56 to -0.51)	0.005
Education						
GCSEs/equivalent or lower	-1.50 (-3.10 to 0.104)	0.065	-0.93 (-2.53 to 0.697)	0.237	-1.25 (-3.47 to 0.97)	0.241
A levels/equivalent or higher	-2.73 (-3.74 to -1.73)	0.000	-0.94 (-2.68 to 0.79)	0.267	-1.72 (-2.81 to -0.63)	0.004
Rank						
JNCOs or lower	-2.65 (-4.13 to -1.16)	0.002	-2.17 (-4.26 to -0.71)	0.044	-0.67 (-2.11 to 0.775)	0.331
SNCOs	-1.96 (-3.20 to -0.70)	0.004	-0.13 (-1.79 to 1.53)	0.866	-2.07(-3.84 to -0.30)	0.025

JNCO = junior noncommissioned officer; SNCO = senior noncommissioned officer

Note: No paired differences of the mean for officer's wives, because the sample size ($n = 3$) was too small for meaningful analysis.

news from Iraq. News flowed by wives' word of mouth and through UWOs. Less than one fifth of the wives reported that they had asked for help from the regiment or other military sources in preparing for their husband's departure, with the majority (96 percent) seeking informal support from their own family and other military wives (85 percent). Both during and after deployment, wives sought and received the most help from other military families and, where applicable, work colleagues.

The majority of wives (69 percent) recognized that regimental UWOs were a potential source of support during the deployment largely for more practical issues such as transport. Of the 37 matched husbands, 64 percent believed that the military was providing sufficient support to their family whilst they were deployed. However, some wives whose husbands were attached to a regiment expressed concern that they were not included in the social welfare package provided by the host unit, because they were not perceived to be "one of them." Support services and charities for military families outside the regiment were not utilized.

> I turn to friends here . . . they're going through the same as what I'm going through . . . got children and husband's away. I know it sounds silly but you feel that you're all in the same situation; you're all in the same boat. Back home, they support you but they don't understand because you have to be living this life to really understand I suppose. My life is here and I feel I've got more support with what's happening to my husband by being here.
>
> [W6424]

> I got leaflets, advice etc. [from the base] but I've had no contact with them. It could be down to me, the facilities are there, I could go over there but I'd rather go to my family members.
>
> [W9897]

5. Wives' overall satisfaction with military life

Only 9 of the 47 wives (19 percent) did not share the same views on the deployment and mission of Telic 5 as their husbands. At the start of the deployment, 83 percent of the wives felt proud of their husbands' careers and work, but approximately half of the wives were not glad that their spouse was in the Armed Forces. However the large majority (83 percent) wanted their husband to stay in the military, with financial security (that is, regular income and an attractive pension) being the main reason why. By the end of the deployment, this figure had increased slightly to 88 percent.

> No I'm not glad he's in the Army but I do want him to stay in. He has only got seven years left and it is for financial reasons that I want him to stay in, not for anything else. We have got a family, we have got a

mortgage to pay, we have financial commitments and the moment it [Army] pays well . . . so like everybody else in the UK, I'm sure they don't do jobs that they want to do, they just do them because they are financially rewarding.

[W1182]

Husband's career just revolves around providing food and water and shelter. We look forward to the day he gets out the Army, it's gonna stop at 22 years. Although we're at that point now where we're trapped! . . . But we're at that point where if he left now he would give up his pension.

[W1173, whose husband had four-and-a-half years of service left to complete]

Conclusions

Wives recognized the benefits and costs of Army life, accepting that commitment to their husbands' military career also included the work–life tensions of frequent postings, separation, lack of privacy from community living, and the nonnegotiable demands of the military. Their greatest source of dissatisfaction was separation from their husbands resulting from long deployments, exacerbated by periods of predeployment training. Previous research by Drummet, Coleman, and Cable (2003) found that separation resulted in high levels of stress for U.S. military spouses. However, our sample of wives became *more* mentally robust (as measured by GHQ-12 scores) as the deployment progressed. This may be partly explained by the context of Telic 5. The British Army's previous deployment to Iraq had been particularly stressful, and subsequently soldiers and wives preparing for Telic 5 had expectations of the same kind of operation. The reality turned out to be a relatively quiet deployment with fewer casualties than expected.

In an Army garrison town, wives favored informal social networks to provide a buffer against the stressors of deployment and did not expect or choose the military as their first line of support, whilst recognizing that regimental UWOs were a potential source of help for more practical problems should they occur and appreciating this "safety net." This point mirrors similar results from military families in Australian and American populations, in which informal support groups have been positively linked to military families' separation adjustment (Siebler, 2003; Wood, Scarville, and Gravino, 1995). Further research is required within less institutionalized families of British Army personnel who live outside Army garrison towns (and in the United Kingdom, not Germany, from which U.K. forces are in the process of withdrawing), to see if support networks differ.

Throughout the deployment, a recurring theme was the diverging perceptions between soldiers and their wives, including the wives' abilities to cope during the deployment period and use of formal support networks, the impact of deployment on marriage, and the importance of R&R and family life. For example, husbands' perceptions of the importance of their careers compared to home life differed from those of their wives. Wives made it clear that they disliked some aspects of military life, which often conflicted with family demands, yet over 40 percent of wives conceded that their husbands' careers were of equal importance. This contrasted with the great majority of service husbands, who felt that home life took priority over their military careers. Most husbands believed that their commitment to the Army depended on the level of commitment of their wives. As one soldier in the Telic 5 study stated: "A happy wife makes a happy, long-term soldier."

Wives accepted their husbands' military careers, but not unconditionally: job and financial security play a major role in career decisions, and military wives are no exception. Most wives considered the long-term financial benefits as a counterbalance to the negative aspects of Army life, including unpredictable and frequent demands upon their husbands' time, and non-negotiable compromises in important areas such as their own employment, choice of housing, and children's schooling. Desivilya and Gal (1996) state in their research on military families that competing conflicts and subsequent high levels of tension often result in significant compromises on behalf of the civilian spouse in order to "survive." However, the Army wives in this study were largely willing to compromise in order to "win" financially. The British Army will need to ensure that financial, as well as other, incentives continue to be provided to ensure that military spouses are willing to make the compromises that military life asks of them.

Notes

1   This study was supported by the Economic and Social Research Council Grant RES-000-22-0769 (2004–05).
2   On this theme, see Chapter 9 by Andres, De Angelis, and McCone.
3   See Goldberg and Williams (1988).
4   The EMS Scale provides "a means to obtain both dyadic and individual satisfaction scores. Ten of the scale's items survey ten domains of marital quality. The other five items compose a marital conventionalization scale to correct for the tendency to endorse unrealistically positive descriptions of the marriage" (Fowers and Olson, 1993: 176). The 12-item General Health Questionnaire (GHQ-12) was used as a measure of general mental health. Conventional scoring (0011) was used for each item and a total score generated. Overall score was treated as a continuous variable.
5   Postings involve a change in job; relocation involves a change in residence. The first need not involve the second, but when it does, this can cause difficulties.
6   "Civvy Street" is British slang for life after military service in the civilian world.
7   The size of the mean differences in EMS and GHQ-12 scores are presented in this chapter, along with comparisons between mean differences using the *p*-value. The latter should be interpreted with caution owing to the small sample sizes involved.
8   The General Certificate of Secondary Education (GCSE) is a secondary school qualification achieved, normally, at age 16, after which children may choose either to enter an apprenticeship or to continue into further education.

References

Andres, M.D., and Moelker R. (2011) "There and back again: How parental experiences affect children's adjustments in the course of military deployments." *Armed Forces & Society*, 37: 418–47.

Cohen, S., and Willis, T.A. (1985) "Stress, social support, and the buffering hypothesis." *Psychological Bulletin*, 98: 310–57.

Coser, L. (1974) *Greedy Institutions: Patterns of undivided commitment*. New York: Free Press.

Dandeker, C. (2000a) "On the need to be different: Recent trends in military culture." In H. Strachan (ed.) *The British Army, Manpower and Society into the Twenty-First Century*. Portland, OR/London: Frank Cass, pp. 173–90.

Dandeker, C. (2000b) "The United Kingdom: The overstretched military." In C.C. Moskos, J.A. Williams, and D.R. Segal (eds.) *The Postmodern Military: Armed forces after the Cold War*. New York/London: Oxford University Press, pp. 32–50.

Dandeker, C., and Segal, M.W. (1996) "Gender integration in the Armed Forces: Recent policy developments in the United Kingdom." *Armed Forces & Society*, 23: 29–47.

Deakin, S. (1994) "British civil–military relations in the 1990s." In D. Ashkenazy (ed.) *The Military in the Service of Society and Democracy: The challenge of the dual-role military*. Westport CT: Greenwood Press, pp. 121–8.

Desivilya, H.S., and Gal, R. (1996) "Coping with stress in families of servicemen: Searching for 'win–win' solutions to a conflict between the family and the military organization." *Family Processes*, 35: 211–25.

Drummet, A.R., Coleman, M., and Cable, S. (2003) "Military families under stress: Implications for family life education." *Family Relations*, 52: 279–87.

Eran-Jona, M. (2011) "Married to the military: Military–family relations in the Israel Defense Forces." *Armed Forces & Society*, 37: 19–41.

Fowers, B.J., and Olson, D.H. (1993) "ENRICH Marital Satisfaction Scale: A brief research and clinical tool." *Journal of Family Psychology*, 7(2): 176–85.

Glaser, B.G. (1965) "The constant comparative method of qualitative analysis." *Social Problems*, 12(4): 436–45.

Goldberg, D., and Williams, P.A. (1988) *A User's Guide to the General Health Questionnaire*. Windsor: NFER-Nelson.

Guest, D.E. (2001) "Perspectives on the study of work–life balance." A discussion paper prepared for the ENOP Symposium, March 29–31, Paris [online], available from http://www.ucm.es/info/Psyap/enop/guest.htm [accessed January 10, 2013].

Harrell, M.C. (2000) *Invisible Women: Junior enlisted army wives*. eBook [online], available from http://www.rand.org/publications/MR/MR1223 [accessed January 10, 2013].

Hockey, J. (1986) *Squaddies: Portrait of a subculture*. Exeter: University of Exeter.

Jessup, C. (1996) *Breaking Ranks: Social change in military communities*. London: Brassey's.

Milgram, N.A., and Bar, K. (1993) "Stress on wives due to husbands' hazardous duty or absence." *Military Psychology*, 5(1): 21–39.

Moelker, R., and van der Kloet, I. (2003) "Military families and the armed forces." In G. Caforio (ed.) *Handbook of the Sociology of the Military*. New York/Boston/Dordrecht/London/Moscow: Kluwer Press, pp. 201–24.

Rohall, D.E., Segal, D., and Segal, M.W. (1999) "Examining the importance of organizational support on family adjustment to army life in a period of increasing separation." *Journal of Political & Military Sociology*, 27: 1–15.

Rosen, L.N., and Moghadam, L.Z. (1990) "Matching the support to the stressor: Implications for the buffering hypothesis." *Military Psychology*, 2(4): 193–205.

Rosenberg, F.R. (1989) *The Wife of the First-Term Enlisted: A study of socialization and role.* Washington, D.C.: Walter Reed Army Institute of Research, Department of Military Psychiatry.

Segal, D.R., and Segal, M.W. (2003) "Implications for military families of changes in the armed forces of the United States." In G. Caforio (ed.) *Handbook of Military Sociology.* London: Sage Publications, pp. 219–27.

Segal, M.W. (1988) "The military and the family as greedy institutions." In C.C. Moskos and F.R. Wood (eds.) *The Military: More than just a job?* Washington, D.C.: Pergamon-Brassey's, pp. 79–97.

Shields, P. (1988) "Sex roles in the military." In C.C. Moskos and F.R. Wood (eds.) *The Military: More than just a job?* Washington, D.C.: Pergamon-Brassey's, pp. 99–114.

Siebler, P. (2003) *Supporting Australian Defense Force Peacekeepers and Their Families: The case for East Timor.* Directorate of Strategic Personnel Planning and Research Special Report [online]. available from http://www.dtic.mil/cgi-bin/GetTRDoc?AD=ADA481108 [accessed January 10, 2013].

Wood, S., Scarville, J., and Gravino, K.S. (1995) "Waiting wives: Separation and reunion among army wives." *Armed Forces & Society*, 21: 217–36.

8 The well-being of military families

Coping with the stressors of military
life among spouses of Canadian Armed
Forces members

Sanela Dursun and Kerry Sudom

Introduction

Perhaps more than in any other kind of organization, the interaction
between work and family in the military has a pervasive influence on the
lifestyle of its members and their families. Unlike most organizations, a military member's family is highly involved in the culture and organization of
the military (Wisecarver, Cracraft, and Heffner, 2006). As well, the unique
demands of military service, including operational deployments, the risk of
injury or death, frequent separation from the family, and postings, can significantly disrupt family life (Castro et al., 2001). These realities, combined
with isolation from traditional sources of support such as extended families,
close friends, and stable community relationships (Black, 1993), are associated with personal and interpersonal stress for some military families.

The aim of this study was to assess the impact of military lifestyle demands
on military families. The study focused on the well-being of military spouses
and evaluated the relationship between factors associated with the demands
of military service – deployments, in particular, and the well-being of military spouses.[1] Furthermore, the study examined the effects of military stressors and the mediating effects of appraisals and coping styles on spousal
well-being. To assess the impact of military lifestyle demands on families,
it may be useful to adopt a "stress and coping" perspective. This approach
emphasizes the cognitive-motivational concepts of subjective appraisals and
coping, and a process-centered holistic outlook regarding individuals' well-
being (Lazarus, 2000). From the perspective of the transactional model of
stress and coping (Lazarus and Folkman, 1984), military lifestyle demands
include various stressors that the individual appraises and to which he or
she responds. The processes of appraisal and coping mediate the relationship between the experienced stressors and the individual's well-being.

Despite the attention given to the various components of the stress process
and the interrelations among them, neither has been extensively studied in
the context of the military family environment. Therefore one aim of this
study was to broaden and refine our conceptual understanding of the coping
process by testing, in a military environment, a model of coping that examined these mediating mechanisms, which are central to the coping process.

The challenges experienced by military families

Military spouses face a number of unique stressors as they attempt to meet the demands placed upon them by the military institution. Aspects of military life that can influence the well-being of family members include frequent relocations, temporary housing, spousal unemployment and underemployment, separations, deployments to hostile situations, and long and often unpredictable work hours. Any combination of these factors may be a source of stress for military families. Perhaps the most significant among these stressors is the separation of family members as a result of operational deployments (Westhius, 1999).

Military deployments and duty-related separations are defining experiences for military members and their families. Separations often entail a reorganization of family roles and routines as the spouse remaining at home adjusts to the partner's absence. Stressors may include strain on the marital relationship, childcare concerns, changes in children's well-being, difficulties accessing military services, and practical issues such as those surrounding home and car maintenance (Van Vranken et al., 1984). Nondeployed spouses may experience loneliness, anger, and depression, as well as headaches, weight change, and sleep disturbances (Van Vranken et al., 1984).

Deployment and duty-related separations are challenging for families, and stress is a normal response during such separations (Martin et al., 1996). Families go through a distinctive multistage process when a member is deployed, reflecting the predeployment, deployment, and postdeployment phases (Pincus et al., 2001). Not surprisingly, what is perceived as stressful before a deployment differs from what is perceived as stressful during or after a deployment. Spouses of military members go through a number of feelings and experiences throughout this cycle, including initial shock, departure, emotional disintegration, recovery and stabilization, anticipation of the homecoming, reunion, and reintegration (Pincus et al., 2001). Although researchers disagree on which deployment phase is the most difficult, it is clear that deployment places both the military member and the spouse remaining at home under considerable stress.

Research conducted on military families often adopts an external focus that assesses how the military organization and community services might intervene to help spouses to cope and adjust, rather than the internal resources and coping abilities that individuals themselves bring to the experience of deployment separations (Wright et al., 2006). However, a spouse's appraisal of stressful situations and his or her coping style may both play a role in how well he or she adapts to the various stages of deployment.

Potential mediators in the relationship between stressors and well-being

Appraisals

According to the transactional model, appraisal is a process of evaluating and categorizing the personal implications of events, and it comprises two phases:

primary and secondary appraisal (Folkman and Lazarus, 1980). Each person makes a primary appraisal of a potentially stressful event. An event is stressful if it is perceived as likely to equal or exceed the resources of the person to adapt to the demand. This primary appraisal involves evaluating the stressor as threatening, challenging, or harmful to one's well-being (Lazarus and Folkman, 1984). If the stressor is appraised as a potential threat, secondary appraisal occurs, involving an evaluation of what can be done in the situation, and whether the individual has adequate resources and coping skills to contend with it. Empirical studies of the effects of stress on well-being have generally supported these links (Roseman, 1991; Smith and Lazarus, 1993; Terry, Callan, and Sartori, 1996; Ysseldyk, Matheson, and Anisman, 2009).

In relation to perceptions of event controllability, a substantial amount of evidence suggests that the belief that one has control over a stressor reduces its impact on both physiological and psychological indices of well-being (Lazarus and Folkman, 1984) and facilitates the adoption of effective coping strategies (Terry, 1994; Terry et al., 1996). This occurs presumably because the perception that an event is amenable to personal control reduces the level of threat associated with it and provides a clear basis for the development of problem-oriented coping responses.

As well as appraising the situation in terms of controllability, people's efficacy expectancies or, in other words, their expectations concerning the likelihood that they can perform the behaviors necessary to deal with the event (secondary appraisals) also need to be taken into account. Spouses who doubt their ability to respond to the demands of military life and separations are likely to focus on feelings of incompetence, which will be accompanied by feelings of psychological distress, resulting in a failure to deal with the situation. In contrast, efficacious individuals are unlikely to be distressed by feelings of inadequacy and, for this reason, are expected to persist in their efforts to manage the situation (Terry, 1992). Thus, in assessing the impact of stressors, it is essential to consider that people may respond differently to the same stimulus, owing to the appraisal process (Folkman and Lazarus, 1991).

Coping

Coping and appraisals are intricately related and influence one another during an experience with a stressor. When a stressor is encountered, an individual appraises it in terms of its relevance to his or her well-being, as well as in relation to the coping strategies available to deal with the stressor. An important distinction between coping efforts is whether they are aimed at transforming the stressful situation itself (problem-focused coping), or at altering the emotional responses induced by the situation (emotion-focused coping). Problem-focused strategies include concrete problem-solving efforts, such as improving one's knowledge regarding the sources and implications of the crisis. Emotion-focused strategies comprise both deliberately chosen instrumental actions to alleviate negative emotional distress (such as exercise or substance use), as well as responses that reflect a perception that the experience is beyond personal control (for example denial or "wishful thinking").

Problem-focused efforts are typically considered to be more adaptive than emotion-focused strategies, given that the latter are more closely aligned with depressive mood states (Matheson and Anisman, 2003). The specific coping styles that spouses use are also likely to play a significant role in their ability to deal with the stress caused by separation resulting from the military members' deployment. Spouses who function most effectively during times of separation appear to be those who use active coping styles, such as actively seeking social support and increasing the quality and quantity of family communication (Figley, 1993). Finally, although appraisals may influence the type of coping strategy used (for example Chang and Strunk, 1999), coping and appraisals likely operate in a dynamic, reciprocal fashion, such that the outcome of engaging in a coping activity may in turn modify one's appraisals of a situation (Folkman and Lazarus, 1985).

This study of military spouses was undertaken to assess the impact of military life on families across several dimensions, including well-being, impacts of deployments on children, and conflict between military and family life. The survey also included several variables that may explain the impact of military life on families, including coping strategies and appraisals.

Method

Participants

A paper-based survey was mailed to the home addresses of a sample of 9,792 spouses of Canadian Armed Forces (CAF) members. The final sample consisted of responses received from 2,084 spouses, yielding an adjusted response rate of 21.3 percent. The majority of the spouses were female. Approximately 12 percent of CAF personnel had been deployed at the time of the survey, and the majority of the deployments reported were overseas. About 18 percent reported that their military spouse had returned from a deployment within the previous six months and another 6 percent reported that their military spouse would be deploying within the next six months. The rest of the participants reported that their military spouse had either never been deployed or had returned from a deployment more than six months ago.

Length of relationship ranged from a year to 38 years, with a mean of 13.1 years. In addition, most respondents (68.2 percent) had children living in their home, the majority of whom were living in the home on a full-time basis.

Measures

Deployment stressors

The 14-item Family Issues Scale (Thompson and Pasto, 2001), with wording adapted to reflect the perspective of the spouse rather than the military member, was used to assess issues experienced by families in response to a deployment. Responses to the items (for example "The deployment was stressful for me") were rated on a scale of 1 (*strongly disagree*) to 5 (*strongly agree*). Respondents were also asked whether they experienced a number of positive or negative feelings (such as anger, pride) throughout the deployment.

Military–family conflict

The Work–Family Conflict Scale developed by Netemeyer, Boles, and McMurrian (1996) was adapted as a measure of *primary appraisals* of the impact of military life on family life. This measure assessed the extent to which spouses perceived the demands of the military as threatening to their family life. The original scale consisted of five items, such as "My spouse or partner's job produces strain that makes it difficult to fulfill family duties." Three items measured the perceived threat of military life to the spouses' family life ("My family life has suffered as a result of my spouse/partner's work commitments") and their career ("My employment or career has suffered as a result of my spouse/partner's service in CAF" and "My career progression has suffered as a result of my family obligations"). Participants indicated the extent to which they agreed with the statements using a Likert rating scale ranging from 1 (*strongly disagree*) to 5 (*strongly agree*).

Self-efficacy

The ten-item General Self-Efficacy Scale (Schwarzer and Jerusalem, 1995) was used to measure self-efficacy – that is, the belief that one's own actions lead to positive outcomes. Perceived self-efficacy refers to optimistic beliefs that one can perform difficult tasks or cope with stressors. In previous studies, secondary appraisal was conceptualized and measured in terms of controllability (Peacock and Wong, 1990), and perceived control and self-efficacy (Terry, 1994). In line with this, *secondary appraisal* was assessed using the self-efficacy measure. Responses to the items (for example "I can always manage to solve difficult problems if I try hard enough") ranged from 1 (*not at all true*) to 4 (*exactly true*).

Coping

Coping strategies were measured using the Brief COPE (Carver, 1997). The Brief COPE is an abbreviated 28-item scale based on the COPE Inventory (Carver, Scheier, and Weintraub, 1989). The COPE Inventory was developed to measure a broad range of coping responses, both functional and dysfunctional. The Brief COPE contains 14 subscales of self-distraction, active coping, denial, substance use, use of emotional support, use of instrumental support, behavioral disengagement, venting, positive reframing, planning, humor, acceptance, religion, and self-blame. Responses ranged from 1 (*I usually don't do this at all*) to 4 (*I usually do this a lot*).

Well-being

A shortened (nine-item) version of the Center for Epidemiologic Studies Depression Scale (CES-D) (Radloff, 1977) was used to assess symptoms of depression. Participants rated the frequency with which they experienced each of the nine symptoms on a scale ranging from 1 (*rarely or none of the time*) to 4 (*most or all of the time*). Respondents were also asked whether they or their military partner had been diagnosed with a psychological disorder at any point during the military member's career. Finally, respondents were asked a number of questions regarding how their children responded to deployment. Fifteen behaviors (such as "decline in school performance") were assessed on a scale ranging from 1 (*never*) to 5 (*always*).

Results

Stressors of military life: Postings and time away[2]

Approximately 40 percent of military personnel had been away for at least 5 of the previous 12 months. Another 17 percent of CAF members had been away between three and four months, and 37 percent had been away between one and two months. Only 5 percent of military spouses reported no time away for their military spouses in the previous 12 months. The spouses who reported more time away in the past year were more likely to report the presence of depressive symptoms ($r = .13$, $p < 0.01$).

Over half of families had relocated between one and three times as a result of military postings. Another 20 percent reported experiencing between four and six postings. More frequent relocations were significantly associated with the conflict between family and spousal work ($r = .10$, $p < 0.05$). Medical services was the most difficult factor to re-establish, with almost 40 percent of respondents reporting that they found it "extremely difficult" to re-establish such services after relocating. A substantial proportion also found it difficult to re-establish their seniority at work (29 percent), their support network (28 percent), their employment (26 percent), and child care (21 percent).

Deployment experiences

Approximately two-thirds of CAF military personnel had spent some time away for a deployment in the previous year. The same number had experienced at least one deployment since the start of the relationship. Respondents' feelings across the deployment cycle are presented in Figure 8.1. The feelings most frequently endorsed by the spouses were of a positive

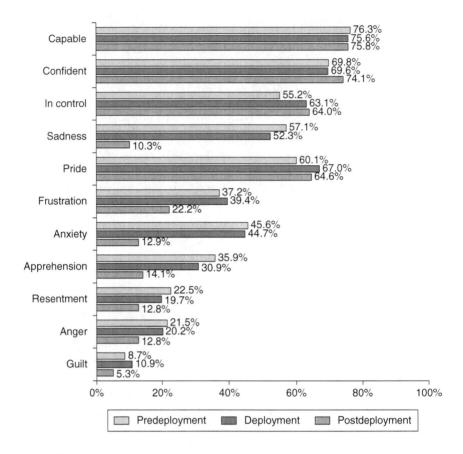

Figure 8.1 Feelings reported by spouses throughout the deployment cycle

Note: Data indicate the percentage reporting often or always experiencing these feelings in association with a deployment. questions were answered by those individuals whose CAF partner had recently returned from a deployment ($n = 384$).questions were those whose CAF partner was currently deployed or had recently returned ($n = 639$). Finally, the postdeployment was currently deployed, or had recently returned from a deployment ($n = 745$). Individuals who answered the deployment Individuals who answered the questions on predeployment feelings were those whose CAF partner was preparing for deployment,

nature, including feeling capable, confident, and in control. Conversely, negative feelings such as resentment, anger, and guilt, were experienced less frequently. Across the stages of deployment, positive feelings of pride and being in control increased from the predeployment to the deployment and postdeployment phases, whereas negative feelings of sadness, frustration, anxiety, apprehension, resentment, anger, and guilt decreased during this time.

Analyses of variance (ANOVAs) were run to determine whether psychological health differed across the deployment cycle. Depressive symptoms were highest for those respondents whose military partner was currently deployed ($M = 1.96$, $SE = .05$), compared to those in the pre- ($M = 1.67$, $SE = .07$) or the postdeployment ($M = 1.68$, $SE = .04$) stages ($F(2, 729) = 12.67$, $p < 001$, $n^2_p = .03$).

Almost all of the spouses (approximately 90 percent) felt that having frequent or regular contact with their military partner during deployment had helped them to cope with the separation. Almost half of the CAF spouses who experienced deployments reported that their children became clingier, while approximately a third reported that their children exhibited behavioral changes such as young children sleeping with the parent, acting out, or exhibiting anxiety. Between 10 and 15 percent of the spouses reported that their children had experienced emotional withdrawal, nightmares, a decline in school performance, and aggression.

Health and well-being

In terms of individual well-being, scores were below the midpoint on CES-D ($M = 1.66$, $SD = 0.67$), indicating, on average, a lack of depressive symptoms ($p < 0.01$). Approximately a fifth of respondents reported that they had been diagnosed with depression at some point during their military partner's career in the CAF, while 12 percent had been diagnosed with an anxiety disorder. For the military member, the most common diagnosis reported by the respondents was also depression, although the rate (5.6 percent) was considerably lower than that of the spouses. Four percent of military personnel had been diagnosed with posttraumatic stress disorder (PTSD), while 2 percent of spouses reported having received this diagnosis.

The correlations between the variables measured in the study are shown in Table 8.1.[3] High correlations (exceeding an absolute value of .30) were found between depressive symptoms, high military–family conflict, lower self-efficacy, and higher avoidant coping strategies. Because the large sample size resulted in substantial power in these analyses, only correlations larger than or equal to .20 were regarded as meaningful.

Role of appraisals in mediating the relationship between deployment stressors and well-being

As noted earlier, the transaction theory of stress and coping (Lazarus and Folkman, 1984) is a process model in which intervening variables such as appraisals mediate antecedent stressor and adaptation outcomes. In line with this perspective, spouses encountering severe stressors were expected to appraise their situation as more threatening and perceive low levels of self-efficacy, and such appraisals would have resulted in a greater likelihood of exhibiting psychological distress. It was expected that deployment stressors would be associated with altered appraisals of self-efficacy, which could lead to variations in psychological distress. Accordingly, the mediating

Table 8.1 Correlations between depression, military career support, coping, and appraisal dimensions

	1	2	3	4	5	6	7	8
1. Depression	—							
2. Deployment stressors [1]	.39**	—						
3. Military-family conflict	.38**	.48**	—					
4. Self-efficacy	-.44**	-.21**	-.18**	—				
5. Behavioural disengagement	.36**	.17**	.14**	-.38**	—			
6. Avoidant coping	.44**	.25***	.22**	-.38**	.68**	—		
7. Active coping	-.29**	-.13***	-.10**	.58**	-.34**	-.28**	—	
8. Self-blame	.39**	.19**	.18**	-.35***	.41**	.73**	-.23**	—
9. Positive reframing	-.28**	-.13**	-.15**	.45**	-.25**	-.29**	.47**	-.25**

Notes
* p < 0.05
** p < 0.01
*** p < 0.001
For correlations involving the deployment stressors variable, only those respondents whose CAF partner had returned from a deployment within the previous 12 months were selected.

effect of appraisals (that is, self-efficacy and perceptions of military–family conflict) on the relationship between deployment stressors and psychological health (that is, depressive symptoms) was assessed.

In order to test the hypothesis that appraisal dimensions mediate the relationship between deployment stressors and depressive symptoms, the mediation approach described by Baron and Kenny (1986) was followed.

- In Step 1 of the mediation model, the regression of depressive symptoms on deployment stressors was significant ($b = .54$, t (1401) = 15.83, $p < 0.001$).
- Step 2 showed that the regression of military–family conflict ($b = .93$, t (1402) = 20.67, $p < 0.001$) and self-efficacy ($b = -.19$, t (1404) = -8.04, $p < 0.001$) on deployment stressors was also significant.
- Step 3 of the mediation process showed that the mediators, military–family conflict ($b = .15$, t (1389) = 8.35, $p < 0.001$) and self-efficacy ($b = -.52$, t (1389) = -14.88, $p < 0.001$), had a significant relationship with depressive symptoms when deployment stressors were controlled for.
- Step 4 of the analyses revealed that deployment stressors were still significantly associated with depressive symptoms ($b = .30$, t (1389) = 8.28, $p < 0.001$) when the mediators, military–family conflict and self-efficacy, were controlled for.

The Sobel *t*-values calculated for military–family conflict ($p < 0.001$) and self-efficacy ($p < 0.001$) indicated that each represented at least a partial path between deployment stressors and depressive symptoms.

Role of coping in mediating the relationship between self-efficacy appraisals and well-being

Appraisals, as measured by self-efficacy and perceptions of military–family conflict, partially mediated the relationship between deployment stressors and depressive symptoms. However, appraisals may also impact upon psychological well-being indirectly, in that appraisals influence the coping strategy used, which, in turn influences psychological well-being (Folkman and Lazarus, 1980). In this regard, spouses who reported increased military–family conflict and lower appraisals of self-efficacy may be more likely to invoke ineffective coping styles (that is, less problem-focused coping, and more emotional and avoidant coping efforts), which, in turn, would be associated with greater psychological distress. The mediating effect of coping on the relationship between appraisals and psychological health was assessed.

Although significant, the correlations between military–family conflict and coping strategies were not sufficiently meaningful to conduct mediation analyses.

- In Step 1 of the mediation model, the regression of depressive symptoms on self-appraisal was significant (b = –.64, t (2037) = –21.82, $p < 0.001$).
- Step 2 showed that the regression of each coping strategy on self-efficacy was also significant: avoidant coping (b = –.31, t (2026) = –18.64, $p < 0.001$), active coping (b = .74, t (2028) = 32.57, $p < 0.001$), self-blame (b = –.58, t (2026) = –16.74, $p < 0.00$), positive reframing (b = .77, t (2028) = 22.66, $p < 0.001$), and behavioral disengagement (b = –.40, t (2026) = –18.33, $p < 0.00$).
- Step 3 of the mediation process showed that the mediators, avoidant coping (b = .36, t (2017) = 5.82, $p < 0.001$), self-blame (b = .10, t (2017) = 4.11, $p < 0.001$), and positive reframing (b = –.10, t (2017) = –2.76, $p < 0.005$), had a significant effect on depressive symptoms when self-efficacy was controlled for. The mediators active coping and behavioral disengagement were not unique predictors of depressive symptoms.
- Step 4 of the analyses revealed that self-efficacy was still a significant predictor of depressive symptoms (b = –.39, t (2017) = –10.66, $p < 0.001$) when the mediators were controlled for.

The Sobel t-values calculated for each of the coping strategies indicated that all represented at least a partial path between deployment stressors and depressive symptoms ($p < 0.001$).

Discussion

Studying military life from the perspective of the spouses of CAF members is crucial, because family life can have an important impact on the well-being of members, for example in terms of psychological well-being, as well as on the organization as a whole, for example in terms of retention (Dursun, 2006; McCreary, Thompson, and Pasto, 2003; Orthner, 1990). The aim of this chapter was to assess the impact of military lifestyle demands on military families. Furthermore, the effects of deployment stressors and the mediating effects of appraisals and coping styles on spousal well-being were examined.

Approximately 40 percent of military personnel had been away for at least 5 of the 12 months prior to the survey for military-related reasons, while approximately two-thirds had spent some time away for deployment. Across the stages of deployment, respondents' positive feelings of pride and being in control increased from the predeployment to the deployment and postdeployment phases, whereas negative feelings such as sadness, frustration, and anxiety decreased during this time. Although reintegration of the military member after a deployment may be stressful for families, it appears from this limited information that spouses are able to adapt well to this period in the deployment cycle. Previous research has documented the adverse effects of deployments on the spouses of military personnel, including marital dissatisfaction, unemployment, divorce, and lower emotional health (Angrist and Johnson, 2000; Schumm, Bell, and Gade, 2000). As well, prolonged deployment was associated with increased risk of depression, anxiety, sleep disorders, acute stress reaction, and adjustment disorders among spouses of military personnel (Mansfield et al., 2010). In the present study, depressive symptoms were significantly higher during deployment than during the pre- and postdeployment stages; nonetheless, the effect size was low, indicating that mental health symptoms were largely independent of deployment status, or that other factors not considered (such as the presence of children at home, or being posted in a location away from extended family) may have played a role in the impacts of deployment on mental health. A possible explanation for this finding may be that military lifestyle demands (such as frequent relocations, separations, and long hours) have a pervasive effect on the well-being of all spouses, including those of nondeployed members, such that deployment itself does not represent a powerful stressor. Overall, there is some indication that military spouses report more mental health issues than the general population (Pierce and Luchsinger, 1986). Another explanation for why deployment did not play a more prominent role in spousal well-being is the length of deployment. The majority of the studies that found deployment to be a distress factor were conducted in the United States, where the length of deployments is at least twice that typically experienced in Canada. Indeed, it has been suggested previously that shorter deployments are associated with modest, temporary behavioral and emotional symptoms in family members, while lengthy separations can result in more persistent negative effects (Jensen, Martin, and Watanabe, 1996).

Approximately one fifth of respondents reported that they had been diagnosed with depression at some point during their military partner's career in the CAF. For the military member, the most common diagnosis, as reported by the respondents, was also depression, although the rate was considerably lower than that of the spouses. Estimates of depression in the general population vary depending on the method used to measure the disorder and whether current or lifetime rates are being assessed; as such, these estimates are not appropriate for comparison purposes. Symptoms of depression were associated with conflict between military and family life, lower self-efficacy, and the use of emotionally focused and avoidant coping strategies.

Following depression, the most prevalent disorders reported both for spouses and military members were anxiety disorder and PTSD. The survey did not examine the event(s) that led to a PTSD diagnosis, so the diagnosis could have been related to military service or to some other traumatic event. It is also possible that some respondents may have confused their spouse's PTSD diagnosis with an operational stress injury (OSI), of which PTSD is only one resulting condition. Such OSIs also include other diagnosed medical conditions, such as anxiety and depression. For spouses, it is possible that posttraumatic stress symptoms resulted from experiences such as a vehicle accident or early experiences of abuse. As in the case of depression, it is not possible to compare percentages with population data owing to differences in the methodologies used. It is recommended that future surveys of spouses include questions on mental health from existing large-scale surveys such as the Canadian Community Health Survey (CCHS), in order to facilitate comparisons of CAF personnel and spouses to the general population.

Deployment stressors, appraisals, and spousal well-being

Many studies have found deployment stressors to be among the most significant predictors of reduced quality of life and well-being among military spouses (Everson, 2005; Medway et al., 1995). Deployment issues include not only an increase in workload and in the responsibilities of parenting, but also a lack of social and emotional support during this stressful time. These factors would contribute to spouses appraising military lifestyle demands as more threatening and uncontrollable. Indeed, in the present study, spousal appraisals of the impact of the military lifestyle on their families and careers appeared to be key to understanding the impact of deployment stressors on spousal well-being. Specifically, employing positive appraisals (lower military–family conflict and higher self-efficacy) of the military lifestyle may provide a psychological respite, allowing the spouse to replenish the energy and psychological resources depleted by deployment stressors. If so, finding ways in which to reduce the threatening aspects of military lifestyle demands and to increase overall perceived control and self-efficacy could attenuate the impact of both deployment and reintegration stressors on spousal well-being.

Appraisals and coping

In the transactional model of stress and coping (Lazarus and Folkman, 1984), appraisal processes of a stressful situation are considered important antecedents to coping processes. In the present study, military spouses reported using problem-solving strategies (that is, active coping, positive reframing) more frequently than either emotional or avoidance coping, implying greater efforts to alter the sources of their stress than to contend with the emotional repercussions.

In line with previous research (Carver et al., 1989; Lazarus and Folkman, 1984; Matheson and Anisman, 2003; Ysseldyk et al., 2009), appraisals and coping styles were predictive of psychological distress. Also consistent with previous research (Amiot et al., 2006; Conway and Terry, 1992; Folkman and Lazarus, 1980; Folkman et al., 1986), increased self-efficacy was related to greater endorsement of problem-solving strategies (that is, active coping and positive reframing), and decreased use of emotional and avoidant coping (that is, behavioral disengagement, self-blame, and avoidant coping). While perceived military–family conflict was associated with higher avoidant coping, it had a weak relation with the use of problem-solving strategies. These findings are consistent with previous research (Mikulincer and Florian, 1995; Portello and Long, 2001), which showed that appraising a situation as threatening will not motivate an individual to use problem-solving strategies.

As anticipated, avoidant coping, positive reframing, and self-blame partially mediated the relationships between self-efficacy and psychological distress. However, it needs to be noted that these data were correlational. As suggested in previous research, it is likely that bidirectional relations exist among the variables, so that not only does appraisal influence coping, but also coping may influence the one's (re)appraisal of what is threatening and whether one has the ability to cope with the stressors (Folkman et al., 1986).

Understanding our own coping style provides important information about how we may react when facing problems, specifically whether we tend to approach or avoid problems, lack confidence in our problem-solving, or feel emotionally in control. For example, a spouse's avoidant strategies may heighten the perceived threat, leading to a lesser sense of control and a diminution of his or her ability to deal with the situation. In such cases, coping-skills training could be an efficient intervention strategy.

Conclusion

Over 60 percent of CAF members are married, and family members outnumber single soldiers by a ratio of 3:2. This means that most military members live at the intersection of military and family institutions. This chapter has identified several classes of factors that underlie the coping patterns of families struggling with the demands of the military lifestyle. This research points to novel and fruitful directions for future work–family research, because it suggests that it is worth devoting more attention to the role that cognitive appraisal processes play in people's experiences of combining work and family roles. It indicates that spousal appraisals of the impact of the military lifestyle on their families and careers appear to be the key to mediating the impact of deployment-related stressors on spousal well-being. Although it was suggested that coping styles would emanate from particular appraisals, it is possible that appraisals and coping work in conjunction with one another in a reciprocal manner. This dynamic pattern of relations has implications for promoting well-being among military spouses and facilitating their adaptation to the military lifestyle. The unique nature of military life sometimes requires that family members subordinate their own needs and desires to military demands, which makes military families unique, and deserving of respect and the best support possible. The military can have a pervasive influence on family life and, conversely, the family can have an impact on the serving member, as well as on the military organization as a whole. Families of military personnel support members' well-being, readiness, performance, and ability to carry out missions; it is therefore important to understand how families adapt to the demands of military life. The results of this survey will enhance our understanding of the impacts of military service on the well-being of the families of CAF personnel.

Notes

1 In order to be as concise as possible, the term "spouse" is used to refer to both married and cohabiting partners.
2 Parts of the results section are based on an internal Canadian Department of National Defense report (Sudom, 2010).
3 Data used in the present study were screened for multicollinearity and singularity by means of the exploration of bivariate correlations among all of the variables. Owing to correlations exceeding .70, several coping strategies were omitted from further analysis, indicating that these variables may be measuring aspects of the same underlying construct.

References

Amiot, C.E., Terry, D.J., Jimmieson, N.L., and Callan, V.J. (2006) "A longitudinal investigation of coping processes during a merger: Implications for job satisfaction and organizational identification." *Journal of Management*, 32: 552–74.

Angrist, J.D., and Johnson, J.H. (2000) "Effects of work-related absences on families: Evidence from the Gulf War." *Industrial & Labor Relations Review*, 54: 41–58.

Baron, R.M., and Kenny, D.A. (1986) "The moderator–mediator variable distinction in social psychological research: Conceptual, strategic, and statistical considerations." *Journal of Personality & Social Psychology*, 51: 1173–82.

Black, W.G. (1993) "Military-induced family separation: A stress reduction intervention." *Social Work*, 38: 273–80.

Carver, C.S. (1997) "You want to measure coping but your protocol's too long: Consider the Brief COPE." *International Journal of Behavioral Medicine*, 4: 92–100.

Carver, C.S., Scheier, M.F., and Weintraub, J.K. (1989) "Assessing coping strategies: A theoretically based approach." *Journal of Personality & Social Psychology*, 56: 267–83.

Castro, C.A., Bienvenu, R.V., Huffman, A.H., and Adler, A.B. (2001) *Soldier Dimensions and Operational Readiness in U.S. Army Forces Deployed to Kosovo*. Frederick, MD: U.S. Army Medical Research & Materiel Command.

Chang, E.C., and Strunk, D.R. (1999) "Dysphoria: Relations to appraisals, coping, and adjustment." *Journal of Counseling Psychology*, 46: 99–108.

Conway, V.J., and Terry, D.J. (1992) "Appraised controllability as a moderator of the effectiveness of different coping strategies: A test of the goodness of fit hypothesis." *Australian Journal of Psychology*, 44: 1–7.

Dursun, S. (2006) "Results of the 2005 spouse Perstempo survey." Presentation to the Military Family National Advisory Board.

Everson, R.B. (2005) "Quality of life among army spouses: Parenting and family stress during deployment to Operation Iraqi Freedom." Unpublished M.Sc. thesis, Florida State University, Tallahassee, FL.

Figley, C.R. (1993) "Coping with stressors on the home front." *Journal of Social Issues*, 49: 51–71.

Folkman, S., and Lazarus, R.S. (1980) "An analysis of coping in a middle-aged community sample." *Journal of Health & Social Behavior*, 21: 219–39.

Folkman, S., and Lazarus, R.S. (1985) "If it changes it must be a process: Study of emotion and coping during three stages of a college examination." *Journal of Personality & Social Psychology*, 48: 150–70.

Folkman, S., and Lazarus, R.S. (1991) "Coping and emotion." In A. Monat and R.S. Lazarus (eds.) *Stress and Coping: An anthology* (3rd edn.). New York: Columbia University Press, pp. 207–27.

Folkman, S., Lazarus, R.S., Gruen, R.J., and DeLongis, A. (1986) "Appraisal, coping, health status, and psychological symptoms." *Journal of Personality & Social Psychology*, 30: 571–79.

Jensen, P.S., Martin, D., and Watanabe, H.K. (1996) "Children's response to parenting separation during Operation Desert Storm." *Journal of American Academy of Child & Adolescent Psychiatry*, 35: 433–41.

Lazarus, R.S. (2000) "Toward better research on stress and coping." *American Psychologist*, 55: 665–73.

Lazarus, R.S., and Folkman, S. (1984) *Stress, Appraisal and Coping.* New York: Springer.

Mansfield, A.J., Kaufman, J.S., Marshall, S.W., Gaynes, B.N., Morrissey, J.P., and Engel, C.C. (2010) "Deployment and the use of mental health services among U.S. Army wives." *New England Journal of Medicine*, 362: 101–9.

Martin, J.A., Vaitkus, M.A., Johnson, M.D, Mikolajek, L.M., and Ray, D.L. (1996) "Deployment from Europe: The family perspective." In R.J. Ursano and A.E. Norwood (eds.) *Emotional Aftermath of the Persian Gulf War: Veterans, families, communities, and nations.* Washington, D.C.: American Psychiatric Press, pp. 227–50.

Matheson, K., and Anisman, H. (2003) "Systems of coping associated with dysphoria, anxiety and depressive illness: A multivariate profile perspective." *Stress*, 6: 223–34.

McCreary, D.R., Thompson, M.M., and Pastò, L. (2003) "The impact of family concerns on the predeployment well-being of Canadian Forces personnel." *Canadian Journal of Police & Security Services*, 1: 33–40.

Medway, F., David, K., Cafferty, T., and Chappell, K. (1995) "Family disruption and adult attachment correlates of spouse and child reaction to separation and reunion during operation Desert Storm." *Journal of Social & Clinical Psychology*, 14: 97–118.

Mikulincer, M., and Florian, V. (1995) "Appraisal of and coping with a real-life stressful situation: The contribution of attachment styles." *Society for Personality & Social Psychology*, 21: 404–14.

Netemeyer, R.G., Boles, J.S., and McMurrian, R. (1996) "Development and validation of work–family conflict and family–work conflict scales." *Journal of Applied Psychology*, 81: 400–10.

Orthner, D.K. (1990) "Family impacts on the retention of military personnel." Paper presented at the Military Family Research Review Conference, Washington, D.C.

Peacock, E.J., and Wong, P.T.P. (1990) "Measuring life stress: The stress appraisal measure (SAM): A multidimensional approach to cognitive appraisal." Stress Medicine, 6, 227–36.

Pierce, M.M., and Luchsinger, M.L. (1986) "Psychological distress among air force wives." In *Proceedings of the 10th Symposium on Psychology in the Department of Defense.* Colorado Springs, CO: US Air Force Academy, pp. 643–48.

Pincus, S.H., House, R., Christensen, J., and Adler, L.E. (2001) "The emotional cycle of deployment: A military family perspective." *Army Medical Department Journal*, 6: 15–23.

Portello, J.Y., and Long, B.C. (2001) "Appraisals and coping with workplace interpersonal stress: A model for women managers." *Journal of Counselling Psychology*, 48: 144–56.

Radloff, L.S. (1977) "The CES-D scale: A self-report depression scale for research in the general population." *Applied Psychological Measurement*, 1: 385–401.

Roseman, I.J. (1991) "Appraisal determinants of discrete emotions." *Cognition & Emotion*, 5: 161–200.

Schumm, W.R., Bell, D.B., and Gade, P.A. (2000) "Effects of a military overseas peacekeeping deployment on marital quality, satisfaction, and stability." *Psychological Reports*, 87: 815–21.

Schwarzer, R., and Jerusalem, M. (1995) "Generalized self-efficacy scale." In J. Weinman, S. Wright, and M. Johnston (eds.) *Measures in Health Psychology: A user's portfolio – Causal and control beliefs*. Windsor: NFER-NELSON, pp. 35–7.

Smith, C.A., and Lazarus, R.S. (1993) "Appraisal components, core relational themes, and the emotions." *Cognition & Emotion*, 7: 233–69.

Sudom, K. (2010) *Quality of Life among Military Families: Results from the 2009 survey of Canadian forces spouses*. Technical Memorandum #2010-017, Ottawa, ON: Department of National Defense.

Terry, D.J. (1992) "Stress, coping and coping resources as correlates of adaptation in myocardial infarction patients." *British Journal of Clinical Psychology*, 31: 215–25.

Terry, D.J. (1994) "Determinants of coping: The role of stable and situational factors." *Journal of Personality & Social Psychology*, 66: 895–910.

Terry, D.J., Callan, V.J., and Sartori, G. (1996) "Employee adjustment to an organizational merger: Stress, coping and intergroup differences." *Stress Medicine*, 12: 105–22.

Thompson, M.M., and Pasto, L. (2001) *Psychometric Assessment and Refinement of the Family Issues Acale of the Human Dimensions of Operations (HDO) Project*. Technical Report #2001-049, Ottawa, ON: Department of National Defense.

Van Vranken, E.W., Jellen, L.K., Knudson, K.H.M., Marlowe, D.H., and Segal, M.W. (1984) *The Impact of Deployment Separation on Army Families*. Washington, D.C.: Department of Military Psychiatry, Walter Reed Army Institute of Research.

Westhius, D.J. (1999) "Working with military families during deployments." In J. Daley (ed.) *Social Work Practice in the Military*. New York: Hawthorne, pp. 217–33.

Wisecarver, M.M., Cracraft, M.L., and Heffner, T.S. (2006) *Deployment Consequences: a review of the literature and integration of findings into a model of retention*. Arlington, VA: U.S. Army Research Institute for the Behavioral and Social Sciences.

Wright, K.M., Burrell, L.M., Schroeder, E.D., and Thomas, J.L. (2006) "Military spouses: Coping with the fear and the reality of service member injury and death." In C.A. Castro, A.B. Adler, and C.A. Britt (eds.) *Military Life: The psychology of serving in peace and combat, vol 3 – The military family*. Westport, CT: Praeger Security International, pp. 64–90.

Ysseldyk, R., Matheson, K., and Anisman, H. (2009) "Forgiveness and the appraisal-coping process in response to relationship conflicts: Implications for depressive symptoms." *International Journal on the Biology of Stress*, 12: 152–66.

9 Reintegration, reconciliation, and relationship quality

Manon Andres, Karin De Angelis, and David McCone

Introduction

Marital separation is ranked among the events that produce high levels of stress in families and couples. Military deployments cause temporary separations and require adjustments from all those involved, before, during, and after the separation, and often with few formal resources to prepare one's self and the family for these transitions. Not only do the temporary absences and subsequent returns of a family member into the household bring with them the need for family restructuring and adaptation, but military-induced separations also involve the potential risks of service members getting injured, or even killed, while performing their duties abroad. This risk is part of the unique combination of demands that military service members face as they seek to balance military service with their familial role.

Because of the stresses involved with military deployments, these separations have the potential to strain family life and relationships. Over the last few decades, and with research demonstrating the importance of family satisfaction with the military lifestyle for retention and performance, both the beneficial and detrimental effects of military deployments on intimate relationships have been a focus area for military leaders and researchers. In particular, research has centered on the impact of deployments on married couples, their marital satisfaction, and the stability of the relationship – that is, whether the marriage ends in divorce. Although this focus is appropriate given the high rate of marriage among military members in general, and particularly officers (McCone and O'Donnell, 2006), it ignores a large group of personnel in other committed relationships, such as those who are in civil partnerships or cohabiting, and how their relationship quality is affected by military deployments. It also does not account for same-sex couples, who, depending on their citizenship, live in a country in which marriage or civil partnership is not an option. In the United States, especially, this is an important consideration in light of the relatively recent repeal of "don't ask, don't tell" policy.

Taking into account the diversity of intimate relationships among military personnel, the aim of this chapter is to enhance our understanding of how military deployments affect the quality and stability of a couple's relationship from an international perspective. We focus first on the stressors that married couples experience during military deployments, using the framework of Karney and Crown (2007) for modeling stability in military marriages. We also present empirical findings from the United States and the Netherlands, in addition to recent international literature, which speaks to the issues experienced by married couples. We then challenge the dominant paradigm used to frame military families as traditional married couples, by considering other types of intimate relationship and how they experience deployments.

This chapter addresses two research questions, as follows.

- How are marital relationships affected by military deployment?
- What are the unique challenges of different types of family/couple?

We also consider the subquestion of how formal military policies regarding families influence relationship outcomes.

Families and the military: How they are connected and recent trends

Although not always the case, the current relationship between the military and the families of its service members includes formal support programs that are often extensive, at least compared with civilian organizations.[1] Research suggests that service member and spousal commitment to the military is directly linked to their perceptions of organizational support for the family. This support must be demonstrated by both military policies and leader actions – that is, the policies and their execution must match. Thus service member and spousal satisfaction with the military's handling of familial needs shape service member commitment to the military. This has a direct impact on retention and, to a lesser extent, on performance. The demonstrated link between families and the military is a major reason why the military tracks trends in marital relationship quality and stability, because increases in negative trends, such as divorce, may impact the retention and overall effectiveness of the force.

The wars in Afghanistan and Iraq, which are unprecedented in terms of duration and are testing the durability of the all-volunteer force, have led to new questions about the effect of military deployments on marital relationships. A 2011 report of the U.S. Department of Defense (Office of the Deputy Under Secretary of Defense, 2012) reveals an annual military-wide divorce rate of nearly 4 percent, which translates to absolute numbers of nearly 30,000 relationships of U.S. military personnel that ended in divorce during that year. This divorce rate among military members is higher than that of the general U.S. population, which has consistently been around 40–50 percent overall (Bramlett and Mosher, 2002; Kreider and Fields, 2001), and around 1.5–2 percent annually (Kreider, 2005). Moreover, the divorce rate for the military has increased over the decade from an annual rate of 2.5 percent in 2001. The increase in divorce rates is even more pronounced among certain subgroups and service branches. Female service members, for example, have an annual divorce rate that is almost double that of their male military peers. At 4.6 percent, Air Force personnel, who overall have shorter deployments and less combat exposure than personnel in other services, have a higher annual divorce rate than personnel in other services.

Because the divorce rates have increased in tandem with the wars in Afghanistan and Iraq, it has been suggested that multiple deployments, extended deployment durations, and the stress involved in the wars have contributed to the rising divorce rates. Relationship stability, as demonstrated by marriage and divorce rates, is one way of gauging the impact of deployments on families. However, the transition from marriage to divorce does not account for different levels of relationship quality – particularly as affected by deployment and stress – which service members may experience in marriages or in other types of relationship. For example, as more service members were called to deploy to Iraq and Afghanistan, anecdotal evidence accrued suggesting that these multiple and extended deployments were taking a toll on marriages, even if these marriages did not end in divorce.

Given that deployments are often viewed as harmful to relationships, it is important to understand not only the factors that negatively impact relationship outcomes, but also the processes that may enhance relationship satisfaction, particularly in the course of prolonged separations. To do this, we argue that Karney and Crown (2007) offer a useful framework that can help to account for the influence of both deployment stress and selection factors (the enduring traits of military couples that have an impact on marital stability), but that the model needs to be reconsidered in light of other relationship types.

How relationships are affected by military deployment: A theoretical approach

Several theoretical perspectives provide explanations of the potential effects of military deployments on couples' relationships. In this chapter, we use the model developed by Karney and Crown (2007: 28) (see Figure 9.1). We selected this framework for the reasons clarified in the authors' report: primarily, that it accounts for the myriad contextual factors that impact military couples, while still accounting for the enduring characteristics of each partner and delineating the possible pathways of influence between them.

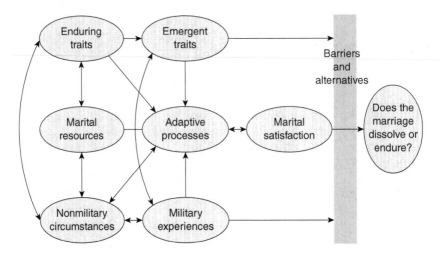

Figure 9.1 An integrative framework to account for success and failure in military
marriages

Source: Karney and Crown (2007); reproduced with kind permission of RAND Corporation.

The model identifies key constructs/factors in the success or failure of
marriages, noting that *marital stability* is predicted by spouses' *marital satisfaction,* which in turn is affected by the way in which they interact, communicate, understand each other, think about each other, and behave towards
each other (that is, their *adaptive processes*). It is assumed that whatever facilitates spouses' adaptive processes promotes their relationship and whatever hinders their adaptive processes strains the relationship. The model
accounts for the influence of both *military and nonmilitary experiences,* such
as how unpredictable tour lengths, possible exposure to violence, feelings
of isolation, ambiguity, and workload may affect both spouses.[2]
    The model also accounts for *enduring traits* (relatively stable traits such
as demographic variables) and *emergent traits* (the personal changes or
changes in well-being that can occur, for instance, as a result of couples'
experiences). Individuals may have changed because of their military and
nonmilitary experiences, or they may develop mental or physical conditions that impact their feelings and behavior. Traumatization from military deployment or secondary traumatization experienced by the spouse
are examples of emergent traits. Changes in well-being are not necessarily
negative – that is, military deployments can also involve positive aspects,
including personal growth.
    Each of these factors shapes the dynamics in couples' interactions and
may result in their being brought closer together or driven apart. Hence
the factors have important effects on the success or failure of relationships. Applying this framework and referring to recent empirical research

findings, the following sections describe in more detail relationship satisfaction and stability, and the factors and mechanisms that affect relationship outcomes in times of military deployment.

Reintegration, reconciliation, and relationship quality after reunion

Notwithstanding the joy of being physically reunited again, upon service members' return from deployment couples find themselves faced with an emotionally complex process of reintegration and reconciliation. This process of re-establishing a close relationship after a temporary separation involves issues commonly connected to the adaptations and transitions undergone during this stressful period. These include the reintegration of military personnel back into the daily rhythms of nondeployed life, the realization that changes have occurred in the family as a result of the service member's absence, and the work involved with reconnecting as a family. Research suggests that the first 90 days after reunion are the most critical for couples as they readjust to being together. This is consistent with the well-known emotional cycle of deployment, which assumes that family relationships typically stabilize within approximately 12 weeks after reunion. Couples negotiating severe problems, such as combat-related injuries, typically take longer.

Demonstrative of these conclusions is longitudinal data collected among Dutch military personnel and their (married or cohabiting) partners before, during, and after four–six-month-long deployments in Bosnia or Afghanistan (Andres, 2010). Just as they had to get used to being separated, these couples had to get used to being back together, despite the initial joy of reunion. These couples described the struggle of making concessions and adjustments as they (re)tuned into each other's daily rhythms, with the nondeployed partners experiencing more difficulties with the readjustment of domestic roles than the deployed partners. During this adaptive period, some couples described becoming estranged from each other. Others enjoyed the presence of their loved one even more than they had before the deployment, suggesting that separations can also cause couples to realize the value of being together. Overall, relationship satisfaction had decreased significantly afterwards, compared with reports predeployment. Although most couples remained fairly satisfied with their relationship, the relationships of 18 percent of the couples had substantially deteriorated, while 11 percent said that their relationships had improved.

Studies of military personnel of other countries make similar findings, despite varying lengths of deployments and mission areas. Generally, researchers found that between 10 and 20 percent of their samples endured marital strain, decreased satisfaction, or considerations of divorce (Newby et al., 2005; Renshaw, Rodrigues, and Jones, 2009; Sharpley et al., 2008). Some studies present more troublesome figures, particularly those conducted among veterans who served in Iraq or Afghanistan and experienced mental health problems (Ponder et al., 2012; Sayer et al., 2010; Sayers et al., 2009).

Studies have also demonstrated deployment benefits that may improve their marriages, such as more financial and job stability (McCone et al., 2011a), personal growth, and mutual feelings of pride, appreciation, and closeness. Baptist and colleagues (2011) found that, for some, the distance and fear of losing their loved one made them value each other more. Also, increased quality in communication and expressions of appreciation led to increased intimacy and closeness.

The impact of couples' interactions on relationship outcomes

According to the model of Karney and Crown (2007), positive interactions play a major role in sustaining satisfied and stable relationships, particularly in times of prolonged physical separation. The effects of interaction on relationships have been well established in the literature. While, in former times, deployed military personnel and their families could stay in touch only by mail, modern means of communication allow for frequent, intense, and "real-time" contact. They enable couples to stay emotionally connected, while being physically separated. The study of Baptist and colleagues (2011), conducted among U.S. male service members and their female spouses, demonstrated that being in contact with each other throughout the deployment helped in building trust and provided them with the opportunity to support each other. Feeling supported, in turn, contributed to a deeper appreciation for each other and for their relationship.

The study among deployed Dutch military personnel and their spouses (Andres, 2010) revealed that couples stayed in touch on a regular basis, and attempted to maintain their intimate bonds by showing affection and asking how the other felt. Not surprisingly, nondeployed partners communicated more openly, which involved sharing their experiences and frustrations. Conversely, deployed service members were not always able or allowed to share all of their experiences, or did not want to burden their partners with the things that they had witnessed and experienced in the theater of operation.

The homecoming usually brings an end to the intense contact by the use of letters, email, or telephone. Physical proximity simply reduces the desire for and necessity of writing elaborate and personal letters and emails to each other. Still, most of the couples engaged in high levels of interactions and adaptive processes after reunion. It was the *quality* (that is, their strategies to remain attached and avoid becoming estranged) rather than the *frequency* of interactions during the separation and after reunion that contributed to smoother reconciliation processes and more satisfied relationships afterwards. Similar to during the separation, after the reunion service members talked less openly and elaborately about their experiences than did their nondeployed partners. It may be too hard for service members to talk about their experiences, they may want to protect their spouses from worrying about what they have witnessed and experienced in the mission area, or they may feel that their spouses do not understand because they simply were not there (Andres and Rietveld, 2012). Often, returned service members feel more comfortable talking to those who shared their experiences. Among nonactive duty service members (such as national guard and reserve troops), this can prove even more difficult. For them, the reintegration process involves not only a transition back into their families, but also often means a return to civilian employment and deactivation of their active military role. These members soon find themselves surrounded by family and coworkers who, despite good intentions, have difficulty fully appreciating their deployed experience (Scott et al., 2011). In particular, respondents noted difficulty finding meaning again in daily activities and discussing this with their friends, coworkers, or spouse. As one respondent stated (Scott et al., 2011: 292):

> The Guard has it worse, because we're just sent home . . . Active Duty, they've still got their [military] routine . . . rather than just, Bam! Fort Living Room . . . That feeling of belonging, that sense of purpose is gone. Completely gone.

Factors affecting couples' adaptive processes and relationship outcomes

Karney and Crown (2007) identified various factors that have protective or detrimental effects on the processes of maintaining well-functioning relationships in times of military deployment. Empirical findings regarding the effect of time away and the frequency of deployments on couples' relationships are inconclusive. While some studies did not find support for the effects of length or extension of deployment on relationship outcomes (Asbury and Martin, 2012; SteelFisher, Zaslavsky, and Blendon, 2008), others studies did (Angrist and Johnson, 2000; McCarroll et al., 2000; Rowe et al., 2013). The study conducted by Karney and Crown (2007, 2011) even revealed that, except for enlisted members and officers in the active Air Force, "effects of deployment were either insignificant or beneficial – i.e., those deployed more days while married were at significantly lower risk of subsequent marital dissolution" (Karney and Crown, 2007: 158). Regardless of the length or frequency of deployments, perceptions of military job demands interfering with family life are shown to be associated with decreased relationship satisfaction (Andres, Moelker, and Soeters, 2012). Because the absences take up all of the service members' time, energy, and involvement, they prevent the service member from adequately fulfilling family responsibilities or spending time together with their spouse and family for prolonged periods.

Furthermore, because of their military and nonmilitary experiences during the separation, service members and their partners may have changed. For instance, they may have become stronger, more independent, and more self-sufficient; they may live more consciously or be more appreciative; but they may also feel emotional, irritated, or restless more rapidly. Deployment and reintegration stressors may also contribute to psychological or behavioral disorders among service members, such as substance abuse, domestic violence, depression, or posttraumatic stress symptoms. In their study regarding deployment and reintegration stress among National Guard soldiers, McCone and colleagues (2011b) found that stress related to the homecoming (for example having difficulty adjusting to life at home) predicted negative coping behaviors (such as excessive drinking or use of drugs) and posttraumatic stress symptoms. Furthermore, stress associated with being in physical danger during the deployment positively predicted posttraumatic stress symptoms, while experiencing positive benefits of deployment and resilience negatively predicted such symptoms.

It may be obvious that adaptive processes are easier when experiences are positive rather than traumatic. Traumatic experiences may have severe effects on interpersonal relationships. There is ample evidence that the probability of relationship problems or divorce is higher if military personnel suffer from mental health problems associated with deployment and combat, such as depression and anxiety, combat stress reaction, trauma symptoms, and posttraumatic stress disorder (PTSD) (Allen et al., 2010; Knobloch and Theiss, 2011; Negrusa and Negrusa, 2012; Nelson Goff et al., 2007). The mechanisms through which these problems affect relationship satisfaction are diminished self-disclosure and emotional expressiveness, negative communication, aggression, and intimacy problems.[3] These may be seen as enduring or emerging traits, as discussed by Karney and Crown (2007).

In addition to military personnel developing mental health problems, their family members, including their partners, can develop similar problems. A study conducted among wives of active duty U.S. Army soldiers (Mansfield et al., 2010), for instance, found that spouses whose husbands were deployed were at greater risk of mental health problems (that is, depressive, sleep, anxiety, and acute stress and adjustment disorders) compared with spouses of military personnel who were not deployed. A study among Dutch deployed military personnel and their wives (Dirkzwager et al., 2005) revealed that wives whose husbands showed posttraumatic stress symptoms reported significantly more PTSD symptoms themselves, along with more somatic and sleeping problems. They also judged the relationship with their spouses less favorable than did spouses of military personnel without PTSD. Empirical research supports several mechanisms or explanations of the process of secondary traumatization (Galovski and Lyons, 2004; Monson, Taft, and Fredman, 2009). Living in close proximity with a person who is traumatized serves as a stressor that impacts one's well-being. Moreover, spouses may feel that their emotional, physical, and social well-being is affected by caring for their traumatized spouse (that is, "caregiver burden"). Furthermore, individuals may identify so strongly with their spouses that they become indirectly exposed to the trauma and either mimic posttraumatic stress symptoms displayed in their spouse or develop a set of symptoms of their own. Through negative interaction patterns, these problems are likely to affect couples' relationships.

Apart from the prevalence of negative outcomes, deployment and reintegration can potentially lead to posttraumatic growth, which implies positive change that results from traumatic events (Tedeschi, Park, and Calhoun, 1998). While similar to the construct of resilience, posttraumatic growth is a distinct and independent construct involving benefit and growth from negative experience, beyond simply enduring it (Scott et al., 2011). It may involve new appreciation for life, changing priorities about what is important in life, and feeling more independent and capable. Successful couples are able to leverage this growth by facing traumatic or challenging circumstances with a "unified front," becoming stronger as a couple because of it (Beasley, MacDermid Wadsworth, and Behn Watts, 2012).

Different types of family and couple configuration and their unique challenges

Although the Karney and Crown (2007) model is helpful in identifying the key constructs and processes that support or detract from marital relationships, we argue for a more nuanced approach to the framework. This will allow us to consider the unique demands, supports, and stressors experienced by married couples who do not fit the traditional family mold (which is typically perceived as a heterosexual couple in which the husband is the service member, while the wife does not have an official, paid role in the military), as well as committed, but nonmarried, couples. We argue for this change because of the different relationship trends by subgroup (such as increased divorce rates) that suggest distinct experiences; we also consider the lack of data on key groups, such as same-sex couples, whose relationship stability and quality is unknown. Additionally, there is evidence that relationship satisfaction is a more powerful predictor of how an individual service member manages stress than is his or her marital status (McCone et al., 2011a). The possible benefits of nontraditional relationships, then, may well be overlooked if research remains narrowly focused solely on marriages.

Typically, marriage is viewed as a social (and, in many cases, religious) contract that binds a man and woman together for life as a family. Marriage remains a popular and desired outcome; however, despite its popularity, it has been decreasing steadily in the United States and especially in Europe. Many couples now choose to cohabit, either as a step toward marriage or as a replacement of it. Others, such as same-sex couples, cohabit if marriage is not an option for them because of religious or legal prohibitions. Regardless of the reason, military couples who are cohabiting in the United States are not eligible for formal benefits or pay allowances, nor are they recognized in the formal and informal supports typically provided to family members when a partner is deployed. This is not the case in many European countries. In the Netherlands, for example, cohabiting partners are eligible for benefits and support so long as they are designated as the "life partner" of the deployed service member.

The differences in how Western militaries account for and support family members provide an interesting critique of the Karney and Crown model, which accounts only for marriage as a relationship starting point and divorce as a measured outcome. Cohabiting couples cannot be easily gauged using this framework because their decision to cohabit may be in place of marriage or as a stepping stone toward marriage; thus there are two different outcomes. Because of this difference, relationships that experience stress and decreased quality from deployment may end and not transition to marriage. There also is the possibility that these couples may stay in a cohabiting relationship because marriage is not an option, or because they are content with cohabitation rather than marriage.

The issue of cohabitation, deployment, and relationship outcomes is especially pressing for same-sex couples in the United States. Gay marriage has only recently become legal in certain states and it is also newly recognized by the military. At this time, however, the same-sex spouses of service members are not recognized as legal dependents and are not part of the formal support networks established by the U.S. Department of Defense. Despite this current setup, there is the potential that the exclusion of same-sex married couples will change, especially with the 2011 end of "don't ask, don't tell." Gay and lesbian service members are now permitted to serve openly in the U.S. military. This change, combined with the possibility of same-sex marriage, means that these service members are bringing family members into the military, with the expectation that their spouses and children will receive the same benefits and support as heterosexual couples, especially during stressful times such as deployment.

The Dutch military, in contrast, handles cohabitation and same-sex marriage differently, providing an important counterexample to the limitations of the American experience. Rather than rely on marriage as the central relationship in military families, the Dutch military provides formal support, such as information briefings and meetings, to those who are invited by the service member. This person is usually the partner or spouse of the service member, but may also be a parent or child. With respect to these types of support, it does not matter whether the couple is married or not. During deployment, it is advised that couples officially register as "life partners" to receive (financial) support in case of an emergency. They do not have to be married to receive this support, but do have to be legally registered. This option is available to both heterosexual and same-sex couples, who are also allowed to wed in the Netherlands. Unlike in the United States, gay and lesbian service members have been allowed to serve openly in the Dutch military for the last several decades. Thus, by incorporating an international perspective, we are able to consider how different countries account for families and integrate them into the military. A comparative perspective also demonstrates the limitations of the Karney and Crown (2007) model for families that are built around relationships, but not necessarily marriage.

An important, but often understudied, subgroup of military members is women. Fluctuating between 10 and 14 percent of the American military, female service members are a growing group. This increase applies to many European militaries as well. In Germany, the Netherlands, and the United Kingdom, for instance, the proportion of military women has risen over the last decades to 9–10 percent. Despite being part of the same organization, research suggests that the experiences of female service members differ greatly from those of their male peers, including in family formation. Overall, women are at much higher risk of marital problems and marital dissolution than their male counterparts (Angrist and Johnson, 2000; Negrusa and Negrusa, 2012), and this trend has been consistent across ranks and services (Karney and Crown, 2011). Military women also experience higher divorce rates than comparable civilian peers. Divorce and possibly remarriage is now experienced by the majority of ever-married military women in the 40–49 age group (Adler-Baeder, Taylor, and Pasley, 2005). This difference in marital dissolution suggests that military women experience increased strain in their marital relationships resulting from the demands of the military lifestyle. When faced with deployments, for example, families may adapt differently to the temporary separation of women because of the different social roles fulfilled by men and women, as spouses and as parents. Consequently, while deployed and upon their return during the reintegration period, female service members and their families may need different formal and informal supports than those designed for traditional families.

Female service members are also more likely to be a part of dual-military marriages than their male counterparts. In the U.S. military, 51 percent of married enlisted women and 44 percent of married female officers are in dual-service marriages. Overall, across the services, 6.5 percent of active duty personnel are in dual-military marriages, with officers (7 percent) having a slightly higher rate than enlisted personnel (6.4 percent) (Office of the Deputy Under Secretary of Defense, 2012). Although research suggests that this does not account for the higher divorce rates among military women, dual-military families have the additional challenge of balancing the unique demands of the military lifestyle for two people versus one.

This can lead to the possibility of increased stress, especially when navigating two deployment cycles. Dual-military couples may request synchronous deployment schedules; however, for those couples with children, it is more common for them to request opposing schedules, so as to make sure that someone is home with the children. This may mean that dual-military couples see each other only for short, infrequent time periods, as they continually replace each other at home between deployments (Booth et al., 2007). Additionally, the resources provided to military families dealing with deployment typically assume a traditional family model. Support services, especially those implemented via spouses groups, tend to focus on civilian spouses (particularly wives) and provide many of their services during the duty day (Harrison and Laliberte, 1997). Thus, although resources are provided to dual-military couples, they are not necessarily the best "fit" for these families, making this factor especially consequential for marital satisfaction and stability.

One strategy that dual-military couples use to balance work and family demands is to have one member transition from the active component into the reserve forces (Smith, 2010). Although this move may alleviate the daily stress of balancing two military careers, reservists still must deal with ongoing deployments, especially in today's wartime environment. Reservists and active duty service members often serve together while deployed and, by law, they are required to receive the same predeployment training. Despite these similarities, there are differences in how regular and reserve service members respond to deployment stress. For example, Browne and colleagues (2007) studied thoughts of divorce among British regulars and reservists in times of deployment, and found that reservists reported lower levels of marital satisfaction. Moreover, among reservists, deployment was associated with increased consideration of divorce; this was not the case for regulars.

Conclusion

Military deployments and the stresses involved have the potential to strain family life and couples' relationships, but it is also important to recognize the potential positive effects and benefits. Research has shown that, generally, between 10 and 20 percent of the couples that experience deployment report marital strain, decreased satisfaction, or considerations of divorce. Hence, in addition to examining trends in marital status and divorce, it is important to account for different levels of relationship quality, because deployments can affect the dynamics in couples' relationship even if that effect does not necessarily result in divorce. Furthermore, relationship problems are likely to be higher among couples negotiating severe problems, such as combat-related injuries, or among couples that experience unique demands and stresses, which pose distinct challenges on their relationships. So, perhaps even more important than having knowledge on the degree of relationship change in times of military deployments, it is important to understand the factors and mechanisms that account for that change. We applied the framework developed by Karney and Crown (2007) to address the question of how military deployments impact couples' relationship satisfaction and stability. According to the model and empirical evidence, remaining connected as a couple, despite the physical separation and the challenges that come with it, is crucial in sustaining satisfied and stable relationships. Although this may sound obvious, the various challenges associated with the separation and reunion are likely to affect couples' interactions and relationships. Most prominent are their experiences and the personal or psychopathological changes that may result from it. If experiences are more stressful or traumatic, and if service members and their families develop mental health issues, interaction patterns are more likely to be problematic, which is likely to negatively affect couples' relationships. But apart from the prevalence of negative experiences and changes, deployment and reintegration can also involve positive experiences, or lead to posttraumatic growth, and bring couples closer together.

Although the framework developed by Karney and Crown (2007) is helpful in identifying and understanding the key constructs and processes that affect relationship satisfaction and stability, we argue for a more nuanced approach to the framework that takes into account the diversity of intimate relationships among military personnel. We advocate a shift in focus not only in research, but also in policies, from the dominant paradigm used to frame military families as traditional married couples to an approach that includes unmarried cohabiting couples, dual-military couples, and same-sex couples, given their diverse demands, challenges, experiences, and supports. Moreover, the international perspective applied in this chapter has shown differences in how Western militaries account for and support family members, and the different approaches to different types of family or couple. Approaching families and couples not solely with a focus on marriage, but also considering nontraditional relationships, prevents ignoring a large group of military personnel in other committed relationships and how their relationship quality is affected by military deployments.

Notes

1 See Albano (1994) for a more detailed account of this relationship.
2 See, e.g., McCone et al. (2011a); Op den Buijs, Andres, and Bartone (2010).
3 See Monson, Taft, and Fredman (2009) for a review.

References

Adler-Baedler, F., Taylor, L., and Pasley, K. (2005) *Marital Transitions in Military Families: Their prevalence and their relevance for adaptation to the military.* Purdue University, IN: Military Family Research Institute.

Albano, S. (1994) "Military recognition of family concerns: Revolutionary war to 1993." *Armed Forces & Society,* 20: 283–302.

Allen, E.S., Rhoades, G.K., Stanley, S.M., and Markman, H.J. (2010) "Hitting home: Relationships between recent deployment, posttraumatic stress symptoms, and marital functioning for army couples." *Journal of Family Psychology,* 24: 280–8.

Andres, M. (2010) "Behind family lines: Family members' adaptations to military-induced separations." Ph.D. dissertation, University of Tilburg. Breda, Netherlands.

Andres, M., and Rietveld, N. (2012) "It's not over till it's over: Sharing memories at the home front." In R. Beeres, J. Van der Meulen, J. Soeters, and A. Vogelaar (eds.) *Mission Uruzgan*. Amsterdam: Pallas Publications, pp. 295–307.

Andres, M., Moelker, R., and Soeters, J. (2012) "The work–family interface and turnover intentions over the course of project-oriented assignments abroad." *International Journal of Project Management*, 30: 752–9.

Angrist, J.D., and Johnson, J.H. (2000) "Effects of work-related absences on families: Evidence from the Gulf War." *Industrial & Labor Relations Review*, 54: 41–58.

Asbury, E.T., and Martin, D. (2012) "Military deployment and the spouse left behind." *The Family Journal*, 20: 45–50.

Baptist, J.A., Amanor-Boadu, Y., Garrett, K., Nelson Goff, B.S., Collum, J., Gamble, P., Gurss, H., Sanders-Hahs, E., Strader, L., and Wick, S. (2011) "Military marriages: The aftermath of Operation Iraqi Freedom (OIF) and Operation Enduring Freedom (OEF) deployments." *Contemporary Family Therapy*, 33: 199–214.

Beasley, K.S., MacDermid Wadsworth, S.M., and Behn Watts, J. (2012) "Transitioning to and from deployment." In D.K. Snyder and C.M. Monson (eds.) *Couple-Based Interventions for Military and Veteran Families: A practitioner's guide*. New York: Guildford Press, pp. 47–64.

Booth, B. H., Segal, M.W., Bell, D.B., Martin, J.A., Ender, M.G., and Nelson, J. (2007) *What We Know About Army Families*, 2007 update. Fairfax, VA: ICF International.

Bramlett, M.D., and Mosher, W.D. (2002) *Cohabitation, Marriage, Divorce, and Remarriage in the United States*. Vital Health Statistics Series 23, No. 22, Hyattsville, MD: National Center for Health Statistics.

Browne, T., Hull, L., Horn, O., Jones, M., Murphy, D., Fear, N.T., Greenberg, N., French, C., Rona, R.J., Wessely, S., and Hotopf, M. (2007) "Explanations for the increase in mental health problems in UK reserve forces who have served in Iraq." *British Journal of Psychiatry*, 190: 484–9.

Dirkzwager, A.J.E., Bramsen, I., Adèr, H., and Van der Ploeg, H.M. (2005) "Secondary traumatization in partners and parents of Dutch peacekeeping soldiers." *Journal of Family Psychology*, 19: 217–26.

Galovski, T., and Lyons, J.A. (2004) "Psychological sequelae of combat violence: A review of the impact of PTSD on the veteran's family and possible interventions." *Aggression & Violent Behavior*, 9: 477–501.

Harrison, D., and Laliberte, L. (1997) "Gender, the military, and military family support." In L. Weinstein and C.C. White (eds.) *Wives and Warriors: Women and the military in the United States and Canada*. Westport, CT: Bergin & Garvey, pp. 35–54.

Karney, B.R., and Crown, J.S. (2007) *Families under Stress. An assessment of data, theory, and research on marriage and divorce in the military*. Santa Monica, CA: RAND Corporation, National Defense Research Institute.

Karney, B.R., and Crown, J.S. (2011) "Does deployment keep military marriages together or break them apart? Evidence from Afghanistan and Iraq." In S.M. MacDermid and D. Riggs (eds.) *Risk and Resilience in U.S. Military Families*. New York: Springer, pp. 23–46.

Knobloch, L.K., and Theiss, J.A. (2011) "Depressive symptoms and mechanisms of relational turbulence as predictors of relationship satisfaction among returning service members." *Journal of Family Psychology*, 25: 470–8.

Kreider, R.M. (2005) *Number, Timing, and Duration of Marriages and Divorces, 2001.* Current Population Reports #P70-97, Washington, D.C.: U.S. Census Bureau.

Kreider, R.M., and Fields, J.M. (2001) *Number, Timing, and Duration of Marriages and Divorces: Fall 1996.* Current Population Reports #P70-80, Washington, D.C.: U.S. Census Bureau.

Mansfield, A.J., Kaufman, J.S., Marshall, S.W., Gaynes, B.N., Morrissey, J.P., and Engel, C.C. (2010) "Deployment and the use of mental health services among U.S. Army wives." *New England Journal of Medicine*, 362: 101–9.

McCarroll, J.E., Ursano, R.J., Liu, X., Thayer, L.E., Newby, J.H., Norwood, A.E., and Fullerton, C.S. (2000) "Deployment and the probability of spousal aggression by U.S. Army soldiers." *Military Medicine*, 165: 41–4.

McCone, D.R., and O'Donnell, K. (2006) "Marriage and divorce trends for graduates of the U.S. Air Force Academy." *Military Psychology*, 18: 61–75.

McCone, D.R., Scott, W.J., Looney, J.D., Sayegh, L., and Jackson, R.J. (2011a) "Resiliency of Army National Guard soldiers: Unique stressors and sources of support." Paper presented at American Psychological Association Conference, Washington, D.C.

McCone, D.R., Scott, W.J., Looney, J.D., Jackson, R.J., and Sayegh, L. (2011b) "Deployment stress in the Army National Guard: The roles of marital status, parental status, and relationship satisfaction." Poster presented at American Psychological Association Conference, Washington, D.C.

Monson, C.M., Taft, C.T., and Fredman, S.J. (2009) "Military-related PTSD and intimate relationships: From description to theory-driven research and intervention development." *Clinical Psychology Review*, 29: 707–14.

Negrusa, B., and Negrusa, S. (2012) *Home Front: Post-deployment mental health and divorce.* RAND Working Paper [online], available from http://www.rand.org/pubs/working_papers/WR874.html [accessed December 20, 2012].

Nelson Goff, B.S., Crow, J.R., Reisbig, A.M.J., and Hamilton, S. (2007) "The impact of individual trauma symptoms of deployed soldiers on relationship satisfaction." *Journal of Family Psychology*, 21: 344–53.

Newby, J.H., McCarroll, J.E., Ursano, R.J., Fan, Z., Shigemura, J., and Tucker-Harris, Y. (2005) "Positive and negative consequences of a military deployment." *Military Medicine*, 170: 815–19.

Office of the Deputy Under Secretary of Defense, Military Community and Family Policy (2012) *2011 Demographics: Profile of the military community.* Washington, D.C.: U.S. Department of Defense.

Op den Buijs, T., Andres, M.D., and Bartone, P.T. (2010) "Managing the well-being of military personnel and their families." In J. Soeters, P.C. Van Fenema, and R. Beeres (eds.) *Managing Military Organizations: Theory and practice.* London: Routledge, pp. 240–54.

Ponder, W.N., Aguirre, R.T.P., Smith-Osborne, A., and Granvold, D.K. (2012) "Increasing marital satisfaction as a resilience factor among active duty members and veterans of Operation Iraqi Freedom (OIF) and Operation Enduring Freedom (OEF)." *Journal of Family Social Work*, 15: 3–18.

Renshaw, K.D., Rodrigues, C.S., and Jones, D.H. (2009) "Combat exposure, psychological symptoms, and marital satisfaction in National Guard soldiers who served in Operation Iraqi Freedom from 2005 to 2006." *Anxiety, Stress & Coping: An international journal*, 22: 101–15.

Rowe, M., Murphy, D., Wessely, S., and Fear, N.T. (2013) "Exploring the impact of deployment to Iraq on relationships." *Military Behavioral Health*, 1: 10–18.

Sayer, N.A., Noorbaloochi, S., Frazier, P., Carlson, K., Gravely, A., and Murdoch, M. (2010) "Reintegration problems and treatment interests among Iraq and Afghanistan combat veterans receiving VA medical care." *Psychiatric Services*, 61: 589–97.

Sayers, S.L., Farrow, V.A., Ross, J., and Oslin, D.W. (2009) "Family problems among recently returned military veterans referred for a mental health evaluation." *Journal of Clinical Psychiatry*, 70: 163–70.

Scott, W.J., McCone, D.R., Sayegh, L., Looney, J.D., and Jackson, R.J. (2011) "Mixed methods in a postdeployment study of U.S. Army National Guard soldiers." *Journal of Workplace Behavioral Health*, 26: 275–95.

Sharpley, J.G., Fear, N.T., Greenberg, N., Jones, M., and Wessely, S. (2008) "Pre-deployment stress briefing: Does it have an effect?" *Occupational Medicine*, 58: 30–4.

Smith, D.G. (2010) "Developing pathways to serving together: Dual military couples' life course and decision-making." Unpublished Ph.D. dissertation, University of Maryland, College Park, MD.

SteelFisher, G.K., Zaslavsky, A.M., and Blendon, R.J. (2008) "Health-related impact of deployment extensions on spouses of active duty army personnel." *Military Medicine*, 173: 221–9.

Tedeschi, R.G., Park, C.L., and Calhoun, L.G. (1998) *Posttraumatic Growth: Positive changes in the aftermath of crisis.* Mahwah, NJ: Lawrence Erlbaum.

10 Stress, wounds, injuries, and meaning

The effects of combat-related PTSD on intimate relationships and partners

Rachel Dekel, Shelley MacDermid Wadsworth, and Laura Sanchez

Introduction

Exposure to traumatic events in general, and to war in particular, is associated with a variety of negative emotional consequences, one of the most common of which is posttraumatic stress disorder (PTSD). For example, according to the U.S. Institute of Medicine, between 4 and 20 percent of members of the U.S. Armed Forces who served in Operation Iraqi Freedom and Operation Enduring Freedom subsequently experienced PTSD (Institute of Medicine, 2013). PTSD has the potential to present severe challenges to close relationships, including loss of intimacy, conflict, and hostility (Institute of Medicine, 2013).

What is "posttraumatic stress disorder"?

According to the Diagnostic and Statistical Manual of Mental Disorders (DSM-IV-TR), PTSD is an anxiety disorder resulting from an individual's experience of a life-threatening or traumatic event. Military service is one capacity in which individuals can be exposed to traumatic events, including witnessing or experiencing serious injuries, being the target of lethal attacks, and carrying out acts of violence.

In the DSM-IV, PTSD is defined as including three symptom clusters: re-experiencing, avoidance and numbing, and hyperarousal (American Psychiatric Association, 2000). *Re-experiencing* symptoms include persistent distressing recollections, thoughts, and recurrent dreams about the traumatizing event(s), and psychological and physiological reactivity to reminders of the trauma. The second symptom cluster, *avoidance*, is characterized by avoiding activities, places, or people that remind the individual of the trauma, and/or inability to remember or talk about important aspects of the trauma, as well as difficulties imagining a personal future. *Hyperarousal* symptoms include sleep disturbances, irritability/anger, difficulty concentrating, hypervigilance, and an exaggerated startle response. Relative to other forms of trauma, those living with military trauma have been found to experience anger and hostility that is strongly associated with PTSD

(Orth and Wieland, 2006). In the fifth edition of the DSM (DSM-V), which is soon to be released at time of writing, the diagnostic criteria for PTSD are expected to be amended to divide symptoms into four clusters: re-experiencing, avoidance, negative cognitions and mood, and hyperarousal (American Psychiatric Association, 2015).

The effects of PTSD on intimate relationships

One of the commonest requests to agencies that provide care for mili-tary service members, such as Military OneSource in the United States, is treatment for relationship distress (Department of Defense Task Force on Mental Health, 2007). This is not surprising, especially when there are many military couple relationships in which one person has PTSD. Several studies have found that, compared to veterans without PTSD, veterans with PTSD are more likely to be physically and psychologically aggressive towards their families (Glenn et al., 2002; Jordan et al., 1992; Sherman et al., 2006; Verbosky and Ryan, 1988). The hyperarousal symptom cluster in particular has been found to be significant with respect to aggressive behavior among Vietnam veterans, with the symptoms in this cluster being strong predictors of intimate partner and general aggression perpetration (Savarese et al., 2001; Taft et al., 2007). The relationship between physical aggression and PTSD has been found to be stronger in military couples than it is in civilian couples (Taft et al., 2011).

PTSD has also been found to influence couple intimacy, defined by Mills and Turnbull (2001: 301) as "the ability to be sensitive and aware of each other's psychological, emotional, physical, operational, social and spiritual needs." Solomon, Dekel, and Zerach (2008) found, in their examination of relationships between PTSD symptom clusters and marital intimacy among Israeli war veterans, that PTSD symptoms impeded marital intimacy. The more the prisoners of war (POWs) suffered from hyperarousal and post-traumatic avoidance, the more likely they were to suffer from intimacy dif-ficulties (Solomon et al., 2008).

The effects of war veterans' PTSD on intimate partners

Being a military spouse can have many consequences for mental health. SteelFisher, Zaslavsky, and Blendon (2008) found that when deployment-induced separations were extended longer than the couple had anticipated, feelings of loneliness, anxiety, and depression increased among spouses. PTSD in military veterans also affects spouses' mental health (Monson et al., 2009).

In their study examining a group of partners of Vietnam War combat veterans, Calhoun, Beckham, and Bosworth (2002) found that partners of veterans with PTSD had poorer psychological adjustment and higher levels of burden than spouses of veterans who were not suffering from PTSD.

While partners were found to have more depression, anxiety, hostility, and obsessive-compulsive symptoms than did the spouses in the comparison group, PTSD symptom severity in veterans was not associated with their spouses' psychological adjustment. Similar to those findings, Dekel (2007) found that, among wives of former POWs, the severity of the husband's PTSD symptomatology was positively correlated with levels of distress and posttraumatic growth among wives. The wives' identification with their husbands' suffering potentially led them to internalize the husbands' symptoms, experiencing them as their own even though they did not personally experience the traumatic event (Dekel, 2007).

Consequences for spouses may depend in part on their own characteristics. Studying spouses' perceptions of combat veterans' PTSD symptom severity, Renshaw, Rodebaugh, and Rodrigues (2010) found that younger spouses reported more psychological distress than their older counterparts. Also, after controlling all other variables, male spouses reported lower marital and psychological distress than females. This suggests that female and younger spouses may be more likely to experience marital and psychological distress when the service member is experiencing PTSD.

The perspectives of the spouses have been found to mediate the effects of veterans' PTSD on the spouses' marital and psychological distress (Beckham, Lytle, and Feldman, 1996; Calhoun et al., 2002; Dekel et al., 2005). The effect of PTSD on a couple's relationship may depend on how the spouse of the service member perceives the severity of the symptoms and the reasons for them (Renshaw, Rodrigues, and Jones, 2008). Renshaw and colleagues (2008) examined spouses of members of the national guard who had recently returned from deployments in Iraq and found that spouses experienced the most distress when they perceived high levels of symptomology in the service members, but the service members themselves did not believe that they had these problems. Spouses reported less psychological distress when service members agreed that they were experiencing severe problems after deployment (Renshaw et al., 2008). These findings suggest that disagreement about veterans' suffering can significantly affect couples' relationships and spousal well-being.

To review, PTSD is one way in which trauma manifests in military veterans. This disorder is associated with higher physical and psychological aggression in military veterans, with the victims of the aggression often being family members. PTSD has effects on military veterans' intimate relationships, as well the partners' mental health and well-being. In addition to having effects on intimate partners, PTSD also leads to traumatization in other members of military veterans' families.

Secondary traumatization

When one member of a family suffers from PTSD, every family member is affected. Charles Figley (1983) coined the term "secondary traumatization" to refer to circumstances in which individuals display symptoms consistent with traumatization in relation to someone else's trauma rather than their own. Although there is controversy about the degree to which PTSD itself is "contagious," there is considerable evidence that one person's trauma symptoms are related to symptoms in both intimate partners and children. In studies of U.S. and Israeli veterans with symptoms of PTSD or combat stress, spouses have reported elevated levels of psychological problems including anxiety, depression, hostility, and somatization (Galovski and Lyons, 2004). Other studies show that children of World War II, Korea, and Vietnam veterans with PTSD experienced higher levels of psychopathology, interpersonal difficulties, and psychiatric treatment than children of veterans without PTSD (Davidson and Mellor, 2001; Galovski and Lyons, 2004). Adult children of Holocaust survivors have been found to report more adjustment problems than their counterparts in comparison groups, although this effect has been confined mainly to studies using convenience or clinical samples (Van IJzendoorn, Bakermans-Kranenburg, and Sagi-Schwarz, 2003).

While many accept that it is distressing to live with someone who has PTSD, the idea that PTSD can be "transmitted" to the spouse and that the spouse is actually traumatized is more controversial and difficult to validate. Some suggest that a part of the distress might be connected with a traumatic event in the wife's own history, rather than with her veteran-spouse's traumatic experiences (Renshaw et al., 2011).

Such ideas are in line with diathesis-stress models of psychopathology (Monroe and Hadjiyannakis, 2002), which suggest that most people, to one degree or another, have predisposing factors that render them vulnerable to the development of a mental disorder. However, individuals are unique in terms of the point at which they might develop a given disorder – a point that depends on the interaction between the degree to which these risk factors exist and the degree of stress experienced by the individual. Applying this model to the lives of spouses of war veterans with PTSD suggests that the spouses' (pre)vulnerability materialized as a result of the extensive stressors that are associated with veterans' PTSD and that this interaction resulted in emotional distress. Others suggest that a spouse's high level of distress could also reflect the difficulties of living with an individual who suffers from PTSD, rather than being a reaction to his or her partner's trauma.

Methods of trauma transmission among family members are not well understood. Shared genetic material may make children uniquely vulnerable to their parents' trauma, but most methods are related to social processes. Researchers have investigated, but found no support for, the possibility that spouses' symptoms predate their partners' traumatization and thus are partial functions of assortative mating (Galovski and Lyons, 2004). Direct methods of transmission are thought to include identification, whereby spouses or children so identify with the traumatized individual that they develop similar symptoms (Galovski and Lyons, 2004). For example, spouses may connect so strongly with veterans' descriptions of dangerous or frightening experiences that they experience intrusive thoughts. Trauma may also be transmitted indirectly by the stress of living with a traumatized individual, whether because of expressions of anger, violence, withdrawal, or overinvolvement by that person, the nature of care needed by that person, or because of hearing about that person's experiences. Stress can also occur as a result of unconstructive family communication patterns, including silence or over-disclosure (Dekel and Goldblatt, 2008; Scheeringa and Zeanah, 2001).

When both partners have experienced traumatic events, they could exacerbate one another's symptoms via "relational PTSD," whereby relationship partners react to one another's symptoms (Galovski and Lyons, 2004). More often discussed in relation to parents and children, patterns are thought to include children's traumatization being exacerbated by parents becoming more withdrawn and unresponsive, or overprotective or constricting, or preoccupied and frightening (Scheeringa and Zeanah, 2001).

Many unanswered questions remain about secondary traumatization. For example, studies of the children of Holocaust survivors are more likely to find PTSD when the focus is on a clinical, rather than more representative, sample (Van IJzendoon et al., 2003). Dekel and Goldblatt (2008) also point out that not enough is known about diversity among families in the reverberating effects of trauma.

Resilience among spouses of war veterans with PTSD

In recent years, a handful of studies have examined positive outcomes of traumatic events among persons close to the individuals who experienced them (Manne et al., 2004; Weiss, 2004). Interest in this issue was sparked by findings that exposure to traumatic events can have a positive effect on those who experience them. Posttraumatic growth (Calhoun and Tedeschi, 2006), manifested in more positive self-perceptions, improved interpersonal relationships, and a greater valuation of life and sense of meaning, has been found among persons who experienced illness and/or natural or manmade disasters.[a#1a#]

While many studies have examined manifestations of distress, only a few have examined the resilience and growth of families in general, and of spouses of traumatized veterans in particular. Two qualitative studies that examined the struggles and coping processes of wives of Israeli (Dekel et al., 2005) and Australian (McCormack et al., 2011) veterans showed that, in addition to distress and secondary traumatization, these women also experienced positive changes and development. These positive changes were documented in several domains.

The women talked about a kind of new and humbling acceptance of themselves and others: a gradual awakening of consciousness that led to a personal re-evaluation and initiation of change, and an acceptance of their own behavior over the years. They talked about finding a new sense of gratitude and appreciation for their husbands and children. In addition, they recognized that their situations had resulted in some positive personal changes. For instance, some of the women learned from their experiences to be less judgmental and more open to other people and experiences, or to become more loving. The women also discussed an increase in personal strength, for example of discovering skills they did not know they had, such as the ability to cope with adversity.

Each of these studies illustrated how a common history with their spouses served as the foundation for the women's current marital relationships, nourishing them and allowing them to give positive meaning to burdensome aspects of their marriages. Lev-Wiesel and Amir (2005) suggested that this type of growth can be viewed as a natural human strength representing a kind of life force in the face of adversity that can compensate for the coexisting posttraumatic stress. These studies indicate that although these women experienced considerable distress, they continued to function and grow.

That said, the positive changes following a trauma did not eliminate the persistent suffering that it caused. In the constant struggle with their husbands' difficulties, these women recognized that they had experienced a great deal of pain, but they also realized that they were stronger for it. Thus the challenges that they faced enabled them to discover new personal strengths in themselves and to learn about new possibilities in their lives (Calhoun and Tedeschi, 2006; Janoff-Bulman, 2006).

This growth could have developed through several mechanisms. One possibility is that the challenges of living with and raising a family with a traumatized husband might have brought the wife closer to him and added a new level of meaning to her life. Furthermore, in both samples, the wives' apparent success in meeting the challenges presented by these difficult marriages might have enhanced their sense of competence. An additional possibility is that watching husbands struggle with their symptoms increased wives' appreciation and love for them, strengthened their own determination to cope with the difficulties created by their husbands' PTSD, and gave meaning to their efforts.

Some professionals in the field, however, suggest that reports of positive changes by distressed individuals may not, in fact, reflect growth and development, but are instead self-delusions that enable them to cope with their unhappiness (Taylor, 1989). Although this explanation cannot be ruled out, some evidence of the validity of the changes has been provided in a study by Park, Cohen, and Murch (1996), in which participants' self-reports of positive changes were validated by others in their environment.

In summary, many of the studies that have assessed the effects of PTSD on family life have focused on the negative consequences of PTSD, rather than on the resistance and growth that can result from it. In addition, only a few have focused on the mechanisms through which the distress of a wife of a man with PTSD emerges and develops. In the second part of the chapter, we suggest "ambiguous loss" as one possible mechanism by which we can understand wives' adjustments to their husbands' PTSD.

Ambiguous loss and boundary ambiguity

It is inevitable that, at some point along the life cycle, families will experience the death of a family member. While such a death might be unexpected and even tragic, and might be associated with complex reactions, this kind of loss is perceived as clear and concrete, and is marked by formal notification rites and rituals of separation that are externally recognized. According to "ambiguous loss" theory (Boss, 1999), however, families can also experience losses that are much less clear. These losses are of two types. The first refers to cases in which the individual is physically absent, but psychologically present. A loved one is not present physically – such as when he or she has been kidnapped, has disappeared, or has gone missing – but is kept present psychologically, because he or she might reappear at any time. Such losses can also result from more common everyday situations, such as divorce, or from less common stressful events, such as war-related deployment (Boss, 2010).

The second type of ambiguous loss refers to cases in which a family member is physically present, but psychologically absent. This type of loss can result from a loved one suffering Alzheimer's disease or chronic mental illness (Boss, 1999, 2007). In these cases, the individual is there, but no longer resembles the person that he or she used to be.

According to this theory, the uncertainty or lack of understanding about the whereabouts, or the mental and functional status, of a loved one is very difficult for most individuals, couples, and families. The ambiguity freezes the process of grieving and prevents cognitive processing from taking place; the ability to cope and make decisions is therefore blocked (Boss, 1999). The ambiguity may also lead to symptoms of depression, anxiety, guilt, and distressing dreams on the part of loved ones. Because family members in these types of ambiguous situation are often uncertain about who is "in" and who is "out" of the family – which family members are performing which roles and tasks within the family system, and which are not – the family itself may become "immobilized." Decisions are put on hold, and tasks that may be beyond the capacity of the "lost" or "missing" person (Boss, 1999) are assigned to the "present" partner or to the children.

Application to military reserve families

Faber and colleagues (2008) examined the longitudinal course of ambiguous loss for families who had a member, or members, serving in the military reserves. Thirty-four reservists, spouses, and parents were interviewed seven times within the first year of the reservists' return from Iraq. During deployment, family members experienced boundary ambiguity that was characterized by the reservist's psychological presence, but physical absence, within the family. The major themes uncovered from interviews with family members about this period revealed boundary ambiguity around the safety of the soldier, the spouse's need to redistribute roles and responsibilities, and, towards the end of the deployment, worries regarding the soldier rejoining the family. Gathering information and attending a family support group provided some relief for families.

A second phase of ambiguous loss occurred upon the reunion of reservists with their family members. Although both reservists and family members had been looking forward to returning to their predeployment lives together, and although most of them expected an initial adjustment period, many of their feelings of loss could not have been expected or predicted. Reservists described feeling disconnected, and many families experienced boundary ambiguity in the form of the reservist's ambiguous presence: although he or she was physically present, family members said that it seemed as if he or she was "not really there." Interviews with family members and reservists following the reunion phase revealed boundary ambiguity around the resumption of roles and responsibilities at home and at work, and around relational communication and expectations.

During the reservist's absence/deployment, it was not surprising that decision-making and role assignment within the household generated heightened boundary ambiguity for families. However, even after the reservist's return, the ambiguity around roles and decisions remained. Family members felt hesitant about asking their reservist to resume certain roles, because they felt unsure about whether he or she was ready to accept these roles back, or how much more time he or she might need before feeling able to do so. Reservists, for their part, wondered about how they could resume their former roles without interfering in their family members' new routines and how exactly they would be able to fit back into their families. Negotiations around roles and responsibilities were particularly complex among reservists and their spouses, because they needed to clarify the boundary around them as a couple (that is, to assess each other's needs and preferences, and to engage in joint decision-making).

Application to military wives

Dekel and colleagues (2005) used qualitative methods to examine the marital perceptions of nine wives of veterans with PTSD. Data were gathered through a semistructured, in-depth focus group. The findings evolved around three themes. The first theme described how the illness shaped the lives of the women, and impacted their functioning both inside and outside the home. Miriam's words best describe the ways in which her husband's PTSD shaped her own life:

Today I simply don't do anything. I'm frustrated, and I can't find the strength to do anything with myself, not even art-like things that I used to enjoy. Once I was very active. For years I haven't gone to an art event. I simply bury myself at home. At night I don't sleep. Today I am connected only to PTSD.

The second theme described the women's conflicts regarding attending to their husbands' needs versus keeping their own physical and emotional space. The women struggled with the question of how to preserve their independence, go to work, and generally maintain a life for themselves, while also taking care of their husbands. Pamela highlighted the difficulty of this mission:

Through all of these years, I refused to treat him like my child or my baby. I really persisted in treating him as my husband, my spouse, a partner for life. But all of a sudden, I see that after all these years of struggling against becoming a caregiver, that's exactly what I am. I have no choice.

The third theme centered on the way in which the wives described their partners as present–absent. On the one hand, the husbands were there and they required intensive care from their wives; on the other hand, they were gone. The wives of these men described the loneliness of being with a partner who is physically present, but psychologically absent. As Mina said:

It's as if I live alone. I have to prepare everything; I have to do everything alone. If I want to go out [he says], "go by yourself," or "go, I'll come later." What am I – am I a widow? Am I divorced? I'm not divorced and not a widow. I have a husband!

All three of these themes make evident the fact that the wives of men with PTSD experience boundary ambiguity, and expend a great deal of energy trying to set clear boundaries for themselves and to reduce ambiguity. These women describe a constant tension between being drawn into a fusion with their husbands and their needs, and a struggle to achieve autonomy and a life of their own.

The women experience the process of their husbands taking over their private space as inevitable, something that they do not have the power to resist. This experience transcends physical boundaries (within the house and also outside it), boundaries of time (day and night), and personal boundaries (minimization of the women's self-expression). The wives engage in an ongoing struggle to preserve their separateness from their husbands as a means of preserving their sanity, their autonomy, and the independence of their spouses.

According to Boss (1999), the deluge of ambiguity often becomes as debilitating as the illness itself. Ambiguity revolves around questions such as whether the spouse is a husband or another child: is he an independent adult, or is he a dependent who needs constant care? The boundaries between the partners are unclear, and thus the rules that shape the couplehood and the roles that each spouse takes on are vague as well (Boss, 1999). Consequently, the women struggle to reduce ambiguity and improve clarity in their spousal relationships.

Application to military couples

A recent quantitative study (Dekel et al., undated) examined the role played by boundary ambiguity among couples in which the male suffered from PTSD. Boundary ambiguity was conceptualized as an intervening variable between a veteran's level of PTSD and his wife's level of adjustment. It was hypothesized that higher levels of veterans' PTSD would be associated with higher levels of wives' boundary ambiguity (that is, with less success in the struggle to make clearer boundaries), which in turn would be related to lower levels of adjustment among wives, manifested in lower levels of functioning and well-being, and higher levels of secondary posttraumatic symptoms.

The study compared two groups: the first – the research group – included wives of veterans who requested mental health assistance after the war; the second – the comparison group – included wives of veterans whose background variables were similar to those of the veterans in the research group, but who had not asked for mental health assistance. No significant differences between women in the two groups regarding the level of their functioning and well-being were found. Surprisingly, there also were no differences in levels of boundary ambiguity between these women. There were, however, differences in the levels of the three subscales of secondary posttraumatic symptoms. Women from the research group reported higher levels of intrusive, avoidance, and hyperarousal symptoms than women from the comparison group.

Tests of the hypotheses revealed that boundary ambiguity fully mediated the associations between veterans' PTSD and wives' levels of functioning and well-being in the research group. Boundary ambiguity also partially mediated the associations between veterans' PTSD and wives' secondary posttraumatic symptoms (that is, there were both direct and indirect associations between veterans' PTSD and wives' secondary posttraumatic symptoms). In addition, there was a direct significant positive association between earlier traumatic events in the women's lives and their secondary posttraumatic symptoms.

Applying the model to the comparison group, however, revealed that veterans' PTSD symptoms were associated only directly with their wives' posttraumatic symptoms (that is, boundary ambiguity did not serve as a

mediator to PTSD). In addition, the association between the earlier traumatic events in the lives of these wives and their secondary posttraumatic
symptoms was not significant.

Discussion

In recent years, as the wars in Iraq and Afghanistan have continued and
many service members have returned home, the recognition that war veterans' distress affects their family members has been validated. Veterans'
own requests for help, family members' calls for assistance, and expansions
of treatment services all reinforce this recognition. The studies presented
in our chapter and two recent meta-analyses (Lambert et al., 2012; Taft
et al., 2011) have documented significant associations between PTSD and
intimate relationship satisfaction, and between PTSD and partner distress.
While recognition of these effects has grown, several questions deserve further exploration, including the definition and manifestations of partners'
distress, and the mechanisms by which it develops.

The literature presented in this chapter documents a variety of effects of
secondary distress on both marital relationships and on spouses. However,
the question of whether distress emerges as a result of veterans' posttraumatic stress needs further examination. Studies are needed that verify the
specific sources of partners' distress; longitudinal studies that control for
spouses' pre-existing distress also will facilitate better understanding.

As noted earlier, most studies of PTSD have focused on the negative
effects of distress rather than the growth that may result or on what might
facilitate resilience. In order to construct a comprehensive perspective,
a better understanding of what encourages coping is needed. Moreover,
existing studies are based on couples who have stayed together. Because
we lack studies focused on couples who have separated, we do not know
what distinguishes couples who split up versus stay together, and what helps
them to stay together.

Finally, this chapter focused on families with male veterans and female
spouses. Studies that focus on female veterans and male spouses are limited
(Berz et al., 2008; Gold et al., 2007; Watkins et al., 2008), but their findings have been consistent with what has been found among male veterans
and their families. Further studies regarding this population are needed to
identify similarities and differences between these groups.

Several factors and mechanisms have already been identified in the
literature and in this chapter as pathways for developing distress. First,
there is a strong association between the severity of a veteran's distress
and the spouse's distress; second, the unique detrimental negative effects
of a veteran's use of physical and verbal violence on family life have been
documented.

In this chapter, we have suggested ambiguous loss as a key mechanism
by which secondary traumatization develops, and we have illustrated

pathways through which it occurs, using both qualitative and quantitative data. Ambiguity regarding the roles, responsibilities, and functioning of veterans when they come home from war is associated with elevations in spouses' distress.

The quantitative findings support the idea that living with someone who suffers from war-related PTSD is associated with both general distress and specific secondary posttraumatic distress. However, while the effects on general distress are fully mediated through boundary ambiguity, the effects of veterans' PTSD on secondary posttraumatic symptoms are only partially mediated through boundary ambiguity, because the direct path is also significant. These findings suggest that there might be several pathways by which spouses' distress is developed. In addition, it has been shown that earlier traumatic events in the wives' lives do play an additional role in wives whose husbands suffer from PTSD. While these earlier traumatic events do not contribute to the distress experienced by the comparison group, they serve as a risk factor and contribute to higher secondary symptoms among the research group. It might be that the husbands' current distress reactivates the wives' earlier traumas, resulting in more severe secondary posttraumatic distress in these wives. These findings provide preliminary support for the diathesis stress model in families in which the husbands suffer from PTSD (Monroe and Hadjiyannakis, 2002). Future longitudinal studies that assess moderating factors and aim to explain the ways in which distress develops are needed.

Recommendations for intervention

Interventions are needed in order to help veterans and spouses, both as individuals and as couples. The veteran needs to become aware of the effects of his behavior on his spouse and family, and learn how to control and minimize these effects. This mission is not an easy one: a recent study (Gould et al., 2010), conducted among soldiers postdeployment from the United States, the United Kingdom, Australia, New Zealand, and Canada, revealed that concerns about stigma and barriers to care tended to be more prominent among personnel who met criteria for a mental health problem than among those who did not, and that this pattern was similar across the armed forces of all five nations.

Regarding spouses, as we have described, ambiguous loss can lead to conflicted feelings and thoughts. Their ambivalence should be recognized, validated, and normalized. Their negative feelings should not be ignored or rejected; spouses should be offered opportunities to express such feelings, rather than to be ashamed of having them. Families need to be encouraged to discuss their feelings and to become more comfortable with the ambiguity (Boss, 1999).

Regarding couples, interventions should include helping couples to revise their attachment systems to include accepting – rather than resisting – the ambiguity that surrounds their relationship. Revision would increase their ability to celebrate what is still available in the relationship, while also grieving connections that are no longer possible (Landu and Hissett, 2008).

Currently, there are several innovative interventions specifically aimed at helping couples in which one member suffers from PTSD. Integrative behavioral couple therapy (IBCT) aims to increase social support, decrease interpersonal conflict, and address the experiential avoidance that maintains posttraumatic symptoms. It also aims to reduce conflict and to encourage intimacy through acceptance and skill strategies (Erbes et al., 2008). Cognitive-behavioral conjoint therapy (CBCT) for PTSD is a disorder-specific conjoint therapy designed simultaneously to improve symptoms of PTSD and to enhance intimate relationship functioning. Recent studies have documented the efficacy of this intervention in reducing posttraumatic distress and increasing marital satisfaction (Monson et al., 2012). These interventions should be further developed and validated.

Note

1   For a review, see Linley and Joseph (2004).

References

American Psychiatric Association (2000) *Diagnostic and Statistical Manual of Mental Disorders* (rev'd 4th edn.). Washington, D.C.: APA.

American Psychiatric Association (2015) "Posttraumatic stress disorder." [online], available from http://www.psychiatry.org/mental-health/ptsd [accessed January 26, 2015].

Beckham, J. C., Lytle, B. L., and Feldman, M. E. (1996) "Caregiver burden in partners of Vietnam War veterans with posttraumatic stress disorder." *Journal of Consulting and Clinical Psychology*, 64(5): 1068–72.

Berz, J.B., Taft, C.T., Watkins, L.E., and Monson, C.M. (2008) "Associations between PTSD symptoms and parenting satisfaction in a female sample." *Journal of Psychological Trauma*, 7: 37–45.

Boss, P. (1999) *Ambiguous Loss: Learning to live with unresolved grief.* Cambridge, MA: Harvard University Press.

Boss, P. (2007) "Ambiguous loss theory: Challenges for scholars and practitioners." *Family Relations*, 56: 105–11.

Boss, P. (2010) "The trauma and complicated grief of ambiguous loss." *Pastoral Psychology*, 59: 137–45.

Calhoun, L.G., and Tedeschi, R. (2006) "The foundations of posttraumatic growth: An expanded framework." In L.G. Calhoun and R. Tedeschi (eds.) *Handbook of Posttraumatic Growth: Research and practice.* Mahwah, NJ: Lawrence Erlbaum, pp. 1–2.

Calhoun, P.S., Beckham, J.C., and Bosworth, H.B. (2002) "Caregiver burden and psychological distress in partners of veterans with chronic posttraumatic stress disorder." *Journal of Traumatic Stress*, 15: 205–12.

Davidson, A.C., and Mellor, D.J. (2001) "The adjustment of children of Australian Vietnam veterans: Is there evidence for the transgenerational transmission of the effects of war-related trauma?" *Australia & New Zealand Journal of Psychiatry*, 35: 345–51.

Dekel, R. (2007) "Posttraumatic distress and growth among wives of prisoners of war: The contribution of husbands' posttraumatic stress disorder and wives' own attachment." *American Journal of Orthopsychiatry*, 77: 419–26.

Dekel, R., and Goldblatt, H. (2008) "Is there intergenerational transmission of trauma? The case of combat veterans' children?" *American Journal of Orthopsychiatry*, 78: 281–89.

Dekel, R., Goldblatt, H., Keidar, M., Solomon, Z., and Polliack, M. (2005) "Being a spouse of a PTSD veteran." *Family Relations*, 54: 24–36.

Dekel, R., Levinstein, Y., Svetlicky, V., and Levy, O. (undated) "The mediating role of ambiguous loss in couples in which the veteran has PTSD." Unpublished manuscript.

Department of Defense Task Force on Mental Health (2007) *An Achievable Vision: Report of the Department of Defense Task Force on Mental Health*. Falls Church, VA: Defense Health Board.

Erbes, C., Polusny, M., MacDermid, S., and Compton, J. (2008) "Couple therapy with combat veterans and their partners." *Journal of Clinical Psychology*, 64: 972–83.

Faber, A., Willerton, E., Clymer, S., MacDdermid, S., and Weiss, H. (2008) "Ambiguous absence, ambiguous presence: A qualitative study of military reserve families in wartime." *Journal of Family Psychology*, 22: 222–30.

Figley, C.R. (1983) "Catastrophes: An overview of family reactions." In C.R. Figley and H.I. McCubbin (eds.) *Stress and the Family, Vol. II: Coping with catastrophe*. New York: Brunner/Mazel, pp. 3–20.

Galovski, T., and Lyons, J.A. (2004) "Psychological sequel of combat violence: A review of the impact of PTSD on the veteran's family and possible interventions." *Aggression & Violent Behavior*, 9: 477–501.

Glenn, D.M., Beckham, J.C., Feldman, M.E., Kirby, A.C., Hertzberg, M.A., and Moore, S.D. (2002) "Violence and hostility among families of Vietnam veterans with combat-related posttraumatic stress disorder." *Violence & Victims*, 17: 473–89.

Gold, J., Taft, C.T., Keehn, M., King, D.W., King, L.A., and Samper, R. (2007) "PTSD symptom severity and family adjustment among female Vietnam veterans." *Military Psychology*, 18: 71–81.

Gould, M., Adler, A., Zamorskim M., Castro, C., Hanily, N., Steele, N., Kearney, S., and Steele, N. (2010) "Do stigma and other perceived barriers to mental health care differ across armed forces?" *Journal of Research in Social Medicine*, 103: 148–56.

Institute of Medicine of the National Academies (2013) "Returning home from Iraq and Afghanistan: Assessment of readjustment needs of veterans, service members and their families." Brief to Congress, Department of Veteran Affairs, and Department of Defense, March 25, Washington, D.C.

Janoff-Bulman, R. (2006) "Schema-change perspectives on posttraumatic growth." In L.G. Calhoun and R.G. Tedeschi (eds.) *Handbook of Posttraumatic Growth*. Mahwah, NJ: Lawrence Erlbaum, pp. 81–99.

Jordan, B.K., Marmar, C.R., Fairbank, J.A., Schlenger, W.E., Kulka, R.A., Hough, R.L., and Weiss, D.S. (1992) "Problems in families of male Vietnam veterans with posttraumatic stress disorder." *Journal of Consulting & Clinical Psychology*, 60: 916–26.

Lambert, J., Engh, R., Hasbun, A., and Holzer, J. (2012) "Impact of posttraumatic stress disorder on the relationship quality and psychological distress of intimate partners: A meta-analytic review." *Journal of Family Psychology*, 26: 729–37.

Landu, J., and Hissett, J. (2008) "Mild traumatic brain injury: Impact on identity and ambiguous loss in the family." *Families, Systems & Health*, 26: 69–85.

Lev-Wiesel, R., and Amir, M. (2005) "Posttraumatic growth among female survivors of childhood sexual abuse in relation to the perpetrator identity." *Journal of Trauma & Loss*, 10: 7–17.

Linley, A. and Joseph, S. (2004) "Positive change following trauma and adversity: A review." *Journal of Traumatic Stress*, 17: 11–21.

Manne, S., Ostroff, J., Winkel, G., Goldstein, L., Fox, K., and Grana, G. (2004) "Posttraumatic growth after breast cancer: Patient, partner and couple perspectives." *Psychosomatic Medicine*, 66: 442–54.

McCormack, L., Martin S., Hagger, M.S., and Joseph, S. (2011) "Phenomenological investigation into decades of 'lived' experience." *Journal of Humanistic Psychology*, 51: 273–90.

Mills, B., and Turnbull, G. (2001) "After trauma, why assessment of intimacy should be an integral part of medico-legal reports." *Sexual & Relationship Therapy*, 16: 299–308.

Monroe, S.M., and Hadjiyannakis, H. (2002) "The social environment and depression: Focusing on severe life stress." In I.H. Gotlib and C.L. Hammen (eds.) *Handbook of Depression*. New York: Guilford Press, pp. 314–40.

Monson, C.M., Fredman, S., Macdonald, A., Pukay-Martin, N., Resick, P., and Schnurr, P. (2012) "Effect of cognitive-behavioral couple therapy for PTSD a randomized controlled trial." *Journal of the American Medical Association*, 308: 700–9.

Monson, C.M., Taft, C.T., and Fredman, S.J. (2009) "Military-related PTSD and intimate relationships: From description to theory-driven research and intervention development." *Clinical Psychology Review*, 29: 707–14.

Orth, U., and Wieland, E. (2006) "Anger, hostility, and posttraumatic stress disorder in trauma-exposed adults: A meta-analysis." *Journal of Consulting & Clinical Psychology*. 74: 698–706.

Park, C., Cohen, L.H., and Murch, R. L. (1996) "Assessment and prediction of stress-related growth." *Journal of Personality*, 64: 1–35.

Renshaw, K.D., Allen, E., Rhoades, G., Blais, R., Markman, H., and Stanley, S. (2011) "Distress in spouses of service members with symptoms of combat-related PTSD: Secondary traumatic stress or general psychological distress?" *Journal of Family Psychology*, 25: 461–69.

Renshaw, K.D., Rodebaugh, T.L., and Rodrigues, C.S. (2010) "Psychological and marital distress in spouses of Vietnam veterans: Importance of spouses' perceptions." *Journal of Anxiety Disorders*, 24: 743–50.

Renshaw, K.D., Rodrigues, C.S., and Jones, D.H. (2008) "Psychological symptoms and marital satisfaction in spouses of Operation Iraqi Freedom veterans: Relationships with spouses' perceptions of veterans' experiences and symptoms." *Journal of Family Psychology*, 22: 586–94.

Savarese, V.W., Suvak, M.K., King, L.A., and King, D.W. (2001) "Relationships among alcohol use, hyperarousal, and marital abuse and violence in Vietnam veterans." *Journal of Traumatic Stress*, 14: 717–32.

Scheeringa, M.S., and Zeanah, C.H. (2001) "A relational perspective on PTSD in early childhood." *Journal of Traumatic Stress*, 14: 799–815.

Sherman, M., Sautter, F., Jackson, H.M., Lyons, J.A., and Xiaotong, H. (2006) "Domestic violence in veterans with posttraumatic stress disorder who seek couples therapy." *Journal of Marital & Family Therapy*, 32: 479–90.

Solomon, Z., Dekel, R., and Zerach, G. (2008) "The relationships between posttraumatic stress symptom clusters and marital intimacy among war veterans." *Journal of Family Psychology*, 22: 659–66.

SteelFisher, G.K., Zaslavsky, A.M., and Blendon, R.J. (2008) "Health-related impact of deployment extensions on spouses of active duty army personnel." *Military Medicine*, 173: 221–9.

Taft, C.T., Kaloupek, D.G., Schumm, J.A., Marshall, A.D., Panuzio, J., King, D.W., and Keane, T.M. (2007) "Posttraumatic stress disorder symptoms, physiological reactivity, alcohol problems, and aggression among military veterans." *Journal of Abnormal Psychology*, 116: 498–507.

Taft, C.T., Watkins, L.E., Stafford, J., Street, A.E., and Monson, C.M. (2011) "Posttraumatic stress disorder and intimate relationship problems: A meta-analysis." *Journal of Consulting & Clinical Psychology*, 79: 22–33.

Taylor, S.E. (1989) *Creative Self-Deception and the Healthy Mind*. New York: Basic Books.

Van IJzendoorn, M.H., Bakermans-Kranenbury, M.J., and Sagi-Schwartz, A. (2003) "Are children of Holocaust survivors less well-adapted? A meta-analytic investigation of secondary traumatization." *Journal of Traumatic Stress*, 16: 459–69.

Verbosky, S.J., and Ryan, D.A. (1988) "Female partners of Vietnam veterans: Stress by proximity." *Issues in Mental Health Nursing*, 9: 95–104.

Watkins, L. E., Taft, C. T., Hebenstreit, C. L., King, L., and King, D. W. (2008) "Predictors of child behavior problems among children of female Vietnam veterans." *Journal of Family Violence*, 23: 135–40.

Weiss, T. (2004) "Correlates of posttraumatic growth in husbands of breast cancer survivors." *Psycho-Oncology*, 13: 260–8.

11 Children and deployment

A cross-country comparison

Manon Andres and Julie Coulthard

Introduction

Temporary parental absence is not unique to military families; various jobs in different industries involve work-related travel. Parental separation as a result of military deployment, however, differs from regular business travel, because it involves the risk that military personnel may be injured, or even killed, while performing their duties abroad. It is one of the unique characteristics and challenges of military life, and, presumably, the most serious concern experienced by spouses and children of deployed military personnel (Booth et al., 2007).

With the evolution of professional all-volunteer militaries in many countries, the workforce demographic has changed from mainly young unmarried men to largely married military personnel who have children. As a result of military deployments, large proportions of spouses and children miss their loved ones on a regular basis and for prolonged periods of time. Moreover, military-induced separations disrupt the daily organization of family life and create temporary single-parent households. Service members' departures and their returns both change the composition of the family, requiring adaptation by children and parents. Today, dual-income families are quite common, and trends in society away from traditional to more egalitarian family relations have led to more equally divided tasks and responsibilities within the household. During military deployments, however, nondeployed spouses typically need to take care of daily household and parenting tasks alone, while managing their careers and work responsibilities. This can result in role overload and conflict between job and family demands. Upon the service member's return, family members face the challenges of reintegration, renegotiation (for example of family roles and rules), and reconnecting. The various challenges and stressors of military-induced separations are likely to impact family members' well-being and family relationships.

This chapter addresses the impact of military deployment on children and parents by providing a cross-country comparison of data collected in Canada and the Netherlands. Guided by the conceptual framework developed by Coulthard (2011) on the basis of earlier theoretical and empirical insights, we describe the stressors that families with children face, the risk and protective factors that can be identified, the impact on children's and parents' well-being, and the potential effects on organizational outcomes.

The conceptual framework

Based on a review of the literature, Coulthard (2011) developed a conceptual model, presented in Figure 11.1, which identifies how the challenges and stressors of military-induced separations are likely to impact children's and parents' well-being and organizational outcomes.

Military deployments have been defined as stressful events, because they create changes in the family structure that require family restructuring and member adaptation. In addition to the physical separation from a loved one, deployments involve various stressors that affect deployed service members and their family members at home.[1] For instance, while being deployed, service members are likely to experience life-threatening situations, sleep deprivation, feelings of powerlessness, and ambiguity about acceptable norms and behavior in the foreign culture. While their family members at home are not involved in life-threatening situations, they do have to cope with the fear that service members might be injured, or even killed, while on deployment. Moreover, additional stressors for families include unclear time frames, increased workloads, worrisome news reports, rumors, reduced communication possibilities, and stressful life events that can occur simultaneously, but which are not related to the deployment, such as illness, death of a close family member, or changes in working conditions.

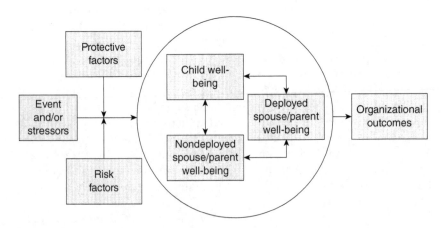

Figure 11.1 Conceptual model

Source: Adapted from Coulthard (2011)

In addition to stressors, protective and risk factors can be identified that can either alleviate or heighten the effects of the stressors on family members' well-being. Among other things, protective and risk factors include family factors, community factors, and (in)effective coping strategies (Watson Wiens and Boss, 2006). For instance, couples who are together for a shorter duration, those who have young children, and those going through a deployment for the first time may be at greater risk of experiencing negative effects. Furthermore, a lack of community networks and social support are likely to increase the negative effects of family separation on family members' well-being. On the other hand, the presence of positive coping strategies in the family, and social support from formal and informal sources, are likely to reduce the negative effects of stressors on children and parents. So, in sum, stressors affect family members' well-being, and the effects may be alleviated or heightened by the effects of protective and risk factors.

Research has demonstrated that military-induced separations have variable effects on children of deployed military personnel. Most studies report adverse effects on children, such as experiencing emotional difficulties, behavioral problems, and decreased school performance (Chandra et al., 2010; Chartrand et al., 2008; Huebner and Mancini, 2005; Mmari et al., 2009). However, studies also show that while a small number of children may exhibit negative behavior during the deployment that is significant at the clinical level, the majority of the children exhibit behaviors within normal limits, and seem to adapt to the separation and reunion fairly quickly (Jensen, Martin, and Watanabe, 1996; Kelley et al., 2001; Orthner and Rose, 2005). Research has also shown that children's and parents' well-being are interrelated (Andres and Moelker, 2011; Flake et al., 2009; Harrison and Vannest, 2008; Lester et al., 2010; Paden and Prezor, 1993; Watanabe and Jensen, 2000). This has been conceptualized as a reciprocal, mutually reinforcing relationship. For instance, if children adjust well to the separation, the parent at home is likely to feel better, which in turn positively affects the well-being of the children. The opposite is also true: if children experience adjustment difficulties, the stress experienced by the nondeployed parent is likely to increase, which in turn negatively affects the well-being of the children. Moreover, despite being physically separated, the well-being of children and spouses affects the well-being of deployed service members and vice versa. Through various communication media, family members remain informed about each other's well-being. More stress experienced at home is likely to negatively affect the deployed family member, and if service members are doing better in the theater of operations, this positively affects their home front, because they will be less concerned and feel less strained. These crossover processes can be explained by family members caring for each other and the strain in one family member producing an empathic reaction in the other, increasing his or her levels of strain (Westman, 2001).

Finally, the well-being of military personnel and their families has the potential to affect organizational outcomes, such as readiness, morale, performance, and retention. For instance, more concerns about their families before deployment has been shown to be related to service members experiencing greater difficulties in performing their operational tasks while deployed (McCreary, Thompson, and Pasto, 2003). Moreover, the perception that their family members are coping well with the frequent separations is likely to positively influence service members' decisions to stay in the military. Overall, research indicates indirect linkages between key organizational outcomes in the military and the well-being of children and the successful adaptation of the family during a deployment (Booth et al., 2007; Orthner and Rose, 2005).

Canadian and Dutch military families

In 2008–09, a study was conducted of spouses and civil partners[2] of Canadian Armed Forces (CAF) members. A paper-based survey entitled "Quality of Life among Military Families" was mailed to the home addresses of a sample of CAF spouses. The goal of the study was to look at the effects of military life on families from the perspective of the families themselves. The final sample consisted of responses received from 2,084 spouses. The majority of spouses were female (87 percent) and spoke English as their first language (77 percent). The length of the relationship with their military spouse ranged from a year to 38 years, with an average of 13 years. Half the CAF spouses were in the Army (50 percent), a third were in the Navy (33 percent), and 17 percent were in the Air Force. Many families were dual-income families, given that 71 percent of the spouses were employed, either on a full-time basis (56 percent) or part-time basis (15 percent). About one fifth of the spouses were CAF members themselves, the majority being part of the regular force. In addition, most spouses (68 percent) had children living in the home. Approximately 12 percent of the spouses (255 spouses) were experiencing a deployment of their CAF partner at the time of the survey, the majority of which were overseas (typically six months long). Further, 6 percent (106 spouses) were preparing for a deployment in the next six months and 18 percent (384 spouses) were in the postdeployment phase (Sudom, 2010).

Deployments of Dutch military personnel typically range from four to six months. Only six-month deployments include a two-week "rest and recuperation" (R&R) leave, which enables service members to spend time at home with their families. Military personnel and their married or cohabiting spouses were surveyed before, during, and after a deployment to Bosnia or Afghanistan. Most of them were spouses of active duty Army personnel. Of the couples with children, the service members were all male and had an average age of 39. Their nondeployed spouses were female and had an average age of 38. Most couples were dual-income couples (83 percent), were

Table 11.1 Numbers of surveyed families with children

Phase			
	Predeployment	*Deployment phase*	*Postdeployment*
Canada	77	186	236
Netherlands	258	219	143

married (84 percent), and on average had two children. The ages of the children ranged from birth to 28. In both research projects, data regarding children's well-being were collected through the parents.

The deployment process comprises three key stages: the predeployment phase, the deployment phase, and the postdeployment phase. Each of these stages involves unique experiences and challenges that the families must manage, from the preparation and anticipation of the absence of the service member, to the actual period of separation, through the eventual reintegration of the military member into the family unit. Table 11.1 displays an overview of the numbers of surveyed Canadian and Dutch military families with children at each of the three key stages of deployment. These are subsamples of the larger research projects conducted in Canada and the Netherlands, given that the focus of this chapter is on families with children.

Stressors faced by families with children

Military deployments are stressful events. Of the surveyed Canadian spouses with children, 78 percent reported that they either agreed or strongly agreed that their spouse's current or most recent deployment was stressful for them. Sudom and Coulthard (2013) examined the stressors particular to each of the three phases of deployment experienced by CAF spouses. In the predeployment phase, they found that many of the challenges that the spouses reported revolved around the practical concerns of managing everyday life in the absence of the service member. During the months before the CAF family member was deployed, a major stressor reported by almost two-thirds of respondents was concern over having to take on sole responsibility for household maintenance and care during the deployment. Spouses also noted experiencing challenges related to the logistics of the deployment. In particular, close to a third of spouses stated that they found the service member's extensive predeployment training requirements and subsequent time away from home to be very difficult. For just over half the spouses, the well-being of the family was also identified as an area of great concern. In particular, issues related to the children were noted, including anxiety over matters such as being solely responsible for childcare arrangements and taking on the role of single parenting, as well as worry over the potential emotional impact that the separation of the deployed parent might have on the children.

Challenges reported by spouses during the deployment phase were similar to those reported during the predeployment period. Approximately two-thirds of respondents reported struggling to manage the household on a day-to-day basis (for example managing household chores, car maintenance, etc.). In addition, nearly a third of spouses reported experiencing strong feelings of loneliness and isolation during the deployment. Ongoing concerns were the well-being of the family and having sole responsibility for the children. Half of respondents also identified concern for the safety of the deployed service member as an ongoing key stressor, with media coverage and news reports an added source of much anxiety for many.

During the postdeployment stage, the key stressors were found to be challenges adjusting to the return of the service members and their reintegration into the family unit after a lengthy absence. For approximately half of the spouses, getting to know each other again after such an extended time apart and trying to rebuild their relationship was a major challenge. Another key source of stress in the reintegration period noted by around two-thirds of spouses was giving up control and sharing household and childcare decision-making after having established new routines and having adjusted to having sole responsibility during the separation period.

Particularly during times of military deployment, when military personnel are temporarily unavailable to the family, military job demands have the potential to interfere with family life. Data collected among the spouses of Canadian and Dutch military personnel with children revealed moderate levels of interference in family life by military job demands,[3] as measured by the Work–Family Conflict Scale (Netemeyer, Boles, and McMurrian, 1996) (see Table 11.2). For both groups, work–family conflict was observed to be slightly higher during the deployment period, which reflects the increased challenges inherent in being solely responsible for managing household and childcare responsibilities. For the most part, however, no significant changes were observed over the deployment cycle among either Canadian or Dutch spouses. This suggests that spouses, despite the demands of deployment, are able to adapt to the challenges posed.

Risk and protective factors

It has been well documented in the literature that social support has beneficial effects on individuals' well-being. In the data collected among

Table 11.2 Mean levels of work–family conflict among spouses with children

Phase	Canadian spouses Mean (SD)	Dutch spouses Mean (SD)
Predeployment	3.2 (0.99)	2.7 (0.99)
Deployment	3.5 (0.95)	2.9 (1.12)
Postdeployment	3.2 (0.92)	2.8 (0.91)

Canadian families, more than half the spouses (56 percent) reported that they would prefer to seek support from outside the CAF, such as from friends, relatives, and civilian support services, during the absence of their military spouse as a result of deployment, while only 12 percent of spouses disagreed that they would prefer to seek support from outside the CAF. Furthermore, the data showed low usage of services during the deployment (Sudom, 2010), suggesting that spouses tend to prefer informal sources of support, such as friends and family, to formal programs and services. For those spouses who did not seek out services, no perceived need was the leading reason given by spouses for not having sought care – a positive finding that suggests that many spouses are capable of coping with the stressors associated with deployment.

Similarly, the study among Dutch families revealed that family and friends were the most important sources of emotional and instrumental support. Other military families were valuable as well, given that they are the ones who know what a deployment means to a family. They are also likely to possess deployment-related or mission-specific information. Furthermore, the military organization was a major source of information, particularly before the deployment. Although levels of perceived social support were quite high over the course of military deployments, the data revealed a significant drop during and after service members' absences when compared with before. Some of the interviewed spouses remarked that they were sometimes disappointed by the attention and support that they had received during their spouse's absence, or that they felt misunderstood by the people in their living environment. In addition to nondeployed parents feeling supported, it is important that children of deployed military personnel receive suitable support, and are not burdened with difficult questions and comments from friends or schoolmates. In the Netherlands, although diverse services are available to younger children (including books on parent–child separation), teenagers are a forgotten group in family support, yet a group who become very aware of the potential risks involved, which is likely to impact their concerns and well-being (Andres, 2010).

Support provided by the military when sending personnel abroad also includes providing and facilitating means of communication, which enables family members to feel connected to and supportive of each other, despite the physical separation. Being able to establish and maintain communication with the deployed service member was found to be of great importance for almost all of the Canadian spouses surveyed. Specifically, 97 percent of respondents reported that the opportunity for their spouses to telephone home was important to them. Communication was also found to have a positive impact on the well-being of spouses. The vast majority (89 percent) reported that regular or frequent contact with their spouses during the deployment made it easier for them to cope during the separation. Similarly, many of the nondeployed Dutch parents who were surveyed mentioned the importance of communication with the deployed spouse/ parent, and emphasized the beneficial effects of regular contact on their and their children's well-being. Telephone and email were the most popular means of communication. Eighty-five percent of the spouses with children reported that they had telephone contact with their deployed spouse/ parent at least once a week, of whom 11 percent had contact on at least a daily basis. Seventy percent had email contact at least once a week, of whom 17 percent had at least daily contact. The telephone enables separated family members to hear each other's voices and speak to each other in real time. Email also provides possibilities to interact fast and frequently. These are the great advantages of modern means of communication, in comparison with former times when family members had to rely on (often slow and uncertain) mail delivery.

While regular and positive communication is a protective factor, a lack or poor quality of communication by phone and email, and difficulty maintaining regular contact with the service member, is a risk factor, as was identified by a quarter of the Canadian spouses (Sudom and Coulthard, 2013).

Family members' well-being

Children's well-being

The absence and return of deployed service members can impact their children's well-being; and the responses vary by age (Andres and Moelker, 2011). Canadian spouses reported many negative effects of deployment on their children, with almost half reporting that their children became clingier (46 percent), while about one third reported that their children exhibited behavioral changes, such as young children sleeping with the parent (34 percent), anxiety (31 percent), and overall behavioral changes (28 percent). However, much smaller proportions of spouses reported more serious negative effects, such as violence (4 percent), nightmares (10 percent), anger (16 percent), or aggression (14 percent) (Sudom, 2010). Nondeployed Dutch parents observed that their children asked for more attention (37 percent), were more disobedient (23 percent), or were edgier (22 percent). They also reported that their children were having sleeping problems (17 percent), or more problems with bedwetting (7 percent); these problems were more prevalent among the youngest children (under 5 years old). Ten percent reported problems in school and 5 percent of the children were ill more often.

In addition to the negative effects on children, positive effects for Dutch children were identified as well, including being more helpful and caring, and feeling more responsible. Furthermore, despite the difficulties, many nondeployed Dutch parents (69 percent) observed that their children adapted quite rapidly and coped quite well with the absence of their parents. These findings are consistent with earlier research that has shown that while a number of children may experience serious problems, the behaviors and feelings of the majority of the children are within normal limits

(Kelley et al., 2001). No effects were found to be related to the duration of the separation or the mission area to which the parent was deployed. The latter suggests that it is the absence that counts.

Nondeployed parent's well-being

Research indicates that the well-being of children during a deployment is closely connected to the well-being of the at-home parent (Harrison and Vannest, 2008; Paden and Prezor, 1993; Watanabe and Jensen, 2000); thus it is also important to examine the well-being of the nondeployed spouses of military personnel.

Table 11.3 presents nondeployed parents' levels of psychological distress in the different stages of deployment, measured by the 12-item General Health Questionnaire (GHQ-12) (Goldberg, 1992).[4] The data revealed that, among both Canadian and Dutch spouses, levels of distress were highest during the deployment, which is to be expected given the stress of the separation. Before the deployment, spouses generally experienced levels of psychological distress similar to those that people usually experience in daily life (scores between 11 and 12 are typical, while scores above 15 point to evidence of emotional problems and scores above 20 indicate severe distress). Compared with the separation period, levels of distress dropped significantly after service members had returned home.

As with the effects on children, the duration of the deployment, ranging between four and six months, did not affect either the Canadian or the Dutch spouses' well-being. With respect to the mission area, the Dutch spouses reported higher levels of distress when their spouses participated in a mission that was perceived as more hazardous (Afghanistan), compared with one that was more routine (Bosnia). These differences were observed only before and after the deployment, which may be explained by spouses' concerns about the risks involved and the impact on their spouse's safety and well-being. This suggests that, during the deployment, it is the separation that produces a certain level of distress, regardless of where the service member is located.

Social support appeared to serve as a protective factor for Dutch spouses, because nondeployed parents who perceived higher levels of social support reported lower levels of psychological distress at each stage

Table 11.3 Levels of psychological distress among spouses with children

Phase	Canadian spouses GHQ score (SD)	Dutch spouses GHQ score (SD)
Predeployment	12.06 (3.72)	11.49 (4.41)
Deployment	13.41 (3.70)	12.39 (4.58)
Postdeployment	12.40 (4.03)	11.14 (4.50)

of the deployment (predeployment, $r = -.23$, $p < 0.001$; during deployment, $r = -.30$, $p < 0.001$; postdeployment, $r = -.20$, $p < 0.05$). The well-being of the nondeployed parent in turn was positively correlated with children's adjustment difficulties ($r = .46$, $p < 0.001$). Thus the better nondeployed parents were coping with the separation, the better the children were doing – and vice versa: if children adjusted well to the separation, the parent at home was likely to have a higher level of well-being.

Deployed parent's well-being

When considering children's well-being, it is also important to examine the well-being of the deployed parent. During the deployment, the great majority of the deployed Dutch parents (91 percent) reported that they were doing (quite) well, whereas the deployment was hard on 9 percent of them. More frequent contact with their spouses and children at home, and their perceptions of how their children and spouses were doing, were significantly associated with their reports about how the deployment was going for them. In addition, the independent reports of their spouses at home regarding their own and their children's well-being were significantly associated with how service members reported they themselves were doing – that is, more stress experienced at home was related to service members reporting more negative deployment experiences (Andres and Moelker, 2011).

The intense (and often violent) experiences in theater, in combination with concerns over their families' well-being and the transition into civilian life after returning home, are likely to impact the psychological well-being of service members. The most common diagnosis of the military member, as reported by the Canadian spouses, was depression (6 percent), followed closely by a stress-related physical or psychological problem (5 percent). It was further reported by the spouses that 4 percent of the military members had been diagnosed with posttraumatic stress disorder (PTSD). However, it is unclear whether these diagnoses were related to military service or some other traumatic event, because the survey did not examine the precipitating event(s) that led to the PTSD diagnosis. In addition, there is a possibility that some respondents may have confused a PTSD diagnosis with their spouses having an operational stress injury (OSI), of which PTSD is one resulting condition among other diagnosed medical conditions, such as anxiety and depression (Sudom, 2010). Research suggests that if service members suffer from problems after returning home, it is likely to impact the well-being of their children, including causing behavioral, social, and/ or emotional problems, or secondary traumatization.[5]

The impact on organizational outcomes

As previously noted, the increased stress experienced at home was related to service members reporting more negative deployment experiences.

Table 11.4 Levels of family–work conflict among Canadian spouses with children

Phase	Mean (SD)
Predeployment	2.5 (1.13)
Deployment	2.8 (0.09)
Postdeployment	2.4 (0.09)

This finding suggests that the better the home front is coping with the separation, the better the service members will function during deployment. It is crucial that service members are able to perform their operational tasks while deployed. In addition, military organizations are concerned with retaining competent personnel, whose families may be paramount factors in decisions to stay in or leave the military. With respect to Dutch service members' intentions and decisions to stay in the military, their children's adjustment difficulties during the deployment were positively correlated with service members' intentions to quit the job after they returned home ($r = .25$, $p < 0.05$). Thus it would appear that if children were to experience more difficulties during the absence of their military parent, service members would be more likely to think about leaving the military.

The stress experienced by family members in times of deployment not only has the potential to affect military organizational outcomes, but may also impact the work of the nondeployed spouse. The reports by Canadian spouses revealed that they experienced interference with their work responsibilities from family demands to a moderate degree (measured by the Family–Work Conflict Scale of Netemeyer et al., 1996), with a slight peak during the deployment phase (see Table 11.4). This can be explained as a result of their being solely responsible for managing the household and childcare arrangements, and taking on the role of single parent during the absence of their deployed spouse, which can interfere with their work responsibilities to a certain degree.

Conclusion and discussion

An effective military depends on maintaining the well-being of not only its service members, but also their families – particularly in times of military-induced family separations, which pose a unique set of stressors and challenges on children and their parents. This chapter presented an international comparison of Canadian and Dutch families' adaptations to these stressors and challenges in times of military deployments.

Various negative effects of the deployment on children were observed by their nondeployed parents, while some positive effects for Dutch children were identified as well. Furthermore, nondeployed parents themselves were found generally to manage fairly well, despite the range of challenges that they experienced throughout the cycle of deployment, such as struggling with a lack of time, greater stress, and difficulty in managing all household and childcare responsibilities on their own. Among both Canadian and Dutch spouses, levels of distress were highest during deployment. The duration of the deployment, which is typically up to six months in both Canada and the Netherlands, did not affect either the Canadian or the Dutch spouses' and children's well-being.

Many families, both in Canada and the Netherlands, were dual-income families. This suggests that many struggle to manage work and family life while one spouse is temporarily unavailable. Nonetheless, Canadian and Dutch spouses with children experienced only moderate levels of interference of military job demands with family life. The reports by Canadian spouses revealed that they also experienced interference from family demands with their work responsibilities to a moderate degree.

Despite the strength and resilience of military families, deployments are perceived as stressful events by family members. As such, efforts should be taken that address their concerns and the challenges that they face. Given that nondeployed spouses were found to have a preference for informal support, for example that provided by family and friends, efforts could be made toward facilitating informal social support networks that meet the specific needs of military families, especially in times of family separation. Communities and schools might also play an important role in helping children and their nondeployed parents to cope with the separation and reunion (Fitzsimons and Krause-Parello, 2009; Mmari et al., 2009). Military organizations should be concerned with suitable support and information for children across diverse age groups.

Furthermore, given the beneficial effects of communication between deployed service members and their nondeployed spouses and children – and that a lack or poor quality of communication is a risk factor – enabling families to remain connected through various means of communication during physical separations should remain a point of attention. In terms of organizational outcomes, the well-being of Dutch children and their nondeployed parents was significantly associated with how well service members were doing during a deployment, while children's adjustment difficulties were positively correlated with Dutch service members' intentions to quit the job after they returned home. As such, the military should also seek to foster a supportive and family-friendly environment, which helps to reduce tensions between work and family life, and helps with the effective management of work and family demands. In short, intervention efforts should be directed towards emphasizing and fostering protective factors, while also seeking to minimize the risk factors. Such interventions will help children and parents to adapt successfully to and meet the demands of military life, especially during military-induced family separations when the challenges are most severe.

Notes

1 See, e.g., Op den Buijs, Andres, and Bartone (2010).
2 From this point on, the term "spouse" will be used to reference individuals who are legally married, in civil partnerships, or cohabiting.
3 On a scale ranging from 1 (*military job demands do not interfere with family life at all*) to 5 (*military job demands highly interfere with family life*). NB: Dutch service members with children were asked the same questions. Similar patterns were shown and, although mean levels were also moderate before and during the deployment, they reported significantly higher levels of interference with family life by military job demands than did their spouses.
4 The 12 items were scored on a four-point scale, ranging from 0 (*not at all*) to 3 (*much more than usual*), and summed.
5 See, e.g., Dekel and Monson (2010) for a review.

References

Andres, M.D. (2010) *Behind Family Lines: Family members' adaptations to military-induced separations.* Breda: Broese & Peereboom.

Andres, M.D., and Moelker, R. (2011) "There and back again. How parental experiences affect children's adjustments in the course of military deployments." *Armed Forces & Society*, 37: 418–47.

Booth, B., Segal, M.W., Bell, D.B., Martin, J.A., Ender, M.G., Rohall, D.E., and Nelson, J. (2007) *What We Know About Army Families*, 2007 update. Report prepared for the Family and Morale, Welfare and Recreation Command by Caliber.

Chandra, A., Lara-Cinisomo, S., Jaycox, L.H., Tanielian, T., Burns, R.M., Ruder, T., and Han, B. (2010) "Children on the home front: The experience of children from military families." *Pediatrics*, 125: 16–25.

Chartrand, M.M., Frank, D.A., White, L.F., and Shope, T.R. (2008) "Effect of parents' wartime deployment on the behavior of young children in military families." *Archives of Pediatrics & Adolescent Medicine*, 162: 1009–14.

Coulthard, J. (2011) "The impact of deployment on the well-being of military children: A preliminary review." *Res Militaris*, 1: 1–30.

Dekel, R., and Monson, C.M. (2010) "Military-related posttraumatic stress disorder and family relations: Current knowledge and future directions." *Aggression & Violent Behavior*, 15: 303–9.

Fitzsimons, V.M., and Krause-Parello, C.A. (2009) "Military children: When parents are deployed overseas." *Journal of School Nursing*, 25: 40–7.

Flake, E.M., Davis, B.E., Johnson, P.L., and Middleton, L.S. (2009) "The psychosocial effects of deployment on military children." *Journal of Developmental & Behavioral Pediatrics*, 30: 271–8.

Goldberg, D. (1992) *General Health Questionnaire (GHQ-12).* Windsor: NFER-Nelson.

Harrison, J., and Vannest, K.J. (2008) "Educators supporting families in times of crisis: Military reserve deployments." *Preventing School Failure*, 52: 17–23.

Huebner, A.J., and Mancini, J.A. (2005) *Adjustments among Adolescents in Military Families when a Parent is Deployed.* West Lafayette, IN: Military Family Research Institute, Purdue University.

Jensen, P.S., Martin, D., and Watanabe, H. (1996) "Children's response to parental separation during Operation Desert Storm." *Journal of the American Academy of Child & Adolescent Psychiatry*, 35: 433–41.

Kelley, M.L., Hock, E., Smith, K.M., Jarvis, M.S., Bonney, J.F., and Gaffney, M.A. (2001) "Internalizing and externalizing behavior of children with enlisted Navy mothers experiencing military-induced separation." *Journal of American Academy of Child & Adolescent Psychiatry*, 40: 464–71.

Lester, P., Peterson, K., Reeves, J. Knauss, L., Glover, D., Mogil, C., Duan, N., Saltzman, W., Pynoos, R., Wilt, K., and Beardslee, W. (2010) "The long war and parental combat deployment: Effects on military children and at-home spouses." *Journal of American Academy of Child & Adolescent Psychiatry*, 49: 310–20.

McCreary, D.R., Thompson, M.M., and Pasto, L. (2003) "Predeployment family concerns and soldier well-being: The impact of family concerns on the predeployment well-being of Canadian Forces personnel." *Canadian Journal of Police & Security Services*, 1: 33–40.

Mmari, K., Roche, K.M., Sudhinaraset, M., and Blum, R. (2009) "When a parent goes off to war: Exploring the issues faced by adolescents and their families." *Youth Society*, 40: 455–75.

Netemeyer, R.G., Boles, J.S., and McMurrian, R. (1996) "Development and validation of work–family conflict and family–work conflict scales." *Journal of Applied Psychology*, 81: 400–10.

Op den Buijs, T., Andres, M.D., and Bartone, P.T. (2010) "Managing the well-being of military personnel and their families." In J. Soeters, P.C. Van Fenema, and R. Beeres (eds.) *Managing Military Organizations: Theory and practice.* London: Routledge, pp. 240–54.

Orthner, D.K., and Rose, R. (2005) *Adjustment of Army Children to Deployment Separations.* SAF V Survey Report [online], available from http://www.mwrbrandcentral.com/HOMEPAGE/Graphics/Research/saf5childreportoct05.pdf [accessed December 28, 2012].

Paden, L.B., and Prezor, L.J. (1993) "Uniforms and youth: The military child and his or her family." In F.W. Kaslow (ed.) *The Military Family in Peace and War.* New York: Springer, pp. 3–24.

Sudom, K. (2010) *Quality of Life among Military Families: Results from the 2008/09 Survey of Canadian Forces Spouses.* Technical Memorandum #2010-017. Ottawa, ON: Department of National Defense.

Sudom, K., and Coulthard, J. (2013) "The impact of deployment on families." In G.W. Ivey, K.A. Sudom, M.A. Tremblay, and W. Dean (eds.) *The Human Dimensions of Operations.* Kingston, ON: Canadian Defense Academy Press.

Watanabe, H.K., and Jensen, P.S. (2000) "Young children's adaptation to a military lifestyle." In J.A. Martin, L.N. Rosen, and L.R. Sparacino (eds.) *The Military Family: A practice guide for human service providers.* Westport, CT: Praeger, pp. 208–23.

Watson Wiens, T., and Boss, P. (2006) "Maintaining family resiliency before, during, and after military separation." In C.A. Castro, A.B. Adler, and T.W. Britt (eds.) *Military Life: The psychology of serving in peace and combat, vol. 3 – The military family.* Westport, CT: Praeger, pp. 13–38.

Westman, M. (2001) "Stress and strain crossover." *Human Relations*, 54: 717–51.

Part III

National social-psychological family support

12 Missions alike and unlike

Military family support in war and peace

Jocelyn Bartone

Introduction

Prior research has consistently shown that, among the challenges faced by military families, those that result from separation and deployments are among the most stressful (Bartone et al., 1993; Bell, Teitelbaum, and Schumm, 1996; Hill, 1949; Segal and Segal, 1993). By their very nature, deployments add stress to the lives of the nondeployed spouse. In the best of circumstances, in which marriages are strong, nondeployed spouses generally have a greater workload to keep the household operating and to have a greater workload to keep the household operating. They miss and worry about the safety of their deployed spouses; and they often struggle with the difficulty and expense of trying to maintain contact with their deployed spouse. In cases in which marriages are in difficulty at the time of a deployment, a spouse may be dealing with all of these challenges *and* the possibility that choices or decisions made while apart may lead to disagreements and fights, resulting in serious problems when families are reunited. In some of the most extreme cases, military families must cope with medical emergencies and life-threatening crises while the deployed soldier – husband/father or wife/mother – is away on deployment. This was the case, for example, for many families in Louisiana and Mississippi during hurricanes Katrina and Rita. And always there is the question of how much to tell a spouse who is away on deployment and in harm's way when problems arise on the home front.

When the U.S. military deployed 20,000 troops to Bosnia-Herzegovina for peacekeeping duty in 1995, many military families stationed in Germany faced the prospect of year-long separations for the first time. These U.S. soldiers had the mission to implement the military elements of the Dayton Peace Accords as part of NATO's Operation Joint Endeavor. While one-year unaccompanied tours to Korea were common at that time, military families in Europe had long been accustomed to shorter six-month rotation cycles. In conjunction with the 1995 peacekeeping mission, one of the most comprehensive studies to date of military family responses to deployment stress was a cooperative effort between the Army Research Institute and the Walter Reed Army Institute of Research's U.S. Army Medical Research

Unit – Europe, in 1996–97 (Bartone and Bartone, 1997; Bell et al., 1996). The study focused on U.S. Army families living in Germany, whose soldier spouses were deployed to Bosnia for peacekeeping duty. Researchers used interview, survey, observation, and open-ended comment data collection methods to assess the impact of the year-long deployment. The study identified the top areas of stress for military spouses, documented a variety of responses and coping strategies, and explored the impact of several major personnel policies.

Then on September 11, 2001 ("9/11"), terrorist attacks brought four hijacked airplanes crashing into the New York World Trade Center, the Pentagon in Washington, D.C., and a field in Shanksville, Pennsylvania. Shortly thereafter, U.S. forces began deploying to Afghanistan to hunt for Osama bin Laden in retaliation for the nearly 3,000 lives that had been taken. Soldiers began deploying routinely for year-long rotations in what came to known as "Operation Enduring Freedom." Later, in 2003, President George W. Bush expanded the military's mission to include the dismantlement of Iraqi President Saddam Hussein's regime and all Middle East terrorist networks, and ordered the deployment of the U.S. military to Iraq and into combat "for however long it takes," beginning "Operation Iraqi Freedom." He explained his decision to the American people thus, during a speech to a national guard audience:

> I made a decision – America will not wait to be attacked again. Our doctrine is clear: We will confront emerging threats before they fully materialize. And if you harbor a terrorist, you're just as guilty as the terrorist . . . We will stay on the offense. We'll complete our work in Afghanistan and Iraq. An immediate withdrawal of our troops in Iraq, or the broader Middle East, as some have called for, would only embolden the terrorists and create a staging ground to launch more attacks against America and free nations. So long as I'm the President, we will stay, we will fight, and we will win the war on terror.

In the years that have passed since this earlier research on deployment stress, the U.S. Department of Defense (DoD) has made widespread changes to policies and programs designed to support soldiers and their families as they face increasingly frequent and hostile deployments. This chapter examines how support for U.S. military families facing long deployment separations has evolved since 1995. It identifies similarities and differences between Operation Joint Endeavor and Operations Iraqi/Enduring Freedom; it summarizes a number of relevant findings from the Bosnia peacekeeping study; and then, utilizing publicly accessible data sources, it explores changes that have been made in support of the military family at war.

During the early phase of the deployment of troops after 9/11 for Operation Iraqi Freedom and Operation Enduring Freedom, more than 1 million service members were deployed for combat (Benjamin, 2005; Chu,

Table 12.1 Demographic profile of dependents of U.S. military forces in 2003

	Army*	Navy	Marine Corps	Air Force	Total
Spouses	263,602	188,154	80,084	216,959	748,799
Children	505,743	341,295	109,010	287,053	1,243,101
Parents	4,772	3,244	318	3,253	11,587
Other	1,945	0	0	0	1,945
Total	**776,062**	**532,693**	**189,412**	**507,265**	**2,005,432**

* Includes reserve and national guard, as well as active duty, troops

Source: Department of Defense, September 30, 2003

2005). One third of these had deployed more than once (Benjamin, 2005). The U.S. combat missions in Afghanistan and Iraq had been shared by both the active duty forces and the reserves and national guard. Official figures show a combined combat force made up 47 percent active duty, 33 percent national guard, and 20 percent reserve troops for a troop strength total- ing more than 1 million. While reviewing the numbers, General Richard Cody, Army vice chief of staff, highlighted the length of military family involvement when he stated that Operations Iraqi Freedom and Enduring Freedom are the largest and longest operations in which the Army has par- ticipated since the Vietnam War (Center for Defense Information, 2001–02; Cody, 2005). At that time, as Table 12.1 illustrates, these men and women claimed responsibility for more than 2 million dependents (Department of Defense, 2003). More than 100,000 Army national guard and nearly 50,000 Army reserve soldiers were mobilized or deployed, in conjunction with a concurrent active duty force of about 200,000. The global "war on terror" left millions of military dependents to cope without their soldiers.

Military families during peacekeeping: Results from Operation Joint Endeavor

Support for the mission

With the signing of the Dayton Peace Accord in 1995, the United States joined with NATO to aid the people of Bosnia in a peacekeeping effort. Approximately 20,000 active duty soldiers participated in Operation Joint Endeavor. Reserve troops were called upon to serve as backfill for the deployed troops. Soldiers sent to Bosnia conducted their mission as guard- ians of the peace among a population that was generally accepting of their task. However, research conducted with the spouses of soldiers deploy- ing at the beginning of the Bosnia mission found very little enthusiasm for participation in the mission (29 percent approved): spouses feared for the safety of their soldiers and had very little confidence in the ultimate success of the peacekeeping effort. Many who disapproved of the mission and feared for their soldier's safety felt that their soldier should not be put in harm's way over a political situation that posed no direct threat to the United States. A comment frequently made was "This is not our fight," and it was asserted that therefore military families were being asked to sacrifice too much in facing a year-long separation. The deployment came on top of more frequent separations for training and other operations. However, as time passed and the mission proved to be fairly safe, the approval ratings increased somewhat (34 percent).

Access to information

The mission to Bosnia was not well known to the general public, in part because the majority of the troops deployed came from the forward deployed troops stationed in Europe. It was carried out with relatively little public and media attention. The general perception seemed to be that of soldiers simply "doing a job." Media attention was very high only at the beginning of the operation, while there was much fear of injury and death. But when the number of casualties remained quite small (U.S. Army Peacekeeping and Stability Operations Institute, 1996), mass media interest quickly tapered off. *Stars and Stripes* (http://www.stripes.com) remained the one media source that maintained a journalistic presence during the entire mission. When surveyed, 71 percent of spouses reported getting helpful information from *Stars and Stripes*, making this their number one media source. CNN was considered a helpful source of information by less than half the respondents.

Half of surveyed spouses reported that getting accurate and timely information from their soldier's unit was a problem. Rumors abound in environments in which accurate information is missing. Without reliable sources of information about the missions on which their soldiers are deployed, spouses accept information wherever they can find it. Therefore they are more susceptible to rumor and the distress that misinformation can cause. This leads to distrust of mission leaders and the military in general. Unit newsletters and mission updates once or twice a month can counteract misinformation and rumors that media stories may foster. More information is always better than less. Spouses greatly appreciated the information that they were given. Keeping the spouses informed about the mission as much as possible helps to alleviate fears of the unknown, and creates much goodwill toward the unit and command.

Overall, only 36 percent of the spouses reported being satisfied with the media coverage. Getting information on the mission and the soldier's welfare was of paramount importance to soldiers' families. Their main source of information was the deployed soldier himself or herself, via phone calls and letters. This dimension provides one of the most striking differences between the Bosnian mission and today's Iraqi war. While phone calls from soldiers provided 93 percent, and letters, 89 percent, of the surveyed spouses with information about their soldiers or their soldiers' unit, the Internet provided only 10 percent with email contact and 2 percent with general information about the mission (Table 12.2). Sixty percent of the spouses surveyed reported that they and/or their soldiers did not have access to email.

A year is too long

The announcement that soldiers and their families could expect to be separated for a year as a result of Operation Joint Endeavor came as a shock to the many families of soldiers deploying from bases in Europe. They had learned to manage without their soldiers for six months at a time, but a 12-month deployment seemed unreasonably long. This was the top issue raised by spouses in the survey comments section. This was also the top stress factor endorsed, with 82 percent reporting the length of deployment

Table 12.2 Operation Joint Endeavor family survey: Utilization of helpful information sources

Source	Utilization (%)
Phone calls from soldier	93
Letters from soldier	89
Stars and Stripes	71
AFN television	62
FSG newsletters	55
CNN or other television	45
Command family briefing	43
Friends/acquaintances not in FSG	42
FSG phone tree	33
AFN radio	33
Rear detachment staff	32
FSG members	28
Unit chain of command	21
Unit videotapes	19
Army Times	16
Email from the soldier	10
Other newspapers	8
Magazines/books	7
Community/town hall meetings	5
Installation family assistance center (FAC)	4
Internet	2
Other	1

AFN = American Forces Network; FSG = family support group

Note: $n = 1,711$

Table 12.3 Operation Joint Endeavor family survey: Top stressors

Ranking	Stressor	% *
1	Length of deployment	82
2	Concern about soldier's safety	78
3	News about the situation in Bosnia	59
4	(Not) Getting timely information	58
5	(Not) Getting accurate information	44
6	Separation from family and friends in United States	43
7	Uncertainty about what the mission is	42
8	Reaching soldier by phone	40
9	Running the household alone	36
10	Problems with children	35
11	Health problems of family members	33
12	Getting mail to soldier	30
13	Not knowing how to contact soldier	30

* Percentage reporting "some," "much," or "very much"

Note: $n = 1,711$

to be a cause of significant stress (Table 12.3). The majority of spouses who expressed negative feelings about Operation Joint Endeavor focused on the negative impact that the year-long separation was having on their marriages and their families. They felt well prepared to handle a six-month rotation separation, but a full year away from the family (and most especially the children) was too much to ask for a noncombat mission. For many, the year-long deployment came immediately after previous long-term training or mission separations. Thus "one year" does not accurately reflect the real time for which soldiers have been separated from their families.

The vast majority of spouses who addressed the issue of length of deployment in open-ended comments were concerned less for themselves ("I'm an adult, I understand that this is my husband's job") than for the devastating affect the year-long loss of a parent was having on their children (Table 12.4). They felt that this particular mission did not justify keeping the family apart for so long. For those who felt the negative impact on parent and children to be too great, and who believed that only more of the same lay ahead, leaving the Army appeared to be the only solution. For those who expressed the intention of remaining an "Army family," the need for clear and consistent deployment and return dates was mentioned again and again. Without relief from ongoing uncertainty, families cannot form plans and "get on with their lives" while their soldiers are deployed. Without a consistent environment in which the children can anticipate routine activities, tensions and conflicts become the norm for the waiting families.

To help to ease the stress on families, and so better protect the time and attention of the deployed soldier, military families were offered support

Table 12.4 Operation Joint Endeavor family survey: Thematic analysis of open-ended comments – Top areas of concern

Ranking	Area of concern	%
1	Deployment length	49
2	Family support/rear detachment	49
3	Impact on family	39
4	Information communication	20
5	Deployment preparation	16
6	Leave policy	14

* $n = 1,711$

from their rear detachments, family support groups, and (to a lesser degree) a number of agencies established to provide assistance (U.S. Army Europe and Seventh Army Headquarters, 1996). While the intention was to give families a single center from which needs could be addressed, less than a third (31 percent) reported utilizing the family assistance center (Table 12.5). Clearly, for the majority (72 percent), the soldier's unit was the spouse's first choice when help was sought. The most heavily utilized service was the military postal service, which provided free mail service to and from Bosnia. Support from the civilian community was virtually non-existent, because these were military families living on- and off-post in Germany and Italy. The Internet also provided almost no support, because only 2 percent of the spouses surveyed utilized the Internet for information and only 10 percent received email from their soldiers.

Table 12.5 Operation Joint Endeavor family survey: Utilization and approval of Army services

Service	Utilization (%)	Approval (%)
Military postal service	95	97
Rear detachment	72	80
Military banking	70	93
Department of Housing Engineering	56	81
Army community services	39	89
Vehicle registration	44	89
Postrecreational facilities	42	85
Legal assistance office	38	90
Auto crafts shop	34	84
Family assistance center	31	81
Child development center	30	77
Youth services	27	79
Chaplains	24	89

* $n = 1,711$

In order to address the problem of length of time away from home, the Army implemented a two-week mid-deployment "rest and recuperation" (R&R) program. Survey responses showed that most spouses favored the home leave/R&R program, but that there were problem areas. A common sentiment was that the leave should not be charged as annual leave, given the length of deployment and typical seven-day work weeks. Some families objected to not having control over when they could take home leave; in most cases, the timing was dictated by the soldier's unit. The actual experience of home leave, although welcome, was disruptive to newly established routines and also required another painful goodbye. Home leave was associated with increased depression scores for spouses surveyed. Overall, these families felt as if they were being asked to shoulder the burden of year-long deployments, in conjunction with an increasingly demanding operational tempo, which kept soldiers from their families for longer and longer periods of time, for a mission that they felt could not justify the sacrifices that they were being asked to make. However, the vast majority did manage to get on with "business as usual" for the military family.

Military families at war: Operations Iraqi and Enduring Freedom

Public support for the Armed Forces

While the military's mission into Bosnia was virtually unknown to the public, Operation Iraqi Freedom received daily media coverage from the start. It became a major motivating issue for voters in the 2004 American presidential election, resulting in record numbers for voter registration. From the beginning, the war in Iraq met with mixed support from the American people. While there was much support for the policy of sending troops into Afghanistan in retaliation for the terrorist attack on the United States, and there was also support for sending troops to Iraq when it was believed that Saddam Hussein possessed chemical weapons of mass destruction (WMDs), at the time of the U.S. presidential election more than half of polled respondents felt that going to war with Iraq had been a mistake. Polls taken in October 2005 revealed the lowest approval rating of President George W. Bush's time in office. Poll results released by CNN indicated that only 39 percent approved, while 59 percent disapproved, of his policies. Political analysts felt that this was largely a result of the loss of public support for American involvement in Iraq (CNN.com, October 18, 2005).

Unlike the role of peacekeepers in Bosnia, which continued for years with very little media attention, the war in Iraq became headline news on a daily basis. Also, unlike Bosnia, which was a mission designed to keep warring factions apart and at peace, Operation Iraqi Freedom was a full combat war. Yet while Americans are as deeply split over the justification for this war as they were during the Vietnam War, there is far less negativity aimed at the military community. Then, soldiers were often condemned for performing the missions that they were ordered to conduct and Vietnam veterans returned home to a harsh, unwelcoming environment. Many veterans suffered for participating in the Vietnam War. Fortunately, the United States has learned many lessons from that period in its history. Public reactions to soldiers have changed dramatically since that time and, in general, citizens no longer blame soldiers for what their mission entails. Today's military service members are being honored as men and women fulfilling their oath to "serve and protect" their country to the best of their abilities. These soldiers are called "heroes" even by those who cannot support the mission. Thus support for the American soldier remained extremely high.

> COLUMBUS, Ohio – A badly battered Marine Corps unit came home Friday to miles of welcoming neighbors, a sea of cheering family members and countless tearful kisses. People waving flags along a 20-mile parade route roared as four buses passed carrying the 140 Marines of Lima Company from Columbus' main airport to the other airport across town. Some of the southern Ohio reservists wrote "thank you" on pieces of paper that they held up to the windows.
>
> (Anderson, 2005)

Perhaps largely as a result of the implementation of the Embedded Journalist program begun by then Secretary of Defense Donald Rumsfeld in 2003, which gave any American with access to a television nearly constant reports on the war's day-to-day progress (Starnes, 2004), both public and institutional support during the early days of Operations Enduring and Iraqi Freedom far outstripped the levels of support available during Operation Joint Endeavor. As daily media reports made clear, those who had deployed lived continually with the threat of injury and death in an effort to defend the people of the United States. For the sacrifices that U.S. service members were making, people could not seem to thank them enough. The Internet played a central role in linking people who felt a need to communicate their appreciation and reach out a hand of thanks with the means to do so. A web search of "support for service members" returned 265 million hits. A look at just one of those hits showed a website listing 50 organizations that allow a person to reach out to deployed soldiers. Public support was coming to soldiers from individuals, families, church groups, civic groups, schools, businesses and corporations, journalists, entertainers, athletes, and medical professionals. Support ranged from cards and letters of support mailed directly to deployed soldiers, to websites filled with messages to any soldier thanking him or her for his or her efforts. Countless care packages, the contents of which ranged from snack and toiletry items for the troops' comfort to small toys for soldiers to distribute to Iraqi children, were sent. At the time, the DoD issued a policy statement saying that the completely overwhelming outpouring of public support was threatening its ability to keep the service members equipped with essential supplies. Therefore, said the DoD, it could no longer accept packages for "any soldier," and would accept only packages mailed to a service member by name. The statement said that the service was bracing itself for 10 million tons of packages to be sent to soldiers deployed for the holidays.

But it is not only the efforts of the soldiers that are being publicly honored. A major difference between Operations Joint Endeavor and Operations Iraqi and Enduring Freedom is the extension of both official and public support of military families to an unparalleled degree. It is not only those who wear the uniform who are being recognized; the role that military families play in support of their service members was acknowledged by the President George W. Bush in a nationally televised speech delivered at Mountain Home Air Force Base, before members of the Idaho National Guard and their families, on August 24, 2005:

> A time of war is a time of sacrifice, and a heavy burden falls on our military families. They miss you and they worry about you. By standing behind you, you're standing up for America – the families are standing for America. And America appreciates the service and the sacrifice of the military families.

In his speech, President Bush not only recognized and thanked these military families for their efforts, but also went on openly to acknowledge some of the specific difficulties that calling the reserves and national guard into combat causes their families. In Operations Iraqi and Enduring Freedom, the reserves contribute approximately 48 percent of the total force. There are more than 50,000 Army reserve soldiers and more than 100,000 national guard soldiers currently mobilized or deployed (Cody, 2005). Unlike families of active duty troops, who are full-time soldiers, families of reserve and national guard soldiers may also lose the income, benefits, and job security that their service members were providing. In an effort to reassure them, President Bush highlighted a number of policy changes that were being put in place to ease the burden on them, including giving at least 30 days' notice prior to mobilization, minimizing the number of extensions and repeat deployments, and extending medical benefits to the guard and reserve forces and their families (Bush, 2005).

The other military family: Parents

While those comments were addressed primarily to soldiers and their spouses, with the declaration of "war on terror," the definition of the military family expanded also to include the parents of the often younger, single soldier. In the active duty Army alone, nearly half the enlisted soldiers are under the age of 25, with 17 percent being between the ages of 17 and 20.

In the national guard, nearly 90 percent are enlisted and the majority are single. Thus, with so many of the younger, single enlisted forces deploying, parents took a much more active role in thinking of their child's "job" in the military. Although these parents may not be "military dependents," they are often the "next of kin" to the single service member. They do not need or qualify for the same kind of day-to-day support that spouses and children do, but they too need access to information and direct communication with their sons or daughters.

The feelings of military parents can run as strong and as deep as a parent's love for a child, and military parents may not feel the same constraints that military spouses often feel about negatively impacting the career of their soldier spouses by speaking out against a particular mission or policy. In fact, military parents became a very visible force both in support of their children going to war, as well as in support of bringing their children home and ending the war. The proliferation of websites such as *Military Moms, Army Moms, Proud Army Moms, Marine Moms, In Our Hearts,* etc., as well as *Gold Star Families for Peace* and *Bring them Home Now,* served to create a community of military parents who could find informational and emotional support from, and reach out to, each other, expressing pride in their daughters and sons, and facing the very real fear of the loss of a child. It was the loss of her child that led to what has become perhaps the most visible example of a parent group protesting the country's involvement in Iraq and Afghanistan: when Cindy Sheehan waited outside the vacation ranch of President George W. Bush and repeatedly asked to speak with him about bringing the troops home, some parents actively supported her efforts, while others saw her as being unpatriotic for not supporting "the president and our troops."

Casualties of war

In the earlier stages of Operations Enduring and Iraqi Freedom, there were daily reminders of the sacrifices that the thousands of service members have made and the devastation of their parents, spouses, children, siblings, and friends, when news networks such as CNN broadcast daily tallies of casualties on television and online. Even today, one can sign onto websites for the DoD, and organizations such as the Iraq and Afghanistan Veterans of America (Iava.org), to see the latest listing of not only the numbers, but also the names, of troops that have died. As of January 2013, the DoD reported 6,574 American troops killed during these two wars. Daily tallies of the number of service members wounded in action are also available on that site. The DoD reports that, to date, more than 50,000 service members have been wounded in action (Department of Defense, 2013). Americans wounded in action cannot be returned to duty within 72 hours, highlighting the potential need for military families to step into a new role of medical caretaker as well (Defense Manpower Data Center, 2003, 2005).

Alleviating the stress on families

For those who have the mission to support military families during their soldiers' absence and return, the Internet has become a central tool. In ten years, since a time when only 2 percent of spouses reported getting mission-related information online, the Internet has become the most heavily utilized resource for disseminating information by both the official agencies, whose job it is to support soldiers and their families, and the public, who want to show their support as well. A web search of "support for military families" in 2005 returned 30.5 million hits. In 2013, the same search returned 149 million possible sites to explore. Whereas getting timely information was a major concern for the spouses of deployed soldiers during Operation Joint Endeavor in 1995, the amount of readily available information today seems to be neverending. From the daily television, radio, and newspaper coverage of imbedded journalists who travel within military units, to DoD links that provide anyone with an Internet connection access, a family member can get plugged in to virtually any operation in which the military is engaged.

Today, there is such a potentially overwhelming amount of information available through the Internet that a worried relative could spend so much of her or his time pursuing information on the web that it interferes with "getting on" with the business of day-to-day living. Whether they be wife or husband, a parent or sibling, or spouse and child, going on with life without the soldier remains the mission of the military family. Today, as with the Bosnia mission, year-long (and longer) deployments are the norm. Once again, military families must find a way in which to cope with the long-term absence of their service members, while living with nearly constant fear for their safety. From the perspective of the military, successful coping involves conducting the family's day-to-day business with a minimum of negative intrusion into the soldier's work life.

When soldiers are deployed for a year at a time, worry about what is happening at home is a major source of stress. It is crucial for the protection of soldiers, their mission partners, and the mission itself that a soldier maintains focus and is not distracted by worries about people or events going on at home. According to those who deal with the impact of long-term separation, facilitating communication between the soldier and the family is one strategy for lowering the risks to all, and the Internet is key (Miles, 2005). For this purpose, the DoD brought the Internet into modern combat. It has become a critical link for often daily communication between deployed service members and their spouses, children, and/or parents. While, generally, only those who had a rear detachment connection to the Internet had access to email during Operation Joint Endeavor (10 percent), a decade later the DoD was creating Internet cafes in combat zones. In an effort to improve morale, and reduce stress, it was announced in October 2003 that the Morale, Welfare and Recreation program would bring 177 cyber cafes, containing more than 3,500 computers with webcams and micro-phones to deployed soldiers in Iraq, allowing free 24-hour Internet access for the vast majority of the 130,000 troops deployed for Operation Iraqi Freedom (Helmer, 2003). Today, soldiers now have the possibility of call-ing home through access to services such as Skype and other online chat services, depending on their location and mission requirements. Donating telephone calling cards with free minutes for soldiers has been a very popu-lar way in which to show support for those troops who have access to more traditional phone services.

Facilitating Internet communication by establishing cafes is one answer to the question of what can be done to support service members and their families while they are separated, so that troubled marriages do not interfere with mission safety or success. The hope is that, by keeping up a fairly steady email exchange, military marriages/families can survive for 12 months at a time as "cybermarriages"/"cyberfamilies" during deployment. While the majority of marriages do manage to survive, the number of divorces rose steadily during the first five years of Operation Joint Endeavor. The Army reported 10,477 divorces among the active duty force in 2004. Among Army officers, the number nearly doubled between 2003 and 2004 (Chu, 2005; Miles, 2005). That trend among active duty officers was particularly disturb-ing, partly because it suggests that some of the more established military families had reached a breaking point and because it may point toward the stress on military families being cumulative. In response to these trends, the DoD offered online referral services, such as its *Army Families* website and *Army Knowledge Online* (AKO), which allowed access to military community instant messaging and chatrooms. In 2005, the DoD established a website called *Military OneSource* as a single resource encompassing all branches of the military, from which family members could seek information and phone numbers on which they could reach a real person for help. In tes-timony before the House Armed Services Committee, General Richard A. Cody, then vice chief of staff of the Army, also announced major policy changes for future operations in an effort to reduce the strain on military families and to reduce the risk of service members choosing to quit to pro-tect their marriages (Cody, 2005).

Attempting to provide as much information about the mission as possi-ble, and providing phone numbers and Internet links to resources that can help ease the burden of going it alone, while acknowledging the stresses caused by war, became key components of the DoD's support of military families during the early stages of Operations Enduring and Iraqi Freedom. One organization that began in 1969 as the Military Wives Association and worked over many decades on behalf of military spouses has grown into one of the most prominent advocacy groups working on behalf of military families: the National Military Family Association (NMFA), as it is known today, made its mission not only to advocate for military families, but also to support them directly as well. Not only can anyone visit the NMFA website for information, but also they can sign up to receive a monthly newsletter via email informing them of all of the latest news regarding military family support. In addition, the NMFA went even further, opening camps to which families and soldiers could go and get a break from the day-to-day stresses of dealing with deployment, and hosting research symposia to help the public and military leaders to be better informed about the nature and consequences of living with war (Bivens, 2013).

Inevitably, as American involvement in these conflicts continued year after year, much of the media attention waned. The big media counts and listings of the fallen disappeared, and the wars began to be covered as news stories only when something major occurred. Whereas, in the early days of U.S. involvement, Americans overwhelmingly supported President Bush's decision to go to war to defend the world against the presence of WMDs, when it was learned in 2004 that there were, in fact, no WMDs in Iraq, Americans' support for the war effort dropped dramatically – including among military leaders (Ricks, 2007). Not only did support for the war drop, but public opinion of President Bush plummeted as well. The Pew Research Center documented the plunge in approval ratings: from the start of his second term until December 2008, Bush's approval rating dropped from 50 percent to 24 percent (Pew Research, 2008). Americans became so disenchanted with the war that support for the war effort became a major political issue in the 2008 presidential election between Senators John McCain and Barack Obama. Yet military families marched on as always.

While it was repeatedly pointed out during the campaign that one candidate had voted to go to war and one had not, fully supporting American service members was always on both party platforms. From the time of his 2008 election, President Obama, who had voted not to go to war, has continually publically thanked those in the Armed Forces and reiterated his pledge to support American troops placed in harm's way by a war that he inherited. Yet it has been the first lady, Michelle Obama, and Dr. Jill Biden, the wife of the vice president, who have stepped up like none before to reach out to, and speak in support of, the military family. Mrs. Obama has said that, when she began campaigning for her husband's 2008 election, she was so touched by the many stories she heard from the families of deployed soldiers that she decided to commit herself to supporting them in whatever way she could (Sweet, 2011). She was joined in that effort by Dr. Biden, who found herself in the role of "military mother" when her son, Beau, was deployed to Iraq. They spoke at every opportunity of the challenges faced by military families in an effort to raise awareness among the American people, who could so easily have forgotten about those who were still deploying as the wars dragged on and as the media lost interest.

The Obama Administration's very public commitment to military families continued throughout President Obama's first term in office. The Obamas have hosted numerous events for military children at the White House, including a Christmas party that gave them the first look at the holiday decorations, a special pre-Fathers' Day movie screening for military dads and kids (White House, 2011), and then (beginning immediately after his re-election) a special inaugural concert held only for military families. The unparalleled degree of support being offered to military families was made even clearer when, on April 11, 2011, Michelle Obama and Jill Biden started the Joining Forces program in support of military families (White House, 2013). Its goal was to get not only the American public, but also American businesses, to actively work in support of these families in ways never before achieved:

> Joining Forces was created to recognize and serve our nation's extraordinary military families who, like their loved ones in uniform, serve and sacrifice so much so that we can live in freedom and security. This is a challenge to every segment of American society not to simply say thank you but to mobilize, take action and make a real commitment to supporting our military families.
>
> (Michelle Obama, quoted in Sweet, 2011)

On the one-year anniversary of the beginning of the campaign, the White House hosted an event to highlight the accomplishments that had been made, and then looked beyond, at what the cost of serving in uniform over the past ten years had been to so many military families – because, as with any war, very quickly the wounded in action began to come home with injuries that would not have been survivable in earlier conflicts. Owing to advances in field combat medical care, wounded service members arrived back in the United States facing a life of serious medical and psychological issues that resulted from their military service. As President Obama was announcing an end to U.S. involvement in Afghanistan, the First Lady was promising to continue to support returning service members and their families with medical, educational, and employment benefits, in an attempt to help them to establish "normal" civilian lives. Even as she was celebrating the prior year's accomplishments, she was reiterating a pledge of support to military families at levels that had never been dreamed of during that first year-long deployment to Bosnia just a decade-and-a-half earlier.

> [T]he outpouring of support that we have seen over this last year – . . . the hours logged, the services donated, the love and devotion and offers to help that have poured in from every corner of the country – all of that has far surpassed even our wildest expectations. Over the past year, more than 1,600 businesses have hired more than 50,000 veterans and spouses, and have pledged to hire at least 160,000 more in the coming years. Technology and employment companies such as Google, Monster and LinkedIn have stepped up to help connect veterans with jobs, and state leaders are passing legislation to ease employment woes for military spouses with professional licenses moving across state borders . . . Additionally, medical

schools are training health care providers so they can better care for military families . . . Joining Forces isn't a temporary initiative, but a forever proposition. We're going to keep driving forward until all of our nation's military families feel in real and concrete ways the love and support and gratitude that we all hold in our hearts. That is our simple promise to you.

(Michelle Obama, quoted in Sanchez, 2013)

References

Anderson, S. (2005) "Battered Marine unit comes home to big welcome." *The Capital,* October 7.

Bartone, J.V., and Bartone, P.T. (1997) "American Army families in Europe: Coping with deployment separation." Paper presented at the International Workshop on the Importance of Research on the Home Front and the Need for Family Support, Brussels, Belgium.

Bartone, J.V., Harris, J.J., Segal, D.R., and Segal, M.W. (1993) "Paratroopers' wives." In D.R. Segal and M.W. Segal (eds.) *Peacekeepers and their Wives: American participation in the multinational force and observers.* Westport, CT: Greenwood Press, pp. 129–40.

Bell, D.B., Schumm, W.R., Segal, M.W., and Rice, R. E. (1996) "The family support system for the MFO." In R.H. Phelps and B.J. Farr (eds.) *Reserve Component Soldiers as Peacekeepers.* Alexandria, VA: U.S. Army Research Institute for the Behavioral and Social Sciences, pp. 355–94.

Bell, D.B., Teitelbaum, J.M., and Schumm, W.R. (1996) "Keeping the home fires burning: family support issues." *Military Review,* 76(2): 8–85.

Benjamin, M. (2005) "How many have gone to war?" *GlobalSecurity.org,* April 12 [online], available from http://www.globalsecurity.org/org/news/2005/050412-gone-to-war.htm

Bivens, M. (2013) "Military families and the men in office." *National Military Family Association* [online], available from http://www.militaryfamily.org/feature-articles/mil-fams-and-presidents.html

Bush, G. (2005) "President addresses military families, discusses war on terror." *U.S. Department of State Archive,* August 24 [online], available from http://2001-2009.state.gov/s/ct/rls/rm/51695.htm

Center for Defense Information (2001–02) "U.S. military deployments/engagements 1975–2001." [online], available from http://www.careforthetroops.org/reports/Report-Military_Deployments_1975_to_2001.pdf

Chu, S. (2005) "Shaping the future of the American military." Unclassified briefing delivered at the Industrial College of the Armed Forces, Washington, D.C.

Cody, R. (2005) "Prepared statement before the House Armed Services Committee." [online], available from http://www.army.mil/leaders/leaders/vcsa/testimony.html

Defense Manpower Data Center, (2003) *Active Duty Military Personnel Strengths by Regional Area and by Country (309A).* [online], available at http://www.dmdc.osd.mil/appj/dwp/dwp_reports.jsp

Defense Manpower Data Center, Statistical Information Analysis Division (2005) *Active Duty Military Personnel Strengths by Regional Area and by Country (309A).* [online], available at http://www.globalsecurity.org/military/library/report/2005/hst1205.pdf

Department of Defense (2013) "U.S. casualty status." [online], available from http://www.defense.gov/news/casualty.pdf

Helmer, K., (2003) "MWR to spread free web site throughout Iraq." *Stars and Stripes*, European edn., October 3 [online], available from http://www.estripes.com/article.asp?section=&article=17227&archive=true

Hill, R. (1949) *Families under Stress*. New York: Harper and Row.

Miles, D. (2005) "Programs aim to reduce military divorce rate." *American Forces Information Service, DefenseLink News* [online], available from http://www.defenselink.mil/news/Jun2005/200520050609_1666.html

Pew Research (2008) "Bush and public opinion." *Pew Research Center for the People & the Press*, December 18 [online], available from http://www.people-press.org/2008/12/18/bush-and-public-opinion

Ricks, T.E. (2007) *Fiasco: The American military adventure in Iraq*. New York: Penguin Books.

Sanchez, E. (2013) "First Lady, Dr. Biden Mark 'Joining Forces' anniversary." *U.S. Department of Defense* [online], available from http://www.defense.gov/News/NewsArticle.aspx?ID=67899

Segal, D.R., and Segal, M.W. (eds.) (1993) *Peacekeepers and their Wives: American participation in the multinational force and observers*. Westport, CT: Greenwood Press.

Starnes, G.T. (2004) *Leveraging the Media: The embedded media program in Operation Iraqi Freedom*. USAW Strategy Research Project [online], available from http://www.dtic.mil/cgi-bin/GetTRDoc?AD=ADA423756

Sweet, L. (2011) "Michelle Obama helping military families: Launches 'Joining Forces.' " *Sun Times blogs*, April 12 [online], available from http://blogs.suntimes.com/sweet/2011/04/joining_forces_and_michelle_ob.html

U.S. Army Europe and Seventh Army Headquarters (1996) *U.S. Army Families in USREUR: Coping with separation*. USREUR Circular #608-2 [online], available from http://www.dtic.mil/dtic/tr/fulltext/u2/a285914.pdf

U.S. Army Peacekeeping and Stability Operations Institute (1996) *Bosnia-Herzegovina after action review (BHAARI)*. Conference Report, May 19–23 [online], available from http://www.au.af.mil/au/awc/awcgate/lessons/bhaar1.htm

White House (2011) "President Obama to host military fathers and children for screening of *Cars 2*." *White House*, June 15 [online] available from http://www.whitehouse.gov/the-press-office/2011/06/15/president-obama-host-military-fathers-and-children-screening-cars-2

White House (2013) "Joining Forces." [online], available from http://www.whitehouse.gov/joiningforces

13 Community capacity and the psychological well-being of married U.S. Air Force members[1]

Gary Bowen, James Martin, Jay Mancini, and Danielle Swick

Introduction

Locally anchored community forces surround families. These forces influence both their everyday life experiences and the way in which the individual and collective lives of their members unfold over time (Bowen et al., 2000). We believe that community context should have a more prominent place in thinking about health and well-being outcomes. Recognized or not, the social environment provides an important context that frames and informs well-being (Bowen, Martin, and Mancini, 2013; Mancini and Bowen, 2013; Mancini, Bowen, and Martin, 2005; Mancini, Martin, and Bowen, 2003).

"Community capacity," a primary idea in our approach to well-being, is one such community force that influences the outcomes that individuals and families are able to achieve (Bowen et al., 2000). Community capacity is represented by a sense of "shared responsibility" among and between community members, and members' "collective competence" in meeting important community goals and challenges (Bowen et al., 2000). These two elements of community capacity reflect the sentiment of making a difference in the community, as well as the action associated with making actual differences.

The social organization theory of community action and change was developed to elaborate the intricate ways in which community members and community institutions affect the quality of life of individuals and families, including health and behavioral health-related outcomes (Bowen, Martin, and Mancini, 2013; Mancini and Bowen, 2013). Community capacity, as defined above, is the core concept that anchors this theory. This theory of action and change is geared toward explaining the differing ways in which people in communities come together and how that coming together makes a difference in what transpires in communities. From this approach, social capital (a social energy for individual and collective efforts) develops as people interact, and therefore fuels the development of shared responsibility and collective competence. Social capital develops from the exchange of information between people, the reciprocity that may also occur in the information exchange, and the trust that develops the more frequently these exchanges are positive (Bowen et al., 2000).

From the perspective of the social organization theory of community action and change, formal systems and informal networks energize and provide the context in which social capital develops (Bowen et al., 2000; Mancini and Bowen, 2013). Whereas formal systems involve agencies and organizations, informal networks involve interpersonal associations and relationships. These systems and networks potentially work together to provide the impetus for the social capital that builds community capacity, which in turn enhances achievement of desired community results (Mancini et al., 2006; Small and Supple, 2001). In our approach, goal-directed change has a better chance of happening when multiple groups or disparate groups are focused on the same issue that requires attention.

The social organization theory of community action and change has been used as a framework for informing prevention and intervention programming in the U.S. military to promote military family and community resilience. The U.S. Air Force (USAF) has used the theory to inform its approach to the prevention of family violence (Bowen et al., 2000; Mancini et al., 2006), as a foundation for the design of the community readiness consultant practice model (Bowen et al., 2009), and as a framework for the development of an online support and resiliency assessment system to inform community policy and practice (Bowen and Martin, 2011). The action orientation of the theory is also reflected in the 4-H/Army Youth Development Project, the Army's Operation Military Kids, and the Essential Life Skills for Military Families family-strengthening program for reserve component families (Huebner et al., 2009).

Purpose and overview

Data from the 2003 USAF Community Assessment (Married Active Duty Member Sample) are used to examine hypothesized linkages in the social organization theory of community action and change between formal systems and informal support networks (agency support, unit leader support, and neighbor support), community capacity, and the psychological well-being of married, active duty, USAF members. The Center for Epidemiologic Studies Depression (CES-D) Index – a short self-report survey measure designed to assess depressive symptomatology in the general population, ranging on a continuum from happiness to depression – is used as the measure of psychological well-being (Wood, Taylor, and Joseph, 2010). The CES-D Index (including the seven-item short form of the original 20-item measure) is widely used in epidemiologic research, and is considered a valuable tool for identifying group-level relationships between depressive symptoms and other variables (Clark et al., 2013; Dooley, Prause, and Ham-Rowbottom, 2000; Golder, Connell, and Sullivan, 2012; Herrero and Meneses, 2006; Williams et al., 2012).

Although depression is not the only indicator of psychological well-being, it is one of the commonest forms of psychological distress and it is a sensitive indicator of life strains (Pearlin and Johnson, 1977). The analysis extends previous analysis of data from the 1999–2000 USAF Community Assessment (Bowen et al., 2003). Compared to these earlier data, the 2003 dataset provides vastly stronger measures of key concepts, as well as important new measures of the core concepts used in this discussion. An earlier version of the social organization theory of community action and change was used as the conceptual model for development of the 2003 Community Assessment Survey (Bowen, Martin, and Mancini, 1999; Martin and Bowen, 2003). These new measures include those assessing community capacity and USAF support agency effectiveness. In addition, new and improved measures of health are used in the 2003 survey, including the use of the seven-item version of the CES-D Index.

Structural equation modeling is used to analyze these data, including a multiple group analysis by gender. As the most comprehensive examination of the social organization theory of community action and change to date, the results have important implications for the science and practice of community capacity-building in military communities, and represent an important examination of these concepts and this practice model.

We open the chapter by briefly discussing current challenges faced by U.S. military personnel. We also present a conceptual model hypothesizing links between key constructs from the social organization theory of community action and change. We conclude by discussing implications of the findings for research, policy, and practice, including a brief overview of the current community capacity training initiative in the U.S. military.

Context

During the past 12 years, the USAF has experienced an unprecedented mobilization of its members and a continuous deployment of forces. While the primary focus has been the "global war on terror," and in particular the overseas contingency operations in Afghanistan and Iraq, during this period there have also been frequent national and international disaster relief missions requiring substantial military involvement. These continuous high-tempo and often dangerous missions have placed enormous stress on the U.S. military. In particular, members of the USAF (active, guard, and reserve) have played an important role in these missions, and have shared in the associated duty and military life challenges, placing unprecedented stress on these service members and their families (Bowen and Martin, 2011). While the war in Iraq has ended and the war in Afghanistan is winding down, there is no doubt that U.S. Armed Forces will continue to have a global reach, and that military service will continue to represent a demanding challenge for America's military members and their families.

Some of the more obvious consequences of this past, current, and future stress are seen in the elevated rates of mental disorders and other mental-health-related problems among military members, including an exponential rise in suicide (Armed Forces Health Surveillance Center, 2012; Mastroianni and Scott, 2011). During the period 2000–11, more than 900,000 active component service members have been diagnosed with at least one mental disorder (Armed Forces Health Surveillance Center, 2012); since 2010, suicide has been the second leading cause of death among all U.S. service members (Armed Forces Health Surveillance Center, 2012).

The high medical and occupational morbidity associated with mental health issues has a deleterious effect on overall readiness; in fact, mental health conditions have been the leading cause of discharge of men from military service and the second leading cause of discharge of women (Hoge et al., 2002). In this context, understanding the many factors associated with the (broadly defined) mental health of military members and their families – in particular, factors that impact their psychological well-being – is considered critical for the promotion and sustainment of current and future military readiness.

The conceptual model

Figure 13.1 illustrates the conceptual model examined here. Respondents' self-reported depression (seen here as being on a psychological well-being continuum from low depression to high depression) is the focal outcome in the model. Variation in respondent depression is shown in Figure 13.1 as influenced directly and negatively by one's sense of leader support (formal system), neighbor support (informal network), and community capacity. Agency support (formal system) is expected to have a direct and positive influence on leader support, neighbor support, and community capacity. Last, agency support, leader support, and neighbor support are proposed to influence depression indirectly by means of their positive influence on community capacity. Support for the central linkages in the proposed model is anchored in our larger community social organizational theoretical perspective, and grounded in the empirical literature and applications of the theory to practice.

Community social organization is a comprehensive descriptor of the contexts in which families live (Mancini and Bowen, 2013: 781): "Social organization is how people in a community interrelate, cooperate, and provide mutual support; it includes social support norms, social controls that regulate behavior and interaction patterns, and networks that operate in a community." From a social action and change perspective, social organization supports building community capacity, in effect shared responsibility and collective competence as primary situations and processes that enable communities to provide desired supports for families (Bowen et al., 2000; Mancini and Bowen, 2009). Within this framework, formal systems, including support from agencies and unit leaders, and informal networks, including support from neighbors, are key social

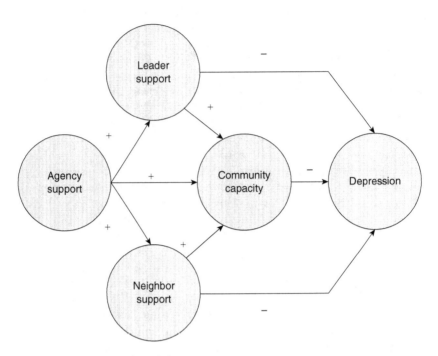

Figure 13.1 Conceptual model

organizational dimensions and function as key leverage points to the generation of community capacity. Service members and their family members are more likely to achieve positive individual and family results in the context of high community capacity, including higher levels of psychological well-being (lower self-reported depression in the current analysis).

A number of studies in the military family literature have found support for the positive influence of supportive formal systems and informal networks on the functioning and well-being of service members and their families (Booth, Segal, and Bell, 2007; Bowen et al., 2003). However, few studies have examined community-level variables, such as community capacity, which may mediate the influence of formal systems and informal networks on proposed dependent outcomes. An exception is an analysis of USAF families conducted by Bowen and colleagues (2003): sense of community mediated the positive and significant influence of unit support and informal community support on the family adaptation of married USAF members.

The present analysis provides an opportunity to extend this prior work, and provides a critical test of the social organization theory of community action and change. It also provides an opportunity to examine the direct and indirect effects of formal systems and informal networks on the well-being of married members beyond the influence of two aspects of the marital relationship (spouse support and relationship cohesion) and in the context of demographic variables that have been shown in prior research to influence either community capacity or indicators of psychological well-being (Bowen et al., 2003; Tanielian and Jaycox, 2008). Finally, the equivalence of both the measurement model and the structural model were examined by gender: the social organizational components of the model and their interrelationship may vary by the gender of the service member. For example, Martin (2004) summarized U.S. Department of Defense (DoD) data showing that female service members report a greater number of depressive symptoms than their male counterparts.

Method

Source of data

Data for the current study were collected in the form of a community assessment of USAF active-duty personnel. Data collection occurred from May to July of 2003 at every USAF base worldwide ($n = 83$), which was during a time of major deployments of U.S. military forces worldwide. Survey items assessed the demographic and social profiles of participants, as well as their perceptions of USAF life, their personal and family lives, and community programs and services. A reference matrix is available that describes the sources of items and scales for the community assessment (Martin and Bowen, 2003).

A random sample of 66,515 active duty members, stratified by rank and gender, were sent an email inviting them to participate in the web-based survey. Junior enlisted, active duty members (airman basic to senior airman) were oversampled, because members from this rank group typically have a lower response rate (Caliber Associates, 2000). The response rate for all participants in the current sample was 61 percent (66,515 participants were contacted; 10,101 emails were undeliverable; 34,381 responses were received). Only data from married active duty members were included in the current study ($n = 22,034$).

Sample profile

Of the 22,034 cases in the data file, 11,932 had data missing on one or more variables of interest. Initially, we imputed missing values with the expectation-maximization (EM) algorithm in EQS modeling software, but there were several imputed values outside the range of data and also several negative values. Therefore we were not confident in these results. Consequently, cases with missing data on one or more variables of interest were deleted from analysis. Cases with missing data did not significantly differ from cases with no missing data with respect to base location, housing location,

Table 13.1 Sample profile

Profile characteristic	Percentage of sample
Base location	
Continental United States	76
Overseas (outside of the 48 U.S. states)	24
Housing location	
Off-base	58
On-base	42
No. of years in current community	
Less than one year	9
One year or more	91
Gender	
Female	17
Male	83
Pay grade	
E1–E4	17
E5 and higher	83
Marital status	
Married to civilian spouse	82
Married to military member spouse	18
Length of time assigned to base community	
Less than one year	11
One or more years	89

Note: $n = 10,102$

community tenure, pay grade, number of children, whether the USAF member had a civilian or military spouse, or gender. The final respondent sample included 10,102 married active duty members. Table 13.1 presents the demographic profile of the sample.

Measures

In addition to nine control variables, five primary variables were constructed for purposes of testing the empirical model: depression, agency support, leader support, neighbor support, and community capacity. Table 13.2 presents descriptive statistics for these variables (mean, standard deviation, and range). Correlations between the five variables ranged from a low of –.18 for depression and agency support, to a high of .64 for community capacity and leader support. All correlations were statistically significant ($p < 0.05$). With the exception of depression, which was coded from low depression to high depression, all variables were coded such that the higher the value, the more affirmative the interpretation.

Table 13.2 Descriptive statistics of variables

Variable	Mean (SD)	Range
Depression	9.58 (3.41)	7–28
Agency support	30.54 (6.17)	7–42
Leader support	21.71 (5.11)	5–30
Neighbor support	24.02 (6.49)	6–36
Community capacity	40.11 (6.95)	9–54

Depression

Depression, as an indicator of the absence of psychological well-being, was measured using seven items from the CES-D Index (Ross and Mirowsky, 1989) (Cronbach's α = .85). The respondent was asked to rate on a four-point scale (1 = *none*; 2 = *one–two days*; 3 = *three–four days*; 4 = *five–seven days*) how many days during the past seven he or she had: (a) "felt that you just couldn't get going"; (b) "felt sad"; (c) "had trouble getting to sleep or staying asleep"; (d) "felt that everything was an effort"; (e) "felt lonely"; (f) "felt you couldn't shake the blues"; and (g) "had trouble keeping your mind on what you were doing." Table 13.3 presents the proportion of respondents by item who reported that they had experienced the depressive symptom on at least one–two days during the last seven.

Agency support

Agency support was assessed using seven items (Cronbach's α = .93). Respondents were asked to rate their agreement on a six-point scale from 1 (*strongly disagree*) to 6 (*strongly agree*) with the following statements about staff from agencies: (a) "have a good working knowledge of the services

Table 13.3 Proportion of respondents reporting depressive symptoms

Depressive symptom	Proportion of respondents who reported depressive symptoms*
Couldn't get going	31.7
Felt sad	26.4
Had trouble sleeping	45.2
Felt that everything was an effort	28.5
Felt lonely	15.5
Couldn't shake the blues	12.0
Had trouble keeping mind on what they were doing	31.0

* On at least one–two days during last seven

offered by their own agency"; (b) "know what other agencies have to offer and can refer me to another agency without a runaround"; (c) "know and understand the needs of active duty personnel"; (d) "know and understand the needs of Air Force families"; (e) "are regularly seen in my unit"; (f) "are regularly seen at community functions"; and (g) "are effective in addressing the needs of members and families."

Leader support

Leader support was measured with five items (Cronbach's α = .94). Respondents were asked to rate their agreement on a six-point scale from 1 (*strongly disagree*) to 6 (*strongly agree*) with the following statements about leaders in their unit: (a) "arrange for classes and programs to address the needs of members and families"; (b) "sponsor social events and informal activities for members and families"; (c) "help new members and families to get settled in the community and connect with other members and families"; (d) "work as a team to support members and families"; and (e) "work with Air Force support agencies, such as the family support center, to address needs of members and families."

Neighbor support

Neighbor support was measured using six items (Cronbach's α = .93). Respondents were asked to rate their level of agreement on a six-point scale from 1 (*strongly disagree*) to 6 (*strongly agree*) with the following statements about people in their neighborhood: (a) "know the names of their neighbors"; (b) "sponsor events and celebrations at which residents come together"; (c) "reach out to welcome new residents and families"; (d) "can be trusted"; (e) "look out for one another"; and (f) "offer help or assistance to one another in times of need."

Community capacity

The two dimensions of community capacity were assessed in the current study with three measures: shared responsibility (Cronbach's α = .89), collective efficacy (Cronbach's α = .88), and collective action (Cronbach's α = .92). Both collective efficacy and collective action reflected the collective competence dimension of community capacity. Each measure had three items.

With respect to shared responsibility, respondents were asked to rate their agreement on a six-point scale from 1 (*strongly disagree*) to 6 (*strongly agree*) with the following statements about members and families assigned to the base: (a) "feel a sense of common mission and purpose"; (b) "evidence teamwork and cooperation"; and (c) "feel a collective sense of community".

For collective efficacy, respondents were asked to rate their agreement on a six-point scale from 1 (*strongly disagree*) to 6 (*strongly agree*) with the following statements that people like themselves can: (a) "have an impact on making this community a better place to live and work"; (b) "have an impact on making the civilian community surrounding the base a better place to live and work"; and (c) "make a positive difference in the lives of other people assigned to this Air Force base."

With respect to collective action, respondents were asked to rate their agreement on a six-point scale from 1 (*strongly disagree*) to 6 (*strongly agree*) with the following statements about active duty members: (a) "join together to solve problems that threaten the safety and well-being of members and families assigned to this base"; (b) "look after and show concern for members and families assigned to this base"; and (c) "take advantage of opportunities to address the support needs of members and families assigned to this base."

Control variables

Although not shown in Figure 13.1, base location (1 = *overseas*), housing location (1 = *residing on base*), community tenure (a year or more), and pay grade (1 = *E5 and above*) were hypothesized to influence community capacity; deployment status (1 = *3 months or more deployed in past 12 months*), spouse support (metric, from low to high), relationship cohesion (metric, from low to high), children in home (1 = *one or more*), and dual-military status (1 = *yes*) were hypothesized to influence well-being as represented by the depression measure. With the exception of spouse support and relationship cohesion, these variables were single items and coded dichotomously.

Spouse support was measured using three items (Cronbach's α = .82). Respondents were asked to rate their level of agreement on a six-point scale from 1 (*strongly disagree*) to 6 (*strongly agree*) with the following statements about their spouse: (a) "understands the demands of my Air Force job"; (b) "is supportive of my being in the Air Force now"; and (c) "is supportive of my making a career of the Air Force." These items were adapted from the 1989 Army Soldier and Family Survey (Martin and Bowen, 2003).

Relationship cohesion was measured with three items (Cronbach's α = .96). Respondents were asked to rate their level of agreement on a six-point scale from 1 (*strongly disagree*) to 6 (*strongly agree*) with the following statements: (a) "My spouse and I have a good relationship"; (b) "My relationship with my spouse is very stable"; and (c) "I feel like part of a team with my spouse." These items were adapted from the measure of marital quality developed by Norton (1983).

Data analysis

Structural equation modeling (SEM) was used as the method of analysis. The dataset was randomly divided into two samples: a derivation sample of 5,033 cases, and a validation sample of 5,069 cases. The models were first tested with the derivation sample, then confirmed with the validation sample, and the final model was fit to the total dataset of 10,102 cases. The two-step modeling approach suggested by Anderson and Gerbing (1988) was implemented in order to test the fit of the measurement and structural models. First, the general SEM was treated as a confirmatory factor analysis (CFA) to test the adequacy of the measurement model for both males and females. In the second step, the general SEM was run as a structural model/path analysis to determine if the model was equivalent for males and females.[2] A 0.05 level of probability was used for purposes of determining statistical significance.

Results

Both the measurement and structural models were invariant across gender, meaning that the models fit equally for both males and females. Results from the validation sample and the total sample were similar to those obtained from the derivation sample. Figure 13.2 presents the results of the

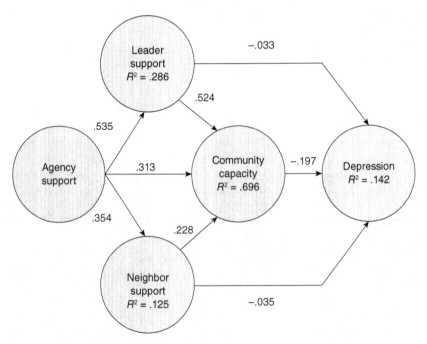

Figure 13.2 Final model results

Note: Standardized path coefficients are presented; RMSEA = .044; CFI = .946; TLI = .942; SRMR = .057; GFI = .934

Table 13.4 Direct, indirect, and total effects on depression for final model

Construct	Direct effect	Indirect effect*	Total effect
Agency support	.000	–.163	–.163
Leader support	–.033	–.103	–.137
Neighbor support	–.035	–.045	–.080
Community capacity	–.197	.000	–.197

* Indirect effects are calculated by multiplying the coefficients associated with the path of influence from the independent construct to the dependent construct (e.g. leader support has an indirect effect on depression via its direct influence on community capacity .524 × –.197 = –.103)

final model for the total sample; Table 13.4 presents the direct, indirect, and total effects. Overall, the model accounted for approximately 14 percent of the variation in self-reported depression ($R^2 = 14.2$). All coefficients are statistically significant ($p < 0.05$).

As predicted, positive perceptions of community capacity had direct effects on depression ($\beta = -.197$). In other words, as respondents' perceptions of community capacity increased, self-reported symptoms of depression decreased. Leader support ($\beta = -.033$) and neighbor support ($\beta = -.035$) had weak, but statistically significant ($p < 0.05$), direct effects on depression. These were the smallest standardized coefficients in the model, although the results were in the expected direction: as respondents' perceptions of leader support and neighbor support increased, self-reported depression decreased. However, as predicted, the primary path of influence of agency support, leader support, and neighbor support on depression was through community capacity. Perceptions of community capacity emerged as a strong and significant mediator of the effects of agency support (indirect effect = –.163), leader support (indirect effect = –.103), and neighbor support (indirect effect = –.045) on depression. In other words, agency support, leader support, and neighbor support exerted a positive influence on respondents' perceptions of community capacity, which, in turn, decreased self-reported depression. Nearly 70 percent of the variance in respondents' perceptions of community capacity was accounted for by these three variables in the model ($R^2 = .696$). Lastly, as predicted, agency support had a strong and direct effect on both leader support ($\beta = .535$) and neighbor support ($\beta = .354$). As respondents reported higher levels of agency support, their perceptions of leader support and neighbor support also increased.

Of the control variables entered into the model, the two substantive predictors of depression scores, spouse support and relationship cohesion, emerged as statistically significant. Spouse support was negatively related to depression ($\beta = -.073$), such that higher levels of spouse support were associated with lower depression. Relationship cohesion was also negatively related to depression ($\beta = -.232$), such that higher levels of relationship cohesion were associated with lower depression. In addition to these findings, the presence of children in the home (1 = *one or more children in the home*) was associated with lower depression ($\beta = -.043$); being in a dual-military couple (1 = *yes*) was also associated with lower depression ($\beta = -.070$). No other control variables in the model were statistically significant.

Conclusions and discussion

The goal of our study was to uncover the potentially significant place that locally anchored geographic community capacity has in the self-reported psychological well-being of married active duty USAF members. We used a short form of the CES-D Index as our measure of psychological well-being. Very often, community-related influences are assumed or alluded to by both researchers and practitioners; however, there are few direct tests of these influences.

Our theory posits that community capacity makes a difference in important results for individuals, families, and communities. As the linchpin in our theory, community capacity is viewed as having a direct relationship to important results – in the instance of this study, to a survey measure of depression commonly used to indicate psychological well-being in public health studies. We also expect community capacity to serve a "gateway" function as well – that is, affecting how other important contextual elements ultimately relate to well-being. Our findings provide clear support for both direct effects and mediating effects of respondents' perceptions of community capacity, as hypothesized in our conceptual model.

The social organization theory of community action and change is robust, and the results suggest that likely leverage points in promoting individual psychological well-being are formal systems (agency support and leader support) and informal networks (neighbor support), which contribute to a sense of shared responsibility and to collective competence (the two dimensions of community capacity). Importantly, these effects are over and beyond the influence of the support that married USAF members receive from their spouses and the marital relationship.

In our sample, those who reported lower levels of depression (an indicator of high well-being) are more likely to see their community as a place in which people are more likely to consider the welfare of others (shared responsibility), to feel personally empowered to make a positive difference in the community and in lives of others (collective efficacy), and actually to come together for positive community change (collective action). As to the intervening function of community capacity in our model, the role that agency, leader, and neighbor support have in psychological well-being is enhanced by how individuals view their community. These findings suggest leverage points for community action and change, in that what leaders and agencies do to further the development of community capacity ultimately filters to individual psychological well-being. In addition, if staffs from community agencies are more intentional about their support of informal networks, such as from neighbors, yet another leverage point is created for capacity-building and for influencing important well-being results.

In the context of U.S. DoD Instruction 1342.22, "Military Family Readiness" (July 3, 2012), and under contract to the DoD Office of Military Community and Family Policy, the Department of Human Development and Family Science at the University of Georgia and the School of Social Work at the University of North Carolina at Chapel Hill are collaborating on developing a community capacity-building online curriculum for program professionals working with military families. This curriculum is derived from the same social organization theory of community action and change that has informed the present analysis. This professional practice curriculum begins with teaching a curriculum on the social organization theory of community action and change as an approach to intervention and prevention efforts. A significant aspect of the curriculum is a results-focused planning approach that is a powerful tool for agencies and organizations to use for building capacity, including bringing formal systems together to support unit leaders in exercising their support function and to develop informal networks with communities. There is an intentional focus on leadership and on service organizations (what needs to occur both within an organization and between organizations). Of pivotal importance in this curriculum are skills for understanding military and civilian communities, for assessing community assets and needs, and for sustaining important community initiatives. Findings from the present analysis align with those from earlier studies (Bowen et al., 2003), and support the potential benefits of such training curriculums for preparing service delivery professionals in building community capacity on behalf of military service members and their families.

In conclusion, while SEM is a powerful statistical tool, several areas of caution should be noted. First, although the results of the analysis were consistent with the data, other potential models may also receive support. For example members with higher psychological well-being (lower levels of depression) may be more likely to seek out support, even though they are less likely to need such support.

Second, our model is based on cross-sectional data. Future research should use longitudinal data to examine the direction of effects over time.

Third, we proposed linear relationships between measures in the model. However, future research should consider the potential for nonlinear effects. For example formal and informal networks may have upper and lower threshold effects in their relationship to indicators of psychological well-being.

Lastly, the amount of missing data encountered in the current study may limit the external validity of our findings. However, comparisons of respondents with complete and missing data were encouraging.

Notes

1 Special appreciation is expressed to Dr. John P. Nelson (USAF colonel, retired), former chief of the USAF Family Advocacy Division, who provided valuable consultation to the authors in this analysis. In addition, the significant contribution of Dr. William B. Ware, Distinguished Professor, School of Education, University of North Carolina at Chapel Hill, is also acknowledged. Dr. Ware served as a consultant on the project, performed the statistical analysis, and helped to prepare a presentation summary from the analysis. An earlier version of this chapter was presented at the 2004 Annual Conference of the National Council on Family Relations in Orlando, FL. The views and opinions contained in this chapter are those of the authors and should not be construed as official Department of the Air Force position, policy, or decision, unless so designated by other authorized documents.
2 See Bowen et al. (2003) for details about this overall analysis strategy and sequence.

References

Anderson, J.C., and Gerbing, D.W. (1988) "Structural equation modeling in practice: A review and recommended two-step approach." *Psychological Bulletin,* 103: 411–23.

Armed Forces Health Surveillance Center (2012) *Medical Surveillance Monthly Report.* June, p. 19.

Booth, B., Segal, M.W., and Bell, D.B., with Martin, J.A., Ender, M.G., and Nelson, J. (2007) *What We Know About Army Families,* 2007 update. Fairfax, VA: Caliber.

Bowen, G.L., and Martin, J.A. (2011) "The resiliency model of role performance for service members, veterans, and their families: A focus on social connections and individual assets." *Journal of Human Behavior in the Social Environment,* 21: 162–78.

Bowen, G.L., Mancini, J.A., Martin, J.A., Ware, W.B., and Nelson, J.P. (2003) "Promoting the adaptation of military families: An empirical test a community practice model." *Family Relations,* 52: 33–44.

Bowen, G.L., Martin, J.A., and Mancini, J.A. (1999) *Communities in Blue for the 21st Century.* Fairfax, VA: Caliber.

Bowen, G.L., Martin, J.A., and Mancini, J.A. (2013) "The resilience of military families: Theoretical perspectives." In M.A. Fine and F.D. Fincham (eds.) *Family Theories: A content-based approach.* New York: Routlege, pp. 419–38.

Bowen, G.L., Martin, J.A., Liston, B.J., and Nelson, J.P. (2009) "Building community capacity in the U.S. Air Force: The community readiness consultant model." In A.R. Roberts (ed.) *Social Workers' Desk Reference* (2nd edn.). New York: Springer, pp. 912–17.

Bowen, G.L., Martin, J.A., Mancini, J.A., and Nelson, J.P. (2000) "Community capacity: Antecedents and consequences." *Journal of Community Practice,* 8: 1–21.

Caliber Associates (2000) *1999–2000 Air Force Community Needs Assessment.* Fairfax, VA: Caliber.

Clark, M.C., Nicholas, J.M., Wassira, L.N., and Gutierrez A.P. (2013) "Psychological and biological indicators of depression in the caregiving population." *Biological Research for Nursing,* 15: 112–21.

Dooley, D., Prause, J., and Ham-Rowbottom, K.A. (2000) "Underemployment and depression: Longitudinal relationships." *Journal of Health & Social Behavior*, 41: 421–36.

Golder, S., Connell, C.M., and Sullivan, T.P. (2012) "Psychological distress and substance use among community-recruited women currently victimized by intimate partners: A latent class analysis and examination of between-class differences." *Violence against Women*, 18: 934–57.

Herrero, J., and Meneses, J. (2006) "Short web-based versions of the perceived stress (PSS) and Center for Epidemiological Studies-Depression (CESD) scales: A comparison to pencil and paper responses among Internet users." *Computers in Human Behavior*, 22: 830–46.

Hoge, C.W., Lesikar, S.E., Guevara, R., Lange, J., Brundage, J.F., Engel, C.C., Messer, S.C., and Orman, D.T. (2002) "Mental disorders among U.S. military personnel in the 1990s: Association with high levels of health care utilization and early military attrition." *American Journal of Psychiatry*, 159: 1576–83.

Huebner, A.J., Mancini, J.A., Bowen, G.L., and Orthner, D.K. (2009) "Shadowed by war: Building community capacity to support military families." *Family Relations*, 58: 216–28.

Mancini, J.A., and Bowen, G.L. (2009) "Community resilience: A social organization theory of action and change." In J.A. Mancini and K.A. Roberto (eds.) *Pathways of Human Development: Explorations of change*. Lanham, MD: Lexington Books, pp. 245–65.

Mancini, J.A., and Bowen, G.L. (2013) "Families and communities: A social organization theory of action and change." In G.W. Peterson and K.R. Bush (eds.) *Handbook of Marriage and the Family* (3rd edn.). New York: Springer, pp. 781–813.

Mancini, J.A., Bowen, G.L., and Martin, J.A. (2005) "Community social organization: A conceptual linchpin in examining families in the context of communities." *Family Relations*, 54: 570–82.

Mancini, J.A., Martin, J.A., and Bowen, G.L. (2003) "Community capacity." In T.P. Gullotta and M. Bloom (eds.) *Encyclopedia of Primary Prevention and Health Promotion*. New York: Kluwer Academic/Plenum, pp. 319–30.

Mancini, J.A., Nelson, J.P., Bowen, G.L., and Martin, J.A. (2006) "Preventing intimate partner violence: A community capacity approach." *Journal of Aggression, Maltreatment & Trauma*, 13: 203–27.

Martin, J.A. (2004) "Depression as an indicator of health and well-being in the context of the community capacity model." Paper presented at the 66th Annual Conference of the National Council on Family Relations, November 19, Orlando, FL.

Martin, J.A., and Bowen, G.L. (2003) *2002 Air Force Community Assessment: Reference Matrix*. Doc. No. F41622–03-M-1026, San Antonio, TX: Brooks Air Force Base (AFMOA/SGZF).

Mastroianni, G.R., and Scott, W.J. (2011) "Reframing suicide in the military." *Parameters*, 41(2): 6–21.

Norton, R. (1983) "Measuring marital quality: A critical look at the dependent variable." *Journal of Marriage and the Family*, 45: 141–51.

Pearlin, L., and Johnson, J. (1977) "Marital status, life-strains and depression." *American Sociological Review*, 42: 704–15.

Ross, C.E., and Mirowsky, J. (1989) "Explaining the social patterns of depression: Control and problem solving or support and talking?" *Journal of Health & Social Behavior*, 30: 206–19.

Small, S., and Supple, A. (2001) "Communities as systems: Is a community more than the sum of its parts?" In A. Booth and A. Crouter (eds.) *Does It Take a Village? Community effects on children, adolescents, and families.* Mahwah, NJ: Lawrence Erlbaum, pp. 161–74.

Tanielian, T., and Jaycox, L.H. (2008) *Invisible Wounds of War: Psychological and cognitive injuries, their consequences, and services to assist recovery.* Santa Monica, CA: RAND Corporation.

Williams, T.T., Mance, G., Caldwell, C.H., and Antonucci, C. (2012) "The role of prenatal stress and maternal emotional support on the postpartum depressive symptoms of African American adolescent fathers." *Journal of Black Psychology*, 38: 455–70.

Wood, A.M., Taylor, P.J., and Joseph, S. (2010) "Does the CES-D measure a continuum from depression to happiness? Comparing substantive and artifactual models." *Psychiatry Research*, 177: 120–3.

14 The influence of the primary social environment on members of the Slovenian Armed Forces

Jelena Juvan and Janja Vuga

Introduction

On the one hand, work represents an important part of a person's life with respect to financial, material, and personal aspects. It enables a better quality of life and influences self-esteem. On the other, the primary social environment (that is, family and friends) plays an inherent part in the formation of one's identity. It is therefore important to balance life and work in order to avoid possible work–life conflict. Regardless of the type of employment, the nature and intensity of the work, or demographic characteristics of the employees and other factors, conflict between work and life occurs in all organizations. However, as we will discuss in the next section, the military organization is exceptional in terms of demands on its members and the potential for work–life conflict.

The issue of work–life conflict is important for members of the Slovenian Armed Forces (SAF) and their family members. The SAF is professionalized, frequently deploys to peace support operations (PSOs), participates in various joint trainings abroad, and expects a high degree of loyalty from its members. By most definitions, Slovenia falls into the category of young and small countries (Grizold and Vegič, 2001; Jelušič, 2007; Zupančič and Udovič, 2011), with armed forces corresponding to its size. The SAF comprises some 7,600 members and, among European countries, has one of the highest proportions of female military personnel (approximately 15 percent). Only two decades old, the SAF is still developing, with the current worldwide economic crisis strongly influencing its functioning. Owing to the financial crisis and mandated public savings, the SAF faced major budgetary cuts that endangered its existence. Under current conditions, family support programs have been left underdeveloped and underfinanced.

We analyzed data collected from four different studies in seeking to answer the question: to what degree are SAF members supported by their families and their primary environment when fulfilling their duties in the military organization at home and during deployment?

The analyses were guided by three research questions stemming from the theoretical assumptions that will be introduced shortly, regarding "greedy institutions," family support during deployments, and the importance of families for the effective functioning of service members and the military organization. The main purpose of the empirical analyses was to test whether the theoretical assumptions also apply to the SAF and its members.

First, we were trying to answer the research question of whether SAF members feel the same level of loyalty to the military organization as to their families, or whether the military organization might take priority.

Second, based on previous empirical findings, it was noted that SAF members are deployed on the foundation of strong support from their primary environment. In what ways does a deployment influence this strong support? Does it diminish the support over time?

Third, we were interested in the question of whether SAF members and their families consider institutional military support important: do they believe it to be necessary?

Greedy institutions

Not only do individuals in traditional family structures face the challenges of balancing work and family life, but also individuals who are single or childless experience these issues: "Balancing professional and family obligations is much more than just an arithmetic function of work demands, family needs, and the number of hours in a workday" (Juvan, 2008: 67). Demands of modern society, such as longer working hours and high female employment ratios, force individuals to interweave personal and professional lives. In most cases, individuals successfully achieve a manageable level of balance. Problems arise if institutions' fundamental conditions for existence and operation are complete loyalty and dedication of their members. Coser (1974) defined such institutions as "greedy." The concept of "greedy institutions" refers to organizations or groups that place high demands on individuals and usually requires a person's full attention. According to Coser (1974: 4), greedy institutions "seek exclusive and undivided loyalty and they attempt to reduce the claims of competing roles and status positions on those they wish to encompass in their boundaries. Their demands are omnivorous."

The demand to sacrifice a personal life toward achieving military goals is probably the greediest demand. Problems arise when the demands of two greedy institutions conflict, which may also lead to strong work–life conflict. As Segal (1986) noted, the military organization and the family, in their exceptional forms, do not have all of the characteristics of Coser's greedy institutions, but they do fit the definition well enough to be so-called. The survival of the military and the family strongly depends on the loyalty of their members. Soeters, Winslow, and Weibull (2003) came to similar conclusions.

What makes an institution greedy is also the dependence of its survival or operation on the complete loyalty of its members. Whereas every institution or group places certain demands and requirements on its members, the military organization is exceptional in terms of demands on its members and, indirectly, their family members. These include, among other things, irregular working hours, unpredictable work tasks, frequent moves, long absences from home and family, and above all, the risk to sacrifice one's life to benefit a country. Although other professions may impose similar demands, the specific risk involved of sacrificing one's life is the factor that makes the military profession one of the greediest of all. However, families also place high demands on their members. Family members are expected to be emotionally devoted, to express love towards other family members, to identify with the family as a whole, and to fulfill their roles within the family system. According to Coser (1974) and Segal (1986), both the family and the military organization are greedy institutions. To a large degree, the family influences individual's decisions regarding employment in a certain organization and the sacrifices that he or she is willing to make.

In Slovenian society, the family has high value (Musek, 2003; Toš, 2003). It is highly esteemed in the everyday life of an individual and represents an influencing factor in decision-making, particularly in the case of employment in a military organization, which is specific in terms of its demands compared to other types of employment. Several studies that are presented later in this chapter demonstrated that SAF members place the highest trust in their families.

When studying the role of the primary environment (defined as one's spouse, relatives, and friends) in the task performance of SAF personnel, the concept of "social support" arises as one of the theoretical concepts that might help to explain the work–life conflict experienced by SAF members and their families. Relationships within the family represent a large share of relationships within an individual's personal network (Musek, 2003; Toš, 2003) and the family remains of key importance for the individual, as well as for society. According to Dremelj (2003: 152): "Family is the fundamental institution of personal life, where the majority of social relationships important to an individual are formed." Close ties with the primary environment are considered a unique Slovenian characteristic. One does not expect high levels of institutional support (for example family support from the SAF), since individuals use their primary environment as a primary source for help and assistance. This unique national characteristic may explain the relationship between the SAF, military personnel, and their family members.

The importance of military families for work outcomes

The way in which family members adapt to the military lifestyle and their satisfaction with the treatment received from the military organization significantly impacts the readiness of the service members: "Soldiers who are worried about their families because the family is having difficulty and/or whose families are dissatisfied with life in the army will not perform well on the job" (Segal and Harris, 1993: 3). In addition, studies have stated that family issues not only reduce the military personnel's degree of readiness, but also may increase the danger of injuries or death in combat. Members of the military organization who are not sufficiently focused on their job for any reason, not only because of family issues, may be paying less attention in the battlefield and consequently will be more at risk of being wounded or killed. Concerns arising from family issues may also prove to be a source of serious stress and may compromise the service member's ability to participate in training in an appropriate manner. However, the most important is that worries may impede service members in carrying out their role in battle (Schneider and James, 1994). The effects of unresolved family issues may have potentially tragic consequences (Pincus et al., 2004) on both the battlefield and at home.

Here, we need to take into account two viewpoints: that of the commander, and that of the family. From the commander's viewpoint, worried service members may be easily distracted and thus have difficulties focusing in critical moments; from the family's viewpoint, unresolved issues may impede service members in performing their everyday family tasks. In noting these two viewpoints, Dandeker and colleagues (2006) conclude that the health and well-being of British military personnel are of key importance for the efficiency in military operations, with the well-being of their families representing an integral component.

Numerous studies conducted in the armed forces of various countries have confirmed the assumptions that family constitutes an important factor influencing the actions and readiness of an individual or unit. Moreover, satisfaction on the part of the family significantly impacts service members' decisions to leave the armed forces or to continue a military career (Bowen, 1989). "Family life affects a service member's military performance during peacetime and during combat" (Schneider and James, 1994: 20), and partner's satisfaction with the quality of military life actually acts as a direct indicator of the partner's support for a job in the military (Pittman and Orthner, 1988).

Retention also negatively correlates with absences from the family. The members of the armed forces that are absent from their families for longer periods of time are less likely to want to continue working in the military. The intention to continue serving the military positively correlates with members' perception of the quality of life in the military community (Segal and Segal, 2003). Various family variables are likely to impact service members' readiness. Service members' perceptions of the degree to which their commander supports and cares for their families has been shown to have a strong impact on unit readiness (Orthner and Pittman, 1986; Rohall, Segal, and Segal, 1999). An important finding from Segal and Harris (1993) is that the capacity of the family to adjust to the military way of life depends on the level to which the military provides official, as well as unofficial, support to the families of its members. The existence of family support groups and other forms of organized family activities has a direct positive impact on unit readiness.

Moelker and van der Kloet (2003) came to similar conclusions regarding the impact of the spouse on the views of military personnel of the Dutch Armed Forces. Similarly, in a study among U.S. military personnel, Bourg and Segal (1999) found that the attitude of the spouse towards military service impacts the recruitment process, personnel retention, and the morale and loyalty of the members towards the military organization. It was precisely the finding regarding loyalty that proved to be extremely important for further studies on military families. Perceptions of the level of family support provided by the military organization affect families' satisfaction with the military way of life and facilitate family adjustment in case of absences resulting from participation in military missions. The perceived level of interference of the military service with family obligations also influences spouses' satisfaction with the military way of life. Bourg and Segal (1999: 636) draw the following conclusion:

> The evidence suggests that married military members' attitudes toward the military organization are influenced by their spouses' satisfaction and commitment, which are shaped by perceptions of the organization's support for families as well as the level of military interference with family needs and demands.

The SAF's institutional family support

When, in July 2007, the new Service in the Slovenian Armed Forces Act was adopted, much was expected from it, especially in the field of family support. Actually, sections determining the rights of SAF members' families and the level of institutional support present a novel step forward from previous conditions. However, some solutions presented in the Act can be considered deficient, for example its definition of "family members" as the "spouse, married and non-married, spouse in a homosexual partnership and children, biological and adoptive until adult age" (article 76). The first main problem with this definition is its exclusion of the parents of SAF members. Research on the participation of the SAF in peace operations (Jelušič et al., 2003, 2005, 2008) shows an important share of military personnel between the ages of 20 and 24, who are single, do not have children, and still live at home with their parents. Thus parents constitute an important part of these service members' families.

The second main disadvantage of the Act is that care for military families is organized as part of the "comprehensive care" for the soldiers and not as a separate care for families. Comprehensive care includes activities that are not implemented directly through command and control, but are necessary for the undisturbed functioning of the military organization, including health care, psychological care, social care, legal help, legal counseling, religious care, and sports and leisure activities (article 76). Family members are entitled to only some parts of the comprehensive care. For example, with respect to health care, they are entitled to attend some lectures on healthy living. What is more important is that family members are entitled to professional psychological help and counseling before and during the absence of service members resulting from missions abroad.

The main novelty of the 2007 Act is that families of the SAF members are mentioned in an official document for the first time. The list of beneficiaries of comprehensive care is extended to include families. The Act also provides for social care as a new benefit not only for the families, but also for the service members themselves. Furthermore, family members are entitled to receive religious counseling and to use the SAF's sport and other recreational facilities; these benefits existed in previous Acts.

A special part of the new Act refers to the rights of families in situations in which service members lose their life while on duty. Families are entitled to financial help and reimbursement of funeral costs. Families of a deceased member can also receive psychological help and counseling, scholarships for children, free legal counseling, and preferential treatment of an unemployed spouse or child when applying for a job at the Slovenian Ministry of Defense (MoD). They also have the right to use the SAF's holiday accommodations for ten years after the death of a serviceman.

During deployments, family members of SAF personnel receive support and assistance, depending on the type of deployment (international headquarters or peace operations and other international missions). If military personnel are stationed at international headquarters, the SAF are obliged to organize visits home at least twice a year, to ensure proper housing facilities for service members and their families, to ensure proper schooling abroad for service members' children, and to help service members' spouses to search for employment. It can be noted that some of the solutions provided for under the Act are highly unrealistic and are undoubtedly out of reach of the SAF and Slovenian MoD. For example, the Act does not provide an answer to how the Slovenian MoD can ensure a spouse's employment in Brussels or Naples.

While participating in peace operations and other missions abroad, the SAF is obliged to assure communication between deployed service members and their families, to arrange free visits home once in a three-month period, to assist with nursing or schooling for children, to take care of a disabled family member, and to provide assistance to an unemployed family member in finding employment. A special "comprehensive care unit" was established in order to ensure that the provisions of the Act were put into practice. Unfortunately, it can be noted that comprehensive care for service members and their families is still underdeveloped at time of writing.

Some years after the adoption of the Service in the Slovenian Armed Forces Act 2007, it is possible to conclude that all executive Acts dealing with family support programs have remained stuck in the wheels of unsuc-cessful harmonization. There were two main reasons for the obstacles to the implementation of the 2007 Act. The first and most important has been the global financial crisis and subsequent economic recession, which in 2008 prevented all forms of new expenditure. The second main reason has been the opposition of civil servants in different ministries and offices, who were supposed to coordinate the proper wording of the executive Acts: they opposed any differences within the almost unique public sector by ques-tioning why military families or the families of SAF members should warrant special treatment.

Service members have regularly complained that the benefits provided for under the Act have never been implemented. In the absence of institu-tional solutions, the SAF continued with those support activities that can be implemented directly through the command and control chain, and which rarely require any additional expenditures, such as the provision of information technology support and communication lines between the sol-diers on missions and their families. Military chaplains continue their duty of care for SAF members and their family members, if requested. Military psychologists organize courses on family reunion after long absences for members of the SAF and their families, and family members are entitled to seek professional psychological help and counseling before and during the absence of service members resulting from a mission abroad. All other benefits that presupposed the involvement of other ministries and offices outside the MoD remain blocked.

Empirical analyses

We analyzed data from four studies to examine family support. The studies were conducted by the Defense Research Center of the Faculty of Social Sciences, University of Ljubljana, between 2003 and 2008. A total of 4,211 standardized questionnaires were completed and 232 structured interviews with SAF members were conducted. When studying and analyzing military families in Slovenia, it is important to note that, in Slovenia, the system of military organization functions the same as any other civil organization or company in terms of relationships towards the families of its members – that is, it does not provide housing facilities (at or near a base), military kindergartens, or schools.

- The study of the "human factor in the military system" (December 2005 to March 2006) was conducted at SAF barracks. The predominant age group among the respondents was 26–30 years (26 percent). The majority of the respondents were male (84 percent); one in six respondents were female (16 percent). The majority of the respondents were childless (41 percent), followed by those with two children (30 percent).

- The studies of the "SAF in peace support operations" (January 2003 to October 2003) and of the "SAF in peace support operations – a social science analysis of factors of influence on peace support operations" (July 2003 to January 2005) were carried out among the population of ten Slovenian contingents carrying out their tasks in the PSO in Bosnia and Herzegovina – that is, the Multinational Battle Group (MNBG) and the Multinational Specialized Unit (MSU) of the NATO Stabilization Force (SFOR). The majority of the respondents were between 26 and 30 years of age (37 percent); all of them were male. The majority were childless (57 percent) or had only one child (20 percent).
- Within the framework of a "social science analysis of the operation of the SAF in missions and at headquarters on international duties at PSO" in the NATO Kosovo Force (KFOR) (February 2007 to August 2008), three Slovenian contingents were surveyed. The majority of the respondents were between 26 and 30 years of age (45 percent) and were male (94 percent), with only 1 in 16 being female (6 percent). The majority were childless (72 percent) and had been deployed to the operation for the first time (67 percent).

The data discussed in this chapter were gathered using a quantitative methodology. Bivariate and multivariate analyses have been performed using SPSS statistical analysis software, to analyze the data collected through standardized questionnaires in these four studies.

Results

Work–family demands

Among a list of social institutions on which people rely and which they trust in everyday life, SAF members placed the greatest degree of trust in their families, with a mean score of 3.60 on a scale ranging from 1 (*do not trust them at all*) to 4 (*trust them completely*). Given the results, we can conclude that they consider family and relatives to be very important, which means that the family represents a factor that cannot be disregarded. A frequency distribution of the responses showed that 96 percent of the respondents "considerably" and "completely" trusted their family and relatives. This high level of trust indicates that the family has an important position in service members' lives. Service members rely on their families and consequently probably expect to be supported by them.

With respect to the relationship between the family and the military organization, we analyzed the impact of SAF members' work obligations on their families' lives and vice versa. To only a small degree did SAF members perceive the family as a factor that causes stress or hinders performance at work: more than 70 percent of the respondents *disagreed* with the claims implying a negative effect of the family on work. At the same time, only 40 percent disagreed with the claims that implied a negative effect of work on family life, while nearly half of the surveyed SAF members (47 percent) felt a negative effect of the job on the family. According to Černič-Istenič and Knežević-Hočevar (2006), SAF members find it somewhat easier to balance work and family obligations compared to those employed in civil organizations or companies.

To examine the demands placed on SAF members by the military organization and by the family conflict, we carried out a detailed analysis of certain claims that defined the members' perception of demands placed by both institutions. The paired *t*-test method was used to analyze what type of conflict is most prevalent among service members: work–family conflict, or family–work conflict. Both were evaluated on the same five-point scale ranging from 1 (*lowest level of agreement*) to 5 (*highest level of agreement*). We noted a significant difference – that is, that SAF members lacked time for family obligations as a result of work obligations (mean = 3.07) more frequently than vice versa (mean = 2.02). SAF members perceived certain burdens in the effect of their job on family life, primarily stress and lack of time, while a negative impact of the family on work obligations was not detected. It can also be noted that service members put their work obligations prior to family obligations.

We further noted that there were no significant differences regarding marital status in the case of the effect of work obligations on obligations at home. The perception of the effect among married members or those living in civil or cohabiting partnerships (representing 55 percent of the sample) differed negligibly from that among members who were not cohabitating, or who were single or widowed (representing 44 percent of the sample). We further used the paired *t*-test method to examine whether work obligations represent a greater source of stress to the SAF members than family issues, and the results revealed significant differences in perception of stress caused by family/military. Both were evaluated on the same five-point scale ranging from 1 (*lowest level of agreement*) to 5 (*highest level of agreement*). Members did not feel that family issues caused stress that interfered with their work (mean = 1.62), whereas certain tensions can be noted in the direction from the work to the family (mean = 2.74).

Furthermore, we assessed the relationship between the family, the military organization, and free time on the basis of the analysis of the question regarding the difficulty of balancing work, family, and free time. Respondents were offered a choice between four levels of difficulty balancing work and nonwork time, ranging from 1 (*many difficulties*), through 2 (*considerable difficulties*) and 3 (*few difficulties*), to 4 (*no difficulties*). SAF members did not perceive balancing work, family, and free time as very problematic; the respondents evaluated the difficulty of balancing these domains with an average of 2.71. Twenty percent of the respondents said that they faced no difficulties balancing obligations, 42 percent faced minor difficulties, 25 percent faced considerable difficulties, and 12 percent faced major difficulties in balancing work and nonwork obligations. There were no significant differences between those members who were married or lived in other partnerships and those who did not live with a partner or were single. This suggests that marital status does not significantly influence the perceived level of difficulties balancing work and nonwork obligations.

Also, no significant differences were displayed between male and female personnel, although women experienced slightly fewer problems than men. The analysis did reveal differences between age groups, with older SAF members (particularly those aged between 55 and 60) having the least issues balancing work, family, and free time. Most difficulties were reported in the age groups 21–25 and 31–35. Furthermore, the analyses showed that having children influenced the level of difficulty experienced in balancing work and nonwork time. Members with no children or only one child predominantly answered, "I have few difficulties balancing work and nonwork time" (45 and 47 percent, respectively), while members with three or more children most often reported "considerable issues" (39 percent). On the basis of the results regarding age and having children, we can assume that military personnel aged 21–25 include inexperienced employees who are new to balancing work, family, and free time, while those aged 31–35 are members with small children, who therefore have more concerns and demands on their time than childless members or members with older children.

Support during deployment

We assessed the degree to which military personnel received family and institutional (that is, military) support during their deployments. We used data from all four studies. The questionnaires were filled out by service members at three points in time: before the peace support operation (PSO), approximately halfway through the deployment, and after their return home.

Service members' perceptions of their social environments' (defined by their partners, parents, and friends) attitude towards deployment were measured with three items. Respondents expressed their level of agreement with the following claims: "My partner agrees with my deployment on a mission"; "My parents agree with my deployment on a mission"; "My friends agree with my deployment on a mission." The answers were given on a scale ranging from 1 (*I completely disagree*) to 5 (*I completely agree*). Parents proved to be particularly important when contingents were primarily composed of members younger than 25, who were on their first mission abroad, and who often were unmarried and childless. In that case, the primary sources of concern for service personnel were the parents, and not the spouse and children. The data showed that military personnel were going on missions with the perception of relatively high level of agreement and support received from friends (59 percent), and slightly lower agreement and support from parents (46 percent) and partners (45 percent). Respondents could declare that they had no parents, partner, or friends. The percentages are the sum of answers "support" and "complete support." Friends appeared to be most supportive, which can be partly explained by the formation of a so-called "military subculture," or a circle of friends that is indirectly or directly connected to the military system (Juvan, 2009). Friends of the soldiers also come from the civil environment, but because of the military subculture, most of their friends are from the military. It needs to be taken into account that the social group of friends is that which suffers the least from a longer absence of one of its members. The impact of the absence on partners and parents is much greater.

In all contingents, we noted the primary environment being less supportive during the mission and growing in support following the return home (Jelušič et al., 2008). It is important to note that the perceived decline in agreement with participation in the mission and the decline in support is usually the highest among partners. The long-term absence causes the most problems for them, especially if they have more than one child. However, the difference in support at different points in time (before, during, and after deployment) was not statistically significant in any of the analyzed groups.

To examine support provided by the SAF to its members and their families, we used the newest data, acquired by measuring opinions of service members in the 17th Contingent of the SAF in Kosovo. Slightly more than 20 percent of the respondents believed that not enough time was made available for the family prior to deployment, while 41 percent of the members claimed the opposite. The question remains whether it is at all possible to determine a sufficient amount of time spent with the family, or would some members and their families always feel that there was "not enough time"? Especially before the deployment, service members must attend preparatory exercises, medical examinations, and psychological tests, which influence families' and service members' perceptions of the time available to them.

The respondents expressed their opinions regarding the institutional support from the SAF to their families during their deployment. Additional interviews conducted during the deployment and after the return home confirmed that it would be desirable to provide certain assistance to families during the members' deployments. The commonest and most basic form of assistance that could be provided by the SAF would be a telephone number that individuals could call in case of psychological issues or concerns arising as a result of the partner's absence. According to service members, the SAF should first and foremost ensure that families are kept informed about developments on an international PSO. The SAF should also organize military centers for family assistance and support in times of deployment. It is evident that, for the majority of SAF members, the definition of a family includes not only the partner and children, but also the parents. According to the respondents, deployments affect family members to a higher degree than it affects the service member: 35 percent of the service members believed that their families suffered because of the separation during the deployment, while 26 percent believed that they suffered themselves because of the family separation. It is interesting to note that financial bonuses represent a very important factor during deployment (Juvan and Vuga, 2011), but the majority of service members (51 percent) did not believe that the money earned could help to solve the family issues arising as a result of their absence.

Discussion and conclusion

In 1991, Slovenia became an independent country with its own Armed Forces (the SAF). Therefore 1991 is the most important milestone in the history of Slovenia as a state. Since 1991, not much institutional or research attention has been given to military families in Slovenia, even though the SAF has been strengthening its cooperation in PSOs in various crisis areas since 1997. The SAF transitioned from conscription to professional force, and has been enhancing its international activities since joining NATO in 2004, which may lead to combat operations in the future. As an important factor in Slovenian society, family is a factor worth taking into account in understanding the relationship with employment, especially in the case of employment within a military organization, which makes specific demands compared to other organizations.

In this chapter, we addressed and answered three research questions by means of empirical data analyses. First, the analyses showed that SAF members believe that work obligations come before family obligations. Primarily, they feel loyal to the military organization and its obligations, with family and family obligations taking second place. However, it must be noted that work obligations are likely to come first only among single service personnel, or service personnel whose spouses take responsibility for the family obligations. Regarding soldiers' perceptions of work–life conflict, the analyses showed that SAF members do perceive certain burdens in the effect of their job on family life, primarily stress and lack of time, while a negative impact of the family on work obligations was not detected. The latter has also been explained in the context of male perceptions of the family–work relationship by Sinacore and Akcali (2000), who found that satisfaction and good family relationships have only a limited effect on work satisfaction of male personnel. Military organizations remain staffed primarily with male service members. In the case of the SAF, the share of female members is relatively high – but it is not sufficiently high to effect swift changes in masculine behavioral and performance patterns. When compared to civilian employment, SAF members seem to find it somewhat easier to balance work and family obligations when they are not being deployed. Work obligations of individual soldiers strongly depend on their position in the military hierarchy: the obligations of a high-ranking officer cannot be compared to those of a soldier. However, in general, working hours in the SAF are strictly defined, from 7 a.m. until 3 p.m., which gives military personnel plenty of time to pick up their children from kindergartens and schools, and to spend quality time with their family members during the afternoons. There are, however, units that must perform weekly 24-hour duty and participate regularly in training, which puts these service members in quite different situations regarding the family obligations. The lack of time for the family is also intensified before and during the deployments.

Second, it was noted that SAF members are deployed on a foundation of strong support from their primary environment. In what ways does deployment influence this strong support? Does support decrease over time? The analyses showed that deployments did not have a strong negative influence on the level of support coming from their families. Even during deployment, SAF members receive fairly strong support from their primary social environment. It is true that family issues arise during deployments, which cause the members stress, especially when families are facing difficulties or extreme situations; this does mean that pressure from the families becomes stronger during deployment. However, this does not significantly influence the support that the family offers. Even though support remains strong during the deployment, some opposition can be identified, which is strongest among partners and parents, and weakest among friends, corresponding to expectations that friends represent the part of the social environment that is least influenced by longer absences.

Third, do SAF members and their families consider institutional support to be important? Do they believe it to be necessary? Certainly, members and their families find the psychosocial forms of support provided by the military organization important – but what is really worrying is that this type of support is not yet functioning efficiently in the SAF. Based on the empirical analyses, we can identify several areas of family care that need to be strengthened on the SAF's and MoD's behalf. First, the definition of the "family" has to be widened. It is evident that, for the majority of SAF members, the definition of "a family" includes not only the partner and children, but also parents. Furthermore, the SAF should include the members' partners in preparatory activities prior to deployment on a PSO. Some special courses for the better preparation of families for deployment are necessary. The SAF should also keep the partners and parents informed regarding developments on the PSO, taking into account the fact that partners and parents are among those most affected by members' work obligations. Furthermore, the SAF should provide centers to assist families during the members' absences. During deployments, families can feel alone, having no one to whom to turn for help or simply socially. In those cases, family centers may be useful.

The primary environment of SAF members must not be ignored. It is of extreme importance given that the family represents the most important source of social support for military personnel, at home, as well as on missions abroad. The issue of families of SAF members has long been prominent, but the austerity measures to which the global financial crisis and subsequent recession led have constrained the SAF's good intentions. It is now unlikely that the institutional attitude toward families will change in the near future – no matter how important the family and primary environment proves to be for military personnel.

References

Bourg, C., and Segal, M.W. (1999) "The impact of military supportive policies and practices on organizational commitment to the Army." *Armed Forces & Society*, 24(4): 633–52.

Bowen, G.L. (1989) "Satisfaction with family life in the military." *Armed Forces & Society*, 15(4): 571–92.

Coser, A.L. (1974) *Greedy Institutions: Patterns of undivided commitment.* New York: Free Press.

Černič Istenič, M., and Knežević Hočevar, D. (2006) "Usklajevanje dela in družine v Slovenski vojski." *Bilten Slovenske vojske*, 4: 215–37.

Dandeker, C., French, C., Birtles, C., and Wessely, S. (2006) "Deployment experiences of British Army wives before, during and after deployment: Satisfaction with military life and use of support networks." Paper #RTO-MP-HFM-134 [online], available from http://ftp.rta.nato.int/public/PubFullText/RTO/MP/RTO -MP-HFM-134/MP-HFM-134-38.pdf [accessed June 13, 2007].

Dremelj, P. (2003) "Sorodstvene vezi kot vir socialne opore posameznikov." *Družboslovne razprave*, 43: 149–70.

Grizold, A., and Vegič, V. (2001) "Small states and alliances: The case of Slovenia." In E. Reiter and H. Gärtner (eds.) *Small States and Alliances.* Heidelberg/New York: Physica-Verlag (Springer Verlag), pp. 145–94.

Jelušič, L. (2007) "Cultural challenges for small countries in mission abroad." In C.M. Coops and T. Szvircsev Tresch (eds.) *Cultural Challenges in Military Operations.* Rome: NATO Defense College, pp. 36–50.

Jelušič, L., Garb, M., Grošelj, K., Juvan, J., and Vuga, J. (2008) "Družboslovna analiza delovanja slovenske vojske v misijah in v poveljstvih na mednarodnih dolžnostih: zaključno poročilo." Defense Studies Research Center, Faculty of Social Sciences, University of Ljubljana.

Jelušič, L., Vegič, V., Garb, M., and Prebilič, V. (2005) "Raziskovalni projekt Slovenska vojska v mirovnih operacijah: Družboslovna analiza dejavnikov vpliva na mirovno delovanje SV – Zaključno poročilo." Defense Studies Research Center, Faculty of Social Sciences, University of Ljubljana.

Jelušič, L., Vegič, V., Garb, M., Trifunovič, J., Grošelj, K., and Ober, K. (2003) "Raziskovalni projekt Slovenska vojska v mirovnih operacijah: Zaključno poročilo." Defense Studies Research Center, Faculty of Social Sciences, University of Ljubljana.

Juvan, J. (2008) "Vojaške družine: usklajevanje zahtev med družino in vojaško organizacijo." Unpublished Ph.D. dissertation, Faculty of Social Sciences, University of Ljubljana.

Juvan, J. (2009) "Širše okolje misije: Skrbi med misijo, kaj se dogaja doma z ženo in starši." *Slovenska vojska*, 17(13): 20–1.

Juvan, J., and Vuga J. (2011) "What motivates Slovenian peacekeepers?" *International Peacekeeping,* 18(1): 96–109.

Moelker, R., and van der Kloet, I. (2003) "Military families and the armed forces: A two-sided affair?" In G. Caforio (ed.) *Handbook of the Sociology of the Military.* New York/Boston/Dordrecht/London/Moscow: Kluwer Academic/Plenum Publishers, pp. 201–23.

Musek, J. (2003) "Raziskovanje vrednot v Sloveniji in vrednotni univerzum Slovencev." In *Pogovor o vrednotah.* Ljubljana: Urad predsednika Republike Slovenije, pp. 151–67.

Orthner, K.D., and Pittman, J.F. (1986) "Family contributions to work commitment." *Journal of Marriage & Family,* 48: 573–81.

Pincus, H.S., House, R., Christenson, J., and Adler, L.E. (2004) "The emotional cycle of deployment: A military family perspective." *Hooah4Health* [online], available from http://www.hooah4health.com/deployment/familymatters/emotionalcycle.htm [accessed March 30, 2007].

Pittman, J.F., and Orthner, D.K. (1988) "Predictors of spousal support for the work commitment of husbands." *Journal of Marriage & Family,* 50: 417–27.

Rohall, D.E., Segal, M.W., and Segal, D.R. (1999) "Examining the importance of organizational supports on family adjustment to army life in a period of increasing separation." *Journal of Political & Military Sociology,* 27: 49–65.

Schneider, J.R., and James, A.M. (1994) "Military families and combat readiness." In R. Zajtchuk (ed.) *Military Psychiatry: Preparing in peace for war.* Washington, D.C.: Office of the Surgeon General, Department of the Army, pp. 19–30.

Segal, D.R., and Segal, M.W. (2003) "Implications for military families of changes in the armed forces of the United States." In G. Caforio (ed.) *Handbook of the Sociology of the Military.* New York/Boston/Dordrecht/London/Moscow: Kluwer Academic/Plenum Publishers, pp. 225–33.

Segal, M. W. (1986) "The military and the family as greedy institutions.". *Armed Forces and Society.* 13(1): 9–38.

Segal, M.W., and Harris, J.J. (1993) *What We Know about Army Families.* Alexandria, VA: U.S. Army Research Institute for the Behavioral and Social Sciences.

Sinacore, A.L., and Akcali, O.F. (2000) "Men in families: Job satisfaction and self-esteem." *Journal of Career Development,* 27(1): 1–13.

Soeters, J., Winslow, D., and Weibull A. (2003) "Military culture." In G. Caforio (ed.) *Handbook of the Sociology of the Military.* New York/Boston/Dordrecht/London/Moscow: Kluwer Academic/Plenum Publishers, pp. 237–54.

Toš, N. (2003) "Pogovor o vrednotah." In *Pogovor o vrednotah.* Ljubljana: Urad predsednika Republike Slovenije, pp. 19–22.

Zupančič, R., and Udovič, B. (2011) "Lilliputian in a Goliath world: The preventive diplomacy of Slovenia in solving the question of Kosovo's independence." *Romanian Journal of Political Science,* 11(2): 39–80.

15 How do military families cope with multiple deployments abroad of loved ones?

The case of Belgium

Philippe Manigart, Valerian Lecoq, and Salvatore Lo Bue

Introduction

Compared to the Cold War period and, to a lesser extent, the era of the mass armed forces, there is a greater need for today's postmodern armies to provide psychosocial support to their personnel participating in military operations abroad and to their families at home. Since the end of the Cold War and even more so after 9/11, there has been a multiplication of crisis response operations carried out by multinational task forces all over the world for more or less extended periods.

In 2011, for instance, the Belgian Armed Forces deployed 776 service members in various operations – that is, 2.4 percent of personnel (totaling 32,182). Only 4 percent of these were female, which is slightly less than the percentage of women in the Belgian Defense as a whole.[1] Usually, service members are away from home for a period of four months; it is important also to take into account the time needed to prepare for the mission, which can vary from four to nine months. During this time, the service member can also be under a lot of pressure, therefore impacting on his or her family.

These extended crisis operations (Belgian troops have been deployed in Afghanistan since July 2003) imply much more frequent separations between military personnel and their families (Adams et al., 2011; Bartone and Bartone, 2005). With the use of more advanced technologies (such as night vision devices), the operational tempo of most of these new operations is much higher than before; soldiers very often operate on a 24-hour basis. The composition of most Western armed forces has also greatly evolved: the old institutional militaries mainly composed of (drafted) young, unmarried people have become occupational, professional organizations staffed by a greater proportion of soldiers who are older, married, and have children. This is particularly the case for the Belgian Armed Forces: for the period 2010–12, the average age of service members involved in operations abroad was 33.18 years (SD = 8.67) and ranged from 19 to 56.[2] Finally, as a result of the social-cultural evolution in Western societies, young people – and their families – are not only less used to the frugal, promiscuous lifestyle that still characterizes most of these military operations (living with others in gated communities for long periods of time), but also, for some, to exposure to death and traumatic events.

From a purely military management standpoint, therefore, the organization of psychosocial support for military personnel and their families has become a necessity, because in the short term the absence of such support negatively impacts the operational readiness of soldiers (Castro et al., 2000); in the longer term, it can have negative effects on recruitment and retention (Reed and Segal, 2000). As a consequence, in all postmodern military organizations, but to a varying degree, services and/or structures have been progressively developed – or adapted – to provide psychosocial support to military personnel in operations and to their families (Moelker, 2005).

Navies naturally were always involved in long-term missions overseas, cruising the oceans; for ground and air forces, this is relatively new. There is therefore an urgent need for scientific assessment not only of the working and effectiveness of the new support structures that have been put in place, but also of the expectations and demands of military personnel and their families. It is in this context that, in June 2005, the Adjunct Chief of Staff for Well-Being (ACOS-WB) – the service that, in the new structure of the Belgian Ministry of Defense (MoD), is responsible for the various dimensions of the well-being of military personnel and their dependents – asked the Department of Behavioral Sciences of the Royal Military Academy to commence a long-term scientific study on the well-being and psychosocial support of military personnel in operations abroad and their families. The aim of this research project was to understand how Belgian military personnel and their families live and experience a tour of duty before, during, and after crisis response operations.

The study started in October 2005 and ended in December 2009. It was carried out by a multidisciplinary team of psychologists and sociologists, and was divided into three parts. In the first phase, the provision of psychosocial support by the organization was assessed. This phase addressed questions such as: who are the various institutional actors? What are their responsibilities and mission? How does the psychosocial support system functions on a day-to-day basis at the level of the various branches and units?

In the second phase, the demand side (that is, the need for support) was analyzed. Military personnel who (at that time or in the recent past) participated in crisis response operations and members of their families were interviewed to examine what kind of social problems (for example management of their everyday lives, material difficulties) and psychological problems (including stress, relational difficulties) they faced before, during, and after long-term operations abroad. Furthermore, their satisfaction with the support provided, and their needs and expectations, were examined.

In the last step of the project, the fit between the (expressed) demand and the existing supply (provision) of support was assessed, on the basis of which specific recommendations were formulated in order to optimize the provision of psychosocial support to families.

The present chapter focuses on two small parts of the research project. First, it addresses how families were experiencing the departure of their loved ones and were coping with their absence during crisis support operations. Second, this chapter discusses to what extent the psychosocial support services provided at the time by the Belgian Defense were known and used by military families before, during, and after long-term operations abroad, and it assesses families' satisfaction with these structures.[3]

Methodology

The data presented in this chapter come from a 2007 cross-sectional postal survey of family members of military personnel who participated in long-term operations abroad (four months) in 2006 and 2007. The survey was carried out, at the request of the MoD and in close cooperation with the Department of Behavioral Sciences of the Royal Military Academy, by a research team of the universities of Ghent (for the Dutch-speaking part of the survey) and of Liege (for the French-speaking part) under a research contract from the Belgian Federal Science Policy Office. To construct the sample, all personnel from the Army, Air Force, and Medical Service who participated in one of the rotations of the three main long-term crisis response operations in which Belgium participated in 2006–07 – that is, the Kosovo Force (KFOR), the International Security Assistance Force (ISAF) in Afghanistan, and the United Nations Interim Force in Lebanon (UNIFIL) – were selected. The target population consisted of the (step)parents and (married or unmarried) partners named by this group of personnel as contact person in case of emergencies. The questionnaire was sent to 1,000 persons (500 French-speaking and 500 Dutch-speaking). The sampling design used was a stratified sample with unequal probabilities of selection. The stratification variable was the linguistic identity (French or Flemish). Within the French strata, all of the French-speaking persons falling into the sampling criteria (that is, kinship ties) were selected for inclusion. Within the Flemish strata, individuals were randomly selected (using systematic selection with a random start).[4] The overall response rate was 36 percent (31 percent among French-speaking respondents and 41 percent among Dutch-speaking ones), which is not a bad rate for this type of survey.[5] Nearly half (48 percent) of the respondents were married to the deployed service member, 18 percent were engaged to be married, 33 percent were the mother or father, and 1 percent had another relationship with the service member. Sixteen percent of the respondents were aged between 36 and 40. The distribution in the other age groups was as follows: 20–25 (6 percent); 26–30 (12 percent); 31–35 (13 percent); 41–45 (15 percent); 51–55 (15 percent); and 55+ (15 percent).

Families and their experience of operations

Before examining to what extent the psychosocial support services provided by the Belgian Defense were known and used by military personnel and their families before, during, and after long-term operations abroad, and how satisfied they were with the support structures and services, we first analyzed how families experienced these missions; more particularly, we analyzed whether these periods of separation represented a difficult time for them.

When a service member departs to operation, life continues for the rest of the family. In addition to the challenges of everyday life, families have to cope with the absence of an important member of the family and the potential impact that it can have on children, the partner, and/or parents.

The impact of deployment on family members

As can be seen in Figure 15.1, 23 percent of the French-speaking respondents (F) and 12 percent of the Dutch-speaking ones (D) said that they had "badly," or "very badly," lived the absence of the service member. Most (48 percent and 60 percent, respectively) said that they had lived it "well," or "very well." The day of the departure of the loved one was even more stressful (50 percent and 39 percent, respectively), particularly among the partners (43 percent and 54 percent of the French and Dutch, respectively) compared with the parents (21 percent and 39 percent, respectively). The return can sometimes be difficult, but is usually very well accepted.

The partner's relationship and professional life

The absence of the service member during the mission has an impact on both his or her partner and his or her children. Concerning the partner,

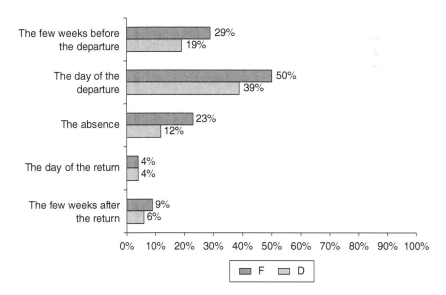

Figure 15.1 Percentage of family members who lived "badly" or "very badly" (by language)

F = French-speaking; D = Dutch-speaking

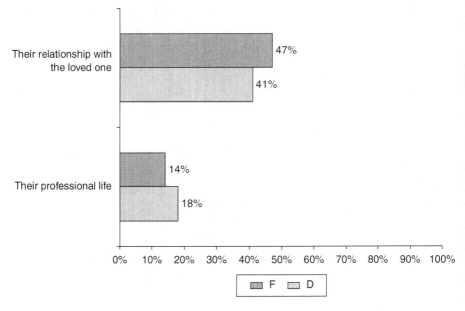

Figure 15.2 Percentage of partners on whom the mission had a "positive," or "very positive," impact (by language)

F = French-speaking; D = Dutch-speaking

Figure 15.2 shows that 47 percent of the French-speaking respondents and 41 percent of the Dutch-speaking ones said that the mission had a "positive," or "very positive," impact on their relationship; only 9 percent and 10 percent, respectively, said it had a "negative" impact.

The professional life of a partner was less influenced by the mission. Apparently, the mission had a positive impact on the professional lives of 14 percent of the French-speaking and 18 percent of the Dutch-speaking partners. Most of them, however, reported no significant change in their work (66 percent and 67 percent, respectively). Unsurprisingly, having children had a negative influence on this aspect: partners who had to take care of children reported a more negative impact of the mission on their professional lives than partners without children (20 percent vs. 8 percent).

The children

More than half (54 percent) of the surveyed family members had one or more children. At the time of the survey, 36 percent had one child, 42 percent had two children, 16 percent had three children, and 5 percent had four children. The mean ages of the children ranged from 11 for the first one and 4 for the fourth one. Almost all children (96 percent) stayed with their nondeployed mother; 4 percent stayed with their non-deployed father.

As shown in Figure 15.3, and similarly to other members of the family, the day of the departure of the service member was the most difficult moment of the mission, with 30 percent of the children living it "badly," or "very badly." The absence was an especially difficult moment for the first and fourth children: respectively, 21 percent and 30 percent lived it "badly," or "very badly."

The reaction of the first child can be explained by two factors. First, it can be explained by generation stress – that is, that the oldest feels that he or she has to take care of siblings. Second, if the child has no brother or sister, he or she can feel lonely during this period of time. Similarly to what was observed among their parents, this reaction was particularly strong in the French-speaking part of the country (that is, 26 percent of the French-speaking vs. 17 percent of the Flemish-speaking first children doing badly). The reaction of the fourth children can be explained by their young age: these children may not yet have developed as many coping strategies as their older brothers

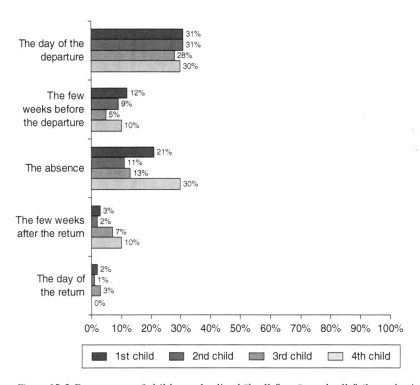

Figure 15.3 Percentage of children who lived "badly" or "very badly" (by order in the family)

and sisters, as a result of which they may experience more difficulties dealing with unusual situations compared with their older siblings.

The way in which children react to the absence of the service member is also influenced by their nondeployed parent: stressed partners have a strong impact on their children – especially on the first and on the second children. Stressed parents reported that 25 percent of their first and 13 percent of their second children lived "badly," or "very badly," the absence of their father or mother, while the corresponding percentages among stress-free partners were only 3 percent and 0 percent, respectively.

Figure 15.4 shows that, according to their nondeployed parents, for 10 percent of the children the mission had a negative impact on their relationship with their absent father or mother.

As for school, the mission also had a negative impact on some children, and older children were more prone to be affected by the absence of the service member than the other (younger) children.

Family life

With an important member of the family far from home, small details of daily life can sometimes become overwhelming. Figure 15.5 shows that 43 percent of the French-speaking and 44 percent of the Dutch-speaking respondents "rather" or "completely" agreed that the daily organization of the family life had become more complicated during the mission.

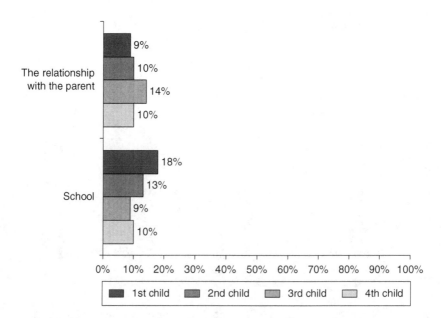

Figure 15.4 Percentage of negative impact of the mission on . . . (by order in the family)

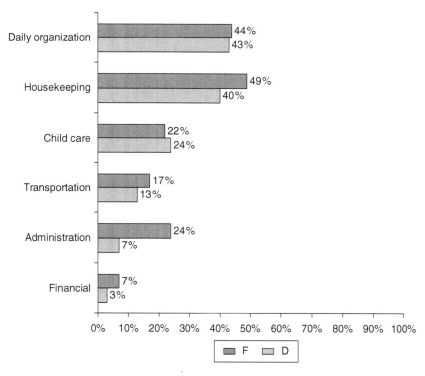

Figure 15.5 Percentage of problems occurring during the last mission (by language)

F = French-speaking; D = Dutch-speaking

Among the list of possible difficulties that the family could face, problems related to housekeeping were reported by 49 percent of the French-speaking and 40 percent of the Dutch-speaking respondents. This category included problems ranging from repairing a lawnmower to fixing a leaking sink. To face these issues, partners and parents used different strategies. Partners tried to solve the problems alone (47 percent) or asked for help within the (extended) family (51 percent). Parents of deployed military personnel, on the other hand, rarely tried to solve these kinds of problems by themselves (10 percent); they first sought help amongst family (44 percent) or called a professional to do the job (40 percent). They almost never turned to professional services offered by the MoD (for administrative or financial problems).

Child care was a problem for 22 percent of the French speakers and 24 percent of the Dutch speakers, and was specific for partners (only one parent of a soldier reported it). A little fewer than three out of ten (28 percent) solved this problem on their own. External help came from the family (80 percent), from friends (27 percent), or, in some occasions, from professionals (11 percent). Only one spouse sought help from the MoD.

Relatively few respondents reported transportation problems (17 percent of French speakers and 13 percent of the Dutch speakers, respectively). Here, help came mainly from family (46 percent) or friends (28 percent), given that the MoD does not provide any professional help in this domain.

Administrative problems were mostly experienced by French-speaking respondents. Most of them tried to solve these on their own (63 percent), whereas a few asked for help from professionals outside the MoD (20 percent) or from specialized MoD services (10 percent). When faced with financial problems, most tried to solve these on their own (60 percent) or turned to family (20 percent).

As one can see from these results, when faced with daily problems, families first tried to find a solution among their inner circles, before widening their search. This strategy hardly included any of the structures that the Belgian Defense had to offer. The kind of problems that families faced also played an important role in the decision to contact professional MoD services or not. With respect to domestic problems, turning to the professional services of the MoD did not seem to be an appropriate response for the families surveyed. Families seemed more likely to turn to the services of the Belgian Defense for help with logistical and administrative problems if no other options were available.

Stress of the mission

As has been seen, missions are stressful events, but they do not affect every family member in the same way. Spouses and partners were significantly more affected than parents (85 percent vs. 61 percent). French-speaking respondents experienced the mission as more stressful (82 percent) than the Dutch speakers (72 percent). An indicator is that more French speakers reported being too sensitive, anxious, worried about problems and things to do, or busy making an effort to make "things work" (see Figure 15.6). The stress experienced forced family members to become stronger, to sort things out by defining priorities and lines of action, and to really show what they were capable of. To release stress, most of the respondents first phoned or saw a friend, while others preferred doing some shopping to clear their mind.

Communications

Generally, families were not very satisfied with the amount of information that the MoD provided during the mission, given that 79 percent of the surveyed families would have preferred more information. The quality of the

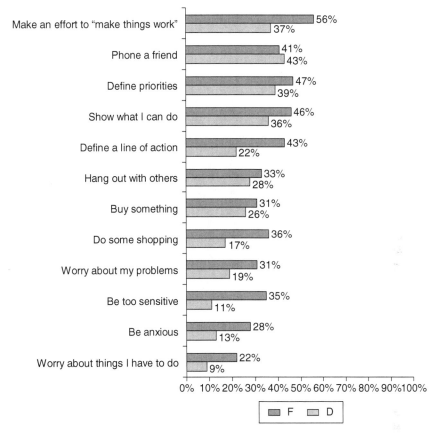

Figure 15.6 "During the last mission, I had tendencies to . . . " (percentages, by language)

F = French-speaking; D = Dutch-speaking

information was, however, rated as good and easily accessible (see Figure 15.7). Most families (58 percent and 64 percent of the French- and Dutch-speaking families, respectively) were "rather," or "fully," satisfied with the answers that they received from someone from the MoD when they asked for information. Furthermore, 69 percent and 68 percent, respectively, "rather," or "fully," agreed that they knew to whom to turn within the MoD when needing information.

Concerning the communications with the service member, if it was logically subject to technological constraints, the frequency of contacts was judged sufficient: more than 80 percent were satisfied (84 percent among the Flemish respondents and 81 percent among the French-speaking ones).

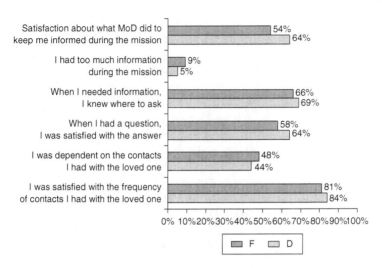

Figure 15.7 Percentages "rather," or "fully," agreeing with statements about communication about and during the mission (by language)

F = French-speaking; D = Dutch-speaking

Psychosocial support

This section analyzes the degree to which family members of military personnel participating in crisis response operations know about the various psychosocial support services that exist within the Belgian Defense, the extent to which they use these before, during, and after these missions, and the extent to which they are satisfied with the services.

In Belgium, there are multiple institutional actors working in the field of psychosocial support, and this sometimes leads to a certain confusion or vagueness about the roles of each actor. The diversity of institutional actors in charge of the psychosocial support of military personnel and their families is largely a legacy. Most of these services were created when the Belgian Armed Forces had a mass army format and were made up of a majority of young, single draftees. After the end of the Cold War and with the multiplication of new constabulary-type missions, these services added the psychosocial support of troops deployed in operations abroad to their core missions. But, until 2001, there was no attempt to develop a really integrated policy toward psychosocial support: each service worked more or less on its own, without caring too much for what the other actors were doing or were supposed to do. A beginning of integration started in 2001, with the creation of a loose structure at the Defense Staff level (the so-called "psychosocial platform"), responsible for the coordination of the various services and the streamlining of their activities. Currently, the Psychosocial Support Section of the ACOS-WB Competence Center is responsible for the well-being and mental fitness of Defense personnel. The section is currently elaborating a general concept of psychosocial support based on the work of the "psychosocial platform." This platform is composed of the four main actors dealing with psychosocial support: the Social Service of Defense, the Centre for Mental Health, the Religious and Moral Assistance Service, and the Mental Readiness Advisors (MRA).[6]

The MRA, created in 1998, is the most recently created service dealing with psychosocial support. Unlike the other services, which initially had – and still have – other missions, this structure has been specifically designed to assist commanding officers in the domain of morale and psychosocial support during operations abroad. In a certain sense, it is therefore the most important institutional actor as far as the provision of psychosocial support to military personnel and their families during operations abroad is concerned. An MRA is an officer with a master's degree in psychology. His or her role is to help commanding officers to optimize the mental readiness of their personnel during operations abroad. The MRA acts as an advisor of the unit commander for matters related to social and psychological well-being, and the motivation of personnel. Specifically, during long-term missions abroad, he or she offers advice in the areas of leadership, group cohesiveness, job satisfaction, and psychosocial support. The MRA team comes under the control of the Assistant Chief of Staff Operation and Training (ACOS Ops & Trg). Teams are divided according to the language communities, with three stationed in Marche-en-Famenne (for the French-speaking community), two in Leopoldsburg (the Dutch Region), and one dedicated to the Navy in Zeebrugge. Depending on the risk and length of a given mission, and the size of the contingent, one MRA is designated to follow an operation according to the language of the pilot unit (generally combat unit, leading the detachment, which is reinforced by support and service support units). The MRA is in charge of accompanying the contingent for parts of the mission (theoretically, two weeks at the beginning of the deployment, two weeks at mid-deployment, and two weeks at the end). His or her colleagues in Belgium coordinate the psychosocial support for the families during the operation.

Additionally, psychosocial teams, consisting of delegates of the four services, are available to families in two centers: the Reception and Information Center Paola (Dutch-speaking), in Leopoldsburg, and the Princess Mathilde Center (French-speaking), in Marche-en-Famenne. Before and during missions, family days are organized in the pilot unit during which family members of the personnel participating in a mission abroad can meet each other, receive news from the theater of operation, talk with their loved ones (via video conferences), etc. Families can call the psychosocial team any time (day and night) 24/7 on a free helpline.

Finally, at the local level, the "rear guard" of the pilot unit is composed of those service members who are not deployed with their unit and stay in the garrison. Even if these personnel cannot be considered to be psychosocial professionals, families can also contact the rear guard if they feel that it can help. The rear guard generally offers a helpline to family members. The rear guard is also responsible for the "family days," organized before and during missions, in the pilot unit. Family members of military personnel participating in a mission abroad can meet each other on that day, receive news from the theater of operation, and talk with their loved ones (via video conferences).

General opinions

Most (60 percent) of the Dutch-speaking respondents, but only 35 percent of the French-speaking ones, "rather," or "fully," agreed that they usually need some kind of support during the mission. Among both groups, parents were significantly less likely than spouses or partners to answer positively. The need for support was greater among younger family members: among those aged under 30, 93 percent of the Dutch- and 64 percent of the French-speaking partners, respectively, acknowledged that they needed support.

As it appears from Figure 15.8, family members were generally satisfied with the various services provided by the MoD before, during, and after the missions. French speakers seemed a little less likely to "rather," or "fully," agree with the three statements.

Opinions on the various services

The 2007 family survey contained a series of questions focusing on the knowledge and use of the various psychosocial services available to families,

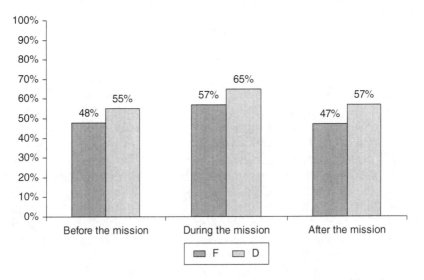

Figure 15.8 Percentage "rather," or "fully," agreeing that MoD provides adequate support for families in case of problems (by language)

F = French-speaking; D = Dutch-speaking

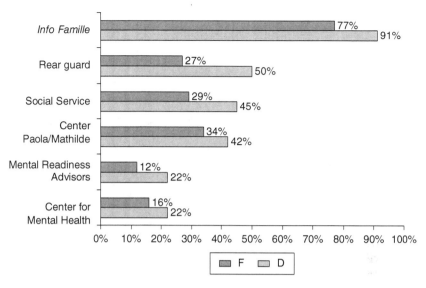

Figure 15.9 Percentage of respondents aware of the service (by language)

F = French-speaking; D = Dutch-speaking

as well as their satisfaction with these services. Figure 15.9 shows to what extent Dutch- and French-speaking family members were aware of the various services.

As can be seen, Dutch-speaking respondents tended to be significantly more likely to be aware of all of the services. The most well-known support structure was the information service specifically tailored for the families (*Info Famille*): more than nine out of ten Flemish respondents and almost eight out of ten French speakers said that they knew of this service. The family structures of the Paola Center in Leopoldsburg (for Flemish families) and Princess Mathilde Center in Marche-en-Famenne (for French-speaking families) were known by, respectively, 42 percent and 34 percent of the respondents. The service specifically designed for the psychosocial support of military personnel (but which cares for their families as well), the MRAs, was known by (respectively) 22 percent and 12 percent of the Dutch- and French-speaking respondents.

Figures 15.10 and 15.11 show the percentages of respondents, among those who had said that they knew of the services, who actually used them and who had been "very," or "rather," satisfied. Given the fact that the numbers on which these percentages are based are very small, one must be extremely cautious with the interpretation. As it appears from Figure 18.10, the two most-used services (proportionally speaking) were those that also happen to be the best known among families – that is, *Info Famille* and the rear guard.

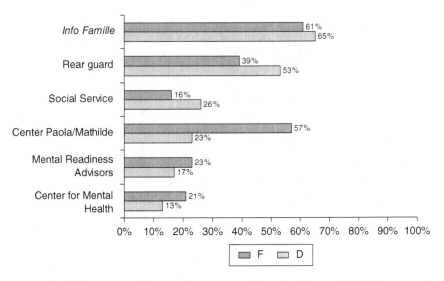

Figure 15.10 Percentage of respondents aware of service who used it (by language)

F = French-speaking; D = Dutch-speaking

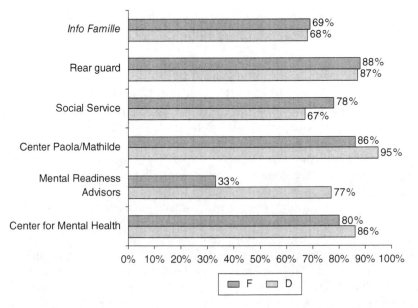

Figure 15.11 Percentage of respondents having used the service and "rather," or "fully," satisfied with it (by language)

F = French-speaking; D = Dutch-speaking

Generally, respondents who had used the services seemed also rather satisfied with what they received (Figure 15.11) – but, again, the number of people concerned is very small. For example, only three French speakers answered the question concerning the MRAs: one was "very" satisfied (33 percent); another was neutral; and the third was "rather not" satisfied.

Discussion and conclusions[7]

It appears that long-term operations abroad – although these have become some routine for a lot of military personnel and their families – remain somewhat difficult moments for families. The survey showed that the period preceding the mission was also quite difficult for some families (29 percent and 19 percent of French- and Dutch-speaking families, respectively). More specifically, the day of the departure seems the most stressful moment for partners and parents of service members. During the separation, families experienced relational tensions and difficulties in the organization of daily life. Furthermore, but to a lesser extent, the period after the return was a sensitive stage for some families, mainly for reasons linked to the reintegration of the soldier within the family. Given the low-intensity nature of Belgian operations (up to now at least), these problems are only rarely linked to posttraumatic stress disorder (PTSD). Deployments posed less strain on service members' parents, while partners of deployed military personnel experienced more difficulties. Not surprisingly, the presence of children made the family separations even more difficult for the partners or spouses. According to 16 percent of the Dutch-speaking and 26 percent of the French-speaking nondeployed mothers or fathers, the absence of soldiers had a negative impact on their children. The survey showed that the children's age and the well-being of the nondeployed parent during the absence of the service member were factors that influenced the way in which the children experienced the absence of their father or mother. Three main categories of difficulty experienced by the families during the missions can be distinguished: emotional; communicational (too much or not enough communication with their loved one); and organizational (coping with practical problems in everyday life, including those related to the presence of children).

Compared to the nondeployed partners, parents of the service members reported fewer problems. It seems that they were less affected by the absence of their son or daughter and that they were less stressed than the partners. When confronted with daily housekeeping problems, they first sought help from within the family or they called a professional; rarely did they try to resolve these problems by themselves, as partners tended to do.

French- and Dutch-speaking respondents did not react in the same way to the stress of the mission. French speakers tended to be more stressed by the departure of the service member and to be more affected psychologically than Dutch speakers. Therefore the French speakers needed to make extra efforts to make things work. They also tended to be less informed about the various services offered by the Belgian Defense. Therefore they also used these less than Dutch speakers. Surprisingly, despite the difficulties encountered, French-speaking respondents were less likely than Dutch-speaking ones to say that they needed support during the missions (35 percent vs. 60 percent, respectively).

The survey demonstrated that, as in most other countries (Bartone and Bartone, 2005; Booth, Segal, and Segal, 2007; Moelker, 2005), families usually coped on their own with all of these problems. When they could not, some tried to find support within their direct social networks (family or friends), and when they did so, they were generally satisfied with this kind of support. Also similarly to other countries, families who find themselves isolated during the mission and cannot benefit from the support of their social networks (family, friends, colleagues) tended to experience more stress during the deployment than families who had an active and supportive social network. Thus, for those families without supportive social networks, a more adapted structure of psychosocial support, mainly in terms of accessibility (physical and psychological), within the MoD could significantly improve their lives during the missions. Several solutions have been considered to try to answer these needs, such as: improving the accessibility and geographic distribution of the family centers; organizing a permanent MRA in the rearguard units; increasing the mobility of the psychosocial actors, who could visit family members at home; and setting up a network of experienced family members, who could act as informal and nonprofessional resources for the other family members. Up to now, however, none of these solutions have been institutionally implemented on a permanent basis.

It appears, however, that the majority of the families who participated in this study were not very familiar with the support services provided by the MoD. Delvaux and Moreau (2008: 122–4) suggest the following reasons to explain the ignorance – at the time of the survey – of existing support structures and their nonuse.

1. The respondents simply were not aware of the existence of the support structures, either because they had not been informed, or because the information had not been transmitted to the right persons. From focus groups conducted before the quantitative survey, it appears that, very often, the information was given to the service member, who, in turn, was supposed to inform his or her family, but failed to do so. It could also be that the information was given to the families, but that, because of its complexity (too many different services), it was not assimilated. Finally, it could be that the families did not intend to use these structures in the first place and therefore did not store the information that they had received during the information session organized before the departure.

2. Given the multiplication of persons and structures dealing with psychosocial support within the Belgian MoD, families could have had a hard time identifying the right service for their problems. The Psychosocial Section of the ACOS-WB Competence Center is currently working to clarify the situation, and should soon publish with a policy document on the psychosocial support available to service members and their families during the deployment cycle. A streamlining of the respective roles of these support structures would therefore improve the situation.

3. Another possibility is that the existing structures did not correspond to what families expected or needed, or that they were not easily accessible (too far from home). In particular, this is the case for families of service members who do not belong to the pilot unit responsible for the organization of the rear guard and who therefore do not have access to all of the rearguard facilities, because the pilot unit is too far from where they live. To limit this problem, a free telephone number has now been offered so that families can call for help. In case of an emergency, social workers can visit families' homes directly to help the household members in need.

4. Finally, some values traditionally associated with the military (in particular, the "macho" self-image of the soldier), as well as the fear of stigma, or the fear of hurting the service member's career, can all be an obstacle to the use of psychosocial support services, not only for soldiers, but also for their families. As one respondent stated: "The fact of trying to find help within the armed forces does not fit with values such as courage, strength, tenacity."

Notes

1 Belgian Ministry of Defense, Directorate-General Communication and Directorate-General Human Resources.
2 Belgian Ministry of Defense, Adjunct Chief of Staff Operations and Training.
3 For a detailed description of the organization of social-psychological support within the Belgian MoD in 2005, especially during long-term operations abroad, see Manigart and Fils (2006).
4 It should be noted that the sample is not representative of family members of the whole Belgian Armed Forces. The Navy was deliberately excluded from this first exploratory survey. The sample is also not representative of the Army, Air Force, and Medical Service, given that an equal number of individuals were selected in the two main linguistic groups, while the linguistic composition of the Belgian Armed Forces as a whole is around 60 percent Dutch- and 40 percent French-speaking. For more details about the composition of the sample, the survey design, and complete results, see Delvaux and Moreau (2008).
5 Generally, response rates for household postal surveys are around 20 percent. See, e.g., Burns and Bush (1998: 266). However, organizational surveys that deal with topics salient for the respondents can obtain higher response rates.
6 For a more detailed description of these services, see Manigart and Fils (2006).
7 This part is based on the conclusions of Delvaux and Moreau (2008: 120–4) to their analysis of the whole family survey.

References

Adams, G.A., Durand, D.B., Burrell, L., Teitelbaum, J.M., Pehrson, K.L., and Hawkins, J.P. (2011) "Direct and indirect effects of operations tempo on outcomes for soldiers and spouses." *Military Psychology*, 17: 229–46.

Bartone, J.V., and Bartone, P.T. (2005) "Missions alike and unlike: Military families in war and peace." Paper presented at the 45th Biennial International Conference of Inter-University Seminar on Armed Forces and Society, Chicago, IL.

Booth, B., Segal, M., and Bell, B. (2007) *What We Know about Army Families*. 2007 update. Report prepared by Caliber for the Family and Morale, Welfare and Recreation Command.

Burns, A.C., and Bush, R.F. (1998) *Marketing Research*. Upper Saddle River, NJ: Prentice Hall.

Castro, C.A., Bienvenu, R.V., Huffman A.H., and Adler A.B. (2000) "Soldier dimensions and operational readiness in U.S. Army Forces deployed to Kosovo." *International Review of the Armed Forces Medical Services*, 73: 191–200.

Delvaux, S.S., and Moreau, P. (2008) *Le soutien psychosocial des familles de militaire envoyé en mission à l'étranger, 2007–2008*. Final Technical Report #AP/057-9850. Brussels: Belgian Federal Science Policy Office.

Manigart, P., and Fils, J.F. (2006) "The Belgian concept of social-psychological support of families of military personnel deployed in crisis response operations." Paper presented at the NATO HFM-134 Symposium on Human Dimensions in Military Operations: Military leaders' strategies for addressing stress and psychological support, Brussels.

Moelker, R. (2005) "Social support systems: A theoretical approach for military families support systems." Paper presented at the 45th Anniversary Biennial International Conference of the Inter-University Seminar on Armed Forces and Society, Chicago, IL.

Reed, B.J., and Segal, D.R. (2000) "The impact of multiple deployments on soldiers' peacekeeping attitudes, morale and retention." *Armed Forces & Society*, 27: 57–78.

16 The invisible families of Portuguese soldiers

From colonial wars to contemporary missions

Helena Carreiras

Introduction[1]

Military families routinely experience separations as a result of frequent moves, hazardous duty, deployments, and exercises, which have potential impacts on the adjustment of both soldiers and the members of their families. Considering that the military and the family can be seen as a "greedy institution" (Coser, 1974; Segal, 1986), requiring enormous commitment and loyalty from its members, possible conflicts between both have been identified as a major challenge to the effectiveness of military organizations. Here, as in other similar situations, social support is considered to have a positive impact on people's ability to cope with the stress of separation, and to develop emotional well-being in the face of uncertainty and change (Andres, Moelker, and Soeters, 2008). Although the structure of social support networks varies (Moelker and van der Kloet, 2003), military organizations have, in many cases, provided services and designed policies to promote positive adjustments and family well-being during the period of separation (Copeland and Norell, 2002; Orthner and Rose, 2005). This chapter addresses the reasons why this has not happened in the Portuguese case.

In 2013, more than one-and-a-half decades after the Portuguese Armed Forces started to send its soldiers into international peacekeeping missions, there was no specific program or policy aimed at supporting military families. Both from the institutional perspective and from the more informal dimension of social networks, soldiers' families are "invisible" components of the military social landscape. However, unlike many other nations, Portugal experienced a rather uncommon pattern of family involvement in military life during the colonial wars in Angola, Mozambique, and Guinea-Bissau, from 1960 to 1974, when thousands of wives with children followed their husbands to long commissions in Africa. What type of factors – social, institutional, cultural – might then explain what seems to be a family withdrawal from military life since that time? Why is there so little institutional attention paid to families, when responses to the few sociological surveys undertaken among deployed soldiers are consistent on the crucial role of family relations to motivation and satisfaction of soldiers during missions abroad? Why do families themselves seem somewhat reluctant to get involved in the military context? The present chapter addresses this puzzle, looking at a problem that has received hardly any attention from researchers and policymakers alike. Through a review of results of surveys among Portuguese peacekeepers, in-depth interviews with policymakers, and soldiers and their wives (from both periods), and a case study of a battalion deployed to Kosovo, this chapter aims to provide some tentative answers to the research questions. This is all developed within the framework of a larger study of the "Portuguese Armed Forces after the Cold War."[2]

The colonial legacy: War in Africa and military families

From 1961 until 1974, the Portuguese authoritarian regime of *Estado Novo*, led first by António de Oliveira Salazar and then by Marcelo Caetano, fought a long war against liberation movements in its African colonies of Angola, Mozambique, and Guinea-Bissau. The full history of these wars – colonial wars to some; liberation wars to others – is still to be written. Although there is an evident lack of information and analysis, the figures offer a perspective on its impact. During these 13 years, Portugal mobilized around 100,000 soldiers, the equivalent of 1 percent of its population. Although military casualties were rather low considering the long duration of the conflict – between 8,300 and 10,000 – the impact of the war was huge, exactly because of its long duration and unpredictable outcome. As noted by Pinto (2001: 48):

> While the social impact of the war measured by the growth of an anti-war public opinion is difficult to identify, due to the dictatorial nature of the political regime, the war and the violence it produced, left lasting marks in the Portuguese society.

Considering that the number of those wounded reached nearly 28,000 and that, in 1992 (the time of the last evaluation), there were in Portugal an estimated 140,000 persons suffering from psychological trauma as a consequence of the war, the persistence of its effects is clear.

The start of the fight in Angola in 1961 took not only the majority of the Portuguese population by surprise, but also the Armed Forces, which were technically and operationally unprepared to face a war (Antunes, 1995: 276). Even the government was surprised, judging from the total absence of any legal tools or institutional structures with which to frame and respond to a set of whole new situations confronted by the military. There was a total absence of regulations related to the wounded or dead in combat, or the deserters, as well as institutional mechanisms to support the families of those deployed to Africa. In the absence of such mechanisms, two very different groups of women became central actors in the provision of support to soldiers and their families (Carreiras, 2007).

The National Women's Movement: A proxy support system

With the explicit aim of overcoming the vacuum, an original solution was put in place in April 1961: the *Movimento Nacional Feminino* (MNF), or "National Women's Movement," the last women's organization of the authoritarian regime. In this year, the war had started in Angola and some Portuguese women – "25 outraged ladies from all social strata" – mobilized to "unite all Portuguese women to give moral and material support to all those that fight for the integrity of our territory."[3] Pluralist in its recruitment rhetoric, the MNF grew rapidly on the basis of an appeal directed mainly to Catholic mothers, of all ages, social conditions, or races, excluding only "the communist and the lazy." Supported by a varied set of regular publications,[4] the MNF integrated directly around 82,000 women and many more indirectly, becoming more influential and mobilizing among Portuguese women than any other women's official organization.

According to its statutes, the MNF was a patriotic organization, without a political nature and independent of the state. However, in its propaganda work in support to the war effort, it reproduced central political values of the *Estado Novo*. The proximity of its main leaders to the power elite – namely, charismatic President Cecilia Supico Pinto, who met regularly with high-ranking officers, and with Salazar himself – had a global impact on the movement's action. Besides, a substantial part of its funding came from the Portuguese Ministry of Defense (MoD).

On the one hand, this connection to power was functional and allowed the movement to reach many of its goals; on the other, it "became dangerous since all of those that joined the movement were immediately associated to its image of a tool of civilian propaganda to colonial politics" (Espírito Santo, 2003: 33).

In any case, the movement had a notable intervention, both in metropolitan Portugal and in the colonies, replacing an absent state unable to respond to a variety of problematic situations, ranging from a soldier's death or physical disability, to payment of salaries and benefits, mail distribution, communication with families, transfer of dead soldiers to Portugal, or vacation leaves. Although the moral and material support that the movement provided was regularly followed by "popular actions surrounded by demagogy" (Afonso and Gomes, 2000: 277), it was effective in solving most of the problems that young soldiers and their families faced. MNF leaders used their preferential relationship with power circles to push for the publication of legal provisions regarding the situation of the wounded in combat, for changes to the pension system to the disabled, for support to the families in case of death, and so forth.

From the point of view of its organization, the movement had a central and several regional commissions, as well as a large number of sections pertaining to specific activity areas. Among these, three were paramount: the "aerogram" section, the "boarding" section, and the "war godmothers" section.

The first had a crucial role in obtaining free circulation of mail between soldiers and their families by means of the issuance of "aerograms," a formatted postcard that became a symbol of the colonial war. The "boarding" section organized the participation of MNF members at the docks before the departure of troops to Africa, offering cigarettes, aerograms, pens, and other small gifts, as well as words of incentive to soldiers. The "war godmothers" section was probably the most famous and effective. Revived from World War I, the MNF embraced the image of the "war godmother," aware of its beneficial effect on soldiers' morale. Through regular and compulsory postal correspondence, the godmother would cheer up the soldier, making him feel proud of the mission, and raising his awareness of the recognition among the Portuguese people. But she should also distract him from "depressing" family messages, transmitting to him confidence and courage. Answering the appeal of the MNF, thousands of Portuguese women lived the war through this experience. In 1963, two years after the start of the war in Angola, more than 10,000 godmothers had already been confirmed. During the war, the total network involved more than 23,750 godmothers and 33,400 "godsons" (Mascarenhas, 2001: 84).

As time went by, the long duration of the conflict reduced progressively the efficacy of the movement's actions and rhetoric. Women responded less and less to its appeals, and at the beginning of the 1970s the erosion of interest in the war caused it to resemble "a megalomaniac representation of a shrinking reality" (Mascarenhas, 2001: 93). Nevertheless, the MNF was an important proponent of official propaganda, and a "powerful front in the psychological and social support to the war and the regime" (Mascarenhas, 2001: 78). It is also generally agreed that the government took political advantage of these women's actions, since "the systematic resorting to public charity obscured its responsibility in support of the most poor [*sic*] families and deployed soldiers" (Espírito Santo, 2003: 33).

Military families that went to war

A second group of women, less studied than the MNF, is that of those who followed their husbands – mainly officers and noncommissioned officers (NCOs) – on their long commissions in Africa. These women, in numbers that are difficult to determine, but estimated to be in the thousands, came from all around Portugal. They traveled usually with their young children, in conditions that were in accordance to the rank of the husband, either by ship or airplane. Although the majority went to live in the bigger cities, many stayed in villages or isolated houses close to the field barracks. Many went on to work in Africa, generally as primary and secondary schoolteachers.

Considering that there existed an official discourse underlining the importance of women's roles in support of the war effort, both in metropolitan Portugal and in the colonies, the question has been put forward as to whether this women's movement towards Africa corresponded to an official policy of conciliating the family mission with the regime's "civilizing" mission (Ribeiro, 2007). There were indeed, during the colonial period, measures aimed at stimulating families to colonize African land, through legislation that encouraged emigration to African destinies, in an attempt to reduce migratory flows towards Europe (Ribeiro, 2007: 25). Loans were granted and free tickets offered through the regional settlers' commissions. However, the meaning and scope of these measures is difficult to interpret. Neither the military wives' testimonies,[5] nor the existing legislation, seem to confirm the existence of a coherent and systematic policy.

On the one hand, many published accounts by military wives call attention to the lack of support and their difficult settlement in Africa:

> Portuguese society ignored the war . . . there was no solidarity whatsoever towards the military and their families . . . In Angola, the only thing that helped was the solidarity among people; generosity was permanent. This is the only explanation for the fact that those who were there by then ended up loving that hell.
>
> (Maria Teresa[6])

> I had no support at all. I didn't even realize that the institution was there.
>
> (Verónica[7])

> One day there was the rumor that there would be an attack in Negage. When it turned dark my husband took his military equipment and a grenade belt and I asked: what about us? He said that he was not there to defend us but the airplanes, that I had my gun. If someone would force the room's door, I should pull the gun against my son's head; He would forgive me everything . . . At that moment I knew how the future would be.
>
> (Maria Luísa[8])

Some testimonies are also revealing of a generation that was increasingly questioning the values of the *Estado Novo* regime under which they had been raised:

> We knew that there were the women from the MNF, an elite . . . They were promoting themselves and making propaganda about their charity. They told us: "we'll visit a soldier that lost a leg." They would take a picture and go to a newspaper . . . It was awful, degrading.
>
> (Verónica)

On the other hand, the way in which the transportation issue was handled shows that state support of the deployment and maintenance of military personnel was not based on an articulated policy. The related legislation dated from 1931, long before the war started, and was updated only by decrees that normalized family transportation. The interviewees referred frequently to this problem:

> I did not enjoy any benefit in my trips to and from Africa. I even think that there were none.
>
> (Madalena[9])

> Well, the money was short and the institution supported only one large trip. All other trips in between had to be paid by us. When I traveled with my daughter, in a military plane from Beira to Lourenço Marques, we even had to take the food. They wouldn't give us anything.
>
> (Maria de Lurdes[10])

It was only in 1969, when there was already obvious erosion caused by the war and it was necessary to attract military personnel, that rights and duties regarding families were established (including the right to free transportation, medical assistance, and lodging). But even then, while career personnel received travel support to bring their families, complementary personnel had to cover all such costs.

Considering the overall lack of institutional support, the movement of these military wives might seem rather surprising. However, an alternative interpretation is that such an absence was at least a partial justification for this unusual pattern. The motivation of these women to follow their husbands to war was clearly related to the perception of a lack of other types of support and possible family disruption resulting from long separation periods. As Maria Teresa noted:

> [T]o stay behind meant having the total burden of raising a family by myself, let alone the terrible feeling of emptiness that could easily lead to deep depression . . .
>
> (Maria Teresa)

While there is still much to be studied with regard to these military wives, their presence is commonly considered to have contributed to family stability, not only because they kept the family together, but also because of the social contribution that they made through their work in the colonial administration.

The scenario post Cold War: Portuguese soldiers' peacekeeping

The importance of international missions

More than three decades later, in the mid-1990s, Portuguese soldiers started to deploy again, but this time for different purposes, and in a very diverse domestic and international context. Although Portuguese troops had already been modestly present in United Nations operations, especially in Angola and Mozambique,[11] it was the presence of a Portuguese contingent in Bosnia in 1996 that signaled a real inflection of policy in this domain. In this year, the so-called "new missions" represented nearly half of the military's operational expenses (46 percent) and approximately 12 percent of the defense budget. Meanwhile, the Bosnian experience revealed a growth in public, military, and political awareness and support of the participation of the Portuguese military in multinational operations and peacekeeping (Carreiras, 1999; Sousa, 1999;Vasconcelos, 1999), paving the way for a permanent presence of the Portuguese military in international missions.

Evolution in numbers of deployed soldiers (always on a volunteer basis) shows a variation between a few hundred and nearly 2,000 soldiers yearly (see Figure 16.1), with two peaks: 1996 (1,521), coinciding with the NATO Implementation Force (IFOR) mission in Bosnia and UNAVEM in Angola; and 2001 (1,736), with the simultaneous presence of military contingents in Bosnia, Kosovo, and East Timor.[12]

Although absolute numbers are modest, the presence of Portuguese troops has been constant and highly significant. During the past two decades, Portugal has been among the 15 largest relative contributors and one of the major European contributors to UN operations (Branco, Garcia, and Pereira., 2009; Carreiras, 2014; Viana, 2002).

At the strategic political level, international military missions have become a core element of Portuguese national defense policy. To a certain extent, they have been used to fulfill what some have called a "strategic vacuum" in

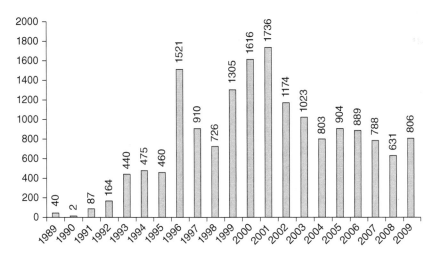

Figure 16.1 Portuguese military personnel deployed to international peace support operations (1989–2009)

Source: Teixeira (2009); UAL (2005)

Portuguese defense policy (Santos, 2001, 2012), becoming a very significant instrument of Portuguese foreign policy and international projection.

(The lack of) Institutional support to families

Considering the centrality of international missions and the increasing importance of these missions for the Portuguese Armed Forces, it might have been anticipated that some attention would be directed toward the development of an institutional support system for soldiers and their families. This is even more the case if we take into account the result of a large sociological survey that had already been carried out in 1996 among the first soldiers deployed to IFOR and SFOR missions (Carreiras, 1999). Data from this postdeployment survey showed that "distance from family" was the main difficulty experienced by almost half of the respondents, with rates higher for NCOs and enlisted personnel than for officers.

However, despite this new focus on international missions, the significant number of soldiers deployed, and the perceived importance of family relations for quality of life during missions, very little specific institutional initiatives (and certainly no policy) have been developed with the aim of providing social support to soldiers and their families. When representatives at the MoD were interviewed about this absence, they underlined the existence of regular social security schemes, including the specific health system for the Armed Forces (ADME), which extends to soldiers' families to different degrees. Besides this, a "green telephone line" was activated in 2002 to provide information about the missions to families of deployed soldiers. Data provided by the Armed Forces' Chief of Staff's Office confirm, however, that the number of calls has been relatively low and has decreased significantly over time, from an average of 50 calls a month in 2003 to 10 calls a month in 2012. The questions posed by those who called regarded the need to contact soldiers and to send packages, and requests of information about dates and timing of the mission. The development of mobile and Internet communications made this line redundant.

Social and psychological support to deployed soldiers themselves, in turn, was recognized to be an area left to the intervention of the Catholic chaplain regularly present in the missions. This dated approach to social support is also evident in the residual role of the psychological unit of the Portuguese Army, the Center of Military Psychology (CPAE), responsible for monitoring all deployed personnel. Paradoxically, this center has seen its competences and mission substantially reduced during the past two decades – the very period of expansion of international operations. The CPAE is the only Army structure specifically oriented towards providing support of a kind not covered by traditional social security schemes, such as psychological help in case of accident or death. This aspect – intervention in the event of critical incident – is curiously the most underlined by institutional actors when the issue of support is brought to their attention, as though family support were something that only really makes sense in such circumstances. This situation is strikingly similar to that of countries that underwent a rapid process of routinization of international deployments, such as Italy, where the military institution:

> . . . was caught relatively unprepared, and it has been able to offer a kind of emergency psychological support in case of dramatic events, but less able to give rise to routine forms of family support for those situations where problems are much less tragic but anyway stressing for the private life of families affected by the professional activity of deployed soldiers.
>
> (Nuciari and Sertorio, 2009: 263)

However, it is important to note that the lack of institutionalized answers goes hand in hand with ad hoc initiatives – more discretionary and selective, but equally more flexible. Military authorities and force commanders developed a pragmatic, reactive attitude aimed at confronting immediate problems and concerns – namely, through the improvement of living conditions during the missions, and communication between soldiers and their families. Thirteen years after the mission in Bosnia, a case study of a battalion deployed to KFOR in 2009[13] showed that communication problems had been largely overcome, by means of effective Internet connections in every soldier's sleeping quarters and in the barracks' area. Although not all missions provide similar conditions, 30 in depth, semidirective interviews conducted on site confirmed that, in this case, such enhanced communication possibilities largely contributed to reduce anxiety over the family's situation back home, allowing soldiers to participate in family decisions and to solve problems at a distance. In general, all interviewees agreed that this was an extremely positive feature of the mission, even if some also underlined the fact that it meant a tradeoff regarding sociability patterns: staying connected in one's premises involved less free time spent with comrades or in group activities.

A survey conducted after the mission confirmed these results, revealing that soldiers' free time was mainly used to communicate with family and friends in Portugal (69.4 percent), rather than to "do sports" (56.8 percent), "talk, watch TV or play in the bar" (56.5 percent), and "stay in one's room reading, watching movies, listening to music or having other hobbies" (42.8 percent). In any case, for almost two-thirds of the battalion, "distance from the family" and the concern over those who stayed home was still the main difficulty experienced during the mission.

But what did these soldiers think about the need for family support during deployment? Did they think that families needed more attention from the Army or, on the contrary, would cope well enough by themselves?

One important conclusion drawn from the interviews was that family networks were the real source of support to families who stayed home. The vast majority of those with family responsibilities indicated that, whenever support was needed, it was provided by other members of the extended family, neighbors, and close friends. Although 87.5 percent of the respondents in the postdeployment survey said that the family did not need additional support during the mission, those who said that it did confirmed that relatives and friends gave such support.

However, when asked in general about the need to count on institutional support to families during missions, survey and interview data revealed some apparently paradoxical results. In the survey, a majority (57.5 percent) considered that the existence of institutional support to families was "important," or "very important." When asked about which type of support, soldiers underlined the need for information about the mission, its goals, and development, as well as support and information in the case of accident, critical events, injuries, or deaths. During the interviews, it was possible to further explore soldiers' opinions about support further. After what seemed to be a ritual approval of the need for family support ("it is always important"), many of the interviewees expressed negative views. Two results are worth signaling. First, those who shared this "in principle" agreement did so without a clear idea about which measures would be appropriate, underlining instead an abstract and symbolic need to have the families back home be given some further care and attention:

> Look, I think there should be support . . . at least some attention, some care, a gesture towards those who stay [in Portugal] . . . and that doesn't happen.
>
> (Male army captain, company commander)

The only exception to this was the general agreement about the crucial role of the institution in the event of critical incidents and emergency situations in terms of the provision of accurate information. Interviews also revealed that there was little awareness of the existence of institutional family support possibilities, which is not surprising, since this perception mirrors the actual absence of significant initiatives in this area.

Second, those who answered negatively with regard to the need for family support from the Army stressed a variety of aspects to justify their opinion, but the existence of easy web-based communication with families – namely, through Skype – was widely identified as a major motive:

> I am not there, that's it. All the rest works perfectly because we have this connection . . . I can take part in the decisions. Although I am not there physically, it is as if I was; everything works in a normal way.
>
> (Lieutenant M., platoon commander)

> Now it is not an issue or something I care about, even because I have all contact I need with my family; I do not need to use [the institutional channel of support].
>
> (Captain S., special operations company commander)

Internet access empowered these soldiers, allowing them to feel present, able to simultaneously exercise control over and relieve the burden on wives or parents who stayed home, helping them to solve problems and make decisions. Even if, for some, it could not replace the "smelling," "touching," and "kissing," and sometimes the perceived obligation of a daily connection was felt to be a burden, its benefits were considered to be much greater than its disadvantages.

But the interviews illustrate another interesting feature pertaining to the meaning of "institutional support" to families: there is a clearly restrictive understanding of what it might be, generally equated with facilitating communication. This restrictive interpretation is better understood if articulated alongside another frequent explanation for the lack of need for support – that is, the idea that the military and the family should be two different spheres, two "separate worlds":

> I separate the two worlds; when I'm working, I completely forget my personal life, otherwise it would affect my work; when I leave work, I am in my space, I totally forget work because if I don't, it would negatively affect my personal life. . . . If we don't do that, we will create very complicated situations for ourselves and those that surround us in both professional and personal life.
>
> (Lieutenant M., platoon commander)

In addition, the idea has been put forward that the military cannot fulfill the true needs of the family, either because it lacks resources or because it cannot provide for the type of need at stake. Sometimes, an institutional intervention might even be felt to be intrusive:

> I agree [that support should exist] but I also ask: why? Ok, we came here and everything that is done to help those who stayed back home is OK, but help them with what? I think that the only support they need, the one thing they miss, which cannot be replaced is ourselves. Should they put somebody else in our place?
>
> (First Sergeant G., personnel)

How did wives feel about this? Although not many wives volunteered to participate in the research, six interviews were conducted that added valuable insights about their perspective regarding institutional support. Wives confirmed the very limited contact between families and the military organization, as well as a lack of awareness of institutional support schemes or initiatives:

> If there is some support to families I do not know. But we do not have kids. For those who do that would probably be important.
>
> (L.F., wife of an NCO)

I do not know if it is needed but it would be nice. My husband is in Kosovo and if I need to send something or if he needs to send winter clothes that are not needed anymore it would be good to have a contact person at the battalion because it is dangerous to send those items by regular mail.

(R.P., wife of a captain)

In general, they did not think that they would need to count on the support of the Army, except in pursuit of such limited and pragmatic objectives. This result mirrors that of other empirical studies – namely, of research into the deployment experiences of British Army wives, which showed they favored informal social support networks to provide a buffer against the stressors of deployment, and did not expect or choose the military as their first line of support (Dandeker et al., 2006).

But what if the question of support relates to the soldiers themselves? What did they do, or to whom did they talk, when feeling psychologically "down"? What kind of support did they look for in difficult moments? The results of both the interviews during the mission and the postdeployment survey are clear in pointing toward informal networks, close comrades, and family as the main providers of help. While 36.3 percent of the survey respondents indicated that they had never felt "down," those who did said that the first person to whom they looked in that instance was a close fellow soldier (59 percent), or family back in Portugal (30 percent). According to the survey results, neither the military hierarchy (3.9 percent), nor the Catholic chaplain (2.6 percent), was an option in such circumstances. Here, again, it is possible to see how formal and institutional channels seem to be devalued, preferably replaced by more informal mechanisms for coping with stress or difficulties.

In sum, institutional support was considered important in the abstract, but almost exclusively associated with information and communication; in practice, soldiers were not aware of the existence of concrete programs or policies, relied primarily on family networks to get support, both to families back home and to themselves, and tended to separate the worlds of work and family.

Explaining the lack of institutional support and the growing invisibility of military families

This chapter started by questioning the reasons for the absence of institutional social support for military families in Portugal, considering an historical experience of great family involvement during the colonial war and the relevance of international deployments in present times. The puzzle regarding the colonial war period is that, considering the dominant institutional model of the Portuguese Armed Forces at the time, as well as the requirements of a war context, it could be expected to see families – and especially spouses who became isolated from their previous social networks – being given more institutional attention and being more integrated than they actually were.

The puzzle for the contemporary period is to understand why this institutional attention is *still* missing, notwithstanding the centrality of international missions and of the family issue for the well-being of deployed soldiers.

Two concrete social processes in Portuguese society might help us to understand both the relative devaluation and absence of institutional support to military families in the two periods. One regards the lack of a strong civil society and the prevalence of what has been called the "welfare society" (de Sousa Santos, 1993). This refers to the existence of strong solidarity among family, friends, and neighborhood networks (sometimes even coresidence), which compensates for the absence of state-funded mechanisms and provides a different kind of domestic support to families. These informal nets have been considered to coexist in Portugal with a weak welfare state, thus fulfilling the additional function of preventing conflicts over limited resources and services to expand. This sociological pattern explains why, although referring to notably different social and political contexts, the empirical data examined in this chapter show the dominance of what has been identified as a "generalized reciprocity" model of social support (Moelker and van der Kloet, 2003). Combining a communitarian dimension and the independence of participating individuals from the provider of support, this model is based on the idea that "there is a large community of friendship circles with members who support each other, but the ties between the members are not so strong that they would cause the support network to become greedy or challenge the independence of the individuals in the network" (Moelker, Andres, and Poot, 2006: 7). Within this framework, where support is supposed to be stable, because it is offered without the expectation of immediate reciprocation, the potential conflict between the military and the family is low exactly because "both believe the relation to be a two-sided affair" (Moelker et al., 2006: 8).

The second process refers to the role of women and their social participation. Since the 1960s, Portuguese women have been entering the labor market in degrees that rapidly surpassed those of other southern European societies. This strong presence of women in the labor market as full-time workers has been a catalyst for the separation between the worlds of family and the military, thus reinforcing occupational orientations in the Portuguese Armed Forces. Even in the colonial war period, it can be hypothesized that, since most military wives worked in the state bureaucracy and educational system in the colonies, they developed personal and professional connections that prevented social isolation, somehow helping them to rebuild social support networks that predated their move to Africa. Validating this interpretation, however, would require more accurate data than that available about the activities and integration of these women into colonial societies. In the case of those women who did not work, institutional support would have been welcomed and, as some of the interviews showed, resentment over the perceived lack of institutional support was expressed. Such a complaint was totally absent from the discourses of peacekeepers' wives.

Nevertheless, the trend towards high levels of female full-time labor participation and family–work separation, which developed hand in hand with the reliance on generalized reciprocal social support networks, have been reinforced in contemporary Portuguese society. In spite of the existence of a political discourse underlining the importance of work–family conciliation, very few changes have taken place in this respect, both in objective and symbolic terms. Therefore it comes as no surprise to find these features present in the military organization at a time when occupational pressures have been at work, following the move towards an all-volunteer force in 2004.

The "strength of weak ties" (Granovetter, 1973), characteristic of the general reciprocity model of social support networks that was mobilized in both occasions (colonial war and contemporary peacekeeping missions), seems to have been effective in making institutional support to families appear to be dispensable.

Concluding remarks

During the Portuguese authoritarian regime, and the colonial war that it waged in its African colonies between 1961 and 1974, military wives and a proxy organization, the MNF, were found to be relatively effective substitutes for a more formal institutional support system. Despite the absence of a policy that stimulated or supported such a risky move, military wives and their children "went to war," with the aim of providing support and keeping the family together.

At present, the historical heritage of absent institutional concern about military families, together with a weak civil society, a still strong welfare society that reinforces a generalized reciprocity model of social support and an occupationally oriented military (from the point of view of the military–family relationship), articulated to explain the lack of institutional support policies, the absence of requests for that kind of support, and the withdrawal of families from military life, both at home and during deployments.

Perhaps one way in which to read these results is that families have become rather invisible components within the military institutional space because they have been, and still are, the backbone of an informal social support system that the Armed Forces have never been pressured or required to institutionalize.

Notes

1 Part of the empirical work on which this paper is based was developed with the assistance of Verónica Neves.
2 A research project funded by the Portuguese Foundation for Science and Technology and run at CIES-IUL (2007–11).

3   Statutes of the MNF.

4   Magazines *Presença* (1963–65), *Mensagem* (1963–68), *Guerrilha* (1967–73), and *Movimento*.

5   A dozen semidirective, biographic interviews were conducted with women who lived in Africa for at least six months during the war, following their military husbands. The empirical material used in this section includes transcripts of these interviews, as well as testimonies published in Ribeiro (2007) and Soares (2008).

6   Maria Teresa lived with her husband, then a lieutenant, in Toto, Angola, between 1960 and 1962, and gave birth to their son there in 1961.

7   Verónica, wife of an NCO, lived in Angola for two periods in 1969 and 1973.

8   Maria Luísa, wife of a lieutenant colonel, commander of an aviation field, lived in Negage, Angola, during the terrible massacres that led to the official start of the war in 1961 (Ribeiro, 2007).

9   Madalena, wife of a lieutenant, lived in Angola (Malange) for six months.

10   Maria de Lurdes, wife of an NCO, lived at different locations in Mozambique between 1960 and 1968.

11   Portuguese military observers joined various UN missions, but in a limited way: the UN Observation Group in Lebanon (UNOGIL) in 1958; the UN Transition Assistance Group (UNTAG) in Namibia in 1989; the UN Operation in Mozambique (ONOMUZ, from the French), in 1992; the second and third UN Angola Verification Missions (UNAVEM II and UNAVEM III) in 1991 and 1995, respectively; and the UN Observation Mission in Angola (MONUA, from the French) in 1997.

12   From a geographical point of view, international missions have taken place mostly in Europe (the Balkans), but also in the Middle East, Africa (mainly Angola and Mozambique), and East Timor. In 2001, for instance, the Portuguese Armed Forces mobilized 1,736 soldiers in peace-related operations conducted under the auspices of NATO in Bosnia (Stabilization Force, or SFOR), Kosovo (Kosovo Force, or KFOR), Macedonia (FYROM), Afghanistan (International Security Assistance Force, or ISAF), and of the United Nations in East Timor (UN Transitional Administration in East Timor, or UNTAET, and UN Mission of Support in East Timor, or UNMISET). In June 2012, a total of 455 soldiers were involved in three main theaters: Lebanon (UN Interim Force in Lebanon, or UNIFIL: 136); Kosovo (KFOR: 162), and Afghanistan (ISAF: 157).

13   The specific research design for this case study consisted of a mixed-method strategy, involving a variety of methodological procedures and tools. Between February and October 2009, a research team followed a Portuguese infantry battalion, from the predeployment phase in the infantry regiment in Vila Real, a city located in Northern Portugal, to its return home after accomplishing a six-month mission as a Kosovo Force Tactical Reserve Maneuver (KTM) battalion in Kosovo. During the predeployment phase, all 292 members of the battalion completed a survey, formal and informal meetings were held with commanders and high-ranking officers, and thirty in-depth semistructured interviews were conducted with men and women of different ranks, seniority, and occupational areas, as well as with a selected sample of soldiers' wives. During the deployment phase, the research team spent two weeks with the battalion in a military camp in Pristina, Kosovo, participating as much as possible in its daily activities. Finally, the postdeployment period consisted of a shorter stay at the battalion's headquarters back in Portugal, a couple of weeks after its return from the mission. Finally, the whole battalion completed an evaluation survey, and more informal meetings and exchanges took place.

References

Afonso, A., and Gomes, C.M. (2000) *Guerra Colonial.* Lisbon: Editorial Notícias.

Andres, M., Moelker, R., and Soeters, J. (2008) "Fulfilling job and family duties: A battle? A longitudinal study to work–family conflict and relationship satisfaction in the military." Paper presented to the ISA RC01 International Conference on Armed Forces and Conflict Resolution in a Globalized World, July 14–17, Seoul, South Korea.

Antunes, J.F. (1995) *Guerra de África.* Lisbon: Círculo de Leitores.

Branco, C., Garcia, F., and Pereira, C. (2009) *Portugal e as Operações de Paz: Uma visão multidimensional.* Lisbon: Prefácio

Carreiras, H. (1999) "O que pensam os militares Portugueses do peacekeeping?" *Estratégia,* 14: 65–95.

Carreiras, H. (2007) "As Mulheres e a Guerra." In N.S. Teixeira and T. Barata (eds.) *Nova História Militar de Portugal.* Lisbon: Círculo de Leitores, pp. 174–238.

Carreiras, H. (2014) "The sociological dimension of external military interventions: The Portuguese military abroad." *Portuguese Journal of Social Science,* 13(2):129–49.

Copeland, A., and Norell, S.K. (2002) "Spousal adjustment on international assignments: The role of social support." *International Journal of Intercultural Relations,* 26: 255–72.

Coser, L. (1974) *Greedy Institutions: Patterns of undivided commitment.* New York: Free Press.

Dandeker, C., French, C., Birtles, C., and Wessely, S. (2006) "Deployment experiences of British Army wives before, during and after deployment: Satisfaction with military life and use of support networks." Paper #RTO-MP-HFM-134 [online], available from http://ftp.rta.nato.int/public/PubFullText/RTO/MP/RTO-MP-HFM-134/MP-HFM-134-38.pdf

de Sousa Santos, B. (1993) *Portugal: Um Retrato Singular.* Porto: Afrontamento.

Espírito Santo, S. (2003) *Adeus, Até Ao Teu Regresso: O Movimento Nacional Feminino na Guerra Colonial (1961–1974).* Lisbon: Livros Horizonte.

Granovetter, M. (1973) "The strength of weak ties." *American Journal of Sociology,* 78: 1360–80.

Mascarenhas, J.M. (ed.) (2001) *O Estado Novo e as Mulheres: O Género como Investimento Ideológico e de Mobilização.* Lisbon: Câmara Municipal de Lisboa.

Moelker, R., and van der Kloet, I. (2003) "Military families and the armed forces: A two-sided affair?" In G. Caforio (ed.) *Handbook of the Sociology of the Military.* New York: Kluwer Academic/Plenum Publishers, pp. 201–23.

Moelker, R., Andres, M., and Poot, G.J.A. (2006) "Supporting Military Families: A Comparative Study in Social Support Arrangements for Military Families (Theoretical Dimensions and Empirical Comparison between Countries)." Paper #RTO-MP-HFM-134 [online]. available from http://www.dtic.mil/get-tr-doc/pdf?AD=ADA472686

Nuciari, M., and Sertorio, G. (2009) "Military families and deployments abroad in Italy: In search of adequate answers for a new issue." In G. Caforio (ed.) *Advances in Military Sociology: Essays in honor of Charles C. Moskos.* Bingley: Emerald Group Publishing, pp. 263–80.

Orthner, D.K., and Rose, R.M.S. (2005) "Social support and adjustment among army civilian spouses." SAF V Survey Report [online], available from http://www.mwrbrandcentral.com/HOMEPAGE/Graphics/Research/saf5socialsupport7dec05.pdf

Pinto, A.C.P. (2001) *O Fim do Império Português.* Lisbon: Livros Horizonte.

Ribeiro, M.C. (2007) *África no Feminino: As mulheres Portuguesas e a Guerra Colonial.* Porto: Afrontamento.

Santos, J. L. (2001) *Segurança e Defesa na Viragem do Milénio.* Lisboa: Europa-América.

Santos, J. L. (2012) *Forças Armadas em Portugal.* Lisbon: FFMS.

Segal, M. (1986) "The military and the family as greedy institutions." *Armed Forces and Society*, 13(1): 9–38.

Soares, A.R. (2008) *A Mulher Portuguesa na Guerra e nas Forças Armadas.* Lisbon: Liga dos Combatentes.

Sousa, T. (1999) "A imprensa Portuguesa e o conflito na Bósnia: Os meses decisivos". *Estratégia*, 14: 97–103.

Teixeira, N.S. (2009) *Contributos para uma Política de Defesa.* Lisbon: MDN.

Universidade Autónoma de Lisboa (UAL) (2005) *Janus 2005: A Guerra e a Paz nos nossos dias.* Lisboa: Ed Público/UAL.

Vasconcelos, Á. (1999) "Europeização da política de defesa." *Estratégia*, 14: 7–19.

Viana, V.R. (2002) *Segurança Coletiva: A ONU e as Operações de Apoio à Paz.* Lisbon: IDN.

17 Family support systems in the Turkish military

Kadir Varoglu, Yavuz Ercil, and Unsal Sigri

Introduction

The Turkish Armed Forces (TAF) is composed of a blended mixture of professionals (210,000), conscripts (380,000), and civilians (54,000), totaling 644,000 personnel among a population of 75 million.[1] While the officers, noncommissioned officers (NCOs), and a core part of enlisted personnel are professionals, the other part comprises conscripts who serve 15 months in the military at the age of 20. Although the wife of the chief commander represents the "mother of the military family" within Turkish military culture, the percentage of women in military is only 2 percent. No women are recruited into the military as conscripts within the system. The most populated service is Land Forces, which is followed by Gendarmerie, Navy, Air Force, and the Coast Guard. Accurate statistics on marriage rates in the TAF are not available in open sources. It is estimated, however, that the majority (80 percent) of the professionals are married; only 5 percent of the conscripts are thought to be married. The goal for the future is to increase the number of professionals, but the conscription system in TAF is likely to continue. The Turkish military focuses both on antiterror operations at home and on participation in multinational peace support operations abroad (as part of the United Nations, NATO, or European Union).

Military families are a significant part of communities in Turkey. More than a third reside within the civilian community; the remainder resides on military settlements. In spite of the obvious psychological implications, however, military populations and their problems and needs have not frequently been the subject of psychological and sociological discourse in Turkey. Apart from attention in the clinical literature to posttraumatic stress disorder (PTSD) among veterans (especially those who fought against terrorism within the country), military-related articles have not appeared in sociology and psychology publications that are widely read by the academics.

A few sociological and psychological investigations related to military populations have been identified in master's or doctoral theses within military academies or civilian universities (Mazici, 1988; Yildirim, 2009). We cannot assert that there is a scientific focus in Turkey on military sociology and military psychology – but we do recognize some first steps, benefiting from scholars in military sociology, organizational psychology, and clinical psychology. But little published work exists, and large gaps remain between these rare academics and the practitioners and policymakers who are responsible from the management of the military system.

The military as a profession and military life as a lifestyle may be considered relatively more difficult in Turkey than in many other countries. Not only does it involve the typical challenges of other countries from a general perspective, but also the Turkish case has some unique characteristics specific to the conditions of the country. In the context of the increasing number of military missions within the country in the fight against terror and outside the country in terms of peace missions, as a natural outcome of Turkey's dynamic international policy, the Turkish military needs to provide social-psychological support to its personnel in military operations abroad and to their families at home. According to the 2012 Uppsala Conflict Data Program (UCDP)/Peace Research Institute Oslo (PRIO) Armed Conflict Dataset (Uppsala University, 2012), 44 armed conflicts have erupted around Turkey (in the Balkans, Caucuses, and Middle East) during the last ten years. Turkey has also contributed to 10 out of 18 UN peacekeeping operations (United Nations, 2012). Additionally, Turkey has been fighting against terrorism in its homeland for many years. Consequently, the Turkish military has experienced the need for a high level of readiness and mobility, which has meant frequent separations for military families.

In addition to increasing demands on military personnel and their families, the nature of civil–military relations has shifted in Turkey (Aydinli, 2012; Heper, 2011; Jenkins, 2007; Karaosmanoglu, 2011; Narli, 2009). With the changing power shift from military to civilians, based on newly experienced political developments and the impact of the changing social and political environment on civil–military relations, the lives of service members have been transformed. The military in Turkey had always been the dominant political actor in the decision-making mechanisms of the country, and had budgetary priority in the eyes of the government and Parliament. Now, the military system is adjusting to being an ordinary component of the whole state, on a level with the other institutions in the country. Also, the covenant between soldier and society has changed radically. New legal and political developments within the country regarding ex-military personnel, assumed to be preparing coup d'état against current government, have paved the way for a shift in the balance of power between military and political systems in society. It is obvious that this power shift has also affected the relations between civil society and the TAF; however, this shift is not considered to have negative implications for the military profession itself or any other negative implications for the military families.

In parallel with the external difficulties for the Turkish military, there appear some internal problems based on the procedures of military itself. Considering the high power distance of the Turkish culture, this cultural characteristic is thought to pave the way for an autocratic management style and centralized decision-making approaches within the military. This indirectly causes the "micro" management of military work, and subordinates cannot find enough space to participate in decision-making and the implementation of these decisions (Sigri, 2010).

In this chapter, we first explore the challenges that are faced by military families in Turkey. Second, we describe the organizational and legal system for supporting military families within and outside the country. Next, the Turkish case will be specifically reviewed in terms of support for both professional service members and their families. Fourth, the specific opportunities that are extended to the families of martyrs and veterans will be discussed. Finally, the impact of national and organizational culture on the application of a military family support system will be analyzed, and some implications for future studies and practices will be highlighted.

Challenges for military families

The nature of the military compels military personnel to follow the rules, orders, and policies of the military system without hesitation. Deployment is a natural requirement of the military system. Changing personal assignments from time to time makes the issue of deployment much more important not only for military professionals, but also for their families. Psychologically, a deployment weighs heavily on both deployed soldiers and families. They may face a different neighborhood and may face new challenges in the context of a new deployment, such as separation. The way in which soldiers and their families deal with these issues is not only a personal matter, but also reflects the way in which these requirements are handled officially by the political and military system in the country.

Most military families in Turkey are resilient and adapt to the unique circumstances of military life, which include family relocation, as well as separation and reunification with an active duty family member. Military families in Turkey face similar financial and emotional stressors as civilian families in the community. Yet the magnitude and the combination of their stressors may be unique, considering the terror problem of the past 30 years and the struggle against terrorism undertaken mainly by the military. For example, military families in Turkey are more likely than civilian families to experience the death, prolonged illness, or disability of a young or middle-aged loved one as a result of Turkey's long-lasting struggle against terrorism. Between 1984 and 2012, Turkey has lost some 6,200 security forces personnel in its fight against terrorism inside the country, according to information from the Turkish Minister of Defense (Yilmaz, 2012).

In addition to illness, disability, and potential loss of life, the struggle against terror results in frequent changes in assignments and increasing number of deployments as well. As deployments away from the family and home get longer, the spouses and children in military families may move through important developmental periods without one parent at home.

Segal (1986) identified four stressors for military families in the United States: the risk of service member injury or death, frequent relocations, periodic separations, and foreign residence. These stressors also have relevancy for military families in Turkey. We consider the most significant challenges faced by families in the Turkish military to be residential mobility, family separation, risk of injury and death of family member in active duty, and comparably high employment rates among spouses (Akyurek, 2010).

Residential mobility

Turkish military families change households more often than civilian families, affecting employment and educational opportunities. For officers and NCOs within active branches, such as infantry, the service period in a garrison is between two and four years, which means at least seven–ten residential moves during 30 years of total service. Moves often bring great disruption, because they are not between neighborhoods, but between cities or even countries.

Family separation

Turkish military families are not immune from the potential difficulties from deployments. More than half of the military families who have experienced the deployment of a loved one have been separated for a year or longer. Almost 20 percent of the garrisons are not suitable for family life and residence, which means that a soldier must experience a new rotation period without his or her family. The more days for which married service members are deployed, the greater their risk of marital problems, and consequently a possibility of divorce when they return. It may also have negative impacts on the education of the children, when service members are unable to offer social and academic help to the child (Akyurek, 2010). In addition, following the veteran's return from duty, the entire family may go through a period transition. This period brings with it potential problems such as readjustment, reintegration, and experiencing feelings such as stress, uncertainty, and concern during and after homecoming.

Risk of injury or death

Since 1984, with the beginning of terrorist activities of the Kurdistan Workers' Party (Partiya Karkerên Kurdistani, or PKK), some 6,200 security personnel have killed and 13,000 personnel injured (Yilmaz, 2012). Of those killed, 200 were policemen and 1,250 were civilian security personnel; the remaining were all soldiers, from recruit level to generals.

Military families whose loved ones are in antiterror combat zones are aware of the risk for death or serious injury. Among the most challenging risks are the loss of organs and "invisible injuries," such as PTSD.

Family members often perform the care of a soldier who has physical or cognitive injuries.

To some extent, the Turkish military experiences a unique situation with a dual impact on the military families. On the one hand, the Turkish military has been dealing with terrorism within its borders for the last 30 years and has lost more than 7,000 soldiers – both professionals and conscripts, meaning that many military families have faced losses. In addition, the struggles with terror and counterterrorism missions have required personnel to be in the theater of operations alone, without their families. Consequently, these military families were left behind. The solution of terror in Turkey has long been the most important issue on the country's political agenda, with some recent developments. On the other hand, Turkey has for quite some time – since the Korean War in the 1950s, in fact – actively supported international peace operations throughout the world.

These two incidents give rise to some important challenges for policy-makers and pave the way for considering military families as an important factor in the Turkish military.

High employment rate among military spouses

In contrast to many Western militaries that face the problem of underemployment of spouses, the military family in Turkey faces the opposite problem in the context of the overall employment rate for women in Turkey: military spouses are more likely to be employed than civilians. According to data released in December 2012 by the Turkish Statistical Institute, the participation of women in the total workforce is 29 percent. It is expected to be even higher among the military population, but no accurate data are available. Long working hours of military spouses may prevent them from taking care of home and children in the absence of an active military member of the family stationed in elsewhere.

The organization of social-psychological support has therefore become a necessity in the context of the challenges faced Turkish military families. In the short term, the absence of such support can negatively impact the operational readiness of soldiers; in the longer term, the absence of support can have negative effects on recruitment and retention. As a consequence, like all postmodern military organizations, family support services and/or structures have been designed by the Turkish military to provide social-psychological support to military personnel and families before, during, and after missions.

Family support systems

The Turkish military offers various programs in family support. The rights provided to the military service member are also available to military family members. The use of military transportation and the use of military facilities to facilitate daily life, such as military restaurants, cafes, holiday resorts, canteens, and maintenance stores, may be considered as some examples of the opportunities. The military health system, with its hospitals and other health units in big and small garrisons, is another privilege for military personnel and families.

The use of military houses ("digs") is dependent upon the conditions of the garrison, city, and the military neighborhood. The total number of military houses is 42,000, which comprises 17 percent of all government housing (236,000) In fact, in some garrisons, the military digs system is a well-designed structure with military canteens (like the post exchange, or PX, and commissary model of the U. S. Army), schools for children, some social clubs, hair salons, restaurants, post offices, and even banks in secure areas. This model makes military life easier, especially for separated families. A limited childcare service is also provided in some situations. The military even provides some sports and hobby courses for the members of the military families.

The fight against terror resulted in thousands of families with martyrs, [2] veterans, and amputees who experienced their losses while in military service. The statutory military family support system provides many rights to families who have lost service members. Financial aid, scholarships for the children, job opportunities for the unemployed family members, and psychological services are some of the rights of the family members of military martyrs and veterans. Counseling personnel and counseling family practices are also designed to help the military family members in the absence of the service member. These counseling resources perform routine or nonroutine visits to listed families.

This counseling practice is also institutionalized by the Turkish military with the help of two military rehabilitation centers in Ankara (TSK Rehabilitasyon Merkezi-Rehabilitation Center) and Ayvalik (TSK Ali Cetinkaya Rehabilitasyon Merkezi-Rehabilitation Center). These two centers provide free medical and mental treatment for all traumatized soldiers and their families. Medical service, as well as transportation and accommodation support, is provided by these centers as an important element of the military family support system.

Foundations also provide support to members and their families, such as the Soldiers Foundation (*Mehmetçik Vakfı*), the Education Foundation, the TAF Solidarity Foundation (*TSK Dayanışma Vakfı*), and the Health Foundation of Military Personnel. These foundations provide financial assistance to military service personnel and/or their families who are in need. These financial aids encompass a wide spectrum, including death benefits, disaster benefits, health benefits, educational benefits, and scholarships for the children of military veterans, along with advocacy assistance to military families in conflict, and some other benefits and aids.

The unofficial practices are as important as the officially designed military family support system. Considering the collectivistic characteristics of the Turkish culture, people are more likely to define themselves as "we." The culture creates small cliques who are bound to each other, protecting members by providing a social identity. This cultural characteristic is also strengthened by the benevolent philosophy of Islam, which is very sensitive to providing help to those in need. So, together with Turkish cultural and religious characteristics, the formal structure of military family support systems is generally supported by the nature of the informal societal structure to build strong communities, including the strong and significant supportive role of extended family (Martin et al., 2004). Bowen and Martin (2011) use the metaphor the "road of life" to highlight the ability of service members and their families to meet their role responsibilities in the context of military life and duties. Their model incorporates a focus on both individual assets and the social context in which individuals and families are embedded, including attention to both formal systems and informal networks of supports. This model is most descriptive of the support system for military families in Turkey.

Concluding remarks

More research is needed on military families in Turkey. We suggest that a needs assessment related to military families and communities in Turkey should be undertaken, with a focus on community capacity-building for strengthening family resilience and the psychological sense of community. In particular, studies are needed of the long-term effects of deployment on families and communities. There is a real need to explore the ability of service members and their families to meet their role responsibilities in the context of military life and duties. We are currently adapting the Support and Resiliency Inventory" (Bowen and Martin, 2011), for use with service members and the civilian spouses of service members in Turkey. This tool will focus on both individual assets and the social context in which individuals and families are embedded.

The multifaceted challenges of military life, however, call for multilevel strategies of prevention and intervention that will extend the focus from family units to the military community and the larger civilian community in building resilience. To help the military to move from a "stovepipe" – that is, top-down – approach toward more coordinated, multilevel assessment and intervention, the assistance of community psychologists is needed. Developing "community psychology programs" that include working with public policymakers can provide them with some of the requisite knowledge and skills to support military families in Turkey. The training of community psychologists, and mental health and human service professionals, should include more focus on the needs of military families, the policies and resources pertaining to the support of military communities, and the institutional structure of organizations and agencies serving military families and communities.

Ultimately, steps need to be taken in developing systems for supporting Turkish military families. Policymakers can initiate legislation, including laws that will address the childcare needs that arise during a parental separation, including facilitating successful school transfers for children in military families, and provide better employment opportunities for spouses of military personnel, and policies that mandate the development of community psychology programs to help to integrate military families more effectively into society as a whole.

Academic research needs to consider the process of developing support systems for military families by participating in "military human resource management improvement projects" undertaken by the TAF in headquarters. Barriers to psychological outreach to military families and communities continue to exist in research and in practice in Turkey. These barriers include assumptions about the self-sufficiency of the military, professional overspecialization, ideological ambivalence toward warfare, lack of knowledge of the military culture, and the support structures and policies pertaining to the military population, and a tendency for the selection of research problems to be guided by academic and theoretical interests rather than by the support needs of service members and their families. It is obvious that these barriers hamper the process of building support for military families as a whole. The fact that military communities are contiguous with civilian communities means that the historical boundaries need to be overcome as well.

In order to bridge this indicated gap between military and civilian communities, and to increase support for military families and the communities in which they live, community psychologists and military sociologists need more involvement. Collaboration within the profession and among psychology, the military, and other stakeholders should be an important guiding principle for the future.

In recent years, attention to "family support systems" in the Turkish military has gained momentum. However, the academic community in Turkey needs to be more fully engaged in this effort. Therefore it is hoped that this review will serve as a stimulus to increased research and attention to military families in Turkey.

Notes

1 January 2013 figures, accessed from the official Turkish Armed Forces website, available at http://www.tsk.tr
2 A "martyr" is a person who is put to death or endures great suffering because of a particular belief (mostly religion, a principle, or a cause).

References

Akyurek, S. (2010) *Zorunlu Askerlik ve Profesyonel Ordu*. Rapor No. 24, Ankara: BİLGESAM.

Aydinli, E. (2012) "Turkey under the AKP: Civil–military relations transformed." *Journal of Democracy*, 23(1): 100–8.

Bowen, G.L., and Martin, J.A. (2011) "The resiliency model of role performance for service members, veterans, and their families: A focus on social connections and individual assets." *Journal of Human Behavior in the Social Environment*, 21: 162–78.

Heper, M. (2011) "Civil–military relations in Turkey: Toward a liberal model?" *Turkish Studies*, 12: 241–52.

Jenkins, G. (2007) "Continuity and change: Prospects for civil–military relations in Turkey." *International Affairs*, 83: 339–55.

Karaosmanoglu, A. (2011) "Transformation of Turkey's civil–military relations culture and international environment." *Turkish Studies*, 12: 253–64.

Martin, J., Mancini, D., Bowen, G., Mancini, J., and Orthner, D. (2004) *Building Strong Communities for Military Families*. Fact Sheet. Minneapolis, MN: National Council on Family Relations.

Mazici, N. (1988) "Türkiye'de Askeri Darbelerin Sivil Rejimler Üzerindeki Etkileri [The impact of military interventions on civilian rule in Turkey]." Unpublished Ph.D. thesis, Istanbul University, Istanbul.

Narli, N. (2009) "EU harmonization reforms, democratization and a new modality of civil–military relations in Turkey." In G. Caforio (ed.) *Advances in Military Sociology: Essays in honor of Charles C. Moskos*. Bingley: Emerald Group Publishing, pp. 433–72.

Segal, M.W. (1986) "The military and the family as greedy institutions." *Armed Forces & Society*, 13: 9–38.

Sigri, U. (2010). "Savasta Yonetsel Karar Verme [Managerial and military decision making in war]." In H. Yalcinkaya (ed.) *Savas [War]*. Ankara: Siyasal Kitabevi, pp. 91–119.

Uppsala University, Department of Peace and Conflict Research (2012) "UCDP/ PRIO Armed Conflict Dataset." [online], available from http://www.pcr. uu.se/research/ucdp/datasets/ucdp_prio_armed_conflict_dataset/ [accessed December 25, 2012].

United Nations (2012) "UN Missions Summary of Military and Police." November 30 [online], available from http://www.un.org/en/peacekeeping/ contributors/2012/Nov12_6.pdf [accessed December 15, 2012].

Yildirim, B, (2009) "Birinci Dünya Savaşında Asker Ailelerine Yapilan Yardimlar [State support given to soldiers' families during the First World War]." Unpublished M.Sc. thesis, Marmara University, Istanbul.

Yilmaz, I. (2012) "28 yillik bilanço." *Finans Gündem*, July 11 [online], available from <URL>http://www.finansgundem.com/haber/28-yillik-bilanco/308109</ URL> [accessed January 2013].

18 "Down under"

Support for military families from an Australian perspective

Philip Siebler[1]

Introduction

> The military is just such a closed book . . . you don't go to unless you really have to. It's like a brotherhood that all just sticks together, and you're just dragged along for the ride and you can't really communicate with them . . . because . . . you'd embarrass your husband . . .
>
> (Nondeployed spouse)

This quote from an Australian family member raises issues about military culture, help-seeking behavior, and the inherent tensions between the military organization and family. Unfortunately, little is known about the situation and needs of Australian military families. This chapter addresses this gap and achieves three main objectives. First, an overview is provided of formal military family support mechanisms in the Australian Defense setting.

Second, findings are presented from the author's qualitative Australian study (Siebler, 2009; Siebler and Goddard, 2014). This investigation took place in the context of Australia's largest deployment since the Vietnam War – that is, East Timor. This study examined the inherent tensions between the family and military organization, family perceptions of formal and informal family support, and stresses on the soldier and the military family.

Finally, the implications of the findings are outlined for policy and practice.

Military family support

Force structure and demands

Australia's operational commitments have increased markedly in recent years. The contemporary Australian Department of Defense (DoD) comprises the Australian Defense Force (ADF) of some 59,000 active duty and 21,500 active reserve force personnel, as well as 22,000 civilian Commonwealth public servants (Defense Census, 2011). The permanent force had been decreasing since a post-Vietnam peak of 73,185 in 1983 (Shephard, 1999). However, the permanent force had a 15 percent increase of 7,675 members between 2007 and 2011 (Defense Census, 2011).

While the precise number of family members, including spouses, children, and parents, is not available, 38 percent of personnel indicated that they were currently married, with a further 20 percent in interdependent partnerships; 37 percent of permanent force members indicated that they had dependent children, and 3 percent reported that they had dependents other than their spouse or children. Of all permanent force members, 56 percent have had at least one deployment since January 1999, with an average of 3.4 deployments (Defense Census, 2011).

A brief history of family support organizations

Defense has a long history of supporting families through the provision of a range of programs and services, and more recently through policy that aims to involve families in mental health service delivery (Commonwealth of Australia, 2011). Historically, the social work profession played the primary role in working with military families. Indeed, work with returning soldiers pioneered many developments in marital counseling in Australia (Wood, 2001). Since the 1950s, social work has been the sole profession providing military family support in the DoD. Until 1996, the Army, Navy, and Air Force each had their own separate family support organizations employing social workers. A fourth organization, the Australian Defense Families Information and Liaison Staff, employed social workers in a community development role. In 1996, these four organizations were restructured to form the Defense Community Organization (DCO).

The DCO is a formal family support organization. According to the current *DCO Commander's Handbook*:

> DCO's strategic direction focuses on a long-term strategy of family self-reliance. The theme "Thriving in the Defense Community" underpins DCO's approach to building opportunities and setting the conditions for success for Defense families. The key to this is the message: A strong family produces a stronger and more capable ADF member.
> (Department of Defense, 2011: 4)

The DCO has five aims. First, regarding critical incident and casualty support, the DCO is responsible for the case management of funerals, and the support of family members and other close associates of ADF members who die or are injured while in service.

Second, "absence from home" support recognizes that separation and deployments are aspects of military life that may require targeted support, such as education pre-, during and postdeployment.

Third, self-reliance support via a community capacity-building approach aims to promote good mental health and well-being, and is a pivotal function of the DCO. This may include support for a partners' education and employment, help with child care, financial support to ADF groups, and educational support for children (Department of Defense, 2012a). In support of self-reliant functioning, the DCO aims to strengthen family connections to informal systems of care.

Fourth, recognizing the importance of military culture, the DCO's command management and policy educates commanders about family needs. Social workers regularly provide written feedback to command regarding factors in families' lives compassionate consideration of which may affect a decision regarding an ADF member, such as a need to return a member from a military operation.

Finally, mobility support acknowledges relocation as an inherent part of military life and provides assistance to families through programs, information dissemination on new posting localities, and education, social work services, and informative literature.

The DCO employs civilian social workers located near a number of ADF facilities around Australia. In 2012, it launched an all-hours Defense Family Helpline (Department of Defense, 2012a), which commanders, ADF members, and family members may call (or to which they may send an email) for information or to access assistance. According to the *DCO Commanders' Handbook* (Department of Defense, 2011), social workers provide assessment, reports, brief interventions, bereavement support, community development, group work, educative programs, and referrals of ADF families to appropriate specialist community services and agencies. Unlike their overseas counterparts in the United States (Beder, 2012), social workers in the DCO do not provide clinical interventions with respect to health and mental health to ADF personnel or their families; instead they refer members and families to appropriate services.

The paucity of family research

While ADF personnel are provided with a system of health care via the DoD, nonmilitary family members utilize the universal services of Australia's healthcare system, known as "Medicare," as well as mental health services in the general community. The DoD has conducted a landmark study into the prevalence of mental health conditions in the ADF population (Hodson et al., 2011). However, as in many overseas countries, no research has been conducted to determine the prevalence of mental health problems with respect to the military family population. One exception, a study from the United States (Chandra et al., 2011), suggested that children whose parents are deployed might have more emotional difficulties when compared to national samples. In Australia, it is unknown if the prevalence rates are higher or lower than the general population.

Findings for the general population in Australia are available and can be used as a basis for extrapolation to the military population, although caution is warranted. The National Survey of Mental Health and Wellbeing of the Australian population reported the following findings:

Of the 16 million Australians aged 16–85 years, almost half (45 per cent or 7.3 million) had a lifetime mental disorder, i.e., a mental disorder at some point in their life. One in five (20 per cent or 3.2 million) Australians had a 12-month mental disorder . . . More than a quarter (26 per cent) of people aged 16–24 years and a similar proportion (25 per cent) of people aged 25–34 years had a 12-month mental disorder compared with 5.9 per cent of those aged 75–85 years old.

(Australian Bureau of Statistics, 2007: 7–9)

Therefore, in Australia and consistently with international findings, the general population has a relatively high prevalence of mental health problems. Children and adolescents also have a high prevalence of mental disorders (14 percent), and a high rate of comorbidity with other mental disorders in all age and gender groups (Sawyer et al., 2000). Children aged 6–12 are more likely to have a disorder than adolescents aged 13–17 (17 percent vs. 12 percent). Children and adolescents with behavioral and emotional problems have a lower quality of life than those with fewer problems. Parents who care for such children and adolescents report greater concern and worry and less time for their own personal needs (Sawyer et al., 2000). Although these findings are only suggestive of what may be the situation for military families, it is reasonable to expect the prevalence and implications of mental disorders to be similar, or even worse, in military families, especially in the context of lifestyle demands. Given the reported notable trend towards a greater level of traumatic symptomatology with each deployment for ADF personnel and their families (Commonwealth of Australia, 2011), the dearth of research regarding these "occupational families," and children in particular, is surprising.

The impetus for change: The Dunt Review

Until 2010, exclusive of families, ADF uniformed and civilian psychologists provided an organizational psychology service to ADF personnel only. A review into mental health care in the ADF, known as the "Dunt Review" (Dunt, 2009), recognized gaps in mental health care for personnel and families. The DoD adopted 49 of the 52 recommendations and allocated AUS$83 million over four years to implement the reform. In particular, a greater involvement of families in mental health care of ADF members was a pivotal recommendation (Dunt, 2009). In concert with Australia's Fourth National Mental Health Plan (Commonwealth of Australia, 2009), multidisciplinary mental health and psychology teams have been created out of the former psychology support sections, in addition to the DCO. These mental health teams are integrated into the DoD's primary care health system, and will be composed of mental health nurses, social workers, psychologists, and occupational therapists. In addition, the review recommended training for this new mental health workforce, an increase in mental health staffing, and a greater capacity to provide mental health prevention and promotion. Regional mental health teams were formed to provide the latter capability, with an additional 32 full-time civilian positions nationally. In addition, the Alcohol, Tobacco and Other Drugs (ATOD) program is a significant component of the ADF Mental Health and Wellbeing Strategy, the intent of which is to be inclusive of families, and which recognizes that the continuum of mental health care, from prevention to treatment, needs "to take into account the environment, culture, social support networks and impact of families" (Commonwealth of Australia, 2011: 7). The extent and nature of involvement of families in mental health care is under development. Notwithstanding, it will be critical for families to receive the assistance that they require. particularly during all of the stages of deployment.

Perceptions of Australian Defense
Force personnel and their families

In the context of recent calls for more in-depth research on military families, especially employing qualitative research designs (Moelker, Andres, and Poot, 2006), an ecological model of the military family was created, modified from a public health model, to inform a qualitative study of deployment in the Australian military (Siebler, 2009). The focus was on the recent deployment of the Australian military to East Timor, and the consequences for service members and the families of these peacekeepers. The model considered the micro-, meso-, and macrosystem levels involved in influencing military family life (Bronfenbrenner, 1979).[2] In the study, microsystem-level circumstances included the uncertainty of deployment, concerns about children and adolescents, physical and mental health and family functioning problems, the advantages and disadvantages of communicating during separation, and finding meaning in the experience. Living and working conditions in East Timor of ADF personnel, the communities in which nondeployed respondents lived, social support and networks, and perception of military family support organizations were important aspects at the mesosystem level. Finally, macrosystem-level circumstances included the military institution, culture, and policies.

The research posed an overarching question to yield a rich description of family life: what are the experiences of ADF peacekeepers and their families in relation to an overseas deployment? As Fraser (2004: 184) has suggested, research needs "to delve beneath statistically driven generalizations" and validate the knowledge of "ordinary people." Moelker and colleagues (2006: 1) contend that research is often based on quantitative data collection, and that "thick" sociological analysis is required of the military family.

Method

The research was conducted during the period from 2001–06, and arose because of the researcher's employment as a civilian social worker in the Australian DoD at the time of the deployment and as a doctoral candidate in social work. Hence the author conducted all components of the research with ethics approval of Monash University and the DoD.

The military service interviewees had deployed as part of the International Force for East Timor (INTERFET) and/or the United Nations Transitional Administration for East Timor (UNTAET). The Australian government deemed these operations "warlike" and "nonwarlike," respectively. Although the findings of this study cannot be generalized across the ADF, the findings provide insights into the phenomenon of deployment. The potent stories of the interviewees have enabled greater understanding to be gained of the multifaceted nature of the deployment experience.

Participants

Participants who had deployed to East Timor and/or their spouses were recruited by advertising the research in a wide variety of military settings, such as newspapers and newsletters sent to families. Using in-depth interviewing (Minichiello et al., 2004), a total of 44 interviews were conducted, involving 76 participants. Of the 76 participants, 40 had deployed and 36 were nondeployed spouses. Thirty-two of the interviews were undertaken with couples; 12, with individuals. The average length of the interviews was approximately 90 minutes. Forty participants were Army personnel and their spouses. Twenty-two respondents were Air Force personnel and their spouses, and 14 respondents were Navy personnel and their spouses. Four females and 36 males were deployed, which reflects the ratio of males to females in the ADF. Only one of the 36 nondeployed spouses was male. Single members, sole parents, married/de facto couples, dual-serving couples, and reservists across all ranks participated.

Analysis

Quotes are used to illustrate four major themes: perceptions of the deployment; positive and negative effects on physical and mental health, and family functioning; helpful and unhelpful experiences of formal support mechanisms; and helpful and unhelpful experiences of informal support mechanisms. The transcripts were coded and categorized, and compared and contrasted, to integrate into themes. Using NVivo software for electronic storage, filing, and retrieval of the large amounts of text, data analysis thus led to the major themes.

Findings

Perceptions of the deployment

> We both work in the Intelligence Field so we've probably got a heads up more than what normal people would . . . no time to think, no time to prepare, no time to do anything especially at that hour of night, coming home and saying "I'm leaving tomorrow morning . . . " It was just shocking.
>
> (Nondeployed spouse)

> I've made a difference . . . We went to a couple of villages . . . The unit adopted this particular village, had not had any medical attention for 20, 25 years . . . this elderly gentleman came in, he sat down and I said "what's the problem?," he goes his foot hurts, he had these ratty old shoes on, takes his shoe off. He had no foot.
>
> (ADF member)

A number of family theorists posit that researchers need to listen to family members' interpretations of their situations to understand why some families remain resilient and others struggle (Boss, 2002; Patterson, 2002). Deployed and nondeployed respondents found meaning in their experiences in nuanced ways, and displayed an array of thoughts and emotions about military family life, deployment, and its consequences. Unlike previous research that has categorized deployment in binary terms as "positive/negative" (Newby et al., 2005), respondents in this study did not describe their experiences in terms such as "good/bad," or "compatible/incompatible" with family life. As the first quote above crystallizes, a lack of preparation was found for deployment on the part of personnel and family members. To name a few aspects, the need for wills, powers of attorney, organization of child care, and a lack of knowledge of family support available through the DoD policy was an unexpected finding, given that the ADF trains for this eventuality. This raised questions about how families understood the need for preparedness and DoD's assistance in this regard.

Similar to previous studies (Thomas et al., 2006), ADF personnel expressed an appreciation of "life in Australia," great pride in their deployment achievements (as the second quote above illustrated), and appreciation for the opportunity to utilize their training and skills in an operational setting. Nondeployed spouses expressed pride in managing a lengthy separation and pride in their partner's achievements. An interesting finding was that nondeployed family members displayed considerable empathy and philanthropy towards the community of East Timor by sending mail packages of resources to schools and villages. This notion of reciprocity in giving and receiving social support is one characteristic of a strong social network (Harms, 2005), which is linked to positive physical and mental health outcomes (Berkman et al., 2000). Overall, attempting to find meaning in the deployment was characterized by ambiguities as respondents weighed the costs and benefits of the experience.

Positive and negative effects on physical and
mental health and family functioning

> . . . He would just be running into his bedroom, running into the walls at full pelt . . . He threatened to stab himself with a really sharp knife in the kitchen . . . And she [family support worker] rang the psychiatrist and said: "look, this is getting to breaking point." He said "well I can put him in the psychiatric facility at the children's hospital or we can put him on some drugs or we can try and get the husband back."
>
> (Nondeployed spouse, about her 8-year-old son)

> . . . One weekend he was so bad that I rang up the Vietnam Vets Association because I believed that they do counseling and I just told them the situation . . . "He is a very depressed person, saying that he hates his life and hates everything . . . to see it affect everyone in the house and you can only sort of put up with it for so long . . . but when I told him that he went off his brain . . . he won't even talk to anyone about it . . . ."
>
> (Nondeployed spouse)

A range of concerns relating to physical and mental health, and family functioning, were critical issues for most respondents. An array of physical and mental health problems were apparent for deployed ADF personnel and their nondeployed spouses, as well as children and adolescents. It was apparent that nondeployed participants developed or experienced exacerbation of existing mental health problems, such as depression, across the full spectrum of diagnoses from mild to severe, including one diagnosis of posttraumatic stress disorder (PTSD) that led to 12 months off paid employment for one spouse. Physical health problems affected a number of interviewees and placed respondents at risk of mental health problems, as well as difficulties with daily managing. One ectopic pregnancy and two miscarriages were reported while partners were deployed. Sleep problems were paramount for nondeployed respondents in particular. Evidence that the mental health of respondents negatively affected family and couples' relationships was apparent. As the first quote above illustrates, one ADF member was returned from East Timor when his 8-year-old son threatened self-harm.

Respondents' living and working conditions in East Timor provided the environment for the traumatic events associated with a diagnosis of PTSD (Keane et al., 2011). Consistent with previous research regarding the stressors of peacekeeping (Shigemura and Nomura, 2002), experiences at this level for deployed participants were characterized by uncertainty, a sense of "not knowing" who the real enemy was, and the constant threat of harm. This uncertainty contributed to conundrums for respondents in deciding to exercise restraint or to use force. Conditions were harsh and respondents confronted numerous environmental hazards. A number of respondents were involved in recovery of bodies from wells, combat resulting in death, and handling and transporting bodies.

Children and adolescents were aware of, and worried about, their parents' military employment and deployment. As the second quote above indicates, this family member was desperate for assistance and sought help for her partner outside of the DoD when problems were negatively impacting on the whole family. A disturbing finding was the enduring suffering before, during, and after deployment of a significant number of young children. Children's and adolescents' symptoms were consistent with undiagnosed mental health conditions, including depression. The evidence that some interviewees sought assistance for their children and did not receive adequate help was a cause for concern.

Helpful and unhelpful experiences of formal support mechanisms

> She [social worker] didn't actually speak to me. "And how will your wife cope?" and "Has she been on her own before?" . . . I'm sitting here thinking that I've suddenly gone invisible.
>
> (Nondeployed spouse)

> The counselor . . . in Psych Corps . . . basically said it's not our responsibility to find these people that are having troubles. You've got to identify it and come and see us, and I snapped straight back at him I said "I didn't even know I had a problem."
>
> (ADF member)

The study adopted a broad definition of formal support mechanisms that included policy, the DCO, command, psychology, the ADF Chaplaincy, and an organization that was created at the time of the East Timor deployment, the National Welfare Coordination Center. This ADF-staffed organization was a 24/7 free call linkage point for families and personnel in situations such as casualty notification and repatriation of ADF personnel to Australia, in circumstances of injury or serious illness, or death of a family member at home.

Military family support organizations were helpful for some respondents, and strongly dismissed as unhelpful and irrelevant for others. Information flow between organizations limited their effectiveness. Most nondeployed respondents wanted and expected some form of contact from the DoD, particularly the DCO or command, even if they were managing well. Many received no contact. ADF respondents expected the DoD to "look after their families." Some respondents were very critical of both ADF welfare staff and civilian service providers, such as psychologists and social workers, as illustrated by the quotes above. Respondents spoke about the inability of professionals to listen, empathize, and establish a relationship, which are foundational skills in the helping professions. Respondents also wanted staff to be knowledgeable about the strains of deployment, to know about available resources, and to know how to access these resources.

Helpful and unhelpful experiences of informal support mechanisms

> I wasn't in the clique plus I was only a corporal's wife. Comes down to the rank, my husband didn't have enough rank to warrant being looked after a little bit better.
>
> (Nondeployed spouse)

> But living in the village where we were, we were all . . . you know we had SAS wives around us as well . . . Everybody understands . . . civilians don't really understand like the military.
>
> (Nondeployed spouse)

With few exceptions, a striking finding of the current study was a theme of disconnectedness from any notion of a military community, with consequent loneliness. Some respondents' networks were composed of few people, which may have contributed to isolation and loneliness for some, and influenced mental and physical health and family functioning (Berkman et al., 2000). This study finding contrasted with a report from the United Kingdom (King's Centre for Military Health Research, 2010), which noted the general strength of informal social support networks.

The mobility of respondents in this study acted to sever affiliations for some, such as those who relocated when their partners deployed. Communities had a number of assets that some respondents utilized, such as family centers. For those with a strong sense of affinity as a "military family," there was a strong sense of connection to military family resources on bases and the notion that the ADF community "understood" their concerns. For those with less of an affiliation, they had some or no contact with these facilities. Families at the greatest risk for problems were those who were disconnected from both the military community and the larger general community.

Social supports such as family, friends, church, and use of the Internet sustained a small number of respondents throughout deployment in particular. Self-help groups were reported as helpful for a small number of respondents. However, negative perceptions of self-help groups served to exclude and alienate some nondeployed respondents. Notions of "cliques" and "gossip" acted to inhibit the formation of social networks for some, and may be likened to what Goffman (1982: 18) termed "surveillance," since some respondents felt that they were under the scrutiny and judgment of others. This explains why some respondents withdrew or would have nothing to do with groups or their neighbors. A perception that support was available for some respondents, even though in practice it was quite limited, was an important finding. In some cases, weak ties, such as contacts with others that respondents barely knew, were perceived as very supportive, which suggests that the small actions of people made a difference. Many of these weak ties were via the Internet, which suggest a host of options for policymakers that may be helpful in sustaining families throughout deployment.

Lessons learned and ways forward

> (My) family is also part of that person over in Timor or on deployment . . . And unless they're looked after, the one over there is not looked after either. That's something Defense has got to realize.
>
> (ADF member)

The notion that war (Leed, 1979) and peacekeeping operations (Weisaeth, 1979) affect military personnel's mental health and well-being is a long-standing theme in the literature, and this was a significant finding of this study. As a case in point, Waller and colleagues (2012) found, in their East Timor peacekeepers' sample, that those who reported more traumatic exposures, such as fear of injury or death, or observing dead bodies and human degradation, had a greater likelihood of physical and mental health outcomes more than eight years after deployment.

Significantly, until this study was undertaken, the perspectives of nondeployed spouses had received little attention in Australian research. Indeed, family systems, ecological, and intergenerational family theories place the family as the "unit of attention" (Hartman and Laird, 1983: 4), which was a resounding theme of respondents in the study. As the above quote illustrates, not only is the family important to military personnel, but ADF respondents also want and expect attention to be paid to their family's needs as well as their own, particularly in the context of a deployment. Findings from the current study suggest that deployment is a challenging event for families. Although many families managed the experience adequately, some experienced family dissolution, and significant physical and mental health problems. As noted previously, current research is emerging of the enduring consequences of this peacekeeping operation for ADF personnel exposed to trauma. In some cases, ADF personnel and their families did not receive the assistance that they required to ameliorate family difficulties, since processes were not in place to identify families requiring support and intervention throughout the stages of deployment.

Military families that undergo the experience of deployment are subject to a number of risk and protective factors, and constitute a subgroup within the overall ADF population that requires nuanced policy and service consideration. Given that notions of belonging to a community were problematic for participants in this study, DoD social workers can do more to strengthen communities via community capacity-building. As Bowen and colleagues (2000) suggest, a crucial function of formal systems, such as the DCO, is to strengthen informal networks, which are often untapped resources in building communities (Mancini, Martin, and Bowen, 2003). In essence, in such a model, social workers would work to form partnerships with military unit leadership, strengthen the interface of the DCO with informal networks, and work collaboratively with community agencies internal and external to the ADF (Bowen, Martin, and Nelson, 2002). Social workers are also encouraged to model, teach, and support skill identification and development throughout the military family life cycle (Kemp and Scanlon, 2002). As a case in point, DCO social workers have begun to provide psycho-educational resilience training for families, children, and adolescents, known respectively as "FamilySMART," "KidSMART," and "TeenSMART" (Department of Defense, 2012b). In addition, the burgeoning of social media and other information technologies offers opportunities to develop assistance for ADF families in online communities.

Implementation of the ADF Mental Health and Wellbeing Strategy (Commonwealth of Australia, 2011) and the DCO Strategic Direction will require a largely civilian workforce of social workers, mental health nurses, and psychologists, with a skillset and knowledge base for being able to work effectively with families. The DoD will need to create viable educational programs for its staff in family-sensitive practice, in accordance with recommendations made in a seminal review into mental health in the ADF, the Dunt Review (Dunt, 2009). In particular, as the study has shown, the DoD's civilian providers need to better understand military culture (Hall, 2011).

Since this study was undertaken, the DoD has made a number of significant advances in mental health and family support. The DCO has developed a comprehensive "Absence from Home" program, which provides a wide range of resources to help families, has conducted further family research, and has hosted its first "Family Conference" to consult with families (Department of Defense, 2012b). As a case in point, ADF members can access the new Defense Family Helpline while on deployment and request assistance for their families. The ADF Mental Health and Wellbeing Strategy (Commonwealth of Australia, 2011) has mandated the development of a number of initiatives, such as involving family members in postoperational psychological screening (Defense Community Organization North Queensland, 2012), and of a family-inclusive strategy as priorities.

Further qualitative and quantitative research into Australian military families is required to develop better programs and services for families, particularly with respect to children and adolescents. Many unanswered questions remain: what is the prevalence of mental health disorders in this population? In the context of a deployment, to what extent is family violence/ child abuse an issue, how do they intersect with veteran and family mental health, and what programs are effective in addressing these problems? The DoD needs to develop and fund external military family research collaboration similar to existing partnerships, such as the Australian Center for Posttraumatic Mental Health and the Center for Military and Veterans' Health. A primary focus would be to promote the well-being of the Australian military family at family, community, and population levels. This would further inform the DCO and the ADF Mental Health and Wellbeing Strategy. The DoD could create an international collaboration, enabling researchers to access its personnel and families to undertake independent military family research that could be disseminated and utilized both internationally and within the DoD. This research would be evidence-informed, with an emphasis on effective program development. Finally, the perspectives and insights of ADF families need to be listened to, validated, and acknowledged, in order to develop appropriate programs and services that address their complex needs.

In conclusion, and in contrast to previous research, the findings of this study suggest that ADF personnel and their spouses find meaning in the deployment experience in nuanced ways, and display an array of thoughts and emotions about military family life, deployment, and its consequences. Perhaps the most important conclusion of this study is that the military family lifestyle, in the context of deployment in particular, needs to be understood, validated, and addressed by government policymakers.

Notes

1 The views expressed in this chapter are those of the author and should not be taken to represent the policy or standpoint of the Australian Department of Defense.
2 See Siebler (2009) for a fuller exposition.

References

Australian Bureau of Statistics (2007) *National Survey of Mental Health and Wellbeing: Summary of results, 2007.* [online], available from http://www.abs.gov .au/ausstats/abs@.nsf/mf/4326.0 [accessed December 23, 2011].

Beder, J. (2012) "Social work in the Department of Defense hospital." *Advances in Social Work,* 13: 132–48.

Berkman, L.F., Glass, T.G., Brissette, I., and Seeman, T. (2000) "From social integration to health: Durkheim in the new millennium." *Social Science & Medicine,* 51: 843–57.

Boss, P. (2002) *Family Stress Management: A contextual approach* (2nd edn.). Thousand Oaks, CA: Sage.

Bowen, G.L., Martin, J.A., and Nelson, J.P. (2002) "A community capacity response to family violence in the United States Air Force." In A. Roberts and G. Greene (eds.) *Social Workers' Desk Reference.* New York: Oxford University Press, pp. 551–6.

Bowen, G.L., Martin, J.A., Mancini, J.A., and Nelson, J.P. (2000) "Community capacity: Antecedents and consequences." *Journal of Community Practice*, 8: 1–21.

Bronfenbrenner, U. (1979) *The Ecology of Human Development: Experiments by nature and design.* Cambridge, MA: Harvard University Press.

Chandra, A., Lara-Cinisimo, S., Jaycox, L., Tanielian, T., Han, B., Burns, R., and Ruder, T. (2011) *Views from the Home Front: The experience of youth and spouses from military families.* Santa Monica, CA: RAND Corporation.

Commonwealth of Australia (2009) *Fourth National Mental Health Plan: An agenda for collaborative government action in mental health, 2009–2014.* Canberra: Department of Defense.

Commonwealth of Australia (2011) *Capability through Mental Fitness: 2011 ADF mental health and wellbeing strategy.* Canberra: Department of Defense.

Defense Census (2011) *Department of Defense Census 2011.* Melbourne: Roy Morgan Research.

Defense Community Organization North Queensland (2012) *Gone Troppo* (May/June edn.).

Department of Defense (2011) "The commanding officers' handbook." *Defense Community Organization* [online], available from http://www.defence.gov.au/dco/documents/CO's%20Handbook%202010-2011.pdf [accessed December 20, 2011].

Department of Defense (2012a) "Support for families during deployment." *Defense Community Organization* [online], available from http://www.defence.gov.au/dco/Family_support_during_deployment.htm [accessed January 21, 2012].

Department of Defense (2012b) "Defense family matters." *Defense Community Organization*, Autumn [online], available from http://www.defence.gov.au/dco/documents/dfm/DFM_Autumn_2012.pdf [accessed August 26, 2012].

Dunt, D. (2009) *Review of Mental Health Care in the ADF and Transition through Discharge.* Canberra: Department of Defense.

Fraser, H. (2004) "Doing narrative research: Analyzing personal stories line by line." *Qualitative Social Work*, 3: 179–201.

Goffman, E. (1982) *Asylums: Essays on the social situation of mental patients and other inmates.* Harmondsworth: Penguin Books.

Hall, L. (2011) "The importance of understanding military culture." *Social Work in Health Care*, 50: 4–18.

Harms, L. (2005) *Understanding Human Development: A multidimensional approach.* South Melbourne: Oxford University Press.

Hartman, A., and Laird, J. (1983) *Family-Centered Social Work Practice.* New York: The Free Press.

Hodson, S., McFarlane, A., Van Hooff, M., and Davies, C. (2011) *Mental Health in the Australian Defense Force: 2010 ADF Mental health prevalence and wellbeing study – Executive report.* Canberra: Department of Defense.

Keane, T., Niles, B., Otis, J., and Quinn, S. (2011) "Addressing posttraumatic stress disorder in veterans." In A. Adler, P. Bliese, and C. Castro (eds.) *Deployment Psychology.* Washington, D.C.: American Psychological Association, pp. 243–73.

Kemp, S., and Scanlon, E. (2002) "Practice with communities." In M. Mattaini, C. Lowery, and C. Meyer. *Foundations of Social Work Practice.* Washington, D.C.: National Association of Social Workers Press, pp. 230–61.

King's Centre for Military Health Research (2010) *What Has Been Achieved by Fifteen Years of Research into the Health of the UK Armed Forces?* London: King's College London.

Leed, E. (1979) *No Man's Land: Combat and identity in World War I.* Cambridge: Cambridge University Press.

Mancini, J.A., Martin, J.A., and Bowen, G.L. (2003) "Community capacity." In T. Gullotta and M. Bloom (eds.) *Encyclopedia of Primary Prevention and Health Promotion.* New York: Kluwer Academic, pp. 319–30.

Minichiello, V., Madison, J., Hays, T., and Parmenter, G. (2004) "Doing qualitative in-depth interviews." In V. Minichiello, G. Sullivan, K. Greenwood, and R. Axford (eds.) *Research Methods for Nursing and Health Science.* French Forest, NSW: Pearson Education, pp. 411–46.

Moelker, R., Andres, M., and Poot, G.J.A. (2006) "Supporting Military Families: A Comparative Study in Social Support Arrangements for Military Families (Theoretical Dimensions and Empirical Comparison between Countries)." Paper #RTO-MP-HFM-134 [online]. available from http://www.dtic.mil/get-tr -doc/pdf?AD=ADA472686 [accessed November 8, 2007].

Newby, J., McCarroll, J., Ursano., R., Zizhong, F., Shigemura, J., and Tucker-Harris, Y. (2005) "Positive and negative consequences of a military deployment." *Military Medicine,* 170: 815–19.

Patterson, J. (2002) "Integrating family resilience and family stress theory." *Journal of Marriage & Family,* 64: 349–60.

Sawyer, M., Arney, F., Baghurst, P., Clark, J., Graetz, B., Kosky, R., Nurcombe, B., Patton, G., Prior, M., Raphael, B., Rey, J., Whaites, L., and Zubrick, S. (2000) *The Mental Health of Young People in Australia.* Canberra: Mental Health and Special Programs Branch, Commonwealth Department of Health and Aged Care.

Shephard, A. (1999) *Trends in Australian Defense: A resources survey.* Canberra: Australian Defense Studies Centre.

Shigemura, J., and Nomura, S. (2002) "Mental health issues of peacekeeping workers." *Psychiatry & Clinical Neurosciences,* 56: 483–91.

Siebler, P. (2009) " 'Military people won't ask for help': Experiences of deployment of Australian Defense Force personnel, their families, and implications for social work." Unpublished Ph.D. thesis, Monash University [online], available from http://arrow.monash.edu.au/hdl/1959.1/157678 [accessed December 21, 2011].

Siebler, P., and Goddard, C. (2014) "Parents' perspectives of their children's reactions to an Australian military deployment," *Children Australia,* 39: 17–24.

Thomas, S., Dandeker, C., Greenberg. N., Kelly, V., and Wessely, S. (2006) " 'Serving in Bosnia made me appreciate living in Bristol': Stressful experiences, attitudes, and psychological needs of members of the United Kingdom Armed Forces." *Military Medicine,* 171: 376–80.

Waller, M., Treloar, S., Sim, M., McFarlane, A., McGuire, A., Bleier, J., and Dobson, A. (2012) "Traumatic events, other operational stressors and physical and mental health reported by Australian Defense Force personnel following peacekeeping and war-like deployments." *BMC Psychiatry,* 12: 88.

Weisaeth, L. (1979) *Psychiatric Disease and Stress among UN soldiers in South Lebanon (UNFIL).* Oslo: Forsuarets Saniets.

Wood, A. (2001) "The origins of family systems work: Social workers' contributions to the development of family theory and practice." *Australian Social Work,* 54: 15–29.

19 Family support and the Japan Self-Defense Forces

Challenges and developing new programs

Hitoshi Kawano and Atsuko Fukuura

Introduction

The Japan Self-Defense Forces (JSDF) has engaged in various types of new mission overseas since 1992, stretching globally from Haiti, to Golan Heights, Iraq, South Sudan, and the Gulf of Aden. More than 20,000 personnel have engaged in peacekeeping, international disaster relief, humanitarian assistance, maritime refueling, and antipiracy operations in the last 20 years. In particular, the operational tempo has dramatically increased since the 9/11 terrorist attacks in the United States in 2001. The operational history of the JSDF has shifted into a new phase of "active international cooperation" after a half-century, inactive, domestic-focused phase.

Owing to the mission expansion and increased operational tempo, the Japanese government, led by the Democratic Party of Japan, adopted a new national security strategy, outlined in the 2010 National Defense Program Guideline (NDPG). The 2010 NDPG introduced a new concept of the "dynamic defense force," emphasizing its transformation into a more agile and effective force with enhanced capabilities for various overseas missions. Of course, the call for transformation derived not only from the new missions, but also from the changing security situation in the Asia-Pacific region.

In addition to increased overseas missions, the Great East Japan Earthquake in 2011, subsequent tsunami, and nuclear power plant disaster in Fukushima resulted in the largest ever domestic disaster relief operation in JSDF history, mobilizing more than 100,000 personnel at its peak. Given a further increased operational tempo for both domestic and overseas missions, the JSDF has committed to improving institutional family support and mental healthcare programs.

This chapter describes how the social-psychological support programs have developed, focusing on the Japan Ground Self-Defense Force (JGSDF). In particular, we examine the institutional programs of the Family Support Center, Mental Support Center, and a "Mobile Counseling," or outreach, program, intended to provide mental health care to JGSDF personnel and their families. We also explore the effectiveness of the institutional

programs from the soldiers' and their families' perspectives, based on qualitative data, including interviews with military wives. The issue of the "stigmatization" of mental disorder is also examined.

New missions and family support programs

Early history

When the new overseas missions began in 1992, including UN peacekeeping and international disaster relief operations, there was no institutionalized family support program. In contrast to the well-developed institutional
family support programs established by the Imperial Japanese Army before
and during World War II, the JSDF had no clear concept of family support
because of its basic policy of no overseas deployment. Having rebuilt the
nation as pacifist after the war, Japan's Constitution renounces war and
the right of belligerency by the state. The official interpretation of the
Constitution would not allow overseas deployment for the sake of "using
force." Engaging in a war or collective self-defense activities is considered
against the Constitution. Thus, when the government decided to send the
JSDF troops overseas for UN peacekeeping operations, strong opposition
was voiced within the nation (Kawano, 2002, 2004). Even among the families of JSDF personnel who were deployed overseas on peacekeeping missions, more than one in three were against the deployment.[1] In particular,
the mothers who experienced World War II were seriously worried about
their sons' safety during the mission, assuming that it would be similar to
the wartime deployment.[2]

　In 1992, the communication between the peacekeepers and their
families was difficult owing to underdeveloped information technology.
Cellphones and the Internet were not available at the time. The JSDF
allowed the soldiers to call home via satellite communication systems, but
the calls were limited to 10 minutes at a time. The cost of these calls could
add up as much as US$1,000 per month if soldiers called too often. Thus
the means of communication were, in large part, ordinary mail, along with
additional shipments from home. The local units that sent troops overseas
had to take charge of those mails and shipments, as well as keep the families
informed about how the operations were going. In principle, the units for
a UN peacekeeping operation rotate every six months. Meeting the needs
of families required further improvement of family support measures. Thus
institutional family support programs began to develop in the JSDF.

The Iraq operation

Another significant step toward further institutionalization of family support programs was the humanitarian aid and reconstruction assistance
operation in Iraq. After 12 years of UN peacekeeping operations, JSDF

joined the non-UN multinational operation. From 2004 to 2006, more than 5,000 troops were sent to Iraq on a three-month rotation. Each soldier was allowed to use a TV phone for up to 10 minutes (later extended to 20 minutes) per week for free. Although the number of computers was limited, Internet access was also granted to send emails.

Because the mission seemed much more dangerous than a UN peace-keeping operation, family support was an even more significant aspect of the operation. For instance, a 36-year old sergeant of the 14th Infantry Regiment, 10th Division, JGSDF – the father of three children – told his wife that he was selected to join the unit deployed to Iraq over the telephone in May 2004. Later on, he learned from his son that his wife had cried after the telephone conversation. The son was also worried about him being killed in Iraq. It took a long time for the sergeant to explain to his family why the JGSDF had to go to Iraq.

Another 39-year old Sergeant also had difficulty in explaining why he needed to be deployed to what seemed a country "in war" in the eyes of his children. "It was a lot harder to persuade them than when I was deployed to East Timor on a UN peacekeeping mission in 2003," said the veteran peace-keeper. The JGSDF operation in Iraq was one of the most controversial operations in terms of its legitimacy, while facing strong public opposition before deployment (Kawano, 2012; van der Meulen and Kawano, 2008).

The social constructionist perspective on family support

Each time a new mission is added to the JSDF, the social construction processes of the meaning of the new mission are called into discussion for all parties involved. The meaning of a new mission will be socially constructed through continuous social interaction (Segal and Segal, 1993). As the social processes develop, the values and norms regarding the new mission will be shared and, eventually, institutionalized. Soldiers, families, politicians, the state, the military, veterans' associations, local communities, the mass media, and other social organizations take part in the social construction processes. Owing to the strict legal provision set forth by article 9 of the Japanese Constitution, this social construction process is indispensable for developing a public consensus toward and shared meaning of the new mission, and thereby securing the public sense of legitimacy and social support for the mission.

Work, the state, and the military are such "nomic instrumentalities," or "nomos-building instrumentalities," that the "create for the individual the sort of order" in which people can experience their lives as "making sense" (Segal and Segal, 1993: 49). Marriage and family are also "nomos-building instrumentalities" (Berger and Kellner, 1964; Gramling and Forsyth, 1987). The social constructionist perspective on marriage allows us to examine the social processes of marriage- and family-making. While marriage can be the "least scripted" or "most undefined" of interaction situations, the two individuals keep working on matching their own definitions of the situation and on constructing the reality through various types of symbolic interaction. The ongoing negotiation processes result in making a new set of norms (that is, "nomos") or rules that define appropriate/inappropriate behaviors and the meaning of the behaviors to each other (Gramling and Forsyth, 1987). Whenever the taken-for-granted definition of social reality changes, conversation among significant others takes place in order to sustain or reconstruct the reality of the social world in which they live. Any nontraditional work scheduling, such as overseas deployment for a peacekeeping, humanitarian aid, or peacebuilding mission, can be "problematic for family interaction" (Gramling and Forsyth, 1987). The social constructionist perspective on family issues allows us to analyze the family as a "microsocial unit" and how nontraditional work scheduling affect the family interaction (Gramling and Forsyth, 1987).[3]

The JGSDF families are no exception. Without mutual understanding and consent regarding the parent's deployment, spouses and children may suffer from anxiety, depression, and other mental disorders (Palmer, 2008; Saltzman et al., 2011). At one farewell ceremony to send off the deploying unit, the JGSDF camp commander asked the local municipal officers to "take good care of the families left behind" (Chunichi Shimbun-sya, 2005). The camp commander was well aware of the potential issues regarding the overseas deployment.

In Asahikawa, Hokkaido, the hometown of the 2nd Division, JGSDF, the issue of family support involved the whole town. While public opinion was divided because of the questionable legitimacy of Iraq operation, a group of citizens led the "Yellow Handkerchief" movement to show their support for the troops of the first Japanese contingent to be deployed for the humanitarian aid and reconstruction assistance mission in Iraq. This is another example of a "nomos-building" social process through symbolic interaction. Raising a yellow handkerchief, which conveys similar meaning as a yellow ribbon in the United States or United Kingdom, symbolized social support for the troops. The spread of this movement all over Hokkaido, and later to other areas of Japan, meant that social support was being institutionalized. In March 2005, 19,000 yellow handkerchiefs were distributed all over the Kyushu and Okinawa areas, the southwestern islands of Japan.

In Kumamoto, Kyushu Island, 700–1,000 citizens joined public demonstrations in support of the JGSDF in Iraq on June 18 and June 22, 2005. In addition to the Yellow Handkerchief movement, women's divisions of defense associations in Miyagi and Kumamoto invented a small motif: the handmade green felt frogs were handed out to deploying JGSDF personnel, wishing their safe return from Iraq. In Japanese, *Kaeru* has a double meaning: both "frog" and "return" (Kawano, forthcoming).

The local press also played a part in the social processes of nomos-building. However, the narrative framing of the news was not necessarily supportive of the Japanese military (Dauber, 2006). The stories of JGSDF personnel and their families were reported from the local residents' perspective, often with a critical tone. In protest at the too-often critical portrayals of the JGSDF operation in Iraq, a conservative national newspaper closely reported the realities of JGSDF families with passionate sympathy. The stories included a mother who kept visiting a local Shinto shrine to pray for her son's safe return every day for three months, a wife who kept serving dishes for the deployed husband who was in Iraq, which is a symbolic act of wishing his return, a father and a daughter who deployed to Iraq on the same mission, and a married couple in the same unit deployed to Iraq.

Limited gender mainstreaming

Among the 5,500 JGSDF personnel who served in Iraq, about 2 percent of them were female soldiers. The first JGSDF overseas operation involving female soldiers was the UN peacekeeping operation in East Timor in 2002–03. The Iraq operation was the second gender-integrated overseas JGSDF operation. The roles played by the female personnel, however, were limited, for example interpreters, coordinators, liaison officers, cooks, and nurses. The gender ideology of the JGSDF is still quite conservative: women are not allowed into positions that involve direct combat activities, such as infantry platoons, special operations units, and field artillery batteries.

Nonetheless, the female personnel carried out important tasks that could not be performed by males owing to the conservative Islamic gender ideology. They are also said to have eased the otherwise very tense working environment of the overwhelmingly male-dominant military organization by "taking good care of male personnel," serving tea, attending parties wearing *Kimono*, and so forth. Certainly, the use of female JGSDF personnel was not based on the concept of "gender mainstreaming" urged by UN Security Council Resolution 1325. Yet the increased female participation in JGSDF peace operations did indeed increase the effectiveness of the Iraq operation by engendering trust in the host nation (Bridges and Horsfall, 2009).

Family support programs

Institutional family support programs

Learning lessons from the past 20 years of international peace operations, that JGSDF has established various family support programs and measures so that the personnel can focus on their missions without worrying too much about the well-being of their families during their deployment. The purposes of these programs are to keep the families well informed about the missions and operations of the JGSDF, as well as to maintain awareness of their needs and to assure social support for them. In particular, after the Iraq operation, the organizational concept of family support shifted from "support during the operation" toward "continuous support," which is similar to the idea of "family readiness" in the U.S. Army. An important lesson learned from the JGSDF operation in Iraq is that a well-established family support system needs to be developed in peacetime for effective overseas operations in an age of increased operational tempo.

Current institutional family support programs for the families of deployed personnel include the following.

1. *Family support centers*   At the area command level, a family support center is established, and family liaison officers at the unit and regional recruitment office level are in charge of various family support activities.
2. *Family meetings*   Before and during the deployment, the families receive briefings regarding deployment and operational activities in detail. Pictures and video images are shared with the families.
3. *Ceremonies assistance*   The families receive organizational assistance from the local units when the family members attend farewell and welcoming ceremonies for the deployed units.
4. *Information sharing*   Whenever available, any information regarding the activities of deployed units is shared as far as possible.
5. *Shipment assistance*   Letters and items to be shipped to the deployed units are collected and sent to the deployed personnel, free of charge.
6. *Communication assistance*   The use of satellite telephones, emails, and TV phones will be available for use at the local units. If there are emergency calls or messages to be communicated, they will get through.
7. *Ministry of Defense (MoD) Mutual Benefit Society (MBS) business support*   Advice and assistance will be offered regarding the use of the MBS cooperative businesses, such as management of saving accounts, life insurance claims, application of loans, and so forth.

Besides these programs, the JGSDF encourages further development of "unit-family communities" at the local unit level by means of various family support activities in peacetime. For instance, the activities include periodical briefings to the family members, meeting with the commanding officer, occasional talks by guest speakers, guidance seminars on the various MBS businesses, base events, group tours to the base facilities, training sites, displays of weaponry, and trial rides on military vehicles and helicopters. For those who are newly relocated to the unit, information regarding living conditions, local areas, shopping centers, schools, kindergartens, local housings, municipal offices, and other facilities will be provided.

Developing the family support network

The institutional family support programs are still developing. According to the Ground Staff Office, JGSDF (2012), programs to enlighten unit commanders and families by means of education and public relations, and confidence-building measures between units and families, as well as cooperation with municipal offices, veterans and civil organizations are already in place. The ideal image of the JGSDF family support network is illustrated in Figure 19.1.

According to this image, the families of deployed personnel are supported by each other or by themselves (mutual and self-support), while receiving formal support from the MoD, the MBS, local JGSDF bases and units, as well as further formal or informal support from the local government, veterans' associations, the Self-Defense Forces Parental Association (SDF-PA), other defense-related nonprofit organizations (NPOs), and community associations in the civil society. The ideal support system consists of "multiple-layered support networks" (cf. Bowen and Martin, 2011; Huebner et al., 2009). Using a "road of life" metaphor, Bowen and Martin (2011) describe these formal and informal support networks as "guardrails" that help to keep military members and their families on the road (that is, within functional patterns of adaptation and resiliency) when the going gets tough.

In past operations overseas, numerous types of civilian organization, ranging from local chambers of commerce and local voluntary associations to the All Japan Defense Association (*Zenkoku Boueikyokai*), the Japan Veterans' Association (*Goyukai*), the [J]SDF Friendship Association (*Taiyukai*), and other small NPOs offered support for the families of deployed personnel, although their support activities were not always coordinated or systematic. Ad hoc family and troop support activities were planned and conducted independently.

However, there are some moves at the local level to coordinate the efforts to support JSDF families. For example, in Tokushima Prefecture in Shikoku

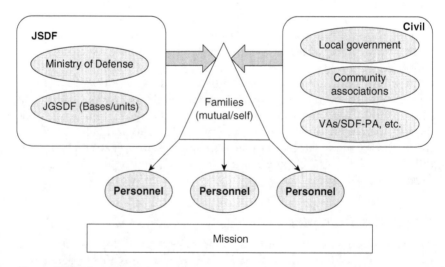

Figure 19.1 Ideal JGSDF family support network

Source: JGSDF document GSO, JESDF, 2012

Island, the All Japan Defense Association, the Japan Veterans' Association, the SDF Friendship Association, and the SDF-PA have agreed to cooperate in terms of family support activities, when needs arise.

The family support project hosted by the SDF-PA is the latest development. The members SDF-PA comprise the 80,000 parents of the 240,000 JSDF personnel. In 2011, a few months after the Great East Japan Earthquake, the JGSDF contacted the association for help in family support cooperation. While mobilizing more than 100,000 personnel for the domestic disaster relief operation, the JGSDF acknowledged growing demands for various family support measures, such as "Please make sure that my parents at home are OK," "Could you see if my kids left at home are doing well?" or "Can you go talk to my parents who lost their home and at a loss?" (SDF-PA, 2012a). In order to extend the existing family support programs to accommodate the growing needs, the JGSDF sought help from the parents of the JSDF personnel. Since there was no formal scheme for family support, the nomos-building has begun.

Starting in 2012, two local cities, Omiya in Saitama Prefecture in the larger Tokyo area and Fukuoka in the Southwestern Island of Japan, were selected to develop a new family support program based on close cooperation between the local JGSDF unit and the local offices of the SDF-PA. The details of programs are yet to be determined by means of discussions among the local units and the local SDF-PA branches. Current plans include measures to check the safety of the family members of JGSDF personnel in case of emergency or natural disaster. Nonetheless, a survey of JGSDF personnel who want the family safety check service and thereby agreed to disclose the personal information of their family members remained at 22 percent in Omiya, a part of the metropolitan city of Saitama with a population of more than 1 million (SDF-PA, 2012b). The urban residents would hesitate to disclose their private lives to strangers. In contrast, at another location in northeastern Japan (Tagajo, Miyagi Prefecture), where the 62,000 residents suffered the tsunami disaster in 2011, 85 percent of the JGSDF families agreed to seek help through the SDF-PA (SDF-PA, 2012c). Thus the needs for family support vary depending on the local situation surrounding the JSDF families.

A further challenge is how to enhance and promote mutual support among the JGSDF families. Despite the organizational efforts made by JGSDF and local units, the rate of participation by the families is relatively low, ranging from 10 percent to 30 percent, depending on the nature of events. According to the statistics of a division in the Northern Army, the average participation rate was 21 percent for the unit-family community activities in the first quarter of 2009. The most frequently cited reasons for not joining the activities were "work" (23.4 percent) and "school events" (15.2 percent). Owing to the prolonged economic recession in Japan of recent years, more spouses are at work to support families than were decades ago. The low participation rate may therefore also reflect the increase in dual-income families.

However, as Robert Putnam (2000) argued of the United States in the 1970s, a trend toward the deterioration of social capital can be observed in the Japan of the late 1990s and early 2000s. Although general trust in others is relatively higher in Japan than in the United States, affiliation to voluntary associations, including neighborhood associations, is much lower in Japan. In fact, the rate of participation in neighborhood associations was almost halved, from 70 percent to 40 percent, between 1986 and 2007 (Sakamoto, 2010). The number of SDF-PA members also decreased, from 120,000 in 1996 to 80,000 in 2012 (SDF-PA, 2012b).

As for the institutionalization of family support by the JGSDF, the objective is to establish and enhance formal and informal networks of cooperation among different groups of organizations and associations. The nomos-building is still under way in terms of JSDF family support programs. While the JGSDF is taking the lead, the Maritime Self-Defense Force and Air Self-Defense Force are following in its footsteps.

Mental health care and family support

For most JGSDF personnel, overseas missions are quite challenging jobs, but they desire to participate in the "real world" missions. Since its establishment in 1952, the JSDF has never been in a combat operation. Even for the last 20 years of overseas operations, the JSDF suffered no casualties as a result of hostile aggression. Having retired the World War II generations, no JSDF personnel have a real sense of war or combat. When asked about their subjective definition of the situation in peacekeeping mission, the majority of the Japanese peacekeepers replied "rather peacetime," and "in-between peacetime and wartime," while a low percentage of those who had served in Cambodia on the UNTAC mission perceived it as "the same as wartime," and more than one in five thought it "rather wartime" (Kawano, 2004). Despite risks of getting injured or killed, the professionally trained military service member would seek opportunities to prove himself or herself in a "real" operation rather than in maneuvers.

However, joining overseas missions inevitably involves stressors for both the deployed personnel and their families. They all are required to cope with stressors effectively, but they are not always successful in their attempts. In general, the military and the family are "greedy institutions," making great demands of individuals in terms of commitments, loyalty, time, and energy (Segal, 1988). When the military personnel get deployed overseas, the military–family tension grows even greater. This, in turn, will affect both the service members and their families. According to a study of the wives of JGSDF personnel, when a deployed husband returns with a mental health problem, the spouse is also affected and suffers from psychological disorder (Fukuura, 2007, 2012a, 2012b). The suicide rate among those who return from overseas missions is higher than the average rate among JSDF troops in peacetime (Kawano, 2007).

In addition to overseas deployments, the largest ever domestic disaster relief operation after the Great East Japan Earthquake in 2011 shed light on the issue of mental health among those JGSDF personnel who served on the heartbreaking mission. The number of civilian victims reached 16,000, while nearly 3,000 were missing and 6,000 injured. More than 1 million houses were partially or totally damaged by the earthquake and subsequent tsunami. The search and rescue missions by the JSDF troops, which saved the lives of nearly 20,000 people, while recovering 9,500 bodies, were emotionally challenging and often traumatic. Quite a few JSDF personnel themselves and their family members were also victims of the earthquake and tsunami. The MoD organized a special taskforce for mental health care for troops who engaged in the psychologically demanding domestic disaster relief operation. Nonetheless, a large-scale survey of JSDF personnel mobilized for the operation uncovered a troubling fact: 3.3–7.5 percent of the nearly 70,000 personnel who replied to the survey were considered to be at "high risk" of traumatic disorder, including a few cases of posttraumatic stress disorder (PTSD) (*Yomiuri Shimbun*, 2012). However, how many family members of the JSDF personnel suffered from mental health disorder is unknown.

Owing to the increased operational tempo for both overseas and domestic operations, the MoD and JSDF are trying to further enhance institutional programs for mental health care of the personnel and their families. In order to illustrate the realities at the local unit level, we now take a close look at two cases of individual JGSDF personnel and their families who suffered from mental health disorders as a result of overseas deployment (Fukuura, 2007, 2012a, 2012b).

Family suffering

As noted, overseas deployment not only affects the deployed personnel, but also the spouses and family members, including children. The military is indeed a "greedy institution," which requires its members' wholehearted devotion and 24/7 commitment, in national emergency or contingency situations, and further demands their spouses' commitment, thereby making it a "two-person career" (Mederer and Weinstein, 1992; Papanek, 1973). According to a survey of U.S. Army couples, wives at home tend to experience greater stress than deployed husbands, worrying about their husbands' involvement in combat, getting injured or dying, or developing psychological problems or otherwise becoming a "changed person" (Allen et al., 2011). We find similar cases among JGSDF families.

Case one

The first case is the wife of a lieutenant colonel, JGSDF. Her husband had studied at a military staff college in Europe before he deployed to Iraq.

When he came back to Japan from Iraq after seven months in 2006, he was hospitalized for treatment of chronic stress disorder. The wife recalls:

> He suffered from chronic headache due to low blood streaming in his brain. His character also changed completely. It gradually became apparent after he came back to Japan. Since his return from Iraq, he has kept irregular hours. He seemed to be stressed out. A doctor prescribed him tranquilizers, so he was sleepy all the time at home. When one family member has a stress disorder, the rest of the family also builds up stress, I thought. Whenever I spoke with my husband, I chose my words with great caution.
>
> One day, when we visited one of my relative's house near my hometown, he decided to come back early by himself. He stayed alone at home, and the next day he was absent without leave. A colleague wondered why, and came to see what happened to him. They went to a hospital, and then, he was hospitalized for a few months.
>
> (Fukuura, 2007, 2012a)

Despite the fact that she was depressed and despite a doctor's suggestion that she seek help from a psychological counselor, the wife declined, saying that she was too busy taking care of her child.

Case two

The second case is the wife of a major, JGSDF. She suffered from nervous gastritis when her husband was deployed overseas for nine months on a UN peacekeeping mission a few years ago. Later on, when her husband returned from his three-month deployment to Iraq, he suffered from mental disorder and depression. As a result, the wife also suffered from depression (Fukuura, 2007, 2012a). She describes how it happened:

> He said that his problems were not all caused by work in Iraq. Normally, when a soldier comes back from Iraq, they get some time off, but he could not have holidays. Instead, he immediately went on to military maneuvers. When he returned, I noticed that he was in a somewhat strange state. That was about one month after his return from Iraq. He had no time for cooling down.
>
> In Iraq, he did not have many subordinates, so he had to handle most of the work on his own. He was so busy that he often slept only for two or three hours a day. When he was not able to return to his living quarters to lie down, he slept on the newspapers on his office floor. What caused his mental illness was overworking, not frightening experiences, I suppose. Because we did not want the JSDF to know about his mental illness, he visited a civilian hospital in a neighboring town for psychiatric treatment.
>
> (Fukuura, 2007, 2012a)

Mental health care for JGSDF personnel and their families

The JGSDF has institutionalized mental health checks during and after return from overseas deployment, sending mental health questionnaires to the deployed personnel and their families. However, in the second case study above, the couple did not want to disclose the husband's mental health problems to the JSDF because they felt that "it was a private matter." They chose to visit a civilian hospital instead of JSDF hospitals at which the husband would have received treatment for free.

The issue of a "stigma" attached to mental health illness is prevalent not only in the JSDF, but among Japanese society in general (Fukuura, 2012a; Hoge et al., 2004; Kawano, forthcoming). The JGSDF personnel who were deployed to Iraq on a three-month humanitarian aid and reconstruction assistance mission in 2004, from Hokkaido, the Northern Island areas, also stated that they had strong sense of hesitation when they recognized their own mental health symptoms. For instance, a warrant officer had experienced trench mortar attacks twice while he was in Iraq. The second attack, which took place at 0200 hours on April 29, 2004, particularly impressed him, since the sound of the strike was so loud that he woke up. "I thought as if it had hit inside of our camp," recalls the warrant officer. After returning from Iraq, he became "too sensitive to the sound similar to the trench mortar hit," and when he heard the sound of an oil drum dumped from a truck, his heart was "pounding so hard." This symptom persisted for more than a year, according to the Iraq veteran, who is also a UN peacekeeping veteran deployed to Cambodia in the early 1990s (Kawano, forthcoming).

On the other hand, another Iraq veteran sergeant who had also deployed to Rwanda in 1994 on a humanitarian aid mission says, "I did not care about it too much because we had much worse experiences in Rwanda." In his case, when a car tire hit a small stone, it reminded him of the sound of gunshots he heard in Rwanda, so he would automatically duck and take cover as he did in Rwanda. Compared to the situation in Rwanda, however, the situation in Iraq was not so much to worry, or to "be panicky," about, like his colleagues (Kawano, forthcoming). Nonetheless, not one out of the 16 JGSDF personnel who were interviewed attempted to see a psychiatrist or to consult with a psychological counselor, even when they recognized some stress-related symptoms.

In general, it is quite common to fear stigmatization because of mental health disorders among JGSDF personnel. For instance, when a mental health checkup was conducted at four JGSDF bases in the Northeastern Japan area in 2009, 254 out of 7,520 personnel (3.4 percent) were identified as "positive" in the standardized self-diagnosis questionnaire for accumulated fatigue and stress. Among those 254 personnel, 107 (1.4 percent) were interviewed by clinical psychologists and 7 further went on to see a psychiatrist at a JSDF hospital, while 38 were required to continue psychological counseling. The JSDF medical report points out a notable tendency toward "stigma avoidance" among the young personnel (26–30 years old;

enlisted), who would worry about negative consequences regarding their promotion opportunities if they were to receive psychological counseling (Ohzeki et al., 2011).

Besides periodic medical and mental health checkups, guest lectures on mental health, education and training for troops, and a counseling service offered by both civilian and JSDF clinical psychologists are available at the unit level. In addition, some new programs can be introduced, depending on the commanders' initiatives. In the case of 2nd Division, JGSDF, a "work–life care team" was established in 2010to support, and intervene effectively at an early stage if necessary, those who are suffering from various social, financial, or mental health issues. The division commander also took the initiative to teach and train individuals to be adept in self-control. The official idea of a "multilayered mental health care networks" for 2nd Division personnel is that the individual JGSDF service member first takes care of himself or herself by exercising self-control, while being supported by his or her family, units at several levels, medical professionals, local government and communities, and the NPOs for alcoholics or heavy smokers, or other types of intervention and prevention program.

The Crisis Management Support Association is a small NPO consisting of more than 20 JGSDF veterans in Hokkaido. This NPO offers an outreach program as a part of its mental health services, which also offer telephone and online consultations. The "Net 99" program, or an "active mental health care" program, provides "mobile counseling" for those who are in need of psychological help. Mutual aid associations and life insurance companies sponsor the free service. The counselors are not clinical psychologists, but JGSDF veterans experienced in "work–life guidance" (*Fukumu-shido*) – a notion that superiors in the JSDF use to help and support their subordinates in both work and private lives. The goal of the counseling is not only to focus on "listening" and alleviating psychological pain, but also on "solving" the underlying problem of a mental health disorder. This work–life guidance approach to "solving a problem" is similar to the "problem resolution" approach in clinical sociology (Enriquez, 1997; Kawano, forthcoming; Sevigny, 1997). The JGSDF veteran counselors play the roles of "sociotherapist," "process consultant," or "facilitator" to promote "conscientization," which means "the process by which individuals as knowing subjects, and not as recipients, achieve a deepening awareness both of the sociocultural reality which shapes their lives and of their capacity to transform that reality" (Glass, 1979: 514). Nonetheless, no other NPO is following its steps yet.

The Mental Support Center Project

In 2009, the first mental support center (MSC) was established in Sapporo, Hokkaido. Located in the vicinity of a JSDF hospital, the MSC took an initiative in orchestrating efforts to help some JGSDF clients who had been unable to work as a result of mental illness. The goal of the center's intervention was to assist the recovering process of mentally disabled personnel. After three years of trial, the first project succeeded, and the JGSDF decided to expand the Mental Support Center Project to the other areas of Japan to cover all five regional armies.

The most innovative aspect of the MSC's social function is to "connect" different actors in the social support networks surrounding a mental health patient. The center plays the role of "coordinator," while offering clinical counseling. The scheme is illustrated in Figure 19.2.

The MSC comprises medical (clinical counselors) and administrative (personnel/human resources) staff. The services provided include assessment (information for assisting patients), counseling, (psychological education (for patients, superiors, and families), and consultation (for all parties). The process of recovery does not involve a fixed format; rather, each patient needs a tailor-made plan if he or she is to recover from a mental disorder.

Conclusion: Developing the multiple support networks

This chapters has demonstrated that the JGSDF has tried to develop multiple support networks to enhance family support and mental health care for troubled personnel. The number of clinical psychologists assigned at local levels has been increasing. We believe that those formal institutional support systems need to develop further.

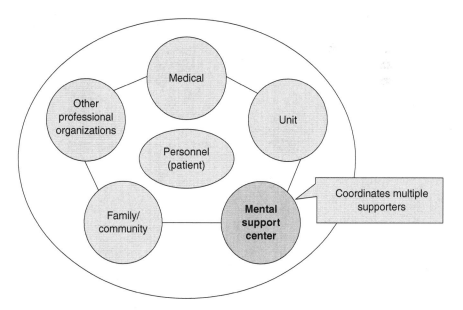

Figure 19.2 Mental health support network

Source: Sapporo Mental Support Center document, Kawano, 2013: 5

However, we find that the sense of stigma attached to mental health disorders among the personnel and their families is still prevailing. Therefore, in addition to formal institutional support system, semiformal or informal networks of social support will also be needed. In this sense, it may be a good idea to introduce a peer counseling system, such as the "Trauma Risk Management" (TRiM) program of the British military (Frappell-Cook et al., 2010; Greenberg et al., 2010). We recognize the organizational efforts to promote social cohesion between units and families by the unit-family community project encouraged by the JGSDF. Notwithstanding, further expansion of the networks by incorporating support from other veterans and civilian groups and associations is required.

Furthermore, the MSCs established by the JGSDF limit their services to JGSDF personnel only. The development of strategies to offer mental health support jointly for those who are in need of help will be future challenges for the JSDF.

In terms of family support, the nomos-building process in Japan is still under way. In an age of increased operational tempo, we expect further policy development to enhance family readiness and mental health care for deployed personnel, as well as for nondeployed personnel and the JSDF families.

Notes

1 According to my own survey of the Japanese peacekeepers conducted in 1999, 35 percent of those who were sent to Cambodia (UN Transitional Authority in Cambodia, or UNTAC), and 38.5 percent of those who were in Mozambique (UN Operation in Mozambique, or ONUMOZ, from the French) met family opposition, mostly from mothers and wives (Kawano, 2004).

2 A Japanese noncommissioned officer (NCO) who participated on the peacekeeping mission to Cambodia recalled that his mother was "crying so hard as if I was going to a war," despite his explanation to her that "it's only a peacekeeping mission that means repairing roads and bridges so that there is no danger at all" (Kawano, 2004: 219–220). To avoid public misconception, the Japanese government carefully chose the word "dispatch" instead of "deployment." In this chapter, we use the internationally standard term "deployment" as simply meaning "sending troops" for various noncombat overseas operations.

3 According to Gramling and Forsyth (1987), the basic assumptions underlying the social constructionist perspective are as follows: a) in Western industrialized cultures, the family has become a place of private existence more than any other interaction situation; b) to realize the individual potential of members, the situation, interaction within the situation, and relationship of members to each other must be ordered and constructed; c) the construction process is essentially one of negotiation and occurs primarily through symbolic interaction or talk; d) the results of negotiations are a continually updated set of rules, which define appropriate interaction, the meaning of that interaction, and, to a larger extent, who and what family members are; and e) the longer the family operates as a social system, the greater the extent to which these roles become shared and objectified, and thus normatively constrain interaction.

References

Allen, E., Rhodes, G.K., Stanley, S.M., and Markman, H.J. (2011) "On the home front: Stress for recently deployed Army couples." *Family Process*, 50: 235–47.

Berger, P., and Kellner, H. (1964) "Marriage and the construction of reality." *Diogenes*, 46: 1–24.

Bowen, G.L., and Martin, J.A. (2011) "The resiliency model of role performance for service members, veterans, and their families: A focus on social connections and individual assets." *Journal of Human Behavior in the Social Environment*, 21: 162–78.

Bridges, D., and Horsfall, D. (2009) "Increasing operational effectiveness in UN peacekeeping: Toward a gender-balanced force." *Armed Forces & Society*, 36: 120–30.

Chunichi Shimbun-sha (2005) *Samawah Dayori [Letters from Samawah]*. Aichi Prefecture: Chunichi Shimbun-sha.

Dauber, C. (2006) "Life in wartime: Real-time news, real-time critique, fighting in the new media environment." In C.A. Castro, A.M. Adler, and T.W. Britt (eds.) *Military Life: The psychology of serving in peace and combat, vol.4 – Military culture.* New York: Praeger Security International, pp. 180–210.

Enriquez, E. (1997) "The clinical approach: Genesis and development in Western Europe." *International Sociology*, 12: 151–64.

Frappell-Cooke, W., Gulina, M., Green, K., Hacker, J., Hughes, H., and Greenberg, N. (2010) "Does trauma risk management reduce psychological distress in deployed troops?" *Occupational Medicine*, 60: 645–50.

Fukuura, A. (2007) "Haigusha no Katari [Narratives by the spouses: Imagination and memory about the violence]." *Kokusai Anzenhosho [Journal of International Security]*, 35: 49–72.

Fukuura, A. (2012a) *Getting Involved: Relocation, overseas deployment and spouse clubs for Japan Self Defense Force officers.* Working Paper No.173. Shiga Prefecture: Faculty of Economics, Shiga University.

Fukuura, A. (2012b) "Combat stress and armed forces: Transnational and local dimension on the Japan Self-Defense Forces." *Annals of Human & Social Sciences*, 19: 75–91 [in Japanese].

Glass, J. (1979) "Reviewing an old profession: Clinical sociology." *American Behavioral Scientist*, 22: 513–29.

Gramling, R., and Forsyth, C. (1987) "Work scheduling and family interaction: A theoretical perspective." *Journal of Family Issues*, 8: 163–74.

Greenberg, N., Kingston, V., Everitt, B., Iversen, A., Fear, N. T., Jones, N., and Wessly, S. (2010) "A cluster randomized controlled trial to determine the efficacy of trauma risk management (TRiM) in a military population." *Journal of Traumatic Stress*, 23: 430–6.

Ground Staff Office, JGSDF. (2012) "Kazokushien no Mokuteki [Briefing Document: Purpose of Family Support]." Family Support Section, June 19.

Hoge, C., Castro, C., Messer, S., McGurk, D., Cotting, D., and Koffman, R. (2004) "Combat duty in Iraq and Afghanistan: Mental health problems, and barriers to care." *New England Journal of Medicine*, 35: 13–22.

Huebner, A., Mancini, J.A., Bowen, G., and Orthner, D.K. (2009) "Shadowed by war: Building community capacity to support military families." *Family Relations*, 58: 216–28.

Kawano, H. (2002) "The positive impact of peacekeeping on the Japan Self-Defense Forces." In L. Parmar (ed.) *Armed Forces and International Diversities*. Jaipur: Pointer, pp. 254–83.

Kawano, H. (2004) "Jieitai PKO no Shakaigaku [Sociology of peacekeeping operations by SDF]." In H. Naka (ed.) *Sengo Nihon no Nakano Senso ["War" in Post-WWII Japan]*. Kyoto: Sekai-Siso Sha, pp. 213–58.

Kawano, H. (2007) "Guntai to Shakai Kenkyu no Genzai [Contemporary studies on armed forces and society]," *Kokusai Anzenhosho [Journal of International Security]*, 35: 1–22.

Kawano, H. (2012) "Japan Self-Defense Force in Iraq: Commitment to international peace and leadership challenges." In H. Haas, F. Kernic, and A. Plaschke (eds.) *Leadership in Challenging Situations.* Frankfurt am Main: Peter Lang, pp. 161–81.

Kawano, H. (2013) "Jieitai no Kokusai-katsudō nikansuru Rinshōshakaigakuteki Kenkyū: Jyosetsu [Clinical Sociological Issues in the International Activities by JSDF]." *Bōeidaigakkō Kiyō [Studies in Humanities and Social Sciences: Social Sciences Series]*, 107: 1–21.

Mederer, H., and Weinstein, L. (1992) "Choices and constraints in a two-person career: Ideology, division of labor, and well-being among submarine officers' wives." *Journal of Family Issues*, 13: 334–50.

Ohzeki, M., Hori, A., Sato, M., Saito, K., Watanabe, M., Shibata, Y., and Morisaki, Y. (2011) "Mental health checkup performed in conjunction with an annual physical checkup in Northeastern Army in 2009 (second report)." *National Defense Medical Journal*, 58(8): 143–9 [in Japanese].

Palmer, C. (2008) "A theory of risk and resilience factors in military families." *Military Psychology*, 20: 205–17.

Papanek, H. (1973) "Men, women and work: Reflections on the two-person career." *American Journal of Sociology*, 78: 852–72.

Putnam, R.D. (2000) *Bowling Alone: The collapse and revival of American community.* New York: Simon & Schuster.

Sakamoto, H. (2010) "Nihon no social capital no genjo to kadai [Social capital in Japan reconsidered]." *Kansai University Kenkyu Sosho*, 150: 1–31.

Saltzman, W.R., Lester, P., Beardslee, W.R., Layne, C.M., Woodward, K., and Nash, W.P. (2011) "Mechanisms of risk and resilience in military families: Theoretical and empirical basis of a family focused resilience enhancement program." *Clinical Child Family & Psychology Review*, 14: 213–30.

SDF Parental Association (SDF-PA) (2012a) *Oyabato.* Monthly Newsletter No. 378, June 15. Tokyo: SDF Parental Association.

SDF Parental Association (SDF-PA) (2012b) *Oyabato.* Monthly Newsletter No. 380, August 15. Tokyo: SDF Parental Association.

SDF Parental Association (SDF-PA) (2012b) *Oyabato.* Monthly Newsletter No. 382, October 15. Tokyo: SDF Parental Association.

Segal, D., and Segal, M. (1993) *Peacekeepers and their Wives: American participation in the multinational force and observers.* Westport, CT: Greenwood Press.

Segal, M. (1988) "The military and the family as greedy institutions." In C.C. Moskos and F.R. Wood (eds.) *The Military: More than just a job?* New York: Pergamon-Brassey's, pp. 79–98.

Sevigny, R. (1997) "The clinical approach in the social sciences." *International Sociology*, 12(2): 135–50.

Van der Meulen, J. and Kawano, H. (2008) "Accidental neighbors: Japanese and Dutch troops in Iraq." In J. Soeters and P. Manigart (eds.) *Military Cooperation in Multinational Peace Operations.* New York: Routledge, pp. 166–79.

Yomiuri Shimbun (2012) "JSDF personnel earthquake trauma." Evening edn., March 7, p. 2.

20 Epilogue

Manon Andres, Gary Bowen,
Philippe Manigart, and René Moelker

Introduction

With this book, we aimed at enhancing our knowledge and understanding of military families, by focusing on the most important issues that touch upon families when military personnel are being deployed, from a global perspective. The volume includes contributions from authors from 12 different countries on five continents. It includes research on personnel and families from different services (army, navy/marines, air force), as well as families from active and nonactive duty personnel (reserves, national guard). In doing so, it provides insights into the extent to which the experiences and reactions of military families, and the support provided to military families, are similar or differ across nations and family types. The chapters not only present new research, but also discuss and bring together a large amount of contemporary international literature.

This final chapter presents a synthesis of the main findings and insights presented in this book: what do we know and where do we go from here?

Military organizations and families in transition

Over the past several decades, various trends and developments have changed the character of the military and the family. One major organizational change is the transition from a conscription model to a professional all-volunteer force in most Western countries. This change affects the nature of the workforce: in all-volunteer forces, employees tend to be older, more personnel are married and have caregiving responsibilities, and the workforce includes more women, compared with conscription forces, in which draftees are usually young, unmarried men. In some nations that rely upon a conscription model, women are recruited as conscripts (for example in Israel), while in other nations (such as Turkey, which has a mixed model), they are not. In addition to changes in the nature of the workforce, members of professional all-volunteer forces tend to be more career-oriented. Qualified and competent personnel are recruited in the labor market, and their families' well-being may be paramount in their decisions to join or to stay in the military.

In many countries, the military profession is increasingly perceived as "just another job," rather than as a "way of life." Many military organizations have (to a greater or lesser degree) flexed from an institutional model toward a more civilian model of organization (Moskos, 1977, 1986). The notion of a "company town" and "one big family" in which everything revolves around (the demands of) military life has faded away (Dursun and Sudom, Chapter 8). Nevertheless, the military still strongly claims the commitment of its members (Coser, 1974). The character and organization of new military missions involve new challenges, stressors, and risks for military personnel and their families (De Angelis and Segal, Chapter 2). Moreover, the increase in operational tempo, in combination with trends toward downsizing and restructuring that have occurred (or still occur) in many defense organizations, imply smaller forces – that is, fewer human resources performing an increased number of operations. This implies more frequent family separations, sometimes with little recuperation time in between. Finally, with respect to developments within the military sphere, in many countries military organizations now more often appeal to reserve forces. Deployments bring with them unique dynamics and challenges for reserve personnel and their families, who regularly shift between military and civilian worlds (De Angelis and Segal, Chapter 2; Andres, De Angelis, and McCone, Chapter 9).

The family as an institution, as well as the military, has undergone change. Owing to various social and demographic trends, a diversity of family structures exists in addition to the traditional family structure of a married male service member and female civilian, with children, running a household together. Single-parent households, childless couples, gay couples (with or without children), and other family structures are quite common nowadays. In some countries, at least until recently, the military designated families that did not meet the traditional family model (such as couples who were not legally married, or single parents) as "irregular families" (Frederic and Masson, Chapter 5). Furthermore, the higher (military) employment rates among women in many countries have increased the number of dual-earner couples and dual-military couples.[1] Because of the higher participation of women in the (military) workforce, men are expected to assume a greater role in childrearing.

Despite these changes, however, and despite household and childcare tasks often being more equally divided in modern families, one still clings to traditional thought regarding gender and work–family roles. Traditional role divisions and expectations within (military) families are often still visible (Eran-Jona, Chapter 3). The traditional view also tends to prevail in military organizations, which expect families to support and give priority to service life. Families are assumed to adjust to the military demands and not the other way around. However, today's families tend to have lives of their own (spouse's employment, social networks) and tend to be less dependent upon the military. Military personnel and their families place more emphasis on the quality of life, and satisfactory work and life conditions; they more often compare the quality of military life to what is perceived as normal in civilian society. Service members' military careers are accepted by their families to a high degree, but not unconditionally.

The work–family interface

These changes that have shaped the military and the family have important implications for how they intersect. For instance, organizational changes have a profound impact on the working conditions of military personnel and, by extension, their families. Work experiences are likely to spill over and cross over to family experiences (and vice versa). The framework of "greedy institutions" (Coser, 1974; Segal, 1986) has been used extensively to study how military and family lives affect one another. In Chapter 2, De Angelis and Segal discussed the usefulness and applicability of this framework in light of the changes that the military and the family have undergone. They argue that the unique combination of demands posed by the military on the family, outlined by Segal (1986), still apply today, and that today's military families face even more frequent separations as a result of deployments, training, and education, in addition to ongoing frequent relocation. Hence, according to De Angelis and Segal, in the past decades the greediness of the military lifestyle has grown.

When comparing different nations, we see that the military institution is not as greedy everywhere. In some nations, such as Belgium (Manigart, Lecoq and Lo Bue, Chapter 15), the military demands less from its employees and their families than in other nations, such as the United States (De Angelis and Segal, Chapter 2), Turkey (Varoglu, Ercil, and Sigri, Chapter 17), or Israel.[2] Still, we often see that the military governs service members' time, while not taking into consideration private or family time. Family decision-making is often adapted to fit the military, while military decision-making usually does not account for family needs. For instance, family plans or vacations need to be cancelled or rescheduled, and families to adjust their places of residence and work, to service members' assignments and postings. In some countries, families have been able to influence change within the military institution by challenging the military cultural and institutional structures (Smith, Chapter 4). These changes include policy changes, for example related to extended parental leaves or operational deferment for young parents, which meet family needs, and contribute to managing work and family life.

Additionally, transitions within the family (for example with respect to spousal employment and long working hours of spouses, role divisions and expectations, and attitudes and needs) may result in higher demands being placed upon family members. The demanding traits of both the military and the family are likely to create tensions and conflict between the work and family domain. Work–family conflict is likely to occur in both civilian and military families; today, many men and women face the challenges of managing work obligations and domestic responsibilities. However, the extraordinary combination of military lifestyle demands (not only family separations as a result of deployment and training, but also frequent relocation are both inherent parts of military life) make military families more vulnerable to experiencing (increased) work–family conflict.[3] Research has demonstrated that conflict between military and family demands are associated with family members' health and well-being (Dursun and Sudom, Chapter 8).

In many countries, military organizations have become more concerned with the overall well-being of military personnel and their families. They have increased their efforts to support military families, helping them to cope with the stressors of military life and military deployment in particular. This is assumed to benefit the well-being of military families, as well as the well-being of military organizations (in terms of the morale, readiness, and retention of military personnel). Moreover, the military depends upon the support of military families: among other things, families are critical to military operations.

In the next sections, we recapitulate the most important issues that touch upon families when military personnel are being deployed, from a global perspective, and the organization of family support systems in different countries.

Military families under stress

The studies presented in this book report on deployments to varying operation areas, both abroad (for example in Afghanistan, Bosnia-Herzegovina, East Timor, Iraq, and Kosovo) and within own national borders (for example in Israel), either pertaining to conflict or domestic disaster relief (for example the Great East Japan Earthquake in 2011, the subsequent tsunami, and nuclear power plant disaster in Fukushima). Interestingly, "objective" characteristics of deployments, such as length, frequency, and recuperation time, vary between countries (and service branches within countries), while "subjective" experiences of military families show certain common patterns.

Durations of the deployments that were the subject of study in this book varied between several weeks up to 24 months, sometimes including a time of rest and recuperation (R&R). An extraordinary type of deployment is the Israeli combat officers' field assignment, which can last up to two years. The service members are able to return home once a week, or once every two weeks, with their home often being just a few miles away from the battlefield. Despite the differences in deployment characteristics, every departure and return creates change in the family structure, and therefore requires adaptation by all family members. Moreover, service members' absences hinder their ability to take an active part in family life for a certain period of time. Lengthier separations (such as year-long or longer deployments, as in the United States) seem to be associated with more persistent negative effects compared with four- or six-month deployments (for example in Canada, Germany, or the Netherlands). Evidence also suggests that adverse effects increase if deployments prove to be longer than originally anticipated (Dekel, MacDermid Wadsworth, and Sanchez, Chapter 10).

Each deployment stage brings with it certain stressors and challenges that seem to be common among families in different nations, such as uncertainty about deployment lengths, concerns about the service member's safety, and the (re)adjustment of family roles. The stages of deployment, and the stressors and challenges associated with them, are commonly known as the "(emotional) cycle of deployment."[4] Across the various stages of deployment, families can experience boundary ambiguity as a consequence of ambiguous loss (Dekel et al., Chapter 10) – that is, a family member being either physically present, but psychologically absent (before or after the deployment), or physically absent, but psychologically present (during the deployment). There is no consensus on what stage of a deployment is most stressful; the contributions in this book demonstrate that all stages of deployment are stressful for families in the nations studied. Families with younger partners and (military) women seem to be most at risk for negative outcomes (Dekel et al., Chapter 10; Andres et al., Chapter 9).

In addition to stressors and challenges, positive experiences and gains have been identified as well. Positive experiences and effects that are identified by the studies presented in this book include, among other things: personal growth and development, (mutual) feelings of pride, appreciation, and closeness, rejuvenated relationships, and expanded social networks (Dursun and Sudom, Chapter 8; Tomforde, Chapter 6; Dekel et al., Chapter 10; Andres et al., Chapter 9; Dandeker, Eversden, Birtles, and Wessely, Chapter 7). However, the positive experiences do not eliminate the difficulties associated with being separated for a long period of time.

The challenges associated with deployment have varying effects on different members of the family: the service member and his or her spouse/partner (Dursun and Sudom, Chapter 8; Tomforde, Chapter 6; Dekel et al., Chapter 10; Andres et al., Chapter 9; Dandeker, Eversden, Birtles, and Wessely, Chapter 7), their children (Andres and Coulthard, Chapter 11), and (the service member's) parents (Bartone, Chapter 12). Various family dynamics and reactions seem to be common across nations, as is demonstrated in the comparative study of Canada and the Netherlands, which reports on the effects on children (Andres and Coulthard, Chapter 11). Apart from the effects on children, deployments – and, in particular, traumatic experiences associated with deployment – have the potential to severely affect the dynamics in couples' relationships (Dekel et al., Chapter 10; Andres et al., Chapter 9), and may result in their being brought closer or driven apart. Furthermore, family members' experiences and adaptations are interrelated. For instance, if a family member suffers from posttraumatic stress symptoms, it affects all members of the family (Dekel et al.,

Chapter 10). Even when family members are physically separated, stress experienced by one member of the family is likely to affect the other(s).

Experiences and effects can be different for different groups of families. For instance, experiences of active duty service members and their families can differ from those of nonactive duty service members and families (national guard and reserves). Among other things, the latter have different reintegration challenges, because returned service members not only need to reintegrate into family life, but also into civilian employment – that is, to deactivate the military role (Andres et al., Chapter 9).

In order to cope with the separation, families seem to apply various strategies, of which the commonest are exchanging information and experiences (for example through attending meetings or using Internet sources), engaging in social contacts (with one's "own" social network or fellow military families), seeking social support, and communicating with the deployed service member. Less is known about how families cope with the (physical) injury or death of a family member. This is an important aspect that should be addressed in future research, bearing in mind the nature of today's military operations.

Family stress and resilience theory, which has evolved over the years, but has its origin in a seminal study of U.S. military families during World War II (Hill, 1949), has been most commonly used to study the adaption of military families to the stressors and demands of military life. Bowen, Martin, and Mancini (2013) recently discussed how life course theory and symbolic interaction theory can be integrated with family stress theory to provide a broader and more dynamic lens through which to understand what distinguishes military families that positively adapt to the demands of military life from those who adapt less well. Other theories, such as bioecological theory, which places emphasis on the dynamic interaction of families in context, and the stress-diathesis model, which addresses genetic and hereditary influences, also provide possible extensions to family stress theory.

National social-psychological family support

With the exception of chapters in this book, families' needs and the organization of family support have received little attention in some countries (such as Argentina, Australia, Japan, Portugal, and Turkey). By bringing together (new) research and knowledge on the evolution and organization of family support systems in different countries, we can learn from each other and make international comparisons, which might inform national policies and practices, and add to international literature.

In various countries, family support systems originated or developed out of grassroots movements. Military families demanded (new) support services because of the nature of (new) military operations and the increased operational tempo. Families worried about the safety of the deployed service members during an operation and their well-being afterwards, asked for mission-related information, and requested regular communication with their deployed family member while he or she was deployed.

In many countries, family support has evolved in the past decades. Although formal family support services vary by nation, they typically include providing deployment-related information (for example through meetings, briefings, newsletters), facilitating communication between deployed service members and their families at home (by telephone, Internet, and mail), providing socio-psychological support (through social workers, psychologists, therapists, and chaplains) from prevention to treatment, and providing critical incident and casualty support in case of injury or death of a service member, or critical family situations at home (such as repatriation because of the birth, illness, or death of a family member). Providing accurate, reliable, and timely (deployment-related) information is crucial, because it reduces uncertainty and rumors, and the distress that misinformation can cause (Bartone, Chapter 12). Communication between deployed service members and their families at home not only helps them to cope with the separation, but also has important effects on relationship outcomes (Andres et al., Chapter 9). With respect to socio-psychological support, families can turn to "civilian" support and health-care systems, but military professionals can address the specific needs of military families in times of deployment, because of their knowledge and experience. However, concerns about stigma and barriers to care remain an issue (Siebler, Chapter 18; Kawano and Fukuura, Chapter 19). One may be afraid of negative consequences when appealing to support provided by the military, such as embarrassing the service member or affecting the service member's career.

In addition to the foregoing, in some countries formal family support services also include the use of military transportation and other military facilities (such as schools, social clubs, restaurants, and hair salons), spousal education and employment services, help with child care, (legal and/or financial) advice and assistance, and unit leader support (commanders being educated about family needs). In many cases, the unit chain of command is an important conduit to supporting both service members and their families in accessing services and supports (Bowen, Martin, Mancini, and Swick, Chapter 13).

Although military organizations in various countries tend to respond to the demographic changes that have shaped modern families and recognize that no single (or ideal) type of military family exists, formal military support systems still tend to rely upon the traditional family model – that is, a breadwinner (military) husband and homemaker (civilian) wife. They hardly account for the diversity of modern family types, including unmarried cohabiting couples, dual-earner couples, dual-military couples, single-parent families, same-sex families, and their (unique) needs.[5] Furthermore, service members' parents are an important component of military families, particularly among younger military personnel. While, in some countries, military organizations have expanded the definition of the military family to include service members' parents (Bartone, Chapter 12), in other countries these family members are still forgotten or ignored in support systems (Juvan and Vuga, Chapter 14).

The key motive of the military with respect to family support usually is that strong and healthy families produce stronger and more capable service members, who are able to focus on the mission without worrying too much about the family. Therefore formal support systems are primarily aimed at helping families to cope with and adapt to the demands associated with military life, not at reducing those demands, and at decreasing conflict between work and family demands, and promoting family satisfaction, because this is crucial for organizational outcomes such as operational readiness, performance, and recruitment and retention. The focus is on dedicated families that support service members in performing their jobs. While this view (in which the support arrangements are embedded) may work in nations with a more collectivistic society and in which families are closely connected to (and dependent on) the military, it may not be that effective in nations that are characterized by more individualism and independence, and in which work is often no longer the family's number one priority. In these nations, families will be dedicated and supportive to the military to a certain degree, but not unconditionally. Most importantly, for family support systems to be effective (and to ensure family and organizational well-being), they should match a nation's and families' social and cultural structure, developments, and values. In Mediterranean countries, for instance, we see family support that principally relies on informal networks (Carreiras, Chapter 16; Varoglu et al., Chapter 17). This is effective because of the strong family ties and involvement. Less need exists for formal support offered by the military in the context of strong informal networks of support.

Countries that have the most formal support services may not be the most supportive to military families. Although formal family support systems are important, they cannot meet every need. But neither can families' "own" social networks (on which families often heavily rely) meet every need, simply because they lack the information, knowledge, or experience related to military deployments in particular. More attention is being given to ways in which formal support services can work in concert to promote informal networks and supports (Bowen et al., Chapter 13; Siebler, Chapter 18). Formal systems and informal networks can strengthen one another, when bringing together the expertise of professionals and accessibility of informal social relations. Support agencies, (virtual) family support groups, rear detachments, and military and civilian communities – including schools (Dandeker et al., Chapter 7) – play an important role in helping military families to cope with the separation and reunion. Research on community capacity (which centers on building resilience not only in families, but also in communities) demonstrates that formal systems and informal networks, through building a sense of shared responsibility and collective competence (the two dimensions of community capacity), positively affect the well-being of service members and their families (Bowen et al., Chapter 13).

As missions have changed, so has the role of unit commanders. Current missions involve more responsibilities for unit leaders. As mentioned earlier, they also play an important role in family support: small actions of supportive commanders can make big differences. Moreover, with respect to community capacity, the role of unit leaders as "community builders' becomes more critical. Unit commanders stand as a quasi-formal system of support between formal social services and informal networks of support, including fellow unit members and families. They assist service members and families in accessing the formal system of services, and work to promote a sense of community among unit members and families. By means of their supportive response to family problems and concerns, and by means of their knowledge of and interface with the human service delivery system, unit leaders can also reduce the stigma that military families may face in pursuing help for problems and concerns.

Although the development of formal social services for military families is unequal across the nations covered in this volume, each nation has at least recognized that military families require support in negotiating the competing demands of work and family life. Future developments across all nations are likely to see greater integration of military and civilian formal social service systems, and greater mobilization of informal networks in support of military families. Unit leaders will continue to play a critical role in support of these families.

What do we know about the science of military families?

The contributions in this book display different research traditions when studying military families: qualitative and quantitative research methods; cross-sectional and longitudinal data collection procedures; and data collection through interviews, focus groups, and (postal) questionnaires, sometimes including a control group in the research design. We witness a trend towards data collection among multiple family members; research is not solely focused on service members or their partners, but also includes children (as respondents, or with their parent as informant) and service members' parents. We see descriptive analyses and more sophisticated data analyses, including the use of structural equation modeling and hierarchical linear modeling.

Yet most research designs continue to focus on "traditional" families and couples – that is, a male deployed service members and a female civilian spouse. Knowledge is limited with respect to deployed female service members (and mothers) and male partners (for example the extent of gender differences with respect to deployment experiences, and the use and effects of family support; the effects of maternal absence on families and family functioning). Knowledge is also limited with respect to nonmarried couples, same-sex couples, and single parents. Also, the role and influence of the extended family (parents, grandparents, siblings, and so forth) on the functioning and adaptation of military families as an informal support system have been surprisingly absent. These are important avenues for future research on military families.

Over the past decades, our knowledge about military families has substantially increased. More international research collaborations, and the development and use of comparative methods and instruments, will promote international comparisons, and further inform literature and practice. International scientific networks and conferences, such as the European Research Group on Military and Society (ERGOMAS), the Inter-University Seminar on Armed Forces and Society (IUS), and the research committee on Armed Forces and Conflict Resolution of the International Sociological Association (ISA RC01), provide excellent forums for (continued) international collaborations and knowledge-sharing.

Where do we go from here?

Many of the chapters have identified avenues for future research; we will not repeat these all here. We do, however, briefly present a number of themes that we believe should have a prominent place in future research.

- As noted above, future research on military families should pay attention to the (unique) challenges of different (modern) family structures, including female service members (and mothers) and male partners, combined families (with children from previous relationships), nonmarried couples, same-sex couples, dual-military couples, and single parents.
- Research should focus on how couples' relationships evolve months, or even a year, after reunion. What mechanisms underlie couples' decisions either to stay together or to part (or to stay in or leave the military)? This will produce valuable (new) information, although it will be difficult to trace people, especially when relationships have been dissolved (and people have moved) or when one has left military service.
- A better understanding of the nature and dynamics of parenting in the military is also required, especially in the context of military deployments. How do service members, for example, continue to parent from a war zone, and what distinguishes children who adapt well and those who do not adapt so well to parental absence?
- Some military families present with particularly high demands, such as families with children and/or adults with special needs, or those with direct or indirect responsibility for aging family members. How do these families cope with these additional demands, especially in the context of relocations and deployments?

- Although we know quite a lot about coping with separation, knowledge is limited with respect to coping with (physical) injury and the loss or death of a family member. This knowledge is particularly relevant in light of the character and effects of new missions.
- Another relevant and necessary line of research relates to the interrelation between family functioning and stress- or trauma-related symptoms (including the prevalence and antecedents and outcomes of secondary traumatization). Service members' stress symptoms have been shown to affect the family, but may it even be likely that service members are more susceptible to (posttraumatic) stress symptoms when things are not going well with the family at home? Fully understanding the nature and direction of this relationship requires gathering longitudinal empirical evidence among a representative and sufficient sample of service members and their families.
- The community context of military families requires more attention. Military families are situated in both military and civilian communities, and these communities have a reciprocal and dynamic impact on these families. More attention to the intersection of military and civilian formal social services, as well as attention to the ways in which these formal systems can work to promote and mobilize informal networks in support of military families, is needed.
- In addition to support provided to service members' families, service members' own (perceived) available support in the course of military deployments (and its interrelations with family functioning) may be a key issue in future research. For instance, their possibilities to address and discuss family-related issues with coworkers and unit leaders, their use and the perceived effectiveness of arrangements that are developed to promote work–family balance, the support available months after their return from deployments, and issues related to stigma are possible avenues of research that will lead to new insights for policy and practice.
- Future research should continue to include methods that focus on both hypothesis-testing (quantitative) and hypothesis-generating (qualitative) designs. For instance, multilevel models make it possible to study dyads, such as husbands and wives, in which both members of the dyad are nested in a relationship and provide parallel information about some aspect of their common reality. However, many nuances of military family life are best explored through in-depth interviews with family members. For example, the ways in which military families socially construct their world and respond to demands on the basis of this construction is open for much greater future exploration. In particular, research designs that track the same families over time will yield new insights into the dynamic nature of family life in the military.

In conclusion, the chapters in this book have revealed many insights into variations in the intersection of work and family life in the military across different countries, including a focus on available formal and informal support mechanisms for services members and their families. In combination, these insights provide a baseline for future research that will lead to new insights about how to best support these families in balancing the dual demands of work and family life before, during, and after missions.

Notes

1 See Smith, Chapter 4, for a more detailed account of dual-military couples.
2 See Chapter 3, in which Eran-Jona describes the characteristics of the "culture of sacrifice" and how this influences the family.
3 In particular, among the younger families: see Dursun and Sudom, Chapter 8.
4 Described in more detail by Tomforde, Chapter 6.
5 With some exceptions: see, e.g., Smith, in Chapter 4, and Frederic and Masson, in Chapter 5.

References

Bowen, G.L., Martin, J.A., and Mancini, J.A. (2013) "The resilience of military families: Theoretical perspectives." In M.A. Fine and F.D. Fincham (eds.) *Handbook of Families Theories: A content-based approach.* New York: Routledge, pp. 417–37.

Coser, L. (1974) *Greedy Institutions: Patterns of undivided commitment.* New York: Free Press.

Hill, R. (1949) *Families under Stress.* New York: Harper & Row.

Moskos, C.C. (1977) "From institution to occupation. Trends in military organization." *Armed Forces & Society*, 4: 41–50.

Moskos, C.C. (1986) "Institutional/occupational trends in armed forces: An update." *Armed Forces & Society*, 12: 377–82.

Segal, M.W. (1986) "The military and the family as greedy institutions." *Armed Forces & Society*, 13: 9–38.

Name index

Subject index